NOVELL NETWARE
POWER TOOLS™

NOVELL NETWARE POWER TOOLS™

Mike Edelhart

Publisher and Editor-in-Chief, *PC Computing*

BANTAM BOOKS
NEW YORK · TORONTO · LONDON · SYDNEY · AUCKLAND

Novell NetWare Power Tools
A Bantam Book / June 1991

ISBN 0-553-348966-X

Published simultaneously in the United States and Canada

Bantam Books are published by Bantam Books, a division of Bantam Doubleday Dell
Publishing Group, Inc. Its trademark, consisting of the words "Bantam Books" and the
portrayal of a rooster, is Registered in U.S. Patent and Trademark Office and in other countries.
Marca Registrada, Bantam Books, 666 Fifth Avenue, New York, New York 10103.

PRINTED IN THE UNITED STATES OF AMERICA

0   9   8   7   6   5   4   3   2   1

Dedication

For DS
Wish you'd been around for this one, buddy

Introduction

People work in groups, and Novell NetWare is the most popular way people can use PCs to work together.

Novell NetWare is installed on more than two-thirds of today's networks. There are a host of technical and marketplace reasons for this, but ultimately they boil down to one fact: NetWare works.

This means different things to different network constituencies. To a network manager, NetWare works because it is so omnipresent. This network operating system offers a multiplicity of menus, screens, controls, options, and commands. This power and complexity guarantees that NetWare has a solution to every situation or problem that managers confront. Network managers can bet their reputations on NetWare and not get burned.

Furthermore, NetWare works for people at PC workstations because it is invisible. The last thing users want from a network is to have to think about it. Users want to think about their applications and work. Users want access to network resources—such as shared printers, large storage space on the network server, group applications—but only if they look and act the same as the resources on their local PCs. Networking is something no one wants to think about. Users can view NetWare as a giant DOS-like application they don't have to think about specifically because the sophisticated tools for managers make it possible to tailor each user's "network" to the individual's needs.

To a business leader, NetWare works because it gets the job done with as few extraneous decisions as possible. Today NetWare runs on virtually any wire, can be configured for groups from 8 to 800 (and beyond), operates across a host of PCs and network interface cards, interacts with communications services of all kinds, extends to Macintoshes and minicomputers, and otherwise makes it possible to take on any business problem no matter what system configuration it requires. NetWare is also robust and far faster to install and reconfigure than ever before. And it is a value, with new simplified pricing and organization across the NetWare family. A business person can start with a tiny NetWare LAN on opening day and expand the network while the company grows, without much trouble at all. A business person doesn't want to have to become a bit twiddler to solve business problems; NetWare has obvious advantages that make it a smart business choice.

This book is designed to help all three of these constituencies—network managers, business leaders, and network users—to better understand and use NetWare.

For the network manager, we offer scads of tips on configuration, installation, troubleshooting, and maintenance, along with batch files and utilities that makes running NetWare easier.

For the user we offer a written, user-friendly guide to the basic parts and functions of a network, along with a straightforward, step-by-step walk through NetWare commands. This allows users to start thinking about and using the network in the same way as the application programs to which they are already accustomed. This helps network managers, as well, because knowledgeable users will pester them with fewer basic questions and avoidable problems.

For the business leader we have detailed forms and procedures that begin with the kind of workers and problems faced by leaders and work back toward the types of network tasks and therefore resources that will work best.

NetWare is a rich, diverse network environment that is both powerful as a practical tool and fascinating as technology. We hope this book will help PC people of all kinds to understand it and use it fully.

Acknowledgments

This book has my name on it, but is truly the work of many. Much of the NetWare expertise that colors the book comes from Craig Ellison, network manager at PC Magazine. Craig was a stalwart in putting the project together and his ideas appear everywhere in the book; without him this manuscript never would have been completed. Carol Ellison, Craig's wife and a noted computer journalist worked closely with me in polishing the words that went into the book. Dale Lewallen, technical editor at PC/Computing magazine proved invaluable at identifying and testing the utilities that went on the Power Tools disk. And Diane Danielle, one of the world's great network managers, provided insights on applications and gateways.

My thanks to them all. Any insight found in the volume is theirs, any rough edges decidedly my own.

Mike Edelhart
Foster City, CA
April 2, 1991

Contents

1

The Basics of Networking

Networking, like baseball, is based on a few, simple fundamentals. In baseball players throw, hit, and catch. In networking PCs link, communicate, and share. And in networking, like baseball, this underlying simplicity results in a complex process, rich with possibilities and dangers.

Making the most of those possibilities and minimizing those dangers is what this book is all about.

But you can't take advantage of the fine points of the game unless you understand the fundamentals.

So, we'll start there.

What Is a Network?

When PCs appeared nearly a decade ago, they had innumerable advantages over previous types of computers, minis and mainframes. They allowed individuals to control their own computing, to create and store their own files, and to program with relative ease, and they initiated an unprecedented explosion in commercial software. But PCs lacked one capability at the heart of those earlier, larger computers: connectivity.

PCs were isolated. Each machine was its own, stand-alone little universe. It shared neither resources nor information with any other machine. And that, of course, meant that PC users didn't share with other PC users either. All mini and mainframe users were connected. They had to be because they worked at dumb terminals; only the central computer could actually do anything worthwhile. This connectivity was valuable. In business much work

1

is done by groups, much information needs to be stored centrally and held available for more than one person. To be affordable, many users must share expensive computer peripherals such as plotters, which print engineering drawings, or laser printers.

PCs could do none of this.

But given the overwhelming advantages of PCs, few people were willing to give up on them and stick with older machines just to get connected. What was needed was a way to maintain the individuality of PCs while still achieving the benefits of group computing.

PC networks were developed to meet that need. A PC network is a system that allows PCs to operate in a group so that they can share access to peripherals, computing resources, and information.

Parts of a Network

As in any system, a PC network is comprised of distinct parts. These are:

1.   A number of PCs. The number can range from two to thousands.
2.   Network boards. Each PC must have a special card to handle communications with the network.
3.   Cable. The network boards must be linked in some way, almost always by a length of wire.
4.   A network operating system. This software oversees all the group operations the system makes possible. Novell NetWare is the most widely used network operating system in the world.

That's it. The basics are simple, but when it comes to networking, the devil is always in the details.

How Networks Work

Imagine yourself sitting at a PC that is part of a network. You are typing a letter that you want to travel through the network and be printed by a laser printer down the hall. What needs to happen?

First, the word processor you are using and DOS, your PC operating system, have to be able to recognize the existence of a network and be willing to cooperate with it. For example, your word processor must be willing to print a document, even though no printer is directly connected to your PC. DOS must be able to forward the document for network processing, because there aren't any printers handy that DOS can reach.

Then there must be software in your PC that can accept the document and put it in a form that will survive network transmission uncorrupted, be routed to the proper place (the laser printer), and arrive in a form the printer can recognize.

Next there must be some way to translate these instructions, which exist in the form of infinitesimal electrical voltages that only a PC can understand, into some physical form that can be passed through a cable over long distances.

At the other end, there must be a way to unravel the message and return it to a form the recipient (in this case, the printer) can recognize.

This electronic bucket brigade represents a tough technical challenge. Imagine it as happening at high speed, in the dark. If even one drop spills from one bucket, it spells disaster.

To cope with this complexity, mini and mainframe manufacturers created a way to divide the process of moving a message through a network into tightly defined tasks. The tasks were organized into layers, to clarify which steps depended on and handed off to which others. In most instances, these models had seven layers, and so became known as seven-layer models. IBM called its seven-layer model Systems Network Architecture (SNA). The International Standards Organization (ISO) called its communications layer cake the Open Systems Interconnect model (OSI).

Rules of operation, known as protocols, controlled each layer of these networking models. Each seven-layer model defined which protocols would be acceptable at each layer—the shape and size of each bucket in the bucket brigade. While the protocols varied with each system, the functions of the seven layers were generally the same. They were:

1. *The application layer* takes information from users or their applications and identifies both the sending and receiving computers for the network communication.

2. *The presentation layer* makes sure the message is transmitted in a form the receiving computer can understand. It also handles compression and encryption of the information prior to transmission.

3. *The session layer* establishes the communication link across the network and sets the rules by which the message is transmitted.

4. *The transport layer* prepares data for network transmission. It breaks the information into discreet segments, adds checksum information to detect information that becomes scrambled within a segment, and backs up the message until transmission is complete.

5. *The network layer* handles message routing. It constructs segments into packets for sending. These packets include the data plus information

about the receiving computer and sequencing. This network layer counts the packets to make sure all are sent and received.

6. *The data link layer* oversees the transmission by confirming checksums and addresses, and duplicating packets. It monitors that the message has been received by the next point along the assigned route.

7. *The physical layer* translates the packets into the form required to travel through a specific medium.

PC networking picked up on the seven-layer idea but shifted away from the notion of tightly defining what happened at each level. Instead, PC networks favored protocol independence, the notion that the layers in between networked PCs or peripherals should be broadly interchangeable.

In the mainframe systems the constant was the layer cake itself—it dictated how all communication occurred—in PC networking, however, the constant became the network operating system, software that linked DOS, the user's environment, and the system's underlying transmission apparatus. As long as the network operating system could understand a message at both ends, all kinds of variations were acceptable in between.

The good news is that this has made PC networking more open, more flexible, more functional, and more economical than earlier group computing systems. The bad news is that it has made PC networking complicated. While the old systems were blue-plate specials, no choices, in a PC network everything is a la carte. In PC networking, choices come with ways to get into trouble at every level. Let's look at some of the choices at critical levels of PC networking systems.

Network Hardware: The System's Bones

There is a profusion of choices at all levels of PC networking, from the lowest level to the highest.

Cable

PC networks can run on cable as simple as phone wire or as complex as fiber optic lines. The variations are innumerable, but for simplicity's sake let's look at the major broad families.

Twisted Pair Cable

This is similar to phone wire. It has the advantage of being cheap, flexible, reliable, and often already present in most offices. When you use twisted pair wire, you plug the PC into the network much as you plug in a phone. The principle disadvantage of twisted pair wire is that it can leak, as anyone who has heard the hiss on a phone line or the echo of someone else's phone call can attest. Twisted pair cable also doesn't work well over long distances. About 100 meters is the typical limit. Still, today probably more networks use twisted pair cable than any other kind of wire, and it's certainly the most familiar, low-cost way to get started.

Shielded Twisted Pair Cable

This is a variation designed to reduce the "leaking" found in regular twisted pair cable. IBM has endorsed one variation, dubbed IBM Type 1 cable, as its network cable of choice. Shielded twisted pair cable is both more expensive and less flexible than the original, but is perfect for Token-Ring networks.

Coaxial Cable

This, consisting of two wires in a thick cable, is what the cable TV company puts in. Coax, as it is called, covers a variety of wire types that the old mainframe and mini systems used, so it is already installed in many offices. (Though not all mainframe wire will work in a LAN.) It is nearly indestructible, can carry messages over long distances at extremely high speeds, and doesn't leak at all. Coax used by LANs comes in a number of types; R6-62, which is used for DOCNET, R6-58, known as "thin" Ethernet, R6-8, known as "thick" Ethernet. All are less flexible than any twisted pair wire. Coax also requires special screw-on connectors that are less familiar and touchier than phone plugs. If you have a mini or mainframe around, with coax you can use one wire for all computing needs.

Fiber Optic Cable

A thin thread of ultra-pure glass, this cable carries network messages not as vibrations in metal but as pulses of laser light. As a result, fiber optic messages travel faster than any others (at the speed of light) and can extend over great distances with no distortion. The problems: Fiber optic cable is fiendishly expensive and qualified installers are hard to find. And fiber optic cable connectors are notoriously finicky.

Cable selection defies generalization. It must be made on a case-by-case basis. There is one sound rule of thumb: If you're starting a network in an already constructed building, the best cable to begin with is the one that's already in the wall, whatever it is. That's because installing cable is usually the biggest expense of getting a network started. Use what you have and then change after you know more about your site's network use and needs.

If you don't have cable installed, consider using twisted pair unless there are compelling reasons to choose another type. But if you are planning to put a network into a new building, think about installing fiber optic. That way you can bundle the installation cost into the initial building expense and you'll be set for the future. Some companies opt for a multiple cable strategy: twisted pair for person-to-person communication, coax cable for network-to-network or network-to-mainframe communication, and fiber optic for building-to-building communication. You should study this issue and make the decision carefully. It is as important as laying the cornerstone on a house foundation.

Topology

Besides considering the type of cable to install, you must consider the physical topology of the network, or how the cables will be arranged. There are three basic network physical topologies: star, bus, and ring.

Star Topology

In a star topology, each workstation is connected directly to a central device, usually the file server, by a cable. This arrangement uses more cable than other schemes because a separate cable length is required for each workstation. But in star topologies it is easy to isolate the source of equipment and system failures—a key advantage. And equipment failure at one workstation rarely affects the operation of the entire network. Only the individual workstation will cease to operate. The rest will continue to operate normally because each workstation communicates directly with the file server. No other workstation is involved in the process of transmitting or receiving information. For that reason, it is also easy to add, move, or remove stations from the star network without interfering or interrupting the work of others on the network.

Bus Topology

In a bus topology all workstations are connected to a central cable, or bus. Bus topologies are easy to install and require less cabling than other schemes. This makes them practical for small networks and small clusters of workstations. But this dependence on a single, central cable poses a risk that you don't get with a star topology. If the central cable fails, all workstations on the bus will go down. And all workstations will have to be disconnected and tested in order to isolate and resolve the problem that was caused by a single workstation. Productivity will be lost in offices where all workstations speak to the file server across a single bus or where large segments of the network operate on a single bus. And, again, for these very reasons, it's also more difficult to add workstations in a bus topology without disrupting the work sessions of other network users.

Ring Topology

In a ring topology the file server and all workstations are physically connected to a ringed cable. Network traffic moves in a single direction around the ring and is controlled by a token-passing scheme, in which an electronic signal—the token—moves around the ring, picking up messages and dropping them off at the appropriate destination. Ring networks are often called token-ring networks and are suited to large offices where networks require an efficient method of traffic control. But, like bus topologies, ring networks depend on a single cable, which makes them more difficult to install and to debug when a workstation fails.

Network Boards

Your choice of network board depends somewhat on your cable selection, because the boards must have connectors for the wire you picked. Besides hooking to different types of cable, boards support different transmission protocols. Protocol determines how a computer message is packaged and transmitted across the wire and also often determines the best pattern in which to arrange the wires. Network boards and protocols form the logical topology of the PC network.

Three main logical topologies are used in PC networks.

EtherNet

Pioneered by Xerox and Digital Equipment Corporation, EtherNet networks are typically wired in a bus topology. EtherNet cards communicate using a technique called Carrier Sense Multiple Access/Collision Detection (CSMA/CD). Here's how it works: Workstations with information to send listen for traffic on the network. When they detect traffic, they pause and listen again. If there's no traffic, they broadcast the packet in both directions over a central cable. Each data packet identifies the destination PC by address. Each PC looks at the message, but only the destination node reads the entire packet. That's the CSMA. However, it's possible that two PCs will send messages at the same time or that one PC will get two messages at the same time, as all workstations can transmit at once. When this happens, the CD part of EtherNet takes over. If messages collide, a warning goes out to all PCs, they all cancel what they just sent, wait a random amount of time, and then retransmit.

The good part of this setup is that it stuffs the network wire with the maximum possible number of messages, so it produces high-speed performance. The bad news is that, on busy networks, collisions and retransmissions can be common. Thus while the number of packets coursing through the wire may be high, the amount of effective information received by each PC may be low.

EtherNet networks have traditionally been installed using coaxial cable, although they can also run over fiber optic cable. For short distances EtherNet uses thin coax known as the RG58 type; for longer runs it uses thick coax, the RG8 type.

In the last couple of years, however, EtherNet also has been adapted to run on unshielded twisted pair cable. When doing so, EtherNet workstations are usually linked to central connection points (called concentrators) in a star topology. This keeps cable lengths short, reducing garble.

EtherNet will undoubtedly provide superior performance in networks where most processing occurs at the workstation and there is little access to network resources. A typical scenario is a local area network (LAN) in which users often run applications from their hard disks. EtherNet handles infrequent bursts of traffic at extremely high speeds. For medium to heavily loaded networks, where the file server's disk receives many simultaneous requests— for continuous database operations, inventory, and accounting transactions, for instance—EtherNet can become bogged down in retransmissions. Other topologies may provide better performance.

ArcNet

ArcNet, developed by the DataPoint Corporation in the mid-1970s, is probably the simplest and least expensive network topology to install. It is also easy to expand and to modify, and it supports both star and bus topology, or a combination of the two. The resulting flexibility makes network installation choices less difficult.

In an ArcNet network, each PC card has a unique node address, ranging from 1 to 255. The number of node addresses defines the maximum number of workstations that can be put on the network, although for most practical applications an ArcNet network should support no more than 100 users; beyond that number performance slows dramatically.

ArcNet is a token-passing network, in which the token travels to each station according to ascending node addresses. When a PC holds the electronic "token," it can query other PCs about their ability to accept messages. If the recipients are free, the token PC can communicate and keep communicating until done. Because only one PC can transmit at a time, and only after getting an all-clear from the recipients, ArcNet eliminates the time-consuming re-transmissions CSMA/CD networks cause.

ArcNet offers a wide range of cabling options, including coaxial cable, unshielded twisted pair, and fiber optics.

If cost is a major factor, look carefully at ArcNet. It supports both star and bus topologies using both coaxial cable and single unshielded twisted pair cabling. ArcNet performance, while theoretically the lowest of the three major topologies, is acceptable if the number of users is moderate and their volume of network messages is relatively light. Electronic mail and occasional printing or file transfer all could be handled ably by ArcNet. It might be bogged down by constant group interaction, heavy transmission, or large files.

Token Ring

While ArcNet is a token-ring topology, it is not *the* token-ring topology. That honor goes to IBM's Token-Ring scheme. This network interface technology uses a token-passing access scheme. But, unlike the logical token-passing scheme ArcNet uses, IBM's can be used only in a physical star layout. A typical token-ring network consists of a series of multistation access units (MAUs) to which multiple workstations are linked. These MAUs in turn are linked to servers.

In this configuration, the token travels in one direction on a logical ring passing physically through every station as it completes the circuit (even though the stations are linked in a star pattern, the token travels in only one direction, creating a logical loop). When a workstation receives the token, it can either transmit a data packet or pass the token to the next physical station. When a transmission occurs, the token becomes part of the description in the packet. As the message passes through each station, that station reads the description, notes that the token is busy, and refrains from transmitting. However, in this scheme each workstation between the originating worksta-tion and the data's destination regenerates the token and all of its data before passing it on. When the message reaches its destination, typically the file server, the receiver reads the data, adds an acknowledgment, and sends the message back into the ring to return it to the sender. Again, each workstation along the way reads and retransmits the token. When the token, with its acknowledgment, returns to the originator, the message is removed and the token passes to the next workstation for use. This scheme creates moderate overhead but assures successful data transmission on a contention-free network.

In practice this means that IBM Token-Ring networks perform less efficiently at low traffic than EtherNet LANs or even than ArcNet in many cases. However, as network loads increase, the lack of contention in this arrangement allows for smooth acceleration. Token-ring networks make the best heavy-duty, large-scale systems. Many companies are choosing to install token-ring networks as the best bet to handle future growth.

IBM Token-Ring networks run over shielded twisted pair cabling that conforms to its Type 1 cable. They can also run over unshielded twisted pair cable that conforms to an IBM specification dubbed Type 3. Token rings can also run over fiber optic cable.

When choosing your network cable and topology, try to establish a single cabling scheme for all devices. This simplifies planning for future growth, cable maintenance, and integration of future devices. Second, try to choose a single logical topology and network card. Two or more logical topologies are more difficult to manage and maintain; each requires separate fault resolution processes. The way you tackle a problem on an ArcNet LAN is different from the way you would tackle it on an EtherNet LAN or a token-ring LAN. Additionally, multiple topology types duplicate hardware and software diagnostic tools. Third, a single topology and cabling scheme reduces the cost of administration, training, and support. The number of spare parts, the types of cable, and network documentation can be standardized and simplified. In addition, fewer vendors are required to support the network.

Novell NetWare works with all these cables and topology types. Figure 1.1 provides a list of vendors of network interface cards for NetWare.

Network PCs

Virtually any PC can be linked to a network. All that's required is a network card and the software that runs with it. However, networks make it possible for PCs to take on roles other than as work handlers for individual users. Also, networks make it possible to link dissimilar kinds of computers, such as PCs and Macintoshes. This can affect how machines are arrayed in the network.

Network Workstation

This is the common name for a PC dedicated to use by an individual that is also linked to a network. In NetWare, it can be any kind of PC or a Macintosh. We talk about how to get the most from a PC workstation in a NetWare network in chapter 3.

3Com Corp.,
3165 Kifer Road,
Santa Clara, CA 95052-8145.
(408) 562-6400.

ACER, Inc.,
401 Charcot Ave.,
San Jose, CA 95131.
(408) 922-0333.

Advanced Digital Corp.,
5432 Production Drive,
Huntington Beach, CA
92649.
(714) 891-4004.

Advanced Micro Devices,
P.O. Box 3453,
901 Thompson Place,
Sunnyvale, CA 94088.
(408) 732-2400.

Allen-Bradley,
555 Briarwood Circle,
Ann Arbor, MI 48104.
(313) 668-2500.

Alloy Computer Products,
100 Pennsylvania Ave.,
Framingham, MA 01701,
(508) 875-6100.

American Research Corp.,
1101 Monterey Pass Road,
Monterey Park, CA 91754.
(213) 265-0835.

AST Research Corp.,
2121 Aulton Ave.,
Irvine, CA 92714.
(714) 756-7793.

AT&T Information Systems,
Inc.,
P.O. Bix 45038,
Jacksonville, FL 32232-9974.

BICC Data Networks Ltd.,
The System Centre,
Brindley Way,
Hemel Hempstead,
Herts HP3 9XJ
England. 44-442-23-1000.

Compex, Inc.,
4065 E. La Palma Ave.,
Unit G,
Anaheim, CA 92807.
(714) 630-7302.

Corvus Systems, Inc.,
160 Great Oaks Blvd.,
San Jose CA 95119.
(408) 281-4100.

Cubix, Inc.,
2800 Lockheed Way,
Carson City, NV 89706.
(702) 883-7611.

D-Link Systems, Inc.,
3303 Harbor Blvd, Suite E-8,
Costa Mesa, CA 92626.
(714) 549-7942.

David Systems, Inc.,
701 E. Evelyn Ave.,
Sunnyvale, CA 94086.
(408) 720-8000.

DFI, Inc.,
3544 Port St.,
West Sacramento, CA 95619.
(916) 373-1234.

Earth Computer
Technologies,
10525 Lawson River Ave.,
Fountain Valley, CA 92708.
(714) 964-5784.

Everex Systems, Inc.,
48431 Milmont Drive,
Fremont, CA 94538.
(415) 498-1111.

Excelan Corp.,
2180 Fortune Drive,
San Jose, CA 95131.
(408) 434-2381.

Gateway Communications,
Inc.,
2941 Alton Ave.,
Irvine, CA 92714.
(714) 553-1555.

Hewlett-Packard Co.,
8000 Foothills Blvd.,
Roseville, CA 95678.
(916) 786-8000.

IBM Corp.,
Entry Systems Division,
P.O. 1328,
Boca Raton, FL 33432.
(305) 241-7614.

IMC Networks Corp.,
1342 Bell Ave., Unit E3,
Tustin, CA 92680.
(714) 259-1020.

Integrated Technologies, Inc.,
126 E. 56th St., 6th Floor,
New York, NY 10022.
(212) 486-7030.

Interlan, Inc.,
155 Swanson Road,
Boxborough, MA 01719.
(617) 263-9929.

Memorex Telex Corp.,
461 S. Milpitas Blvd.,
Milpitas, CA 95035.
(408) 957-9542.

Miniware B.V.,
Beemdenstraat 38,
600 CT Weert,
Netherlands.
31-4950-43135.

Figure 1.1 Vendors of NetWare—Compatible NICs and LAN Drivers

NCR Corp.,
1601 South Main Street,
Dayton, OH 45479.
(513) 445-6638.

Novell, Inc.,
122 E. 1700 S.,
Provo, UT 84601.
(801) 379-5900.

Proteon, Inc.,
Two Technology Drive,
Westborough, MA 01581.
(508) 898-2800.

Racore Computer Products,
Inc.,
2070 N. Redwood Rd.,
Salt Lake City, UT 84116.
(801) 596-0265.

Retix Corp.,
2644 - 30th Street,
Santa Monica, CA
90405-3009.
(213) 399-2200.

Standard Microsystems
Corp.,
35 Marcus Boulevard,
Hauppauge, NY 11788.
(516) 273-3100.

Thomas Conrad Corp.,
8403 Cross Park Drive,
Suite 1-C,
Austin, TX 78754.
(512) 836-1935.

Toshiba America ISD,
9740 Irvine Blvd.,
Irvine, CA 92718.
(714) 583-3850.

Western Digital Corp.,
2445 McCabe Way,
Irvine, CA 92714.
(714) 474-2033.

Networth, Inc.,
8101 Ridgepoint Drive,
Suite 107,
Irving, TX 75063.
(214) 869-1331.

Olicom A/S,
Overodvej 5, DK-2840 Holte,
Denmark,
45-2-42-3388.

Pure Data Ltd.,
200 W. Beaver Creek Rd.,
Richmond Hills,
Ontario, Canada L4B 1B4.
(416) 731-6444.

RCE, Immeuble Ordinal,
Rue Des Chauffours,
95003 Cergy
Pontoise Cedex, France.
33-1-307-34125.

Riverbend Group,
1491 Chain Bridge Road,
McLean, VA 22101.
(703) 883-0616.

Sytek, Inc.,
1225 Charleston Road,
Mountain View, CA 94043.
(415) 966-7300.

Tiara Computer Systems, Inc.,
2700 Garcia Ave.,
Mountain View, CA 94043.
(415) 965-1700.

Ungermann-Bass, Inc.,
3900 Freedom Circle,
Santa Clara, CA 95052.
(408) 496-0111.

Zenith Electronics Corp.,
1000 Milwaukee Ave.,
Glenview, IL 60025-2493.
(312) 391-7000.

Northern Tlecom,
2305 Mission College Blvd.,
Santa Clara, CA 96054.
(408) 988-5550.

PC Office, Inc.,
4631 Viewridge Ave.,
San Diego, CA 92123.
(619) 268-3235.

Quadram Corp.,
1 Meca Way,
Norcross, GA 30093.
(404) 564-2353.

Research Machines, Ltd.,
Mill Street, Botley Road,
Oxford OX2 0BW England.
44-865-796279

Schneider & Koch & Co.
Haid-und-Neu-Str. 7-9, D-7500
Karlsruhe 1, Germany.
49-721-60521.

Tecnetics (Pty) Ltd.,
P.O. Box 56412,
Pinegowrie 2123,
Republic of South Africa.

Torus Systems, Ltd.,
Science Park, Milton Road,
Cambridge
CB4 4BH England.
44-223-862131.

Unisys Corp.,
322 North Sperry Way,
Salt Lake City, UT 84116.
(801) 594-6910.

Figure 1.1 *(continued)* **Vendors of NetWare—Compatible NICs and LAN Drivers**

Network Server

All networks require servers, PCs that can process the messages created by the network. In peer-to-peer networks, every networked PC operates as both a workstation and a server; the network load is spread more or less evenly across the linked PCs. More commonly, however, a specific PC must be designated as the controlling point for the network. This PC becomes the server for all the networked PCs.

Novell NetWare requires a designated server, a PC with an 80286 or 80386 processor; other specific requirements are discussed more fully in chapter 4. While this server can also double as an individual's PC, that is generally discouraged. To keep the network running smoothly, it is best for NetWare to have its own dedicated PC.

Specialized PCs

In addition to the network server—or file server—NetWare networks can support other specialized PCs. Printers, for instance, can be controlled by a PC dedicated as a print server. This print server separates the queuing of print jobs, the storage of fonts, and other printer-specific chores from the main server, freeing it to handle other chores faster. Some of the latest applications require their own dedicated servers. Group databases, such as SQL Server from Microsoft, need database servers—PCs linked to the server that store database files and interpret database queries. The Microsoft-DCA Communications Manager, a vast selection of communications protocols and services, requires its own communications server, a PC that takes over communication chores from the file server. If a mainframe must be accessed, a PC can be dedicated to handling network-mainframe exchanges; these PCs are called gateways and run software that translates mainframe instructions into PC-comprehensible form and vice versa.

Other possible specialized uses of PCs include FAX servers, CD servers, and virtually any other task that requires baby-sitting of a high-powered piece of equipment or process.

Network Operating System: The System's Heart

PC network life isn't quite as complicated as all this might make it sound. Network users and managers don't spend much of their lives dealing with these intricacies of network design. They spend most of their time working with the network operating system. In more than 70 percent of the PC networks installed today, this is Novell NetWare.

The network operating system is the heart of the network. NetWare takes much of the worry out of network design because it runs with all common forms of cable and all three network protocols. It is completely protocol independent. NetWare can, in fact, support an enormous range of protocols at every level of the seven-layer cake.

As a result, once you choose Novell NetWare, you can make all network hardware decisions without worrying what your network ultimately will look like. Whatever you choose, your network will look like NetWare. You can change your network hardware at any level without changing the heart of the system.

What Is a Network Operating System?

A network operating system is actually a set of programs, some of which run on workstations and some of which run on the server. As a whole these programs are designed to create a group environment for PCs that offers a rich suite of peripheral, file, and application-sharing capabilities in a way that is reasonable to manage and that looks to the user as much like native DOS as possible.

What Network Operating Systems Do

Network operating systems provide three key extensions to stand-alone PCs: resources, operations, and applications.

Resources

The network operating system brings the PC access to resources that aren't inside or attached to it, including printers and other peripherals and actual or virtual disk space on the server. So, through the network a PC with two floppy drives could be endowed with drive H:, a multimegabyte space with all the characteristics of a hard drive. The server's processor, too, is a resource available through the network. For example, an old-time 8088 PC can handle high-end 80386 PC operations through software that runs on the powerful server PC but takes all its commands from and shows its results on the old PC's screen. In this way the network can endow weak PCs with fresh power.

Operations

The network operating system brings new commands, filters, utilities, and reports to each linked PC. Most of these appear DOS-like but don't exist in DOS. They allow the network and its resources to be managed much as a PC is overseen by DOS. Some examples from NetWare:

- *Login security.*   Except for the most recent and powerful models, PCs do not come with any security. There is no password protection. Each NetWare PC can add Login and Password routines to standard autoexec.bat startup files.

- *Login scripts.*   Just as batch files and the config.sys file establish how a PC starts and is configured for use, NetWare provides sophisticated script capabilities for setting up the PC-network environment on each workstation.

- *Commands.*   You can discover who is logged on a NetWare workstation with no one present by typing WHOAMI at the prompt. This DOS-like NetWare command displays the logged-in user's name. Similar commands allow for creation of directories on network drives, display of maps of network services, and much more.

- *Utilities.*   Type NPRINT at the prompt of a NetWare workstation and you are transported into a menu-driven printer control utility. It lets you choose your printer, look at what's printing, move your own print jobs around, or troubleshoot printer problems.

- *Reports.*   NetWare keeps track of how the network is utilized in far more detail and much more accessibly than any stand-alone PC does. This is valuable for security but also for efficient system use. Who is using the network a lot? When? What services are being used? Is one printer overloaded and another sitting idle?

Applications

This network operating system benefit has been the slowest to develop, but will be the most important in the future. At its lowest level, which is where most systems are today, the network can deliver to any linked PC any standard PC application, just as the PC would receive it from a local hard disk. There are three main advantages here. First, money. It is almost always cheaper to buy a multiple user license for software loaded on a network server than to buy single copies for many users. Second, consistency. When software is loaded from a network server, everyone is always using one version; it can be upgraded in one operation and protected from user fiddling or corruption. Third, it saves on precious PC resources. An application loaded from the server doesn't have to eat up repetitive multiple megabytes on dozens of expensive hard disks. Those disks can be used to store individual users' files instead. Some installations have eliminated hard drives altogether by switching to network delivery; a few companies have actually eliminated *all* disks— they use diskless PCs and load DOS from the network.

The second level of network application support is a multiple-person application. These have begun to appear in the last year. Here the application is written in the same way as the network operating system—it has modules that run on PC workstations and modules that run on the server. These programs assume they will be used by groups, not individuals, and that they will be in a network environment. Examples include Lotus Notes and Word-Perfect Office.

In Lotus Notes a group can create, move, and modify documents, reports, spreadsheets, notes, and other information. Notes shows a series of file folders on screen. These folders may be personal, group oriented, shared, protected, locked. They may contain information from any member of the group that could be stored anywhere in the group's area, on the server, on a user's hard drive, even on a remote machine reached by telephone. The software aims to enhance group decision making and project operation.

WordPerfect Office extends the familiar interface of the popular word processor into a group setting. A note typed in WordPerfect could become an instant office message to be flashed to another user's PC. Or a letter could be built up by one user with paragraphs created by other users and stored in a common group database.

These products allow users to share in a single process that mimics the way groups actually operate. Such a task is impossible on stand-alone PCs.

The third level of application interaction with networks is just beginning to emerge. Here, software is written that sees the whole network and all of its PCs much as earlier software saw a single PC and all of its resources—as a single exploitable whole. Instead of merely sharing files, documents, or folders, these applications will share every aspect of their operation. Today, any specific software module runs either entirely in the server or entirely in the PC workstation. In the emerging group software, commonly called client-server software or client-server architectures, the software could run in either; tiny parts of it could be running on the PC and server simultaneously or even on a third networked PC. Individual program instructions from the workstation could set off support operations on the server and vice versa. For instance, a spreadsheet could order the server to "Add these two huge numbers and send me back the result" and continue with other operations while awaiting a response.

In this model networks and their applications become as tightly bound together as DOS and traditional PC programs. These new group application processes can squeeze the full power of the network and all the PCs linked with it.

NetWare has become the standard platform for delivering DOS applications over networks. The second-level applications that have appeared, including WordPerfect Office and Lotus Notes, are largely written with NetWare in mind, because it dominates today's network installations. Although very few third-level applications on servers have yet appeared, as we discuss in chapter 6, NetWare has been completely redesigned in its latest and most powerful version, NetWare 386 version 3.1, to take advantage of these application modules. Novell has also created a wide-ranging set of application development tools for group applications, including Btrieve, a development tool for group databases.

Kinds of Network Operating Systems

Essentially, there are two kinds of network operating systems: server based and peer to peer. Peer-to-peer networks are designed so that each PC operates as both a workstation and a server. Server-based networks rely on a central PC to oversee network operations. To date, server-based networks, such as Novell NetWare, have proven far more popular and much more powerful than their peer-to-peer counterparts, such as LANtastic. This is likely to be the case for some time, because new, tremendously powerful PCs have allowed servers to become amazingly fast and efficient at running networks. At the same time, workers' heavy use of PCs has left most desktops unable to handle more than one person's chores.

With the spread of powerful PCs to desktops and the dominance of third-level applications, peer-to-peer networks could become more popular. Because these leading edge applications run in pieces all over a network, the situation they set up is essentially peer to peer, even if one machine has nominal control over network operations. However, server-based networks should hold the lion's share of the market for several years, at least.

Novell NetWare: A Systems Family

One of NetWare's great strengths is that it is not just a single product but a *family* of operating systems. This means that, instead of trying to solve every problem, every situation for every customer, in a single software swat, Novell has tailored NetWare to many different needs. All the products share the same core and operate similarly, but all are focused on specific kinds of networks and users.

Here is a brief overview of the NetWare family.

NetWare 2.2   This version of NetWare replaces four previous versions—Entry Level System NetWare Levels 1 and 2, Advanced NetWare, and Netware System Fault Tolerant. It brings, for the first time, a uniform level of network management, application support and operation to the Novell family from very small networks to very large ones.

NetWare 2.2 comes in versions for 5, 10, 50 and 100 users. For small networks it can operate with a nondedicated server running on virtually any PC, as Netware ELS once did. It can also run as a dedicated server on PCs with 80286 microprocessors, as Advanced NetWare and SFT Netware did. The familiar functions of all those old products are retained in the new version.

However, NetWare 2.2 also provides new methods of installation, fault tolerance, application support, workstation generation and other important LAN tasks that are common in all installations from 5 to 100 users. For the first time, with Netware 2.2, a customer can start with a small network and then smoothly upgrade without having to change the way the network runs.

NetWare 2.2 also brings Mac support to all Netware installations for the first time, and produces an environment much closer to that of Netware 386 than ever before. This makes taking the leap from 286-based NetWare to the more powerful 386-based NetWare less daunting than in the past.

NetWare 386 version 3.11.   The most powerful version of NetWare, this system has been redesigned to take full advantage of powerful Intel 386 microprocessor PC servers. It can support more than 1,000 users per server, can be installed much more quickly than Advanced NetWare, can be reconfigured while the network remains operating, and has a high-performance file system and innumerable other advances. This version also offers new modular application support tools, called NetWare loadable modules and now includes protocol layer with TC pip support.

Portable NetWare.   Minicomputer companies can use this subset of NetWare to build environments that run on their machines and support NetWare services. A number of Portable NetWare systems are due to be announced early in 1991.

For much more detail on the various NetWare versions, see figure 1.2.

By carefully making fundamental network decisions, selecting the right version of NetWare, and mixing and matching the right support software, it should be possible to build a reliable network for any arrangement of PCs, applications, and tasks.

That brings us to a final but critical question. Assuming that, through NetWare, you can achieve a powerful, steady network, what do you want it to do?

	NetWare 286 Ver. 2.2	NetWare 386 Ver 3.11
Scheduled Availability	Now	Now
Operation	286 Ded 286 Non	386 Ded
Bus Support	MCA, AT	MCA, AT
Installation		
Install?	Install	Install
Dynamic (Non-Stop)?	No	Yes
3.5" Disks (720KB)?	No	No
3.5" Disks (1.44MB)?	Yes	Yes
5.25" Disks (360KB)?	No	No
5.25" Disks (1.2MB)?	Yes	Yes
Network Adapters		
Topologies	~30	~30
Add-on LAN Drivers	Yes	Yes
Dynamic Driver Load	No	Yes
Number of LAN Drivers	4	4
Internetworking	Yes	Yes
Network Transports		
Dynamic Transports	No	Yes
File System		
Max. Disk Storage*	2GB	32TB
Max. File Size	255MB	4GB
Max. Opened Files	1000	100,000
Multiple Name Space (DOS, OS/2, Mac, and Unix)	No	Yes
Extended File Salvage	No	Yes
Trustee Rights Granted at File Level	No	Yes
Extensible File System	No	Yes
Bundled Software		
Btrieve VAP	Yes	Yes
MHS	Yes	Yes
3270 LAN Workstation Software	Yes	Yes

Figure 1.2 NetWare Version Guide

	NetWare 286 Ver. 2.2	NetWare 386 Ver 3.11
APIs	Yes	Yes
VAP	Yes	Yes
VADD	Yes	Yes
Queue Mgmt	Yes	Yes
Diag & Net Mgmt	Yes	Yes
Resource Accounting	No	Yes
TCP/IP		

*All maximums may not be supported concurrently, subject to availability of hardware technology.

Figure 1.2 *(continued)* **NetWare Version Guide**

2

Setting Up the Right Network for You

If you understand the fundamentals of networking, you can make a network work. And if you understand the fundamentals of your business, your workers, and your industry, you can make a network work *for you*.

This is a key point. Too often, PC networks have been created because they were possible, not because they were needed. Sometimes uses were found for them after they were installed, and over time the network has become an integral part of how PCs help that group. Other times, though, network installations have led to confusion, doubt, and disappointment, not because the network didn't work technically but because no one had established its purpose.

If you don't have a network, you must consider your reasons for wanting to install one before you proceed. If you already have a network, you still should think through the business case; doing so can reveal both hidden strengths and weaknesses in how your network is deployed. In both cases, knowing the business benefits of the network makes it easier for you to justify initial installation or upgrades to management.

Making the Business Case for a Network

When you consider the business impact of a network, you don't start with wires and boards. That's just plumbing. You begin where all good business decisions begin—with people.

Here, and again later in this chapter, we challenge you with strings of provocative questions. Sometimes we comment on them, but often we won't.

21

This is because the answers to many of these questions will differ with each site, each company. In thinking about a network for your business, ask yourself questions like these and then answer them—on paper—in a manner consistent with your situation.

First, let's ask some questions about the workers who will actually wind up using your network.

People Considerations

Where are the workers? Close together? On one floor? Scattered all over the building? All over several buildings? In individual offices? In cubicles? In an open space? On a factory floor?

What are they like? Educated? Experienced? Raw recruits? In it for the money? Deeply dedicated? Hard-pressed? Lazy? Unionized? All managers? All prima donnas? Cooperative? Surly? Impassive? Out to lunch?

What do they do? Not generally, but specifically, hour to hour. Take orders? Serve customers—face to face or by phone? Make things? Write reports? Hold meetings? Ship goods?

What kind of information do they require? Do they all read the *Wall Street Journal*? Last night's production report? Stock quotes? Real-time production statistics? Field sales reports?

What kind of information do they create? The God of Paperwork decrees that everybody creates information of some kind. Forms? Orders? Invoices? Memos? Research reports? Magazine articles? Spreadsheet entries?

What kind of information do they share? Do they pass around industry journals? Does each sales group post its daily results on a bulletin board? Must engineering know today about quality control's day yesterday?

Where is new information created? Consider this point carefully. In a doctor's office all new information starts with a patient or the medical literature. In a department store new information comes with each sale, each item received, each item returned. At an insurance firm new information comes from actuaries, agents, and field adjustors.

Where is old information stored? In the basement? In individual workers' PCs? In a mainframe? In a warehouse? In the trash?

How is shared information shared? Formal sharing might include meetings and memos. Informal sharing might include conversations, Post-it notes, and bull sessions. Casual sharing might consist of chats over the water cooler, in the bar, on the airplane.

The key in thinking about people and a network is to translate how people's backgrounds, attitudes, and tasks translate into network needs. Novell recommends sorting workers into four groups for network planning purposes:

Type 1 Users.   Included here are those whose needs are largely met by stand-alone applications—word processing, spreadsheets, and so on. They will use the network sparingly, mostly for electronic mail (E-mail) or occasional printing and file transfer.

Type 2 Users.   These include database input people, such as order takers or form creators. They make straightforward use of databases. They create records and forms, forward them, and download information. Their network use will be moderate, but critical.

Type 3 Users.   Project managers, members of a network-oriented group process, heavy mainframe data users, and the like with moderate database use are included here. They tend to spend more of their time on the network, steadily uploading, downloading, creating, modifying, and moving information.

Type 4 Users.   Network managers, engineers, and software developers who use a database heavily are included in this category. These people push the network as hard as they can.

The Network Analysis Form shown in figure 2.1 is designed to help you get started thinking about workers, what they are doing, what PC tools they are using, and how they will interact with the network.

Now let's go on to think about the business itself. The way a business is organized and the way workers and executives view their roles greatly affects the network's role.

Management Considerations

How is your business organized? By region? By city? By product line? By customer group? By acquisition history? By fate? By happenstance?

Which business model are you?

Traditional/Hierarchical   At the top a paternal boss, then a gradually expanding pyramid of upward-seeking management.

Portfolio Managed   Each business for itself. Resources go to the fittest. Operating responsibility rests where profit potential exists. Corporate management advises, adjusts and disposes of the weak.

Spokes in a Wheel   Each business group is tied to a corporate core but with some independence and sibling association to other business groups.

Holy Roman Empire   A loose confederation of bickering states with the group of dukes having more power than the nominal king.

Entrepreneurial Chaos   A one-person operation with 500 people in it.

Company: _____

Location: _____

Analyst: _____ Date: _____

Goal: _____

_____

_____

I. User Profile

Number of users: _____

Major existing application programs: _____

_____

_____

_____

New application programs: _____

_____

_____

_____

Number of User Types:

Type 1	Type 2	Type 3	Type 4
_____	_____	_____	_____
Very light user Word processing Spreadsheets	Light database entry	Moderate database activity	Heavy database activity

Comments:

Figure 2.1 Network Analysis Form

At what level does profit-and-loss responsibility lie? Who generates the money, who gets credit for it, who gets to count it, and who gets to keep it?

At what level does operational responsibility lie? In some companies the money and the power lie together; in other companies one guy gets the money and another guy does all the work.

At what level does project responsibility lie? Are projects owned by local managers? Do they come from corporate initiatives? Do committees choose which are funded and which fade? Are hit squads created to take on new projects?

At what level does new product development lie? Research and development? Marketing? Suggestions from sales? From the boss? From consultants?

Whose customer? This question is a toughie, but the answer is incredibly revealing.

As mentioned, the biggest single problem with new networks isn't technical glitches but the lack of a focused business goal. You are putting in a network. Therefore, you must have business or personal reasons to do so. If you can't articulate those reasons in detail and tie them into the existence and form of your network, you are bound to be disappointed no matter what network you choose.

Networks unquestionably conform to this axiom: If you don't know where you're going, you'll probably wind up somewhere else.

Now let's consider your situation in your business world. Sometimes the fastest way to justify a network purchase is to say simply: The competition has it, and it works.

Strategic Considerations

Who are your competitors and what kind of information do they use?

What kind of information do they provide their customers? Their executives?

What kind of information do you use internally to stay ahead of the other guy?

What kind of information do you provide customers? Executives?

What kind of information do customers and/or executives want?

What kind of management structure do competitors have? What kind of systems do they use?

What kind of management structure do your customers have? What kind of systems are they using?

The aim here is to analyze, as best you can, your competitors and their information approach in the same way that you are analyzing yourself. If the purpose of a network is to provide a competitive advantage, then you must view it in the competitive framework.

All of these questions provide valuable underpinnings to thinking about the whys and wherefores of a network. But even the most sophisticated conjuring must give way to practical plans for anything worthwhile to become real.

Now let's get down to work.

Information Organization Chart

To get from thinking about a network to designing one, we move from questions to exercises.

1. Draw an organization chart of the area of your company you want a network to cover.
2. Put a blue square at those places where new information is created.
3. Put a green triangle at those places where old information is stored.
4. Does a person at the lowest level of this chart generate information of interest to the person at the top? Draw a line to show how the information flows upward.
5. Does the person at the top have information of interest to the folks at the bottom? Draw a line to show how information flows downward.
6. In a different color, draw lines that join those people, at whatever level, who are currently working together on a project or who otherwise share information regularly.
7. Circle in blue those employees who already have a PC. Put an X on those who have an 80386 PC.
8. Circle in red those employees who have Macintoshes.
9. If you can, write in each circle the names of the applications used by that person.
10. Now examine and ask:
    Is this the information flow you want?
    Is information getting to the right people?
    Is information moving in a logical way?
    Do many people share information?
    Should more people share information?
    Are the people who generate information the ones who have PCs?
    Do they have the most powerful PCs?
    Do the places where information is stored have PCs?
    Are these powerful PCs?
    Do many people use the same applications?
    Does much information originate outside this model?

Does much information flow outside this model?

Is this the right organization for our business goals?

Now picture the perfect model of information usage and flow in your company. Ask yourself:

How does it differ from your model?

Is more information created?

Does more information move?

Is more information shared?

Do more people have PCs?

Do more people use more applications?

Are more applications common across the group?

Does more information flow in from outside the group?

Does more information flow out from the group?

How realistic is this model, given your business structure and goals?

Okay, now let's do a model that takes the ideas from your dream that are most practical in the real-world situation and lays them on the as-is chart. This model represents what we think we can realistically achieve in the near future.

Consider your latest model and answer these system questions:

Which workers have PCs?

How many workers use PCs?

How many managers use PCs?

How many executives use PCs?

Are PCs used in manufacturing/production/shipping?

Are PCs used in sales?

Are salespeople or other staff located in remote offices?

What applications do workers run on PCs?

Who manages the PCs?

What other systems must PC workers have access to?

How do they access those systems now?

What applications do they access?

What kind of PCs do workers have?

What kinds of peripherals do they use?

Who controls the PC budgets for these workers?

Does that person have a PC?

Are any networks already in place anywhere in your company?

What kind are they?

How many employees will need PCs to accomplish this?

How many employees will need new applications to accomplish this?

How many more employees will become involved in creating information?

How many more employees will become involved in storing information?

Estimate the volume of information flowing out of the model system. How much more is that than what you are doing now?

Estimate the volume of information flowing into the model system. How much more is there than what you are doing now?

Does your model require a shift in organizational structure, attitudes, or tasks?

Does your model rest on any involvement by suppliers or customers?

Does your model rest on any involvement by people who don't work with or for you?

Does your model involve workers interacting with non-PC systems?

Does your model require applications you don't now use?

Are those applications commercial or company written?

Your answers will provide a description of how a network can address business needs in your particular situation, a sense of the productivity or marketplace value of those benefits, and a list of the elements required to achieve those benefits and their cost. In short, they provide everything necessary to justify a network implementation or to make a midcourse correction for an existing system.

Network Planning Guide

Use the knowledge, surmises, and guesses you have derived from these exercises and fill out the Network Planning Guide, figures 2.2 through 2.5. You might want to photocopy the guide and work on the duplicate or even re-create the form in a PC forms package because it will undoubtedly go through many revisions before you're through.

To the standard form add any questions that you feel matter significantly at your site or situation.

When you have filled in these forms, discussed them with key compatriots, revised them, and feel fully satisfied with them, move on to the Network Recommendation Worksheet, figures 2.6 and 2.7.

Company: _____

II. Hardware Profile

Existing workstations: (Number and type) _____

_____
_____
_____
_____
_____
_____

New workstations: (Number and type) _____

_____
_____
_____
_____
_____

Disk space for workstation application files: _____

_____
_____
_____
_____
_____

Disk space for workstation data files: _____

_____
_____
_____
_____
_____

Figure 2.2 Network Planning Guide

Company: _____

II. Hardware Profile (continued)

File Server

Disk space for file server application files: _____

_____

_____

_____

_____

_____

Disk space for file server data files: _____

_____

_____

_____

_____

_____

Existing cabling available: _____

_____

_____

_____

_____

_____

_____

Number/type of printers: _____

_____

_____

_____

_____

_____

Figure 2.3 Network Planning Guide

Company: _____

III. Other Considerations

Will network be bridged to another LAN?   ❏ Yes   ❏ No

_____

_____

Do you need to document or bill user activity?   ❏ Yes   ❏ No

_____

_____

Can you afford down-time as a result of a power failure?   ❏ Yes   ❏ No

_____

_____

Do you need access to a mini or mainframe?   ❏ Yes   ❏ No

_____

_____

Will it be feasible to shut down the network   ❏ Yes   ❏ No
during backup process?

_____

_____

Will you be willing to spend over $500 to make the   ❏ Yes   ❏ No
backup process quicker and easier?

_____

_____

How much data and how often do you need
to backup files? _____

_____

_____

Figure 2.4 Network Planning Guide

Company: _____

III. Other Considerations (continued)

Do backup files need to be stored at a different site?   ❏ Yes   ❏ No
_____
_____

Local fire codes, building codes, leasehold restrictions?   ❏ Yes   ❏ No
_____
_____

Will you be remodeling within the next six months?   ❏ Yes   ❏ No
_____
_____

Will you be adding PCs within the next six months?   ❏ Yes   ❏ No
_____
_____

Do you have someone available to manage network?   ❏ Yes   ❏ No
_____
_____

What is the level of user proficiency (DOS and networking concepts)? _____
_____
_____

Comments:

Figure 2.5 Network Planning Guide

Company: _____	
Solution	**Cost**
New Workstations:	
Network Scheme **Cabling:**	
Network Interface Card:	
Topology:	
Bridge **Internal or External:**	
Backup System:	
UPS System:	
Total Cost:	
Printer Placement: See floor plan	

Figure 2.6 Network Recommendations Worksheet

Company: _____	
Solution	**Cost**
NetWare Operating System:	
Network Interface Software:	
File Server (Brand and model):	
How many?	
Processor:	
Clock Speed:	
Dedicated or Nondedicated:	
Disk Storage Capacity:	
RAM:	
Disk Coprocessor Board:	
External Disk Subsystem:	

Figure 2.7 Network Recommendations Worksheet

Here, fill in your best estimate of what products you should use for each network component. Your answers can form the basis for a request for proposal, serve as a guide for a conversation among staff members who are interested in networks, or provide you with a menu to discuss with a professional network installer.

Once the preliminaries are out of the way and you've chosen a network, we can move on to the fun part: squeezing more power from the system. That's what the rest of this book is all about.

3

Getting the Most from a NetWare Workstation

The first rule in setting up NetWare workstations is: Be prepared and be consistent. Anyone who's ever been frustrated by conflicting interrupt settings or equipment incompatibilities on a PC can appreciate what it must be like to configure fifteen to fifty PCs on a network. Multiply the complexities of configuring a single PC by the number of workstations you plan to install and you begin to get an idea of the size of the challenge that lies ahead.

A little advance planning simplifies the chore and eliminates tasks that have to be redone when you go about the installation in trial-and-error fashion. In this chapter we give you some tips and strategies to help you go about the installation logically, reduce the potential for hardware conflicts, maximize the usefulness of the network-related software files installed on the workstation, and make it easier to maintain and expand your network.

We begin by giving you a strategy for installing network interface cards (NICs). But the same level of planning and consistency that you bring to the task of assigning settings on the NICs should also apply to the ways in which you name and organize the directories in which you store the network "shell" files on the workstation, configure the workstations' DOS environments, and write the batch files that aid users in logging onto the network. And, for each one of those tasks, we give you tips that should make for easier, more straightforward installations.

Network workstations may or may not have hard disks or floppy drives. They may or may not possess their own, local set of peripheral devices such as a printer, a mouse, or a CD-ROM reader. They can be diskless workstations, aging 8088 PCs, or powerful 80386 PCs. But, to function as workstations on a network, they all must possess two things in common: a network interface card to link their hardware to the hardware on the network and a software "client shell" that sits in memory and functions as a kind of traffic cop, directing communications to the network operating system or the version of DOS installed on the local workstation.

The NIC is an add-in card that provides the hardware link between the workstation and the network cable that leads to the file server (although diskless workstations have no actual "card"; NIC circuitry is built into the motherboard). The client shell provides the software support that enables data to be sent from the workstation's keyboard to the file server via the card and cabling. If either the card or the shell is improperly configured, network communications cannot take place.

The NetWare software shell is made up of two files—IPX.COM and NETx.COM. IPX is critical to the operation of the workstation. IPX, for internetwork packet exchange, is the primary communication protocol used by NetWare to create and maintain connections among network devices such as workstations, file servers, printer servers, and communications servers. The IPX is directly related to the settings on the workstation's NIC. And you must generate the workstation's IPX for the specific hardware settings of the workstation's NIC. You need to know the hardware settings on each workstation's NIC before generating the IPX for that location. For that reason, we look at hardware first. The x in NETx.COM denotes the version of DOS installed on the workstation. (The file is NET3.COM if the workstation is using a version of DOS 3.x, NET4.COM if a version of DOS 4.x is installed.) We discuss this and IPX later. Other software files, including NETBIOS, which is loaded into memory to set up point-to-point communications across the network and is required to run some applications, are installed on the workstation, but unlike IPX and NETx, they are not essential to the workstation's interaction with the network and are not considered part of the network client shell. Nevertheless, as they need to be considered when you configure the workstation, we discuss them in some depth later in this chapter.

Hardware Configuration

A Two-Step Strategy

As noted, IPX.COM is directly related to the settings on the workstation's network interface card and must be generated for the specific hardware settings on the NIC installed in the workstation. But rather than generating separate IPX files for each workstation, you should just identify a common group of hardware settings and set them up on every workstation's card. Make sure all switches and jumpers on the NICs reflect the settings you've chosen before you install the cards in the workstations. With a universal hardware configuration for all workstations, you'll have to generate only one version of IPX.COM and copy it to each workstation.

Be sure that the settings you select will not conflict with other devices on the workstations, such as video memory cards, expanded memory cards, or any of the interface cards needed to operate a bus mouse, tape drive, CD-ROM reader, or scanner. Clearly, the fewer peripherals network users have hanging from their workstations, the easier this job is. Nevertheless, even on a network of power users, by following two simple steps you can keep the chore of configuring workstation NICs from becoming a recurring nightmare of hardware conflicts.

1. Configure all the NICs before you even install one of them in a workstation. There are five possible settings on a network interface card—IRQ (interrupt setting) address, memory address, node address, input/output (I/O) channel address, and DMA (Dynamic Memory Access) channel address. Depending on the type of LAN you are installing—EtherNet, ArcNet, or Token Ring—you may have to set no more than three or four. It's easier to spot conflicts and change the settings before the cards go into the workstations than it is to tear apart the workstations to make changes later.

2. Permanently record the settings on each NIC in a worksheet or database where you can perform sorts and searches to identify conflicts immediately. They'll be easy to spot if you use the same settings to ensure consistency across your network.

Now, doesn't that sound easy? It is if you're installing a new network with new workstations. But what if you're adding workstations to one that's already installed and you have no clue to the settings on the installed cards? The answer is that you should apply the same strategy. Finding a combination of settings that will work may be a bit more time-consuming in a previously installed network. But you'll still simplify the task ahead if you identify a common set of hardware settings and generate a single IPX for the new workstations you're installing.

Figure 3.1 is a worksheet template to help you record the settings on your NICs. Fill in the location of the workstations in which the NICs will be installed and the alphanumeric code of each of the five settings you will assign to the cards. After entering the information in your spreadsheet, you can sort on any range of settings and check for duplicates. Remember, do all this *before* installing a single card in a workstation. That way, you can change duplicate settings on the cards easily. Once the cards are installed in the workstations, it's extremely difficult to trace the conflicts that interfere with network operations. The task generally involves swapping boards in and out of the

RESOURCES

USER NAME	VIDEO STD	DOS VERSION	MISC. PERIPHERALS	NETWORK NAME	NETWORK ADDRESS	NETWORK CONFG.	INITIAL PASSWORD	LOTUS 123	WORD PROCESS.	AGENDA	E-MAIL	UTILITIES	GRAPHICS	PRINTER 1	PRINTER 2	PRINTER 3	GATEWAY TO MINI
TOM SMITH	VGA	3.31	TAPE@280H	TSMITH	03	300H;CC00;IRQ2	TSMITH	X	X		X			PRIMARY		X	X

Figure 3.1 Local Area Network Setup Grid

workstation until things start working. By working it all out beforehand in a spreadsheet or database or on paper, you won't have to disassemble work-stations and your business won't experience a loss in productivity while users wait for you to fix the problem.

As you work to identify the common settings to use on the cards, you'll need to be sensitive to what each setting does and the kinds of conflicts that can result.

Setting #1—The IRQ

The most challenging setting on the card is the interrupt setting. For that reason, it may be best to attack it first. The interrupt setting is sometimes known as IRQ and is shown in decimal digits, normally 2 through 14 or 15. Interrupts are the means through which a device, such as a CD-ROM reader or fax card, calls upon the processor in a PC or workstation. Like video memory or CD-ROM interface cards, most NICs require their own interrupt to function properly.

Eight-bit network interface cards, which can be used in any PC worksta-tion—from an original PC/XT up through an 80486, support interrupts 2, 3, 4, 5, and 7. But often only one or two are available to you. Why so few? Well, consider what DOS does with the interrupts before the network card is ever installed:

Interrupt 3 is COM2, the second serial port.
Interrupt 4 is COM1, the first serial port.
Interrupt 5 is LPT2, the second parallel printer port.
Interrupt 7 is LPT1, the first parallel printer port.

That leaves only Interrupt 2 for the network interface card. The interrupt landscape is less crowded on PCs with only one COM port or one printer port. But if your network will employ a mix of PC types and your goal is to find a common set of hardware settings for all of your 8-bit NICs, IRQ 2 is probably the best choice for an interrupt setting.

The potential for conflicts is not nearly as great if you're installing 16-bit network cards. In addition to interrupts 2, 3, 4, 5, and 7, 16-bit cards have IRQ 9, 10, 11, and 12 available. The 16-bit cards are more expensive but they also offer better performance. Of course, 16-bit cards cannot be used in PC/XT-style workstations that possess only 8-bit slots. They must be installed in AT-style workstations that possess the bus channel to support them. But they are definitely worth considering if your workstations are 80286-class machines or better.

One important note to consider regarding interrupt settings: Be prepared to make exceptions. Many peripherals, such as bus mice, require interface cards with their own interrupts. Individual workstations that have a fair number of such peripherals installed may require different NIC interrupt settings from the common one you establish for all workstations. This should cause no problem as long as you record which stations are the exceptions and which interrupt setting their NIC cards possess. Doing so will simplify workstation maintenance and any later installation of other devices.

Also, pay particular attention to the jumper setting on the boards of any devices you later add to the workstations—even those that use as IRQ the common NIC setting. The factory default settings of many interface boards, such as bus mouse ones, are set to IRQ2. If that's the universal setting on your NICs, these devices will conflict with them. When that happens, you may find that neither device will work. To alleviate the conflict, reconfigure the new peripheral for another interrupt setting. Good alternatives include IRQ3 if the workstation is not using COM2, or IRQ5 if it isn't using LPT2. But before stealing COM2's IRQ3 setting for the NIC, check to see if your computer's motherboard has both COM1 and COM2 built in. Many of the newer slimline computers do, including the popular Dell and Northgate computers. If you're configuring such a workstation, you'll have to dig out the computer's manual and find the instructions for disabling COM2 on the motherboard. Usually all it takes is moving a jumper or changing a switch.

Not surprisingly, given the number of devices users like to attach, workstations often run out of available interrupts. When that happens, all you have to do is configure the device to use *polling* instead of a dedicated interrupt. The Sony CD-ROM players support polling, for instance, if an interrupt is not available. With polling, you can maintain the interrupt setting on the NIC and use polling to operate the device. The user pays a slight performance penalty with any device that uses polling, for polling noticeably slows down the device. However, if all other interrupts are in use, polling may be your only option.

Setting #2—The Memory Address

After finding a common interrupt setting for all cards, the next thing you need to set on the NIC is the memory address. Network cards, like video and expanded memory cards, require a memory address, expressed in hexadecimal and generally in a range of C000h to D000h. The address cannot conflict with the workstation's video memory address or Expanded Memory Specification (EMS) page frame address. In most instances a memory address of CC00h will work .

Important note: Most ArcNet adaptors come from the factory with a default setting of D000h. It is not uncommon to have conflicts at this address with EMS or Enhanced Graphics Adapter/Video Graphics Array (EGA/VGA) video cards, so be sure to change it to CC00h.

Also, some inexpensive ArcNet adapters can be addressed only in 64K segments and are limited to the larger memory boundaries of C000 or D000.

The inability to address memory in smaller, 16K segments limits your ways of configuring around possible hardware conflicts. You wouldn't, for example, be able to configure the ArcNet card to avoid the memory address problem in a system that possessed EGA video with expanded memory.

Setting #3—The I/O Port Address

The third setting you need to determine is the I/O port address. Here, as with the interrupt setting, you need to be concerned about conflicts with other devices. Where the interrupt is the means by which devices grab the attention of the CPU, the I/O port serves as the standard way through which the PC communicates with input/output devices such as serial ports, disk controllers, NICs, and most other interface cards. With the I/O port, as with the interrupt, each device must have a unique address. The port address is generally a three-digit number expressed in hexadecimal. ArcNet's default is 2E0h.

All the same cautions apply here as apply to interrupt settings. Many tape drives and CD-ROM drives have a separate interface card that also requires a port address. As with interrupt settings, there is a high probability you'll encounter conflicts when choosing an I/O address for the NIC—and an equally high probability that you'll encounter conflicts when users add peripherals to their workstations. As you'll be installing network cards in most if not all of your computers, standardize the network card, and configure the peripherals around the NICs. You don't always have to set a port address for NIC cards. But generally a setting of 300h will produce no conflicts.

Setting #4—The DMA Channel

The fourth setting you'll need to make is for the DMA channel. DMA, or direct memory access, is the NIC's method of accessing memory without "interrupting" the central processing unit (CPU) with a hardware interrupt. If you're installing ArcNet or IBM Token-Ring cards, this setting may not even apply, because 8-bit ArcNet and Token-Ring cards generally do not have a DMA channel. Sixteen-bit cards often do. Some EtherNet cards let you choose whether to use DMA or interrupts. The important thing to remember about the DMA channel is that, if the NIC uses DMA, the card must have exclusive use of its own, unique DMA channel. DMA channels are expressed in decimal numbers or integer base 10.

Setting #5—The Node Address

A node address is the network equivalent of a mailing address or telephone number. It identifies the individual locations of workstations on the network and ensures that data packets moving across a network arrive at their intended locations. There can be 255 workstations on an ArcNet network. As with mailing addresses or telephone numbers, each must have a unique node address. Manufacturers of token-ring and EtherNet cards spare you the burden of assigning individual addresses to each NIC on your network by burning individual node addresses into ROM chips on their cards. ArcNet manufacturers, however, use a single factory default setting, usually 2, which you will have to change before installing the cards. Consequently, you'll have to reset the node addresses on all but one of the cards when you go to install them.

Not surprisingly, the node addresses available to you for ArcNet range from 1 to 255. If you're installing an ArcNet LAN, it is absolutely essential that you avoid duplicating addresses as you set the node addresses on the cards. Duplicate addresses will render a network nonfunctional once the cards are installed in the workstation. After the cards are installed, it's difficult to trace the source of the problem and identify where the conflicts are occurring. Thus you should change all the factory default ArcNet settings, double-check the new settings to be sure none conflict, and record the unique node addresses before you install the cards and boot the network. This will help you avoid a lot of trial-and-error at installation time.

A simple way of going about the task is to assign node addresses in sequence: 1, 2, 3, and so on. List the individual addresses on paper as you make the changes. When you're done, double-check the settings on the cards against the addresses on your list to make sure no two are alike.

It's also a good idea to identify workstation locations and permanently record the locations and their node addresses in a database. The database will be of assistance whenever you need to troubleshoot card problems or add workstations to an ArcNet LAN. By listing node addresses on separate records in the database, you can perform sorts and searches to readily identify duplicate addresses. As you add users to the network, you'll need to know you're assigning unique workstation node addresses. If conflicts do occur, you can also sort the database to identify their source. Because you've recorded the location of the workstations that contain those addresses, you'll be able to go directly to the workstations that are causing conflicts and set a new, unique address on one of the cards. To further simplify the task, affix a label to the outside of every workstation that identifies the node address on the card inside. Workstations tend to move around a company as employees are promoted, change jobs, update equipment, or leave. It's tough to update a database every time someone changes jobs or offices. If the database hasn't been updated, the labels will allow you to identify the node addresses inside each machine without having to tear apart the PCs and remove the NICs to check the settings. If you prefer not to deal with labels or if users remove the ones you've applied, you can use the NetWare command USERLIST /A to check the node address of individual stations. Simply type the command from the prompt of the workstation you're attending. (See "Getting the Most from NetWare Commands" in chapter 5.) NetWare will return information on all users who are currently logged into the network, including the node addresses of their workstations. You'll be able to identify the node address of the workstation you're working at as well as the node addresses of all others who are on the network.

A final note on the ArcNet node address: Some of the newer cards make the assignment task a lot easier by placing node address dip switches on the back of the cards where they're accessible. This eases the chore of assigning and checking node addresses because you don't have to remove the cover of the PC to check or reassign the node address. The drawback, though, is that anyone in an office—even someone who jostles the machine—can change the switches as easily as the network manager can. If you're installing such cards, consider ways of ensuring that the settings don't get changed. A simple though crude solution is to put a piece of tape over the access slot.

Software Configuration

Once the network cards are in place, it's time to install the software that enables users to log onto the network. As noted earlier, the software files that do this are known as the network shell. This shell is made up of two files—IPX.COM and NETx.COM. NETx.COM tells the network which version of DOS is running on the workstation and ensures proper communication between that version and NetWare. IPX is the primary communication protocol used by NetWare to create and maintain connections between network devices such as workstations, file servers, printer servers, and communications servers. It is the IPX that addresses the data packets and routes them to their appropriate destination when a user at the workstation sends information across the network. When a workstation receives data packets from elsewhere, it is the IPX that reads the address assigned to the packet and directs the data to the proper area within a workstation's or file server's operating system.

IPX.COM

The IPX is directly related to the settings on the workstation's network interface card. For that reason, IPX.COM cannot be treated as a file you'd simply copy to the workstation's hard disk or onto to a floppy that you leave in the A drive. You must use SHGEN to generate the IPX as you install the network and configure the workstations. SHGEN and the procedures for generating the IPX are discussed in detail in the NetWare installation manual.

It's important to know here, however, that you must generate the IPX for the specific hardware settings of the workstation's network interface card. Here, once again, a database can help out. You can generate the IPX from any workstation as long as you know the settings on the NIC that's installed in the workstation where you plan to install the IPX. When you boot the workstation and log into the network, the IPX identifies the NIC settings for the local system and establishes the hardware links that enable you to communicate across the network. Therefore, it is the first file that must be loaded before network communications can take place.

NETx.COM

The NETx program is the actual network shell. When users log onto a network, they first load the IPX to establish the appropriate hardware connection and then load NETx to set up software communications. NETx intercepts application requests and determines whether they should be routed to the network or handled locally by DOS. If the NETx determines that the application requires a network resource, such as a network printer or a data file stored on the file server, it interacts with the IPX to assign source and destination addresses to a data packet.

Unlike the IPX, which must be generated for the individual workstation, the NETx file is written specifically for the version of DOS that's installed on the individual workstation and can be copied directly to the workstation's hard disk. Unless the workstation is set up with extended or expanded memory, all you need to know is the version of DOS that's installed on the workstation, then copy the correct file. NET3.COM is for all versions of DOS 3.X. NET4.COM is for all versions of DOS 4.X. You'll sometimes find NET2.COM on distribution diskettes, but you really shouldn't use DOS 2.0 on a network workstation unless it's unavoidable—as when the "workstation" happens to be a laptop with DOS 2.x burned into ROM. DOS 2.x predates current versions of NetWare and will not support all its features.

EMSNETx and XMSNETx

With Microsoft's introduction of Windows 3.0 in 1990, it became more and more important that the NetWare shells recognize expanded and extended memory and support the new graphical interface. In May 1990 Novell released the NetWare DOS Client Version 3.01 shells. Rev 3.02A have been released as of March 1991. In addition to providing support for Windows 3.0 and extended and expanded memory, they offer a set of NetWare utilities to support a feature called "fake roots" (discussed later), new shell configuration parameters, and a new SHGEN utility and IPX.OBJ file to generate compatible IPX.COM files.

These shells guarantee your ability to run new versions of software like Windows 3.0 on the network. If you're not using the DOS Client Version 3.01 (or later) shells, contact your Novell dealer and ask for copies. Novell 3.02 also makes new shell files available on CompuServe, so you can download them from the CompuServe Netwire forum. To find the files on CompuServe, type GO NETWIRE at the ! prompt. You'll find the shell files and utilities in four files that have been archived in ZIP format. At 2400 baud, the files take approximately two hours to download.

Even if you're not running Windows and have no plans to install it, you'll find the new files useful. One of the biggest problems network users experience is lack of memory at their workstations. The problem stems from the amount of memory consumed by the network shell. Typically, IPX takes up 16K to 20K of RAM, and NETx takes up another 36 to 40K. If a user needs to load NETBIOS to run an application, another 20 to 25K is consumed. Obviously, being on the network uses up a lot of conventional memory. Some applications are so large that they end up competing with the network shell for conventional memory and simply will not run if the shell is loaded. The 3.01 shells help rectify the problem by offering three versions of NETx for both DOS 3.x and DOS 4.x. You'll need to install the one that best supports the configuration of the workstation.

If the workstation uses DOS version 3.x, install one of the following files:

NET3.COM	For use with conventional memory
EMSNET3.EXE	For use with expanded memory
XMSNET3.EXE	For use with extended memory

If the workstation uses DOS version 4.x, install one of the following:

NET4.COM	For use with conventional memory
EMSNET4.EXE	For use with expanded memory
XMSNET4.EXE	For use with extended memory

When installed on a workstation equipped with extended memory, XMSNET loads about 34K of the NETx shell into extended memory and leaves just 6K in conventional memory to handle interrupts. For the expanded memory shell, 7K remains in conventional memory, and 33K is freed up. EMSNET shell is written to support the LIM 4.0 standard.

Use of the extended memory shell requires a high degree of IBM compatibility. Some workstation users may experience keyboard sluggishness or other hardware problems; others will not. The type and degree of problems relate to the brand of IBM compatible PC that is used. Note, too, that XMSNETx can be used only with DOS 3.0 and above. The current VDISK.SYS from IBM is not compatible with HIMEM.SYS, so do not use the extended memory shell with VDISK.SYS. And do not use the extended memory shell on a machine running nondedicated NetWare.

SHELL.CFG

SHELL.CFG, a file that's also installed on the workstation, allows you to set some of the parameters for the NetWare shell. In a sense, it operates with NetWare a bit like CONFIG.SYS operates with DOS. You create SHELL.CFG with a text editor as an ASCII file, just as you would create or edit CON-FIG.SYS, and store the file in the same directory as IPX.COM and NETx.COM (or XMSNETx or EMSNETx). If you don't create SHELL.CFG, or if you store it in the wrong directory, NetWare will use a set of default parameters.

You'll find a thorough discussion of SHELL.CFG and the various options it offers you in Appendix B of the Supervisor's Reference to NetWare version 2.1x. The documentation gives a straightforward description of what each option does. But to customize the workstation for special options, you can use a couple of tricks on two settings—LOCAL PRINTERS = and SHORT MACHINE TYPE =.

The LOCAL PRINTERS = <number> option identifies the number of local printers on a workstation. It's wise to include this statement in SHELL.CFG even if there are no local printers at the workstation. By adding the line:

```
LOCAL PRINTERS = 0
```

you'll ensure the workstation will not hang if a user presses

```
<SHIFT> <PrtSC>
```

The SHORT MACHINE TYPE = can be set to equal IBM or CMPQ, as in:

```
SHORT MACHINE TYPE = IBM
```

or

```
SHORT MACHINE TYPE = CMPQ
```

These machine types would seem to indicate that you're using an IBM or Compaq machine as a workstation. But, in fact, SHORT MACHINE TYPE = IBM is the system default, and SHORT MACHINE TYPE = CMPQ is useful even if you're not using a Compaq PC as your workstation. The CMPQ setting invokes an overlay that affects which color palette the Novell menu system uses. You can specify SHORT MACHINE TYPE = CMPQ to force the workstation to access to the CMPQ$RUN.OVL overlay file, which determines the color of NetWare screen menus. If you use laptops as workstations on the network, include this setting in the SHELL.CFG file. It makes the Novell menuing system much more legible on laptop PCs that use fluorescent displays.

The DOS 3.01 Client shell also offers new SHELL.CFG options that are not fully documented in the NetWare manuals. Nevertheless, you need to know about them.

The first is MAX CUR DIR LENGTH. DOS defines the "Get Current Directory" call to return 64 bytes of path. In the past, the network shell allowed 128 bytes to be returned. In the 3.01 shell this parameter is configurable to provide compatibility both ways. The default is:

```
MAX CUR DIR LENGTH = 64
```

However, you can now change the default and enter a number between 64 and 255. If you use this parameter, however, keep in mind that some applications, including Windows 3.0, may have problems with path names greater than 64 characters.

Another useful new SHELL.CFG option is MAX PATH LENGTH. DOS defines a valid ASCII path string as 128 bytes, but that may be insufficient for some network paths. This parameter can be changed to allow users to have path names ranging from 64 to 255 characters. The default is:

```
MAX PATH LENGTH = 255
```

This path does not include file or server names. Remember, once again, some applications including Windows may have problems with path names greater than 64 characters.

A third new option you'll find useful is PREFERRED SERVER. The default is No Preferred Server. This option allows users at workstations to specify the server they want to connect to when they log in. This is especially useful in multiple server environments.

Server connections can be a gamble for users if there is no provision in the login procedure to ensure that they connect to a server where they enjoy rights. If you go with the No Preferred Server default in a multiple server environment, NetWare's software shell will poll up to five different servers to find one that the user can attach to. (If all servers are busy, it will return the message: "Server has no available slots.") If your users can attach to a file server other than the one they're authorized to use, you'll need to set the Preferred Server option in SHELL.CFG to direct their login to the appropriate server. If you do not invoke the Preferred Server option, NetWare will simply attach a workstation to the first available file server when the user logs in.

For example, a company may have two different file servers servicing two different departments and connect the two via a bridge. Nevertheless, employees in the production department who enjoy rights on the file server called PRODUCTION may attach to the marketing department's server, MARKET, if they log in without specifying the server name (i.e., LOGIN PRODUCTION/USERNAME). But unless users are also authorized on MARKET, they will be denied access to the applications and files stored there. Even if they enjoy some rights on that server, they may not be able to access the applications and files they need.

However, if you include the line:

```
PREFERRED SERVER = <servername>
```

in SHELL.CFG, the network software shell will attempt to establish its connection to the server specified instead of the first server that responds at login time.

One last new option to consider is SHOW DOTS. The default is:

```
SHOW DOTS = OFF
```

but if you plan to run Windows, you must change the setting to ON for all users to change from their current directory location to a parent or child directory. Unlike DOS, NetWare does not support directory entries for "." and ".." The file server will not recognize the dots unless you set the option at the workstation. The software shell on the workstation must emulate these entries on FindFirstMatching and FindNextMatching DOS calls. By changing the default to:

```
SHOW DOTS = ON
```

you'll enable users to use a mouse to select the "." or ".." entry when they want to change directories on the network.

A good SHELL.CFG file that takes advantage of these new options should look something like this:

```
LOCAL PRINTERS = 0
PREFERRED SERVER = MARKETING
SHOW DOTS = ON
SHORT MACHINE TYPE = CMPQ
```

The Network Files Directory

Novell recommends loading IPX.COM and NETx.COM from a workstation's AUTOEXEC.BAT so that the files are loaded and the user is attached to a server the minute the station is turned on. That works fine if the workstation is a dedicated network workstation with no local drives that contain applications the user will run. But if the user will run local applications from local drives, there's no reason to load the network shell into memory when it isn't needed.

By loading the network files from a batch file that users run at their option, you'll free memory at the workstation. And by keeping the batch file and network files in a subdirectory off the root of the workstation's C drive, you'll promote good hard disk organization.

Most network installers create a subdirectory off the root of the user's C drive (or off the root of the Boot diskette for floppy-only workstations) and give it a name that readily identifies it as the directory that contains the network files—say, NET or NOVELL. NET is a good choice because it's short and users can change to it with a minimum number of keystrokes (CD\NET). You could copy the batch file you wrote to load the IPX and run NETx into this directory. Or if the user has a special directory for batch files, you could copy it there. In either case, it's wise to include the name of the directory on the workstation's DOS path so that users can load the necessary network files from the prompt at any time.

Copy IPX.COM (generated for the hardware configuration of the NIC as discussed earlier), the NETx file that's most appropriate for the version of DOS installed on the workstation and for the type of memory it utilizes, and SHELL.CFG. SHELL.CFG must reside in the same directory as NETx.

Two other files that often end up in the NET directory, but really shouldn't be there, are NETBIOS.EXE and INT2f.COM. NETBIOS was developed by IBM as the protocol to facilitate point-to-point communications between networked devices. INT2f.COM is a small TSR (terminate and stay resident) program that must be loaded after you load NETBIOS.EXE. It "hooks" interrupt 2F and is required for full NETBIOS emulation. It may seem logical to copy these files to the NET directory, but if you do, you may set yourself up for future problems. NETBIOS is frequently revised. In fact, there were *three* revisions from 1989 to 1990. If the files are stored on the hard disks of every workstation, you'll have to update them on every user's hard disk whenever a revision occurs. It's far more efficient to store the files on the network in a directory that is on the network search path. That way you'll only have to change the files once whenever there is an upgrade.

Don't automatically load NETBIOS.EXE as part of your NET.BAT file. NETBIOS takes up approximately 26K of your workstation's memory, and unless you're running an application that depends on NETBIOS as its transport mechanism, you'll be wasting precious memory. It's far better to load NETBIOS from batch files that call the applications needing its services. If you're using the DOS 3.02 Client shells (and you should be), that same batch file will also unload NETBIOS automatically when you exit the application. If you're not using the DOS 3.02 Client shells, NETBIOS remains in memory until the workstation is rebooted.

Installation Checksheet

Now let's review the strategy for standardizing your workstation configurations and some tips that will make the process more efficient.

1. Assemble your network interface cards and identify a common group of switch settings that will allow you to standardize your hardware settings.

2. Use the template provided in figure 3.1 to record the settings in a spreadsheet. You could also do this with a simple flatfile database program.

3. Sort the records in the database to identify conflicts. Make necessary changes in the switch settings before you install the boards in the workstations.

4. Install the NICs in the workstations and generate an IPX.COM file that uses the common settings. If you were unable to use the common settings on particular workstations, generate separate IPX files accordingly.

5. Identify the NETx files that will best serve the DOS and memory configurations on your workstations. We recommend you use those in the most recent DOS Client Version 3.01 shell.

6. Pick a directory name for the subdirectory that will contain the network files on every workstation. We recommend \NET. Create a directory with that name on the hard disks of every workstation or on a floppy "boot" disk that users can insert into the A drive to log onto the network. Store that file in that directory.

What should be in this directory? The directory should contain the following files:

IPX.COM
SHELL.CFG
NET.BAT
NETx.COM

If you're using DOS version 3.x, install one of the following:

NET3.COM   For use with conventional memory

EMSNET3.EXE   For use with expanded memory

XMSNET3.EXE   For use with extended memory

If you're using DOS version 4.x, install one of these:

NET4.COM	For use with conventional memory
EMSNET4.EXE	For use with expanded memory
XMSNET4.EXE	For use with extended memory

The NET.BAT file should be written to automate the login process and make it as transparent to the user as possible. It should call the IPX and NETx files, automatically switch the workstation to the login drive, and invoke the user's login script stored on the file server. It should look something like this:

```
CLS
@ECHO OFF
ECHO CONNECTING TO THE NETWORK . . . . .
IPX
XMSNET3
F:
LOGIN
```

If there is only one server on the network or if the PREFERRED SERVER option is specified in SHELL.CFG, you don't have to specify the server the user should attach to in the NET.BAT file. However, if a user can attach to a server other than his or her "home" server, and you're using network shells prior to 3.01, you should include the user's "home" server as part of the login command. Do this by substituting the line:

```
LOGIN <name of server>/
```

for the line above that says LOGIN. You could even go a step further and change the line to read:

```
LOGIN <name of server>/<user's username>
```

However, to do this you'll need to write an individual NET.BAT file for every user. And when workstations are not assigned to specific users, it's really counterproductive.

In the sample batch file just given, drive F was assumed to be the network drive that will be available when the NetWare shell loads. In fact, drive F is often, but not always, the first network drive. The first network drive follows the last local drive. If a workstation has a large hard disk that is partitioned with C, D, E, and F drives, the first available NetWare drive will be G:. In other words, the first NetWare drive is always the next drive in sequence following the highest locally mapped drive. Or it can be the drive letter in the workstation's CONFIG.SYS file that follows the drive named in the specification statement:

    LASTDRIVE=

For example, if the statement LASTDRIVE=G appears in the CONFIG.SYS, the user at that workstation would have to go to the H drive to login.

Some hardware installation routines, such as CD-ROM drives, will modify the CONFIG.SYS file with a statement of LASTDRIVE=Z. If you don't rid the CONFIG.SYS of the modification, NetWare will map to a drive that is inaccessible to you. When this happens, change the LASTDRIVE specification to a lower drive (G is a good choice), and write the batch file to change to the next drive in sequence after the network shell loads. The LASTDRIVE line in the CONFIG.SYS, if you use it at all, should be kept to the lowest possible value consistent with your installed hardware. By sticking with the lowest possible value, you'll maximize the number of logical drives available for mapping NetWare volumes and directories.

Making It Work

What should you expect after you have booted the file server, run the NET.BAT file from the workstation, and established your first connection? If you've done everything right, a message similar to the one that follows should appear on the workstation screen when you log in:

```
C:\NET>ipx
Novell IPX/SPX V2.15
(C) Copyright 1985, 1988 Novell Inc.  All Rights Reserved.
LAN Option: Proteon ProNET-4 p134X/p1840 Vers 3.00
Hardware Configuration: ProNET-4/AT p1344, IRQ=12, IO=A20, DMA=5

C:\NET>net3
NetWare V2.15 rev. A - Workstation Shell for PC DOS V3.x
(C) Copyright 1983, 1988 Novell, Inc.  All Rights Reserved

Attached to server PRODUCTION
Monday, October 30, 1990    11:11:52 am

C:\NET>f:
F:\LOGIN>LOGIN MARKET/CRAIG
```

This example shows a typical attachment of a workstation using a Proteon Token-Ring board and the "old" or 2.15 shells without a SHELL.CFG file on a network serviced by two servers. Notice that as IPX loads, the hardware configuration is displayed for you. In this case, of the two possible file servers available, MARKET and PRODUCTION, the shell heard the PRODUCTION server broadcast first and attached to it. But since the "Home" server for this user is MARKET, it must be specified explicitly in the login command.

The next example shows how your screen should look if you're using the "new" version 3.01 shells on a workstation with an IBM Token-Ring board and a SHELL.CFG file installed:

```
C:\NET>IPX
Novell IPX/SPX v3.02 Rev. A (900507)
(C) Copyright 1985, 1990 Novell Inc.  All Rights Reserved.
LAN Option: IBM Token Ring  V2.41 (890505)
Hardware Configuration: Self Configurable.

C:\NET>xmsnet3
Using configuration file SHELL.CFG
PREFERRED SERVER MARKET
SHOW DOTS ON
Established Preferred Server connection.
NetWare V3.02 rev. A - XMS Workstation Shell for PC DOS V3.x
(C) Copyright 1983, 1988 Novell, Inc.  All Rights Reserved.

Attached to server MARKET
Monday, October 30, 1990    7:27:42 am

C:\NET>F:
F:\LOGIN>LOGIN CRAIG
Enter your password:
```

Notice in this example that the shell picks up the preferences in the SHELL.CFG file. In this case it reports that it was able to establish a connection with the PREFERRED SERVER.

Tips for the Troubleshooter

If your login was successful, the workstation is ready to use. If it wasn't, you'll need to investigate what went wrong and fix the error. The ease with which you do that depends on the type of LAN you're running and where along the way the problem occurred. Myriad things can go wrong, but in this section we talk about some of the most common network workstation ailments, describe their symptoms, and try to steer you toward a cure.

Can't Get Started

Suppose you just can't get started. The workstation freezes when you execute the IPX command. If you're running EtherNet or ArcNet, there is a high probability that the configuration of the IPX.COM does not match the hardware settings on the network interface card. (On a token-ring network, an incorrect IPX setting will not hang the workstation but it will return an error code.)

Here's what to do. Reboot the workstation. Change to the NET subdirectory, but instead of running IPX, type:

```
IPX I.
```

This will print the IPX settings to screen and allow you to check the settings configured in IPX.COM. Make note of the settings you see onscreen. Open the workstation and examine the NIC. Check carefully to see if the settings on the card match the ones that were displayed onscreen. If they differ, you'll either have to change the settings on the board to match the IPX.COM file or regenerate the file using SHGEN.

If all of your settings match, you may have a hardware conflict with another device in the workstation, such as a bus mouse board. If the workstation is equipped with interface cards for devices (a bus mouse board, a CD-ROM driver board, or a tape interface board), remove them temporarily and run IPX.COM once again. If the computer doesn't hang, you know that the original problem was due to a hardware conflict. Examine the interrupt settings on each of the other boards to identify the source of the conflicts and reconfigure the board that's causing the problem.

The fix for a token-ring network isn't quite so straightforward. On such networks, the workstation itself is in the physical ring. If there's a wiring problem, the network may return an error message. If the NIC installed in the workstation is an IBM Token-Ring board, the error message will look like this:

```
C:\NET>ipx
Error opening IBM Token Ring board.
```

If the NIC is Proteon board, the error message will look like this:

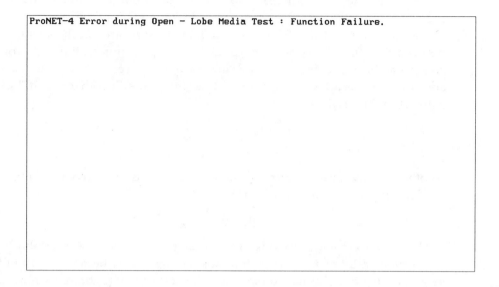

```
ProNET-4 Error during Open - Lobe Media Test : Function Failure.
```

The Forgotten Cable

No matter which card you're using, it's possible that you're getting the error simply because you forgot to connect the cable to the network card. If that's the case, and you're working with an IBM Token-Ring board, you'll have to reboot your computer to try the login after you connect the cable. If you try to execute IPX without rebooting, you'll get another error message that will look like this:

```
Error opening Service Access Point on IBM Token Ring board
```

Be aware that error messages don't always steer you in the right direction. Sometimes they will return wrong or misleading information. In one case, for example, the following error was reported:

```
IBM TOKEN RING ADAPTER NOT INSTALLED
```

But the adapter was properly installed and configured in the workstation. The problem really stemmed from the fact that the user at the workstation had loaded an early version of QEMM's memory manager that caused conflicts. When the memory manager was removed from the CONFIG.SYS file and the machine was rebooted, the user successfully connected to the network.

On initial installations, start with a simple CONFIG.SYS. Write a file that includes only:

```
FILES=20
BUFFER=20
```

You can change the file later. But by keeping CONFIG.SYS information to a minimum, you also minimize the number of potential conflicts that can occur in an installation. Also, keep your AUTOEXEC.BAT short and simple and avoid loading TSRs. That way you'll avoid software conflicts with the network shell files. Once you have established connection with the network, you can go back and add your TSRs and memory drivers. It's a good idea to add them one at a time and, with each addition, confirm that you still can connect to the network.

The Missing File Server

Another common mishap occurs when the IPX loads properly but when you load NETx you get a message that says:

```
FILE SERVER COULD NOT BE FOUND
```

The network shell gives this error message when it cannot establish a connection with any file server. It almost always occurs because (1) the file server is either down or not connected to the network, or (2) there is a physical cabling problem on the network. To diagnose which it could be, first make sure that the file server is up and check to ensure that other workstations can log in. If they can, the problem is at the workstation. If they can't, the problem is at the file server. Wherever you determine the problem to be, examine the cabling connection there. Make sure the cable is attached to the network card. Also, check to see that the cable enters a data socket in the wall. If your network is a bus or star topology, make sure, too, that the network cabling is properly terminated according to the card manufacturer's specifications. If the network cable is improperly terminated, workstations won't be able to find the file server. In a bus topology, improperly terminated cabling can affect all the workstations on the bus. In a star topology it generally affects only individual workstations. Note that your network configuration can affect the way in which the cable should be terminated. For instance, some twisted pair ArcNet cards require a terminating resistor in the second RJ-11 socket when configured in a star configuration. But, when configured on a bus, the resistor should go in the last workstation.

If the connections appear in order and the termination conforms to the manufacturer's specifications, but you still can't attach to a file server, physically move the workstation to where another one has attached successfully to the network. If the workstation logs in successfully from that location, the problem is in the cabling.

4

Getting the Most from a NetWare Server

The file server is up! You've installed its network interface cards. You've generated the network operating system and successfully installed its software. Now you're looking at NetWare's : prompt as it appears on the screen of the file server console. The workstations are online and on their screens you see something like this:

```
Established Server connection.
NetWare V3.02 rev. A - Workstation Shell for PC DOS V4.x
(C) Copyright 1983, 1988 Novell, Inc.  All Rights Reserved.

Attached to server FINANCE
Wednesday, October 24, 1990    8:08:04 PM

F:\LOGIN>
```

How Do You Proceed?

This chapter takes you through the basic activities you need to perform at the file server: setting up new users, assigning passwords, creating groups, setting up directory structures, assigning trustee rights, and choosing printer configurations. The focus in this chapter, as it is throughout the book, is not on the installation procedures you'll find in the NetWare manuals but on the alternatives you should consider when you configure your system to the needs of your particular office. In setting up a file server, sticking to standard ways of doing things will ease the tasks of maintenance and installing future upgrades. But, before we look at how to arrive at those standards, one task you'll encounter during installation deserves comment.

Naming the File Server

Naming the server is one of the more routine things you do during the NetWare installation, but it is one of the most important. Given the opportunity to name the server anything at all, it's always tempting to have a little fun, sticking it with a moniker like LARRY (with a long-term plan of adding file servers CURLY and MOE), or BATMAN or even MUTANT_TURTLE.

But think about it. Do you really want to live with the kind of professional image such a name conveys? Everyone who logs into the network will see the file server's name. Over the life of the network, everyone from the receptionist to the corporate executives will type it countless numbers of times. And once you settle on a name, it's tough to change it; you use the server's name in mappings, batch files, and SHELL.CFG files that you'd have to go back and revise later. It's particularly tough because many of these files are stored on local workstations, and you would have to go from station to station to change each individually. Even at the operating system level, changing a file server name isn't easy. Unless you've installed NetWare 386, you'll have to regenerate the operating system if you decide to change the file server's name. It's often best to choose a name that reflects the kind of workgroup the file server will accommodate.

Whatever type of name you decide on, it's a good idea to keep the file server name short—under eight characters. This makes it easy for you to configure and maintain the server. It also makes life easy for others who'll have to type the name repeatedly when working on the network. If the file server is being set up for the management information department, for example, name the file server MIS rather than something more obscure, such as the department's accounting code. Remember, as the network administrator, you're going to type the file server name more times than anyone else. And, down the road if your LAN grows, a short, meaningful, descriptive name will fit better in a large system than a long, cute, cryptic, or campy name.

What to Do When You First Login at the Server

When you first bring up a server and attach to it from a workstation, you'll find NetWare has created two default users—supervisor and guest. Neither of these user IDs has a password assigned to them. The supervisor ID has complete authority over all network security. To secure the network, the first thing you should do as a network manager is set yourself up as the supervisor and give yourself a password.

To do this, login as the supervisor by typing LOGIN SUPERVISOR at the prompt. Since you don't yet have a password, you will immediately see the NetWare greeting and the default map listing. It will look something like this:

```
F:\LOGIN>LOGIN CRAIG
Enter your password:
Good morning, CRAIG.

Drive  A:    maps to a local disk.
Drive  B:    maps to a local disk.
Drive  C:    maps to a local disk.
Drive  D:    maps to a local disk.
Drive  E:    maps to a local disk.
Drive  F: = FINANCE\SYS:  \

SEARCH1:   = Z:. [FINANCE\SYS:  \PUBLIC]
SEARCH2:   = Y:. [FINANCE\SYS:  \]
```

Notice in the greeting that NetWare continues the login process, even though you do not enter a password. NetWare, by default, creates a public directory on the main, or SYS: volume, as you'll note in the drive mapping. Its default search mappings place the public directory as the first search drive. SYSCON, the main system configuration utility and the one through which you assign passwords, resides in this directory.

As the supervisor, you'll need to execute SYSCON from the prompt and assign a password to the SUPERVISOR's login ID. This is an important first process. So let's go through each step. (In chapter 5, we give you a more complete description of SYSCON's functions and options.) After entering SYSCON at the prompt, you'll see the following screen. As a network administrator, you'll undoubtedly see this screen many times every week.

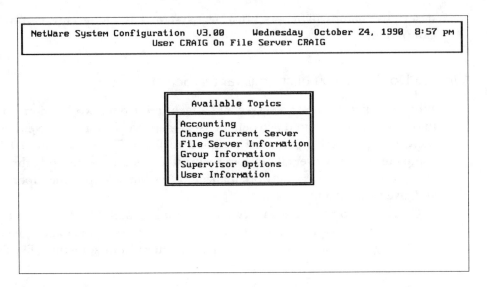

NetWare's menu-driven utilities have a consistent look and feel that you'll quickly recognize as you use the operating system. The menu-driven utilities present you with pop-up windows at every step to show you the options available to you.

At this step, select User Information and, at the next menu, move the cursor down to the SUPERVISOR login ID and press the Enter key. A third pop-up option screen will appear, showing all of the available options for the user SUPERVISOR. Now move the cursor down to Change Password and press the Enter key. You'll see a screen that looks somewhat like the following:

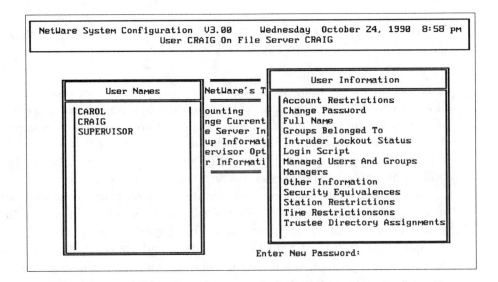

Enter the supervisor's password. As the password you enter does not appear on the screen, NetWare will prompt you to type the password again for confirmation. Be sure to remember this password because there's no way to identify it if you forget. NetWare encrypts all passwords, including the supervisor's.

Establishing Directory Structure

Directories in a NetWare operating system are created in two different ways. Some are created by default as you install the system. Others must be created by you as the supervisor.

When you log in as the supervisor, you'll find the default directories on the SYS: volume of each file server. They include:

SYS:LOGIN   Users have access to this directory after NETx is loaded on their workstation. It contains LOGIN.EXE and SLIST.EXE and is the only NetWare directory that users can access from their workstations before they actually log in. Normally, users execute NetWare's LOGIN.EXE command from this directory to start the login process.

SYS:MAIL   This directory contains a subdirectory for each user. These subdirectories are created when user login scripts are executed or when print job definitions are conveyed to a printer.

SYS:SYSTEM   This directory contains system files and NetWare utilities used only by the network supervisor.

SYS:PUBLIC   As the name implies, this directory is for general network use. It contains the utilities discussed in chapter 5.

The only rights to this directory that are generally assigned to users are R, O, and S (Read, Open, Search) under NetWare 286, and R and F (Read and File Scan) under NetWare 386.

Don't change these directories or move the files that are in them. But you will need to plan the directories and subdirectories that you'll create under them, including the directories you'll create for each application you put on the network. Each application should have a subdirectory of its own. For the sake of organization, you should create a parent directory under which all applications directories will reside. Let's assume that the parent directory is named APPS (short for applications). A good rule of thumb is to keep the parent name short, because you'll probably type it frequently as you set up your applications and drive mappings. Specific application subdirectories should have meaningful names. Let's look at an applications directory structure by examining a typical directory tree on a file server.

```
Y:\
    APPS
        BAT
        CCADMIN
        CCDATA
        CCMAIL
        EXCEL
        LA
        LOTUS
    LOGIN
    MAIL
    PUBLIC
    SHARE
    SYSTEM
    USER
        BSMITH
        JBACH
        SUPERVISOR
        TJONES
        WMOZART
```

Here you can see the beginnings of a structure. Several applications are installed under the APPS directory of this file server. In this example, the applications include the electronic mail package CC:Mail, the Windows-based spreadsheet Excel, the LAN utility Lan Assist, and the DOS-based spreadsheet Lotus 1-2-3. Additionally, there is a directory named BAT for batch files.

Every installation should have a BAT directory for batch files. It's easier to change the batch files and control user access to them when the batch files are grouped together. Include your BAT directory on the network search drives list and create batch files (or use some included on the disk that accompanies this book) to launch all network applications. By storing all batch files in a common directory on the file server and including that directory on all users' search paths, you'll be able to revise applications menus for your users more easily. As all the batch files are centrally located on the file server, you'll only have to make the change once if you add or subtract an application from the users' menus.

In addition to the APPS directory, you can see the NetWare-created directories in the previous example. And notice, too, that there is a directory called SHARE. In any network environment, it's a good idea to set up a shared directory and assign all users' or groups' rights to it. The share directory can be a conduit through which they can pass files because everyone can write files to it and copy files from it.

Setting Up the Users' Directories

In addition to a share directory that all users can access, each user on the network should have a home directory in which only he or she enjoys full rights. Here the user can store confidential or personal files. You'll ease your network administration chores if you set up this home directory to have the same name as your users' login IDs. And if the users' IDs are limited to eight characters, it becomes a simple matter to administer user subdirectories.

Instead of creating all user home directories and applications directories at the root level of a file server volume, where you have to adjust user rights for every individual directory you create, you should first create a control directory as a parent to the others. This control directory should contain no files or applications. Instead, you'll use it to assign all user rights that should flow to the subdirectories under it. Here you can exercise access control for all users. When you're creating a control directory for the users' home directories, you should first delete all access rights and then assign them individually in the users' home directories. The home directory level will be one level lower than the control directory. So, for example, if we have a user ID of BSMITH, his home directory would be:

```
SYS:HOME\BSMITH
```

In this case HOME is the name of the control directory. If you named the control directory USER, the user's home directory would be:

```
SYS:USER\BSMITH
```

Another variation would be to assign a group name to the control directory and assign user directories for everyone in that group under the group name. For example, if user BSMITH belonged to a group named SALES, his home directory would be:

```
SYS:SALES\BSMITH
```

No matter how you structure the subdirectories beneath it, access privileges to a control directory are restricted while users are allowed access one level below in their personal directories. We'll see how this works when we create our sample user, Tim Jones.

Establishing Groups

NetWare provides you with a way to organize your departments or applications into groups, and you should do so. Groups give you the ability to grant, or revoke, network directory access privileges to groups of individuals all at once rather than having to grant or revoke those rights individually. It's logical to set up your groups by establishing them around the departments in your organization. Departments generally need access rights to the same applications.

By creating a group for each department and then assigning all the users within that department to be group members, you can conveniently control access to applications and printers. We investigate methods for controlling access a little later when we discuss the system login script.

Be aware that NetWare establishes a default group named EVERYONE when you install the operating system. As the name implies, each new user you identify is automatically added to this group. You may later choose to remove users from the EVERYONE group. But initially, everyone on the network is a member. This global group provides a ready facility for controlling access privileges that should apply across the network.

The SYSCON command utility is used to add new groups. To illustrate how it's done, we'll create a new group called FINANCE. From the SYSCON main menu, select the Group Information option. Press the Insert key. A window pops up to prompt you for the new group name. It will look like this:

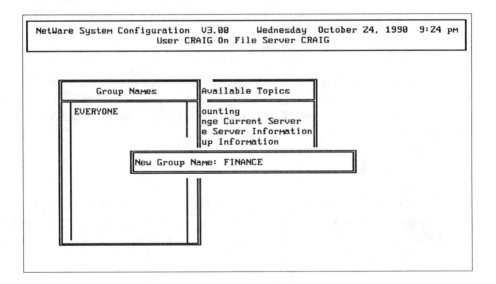

Type in the name of the group, in this case FINANCE, and press Enter. FINANCE now appears in the Group Names listing. Now you'll need to identify the privileges that members of this group will enjoy. With the cursor highlighting FINANCE, press Enter again, and you'll see another pop-up option screen for this newly created group. It will look like this:

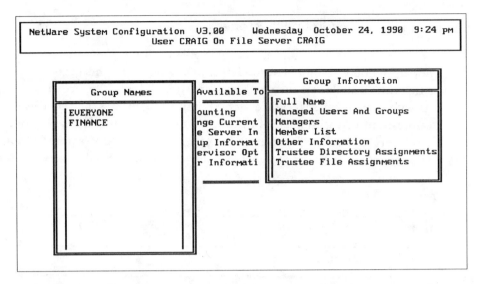

For this sample session, we'll create a Trustee directory assignment. A trustee is anyone—a group or an individual user—who enjoys rights to a directory. Move the cursor down to that option and press Enter. A pop-up box will appear across the top of the screen prompting you for the name of the directory to which the group trustee should be added. In this case, type SYS:FINANCE and hit the Enter key. You'll see a screen that looks like this:

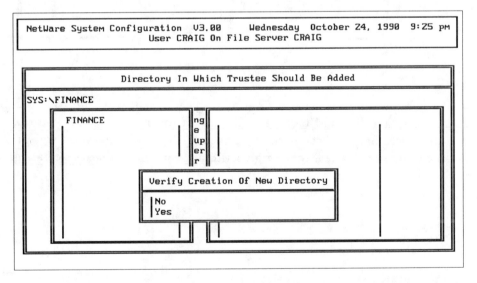

If you answer Yes when you see this message, the directory will be created. Once you've created the directory, you'll have to assign group directory rights to it.

Assigning Rights to Group Directories

With the cursor highlighting the new group name, press the Enter key. A pop-up menu will appear at the left showing trustee rights granted. If this is a first-time installation and you haven't assigned rights, the box will be empty. As with many of the NetWare menu commands, hitting the INS (insert) key will present you with a list of options you can add. In this case, by pressing the Insert key, you will pop up a list of trustee rights not granted alongside those that have been granted. (For a fuller discussion of rights, see chapter 5.)

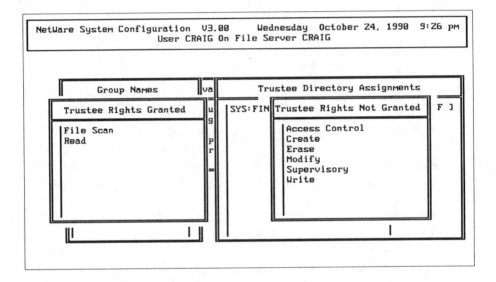

```
┌──────────────────────────────────────────────────────────────────────┐
│ NetWare System Configuration   V3.00    Wednesday  October 24, 1990  9:26 PM │
│                    User CRAIG On File Server CRAIG                     │
└──────────────────────────────────────────────────────────────────────┘

   ┌──────────────────────────┐va┌─────────────────────────────────────┐
   │        Group Names       │  │     Trustee Directory Assignments     │
   ┌──────────────────────────┐u ┌──────┬──────────────────────────┬────┐
   │  Trustee Rights Granted  │  │ SYS:FIN│ Trustee Rights Not Granted │ F ] │
   ┌──────────────────────────┐g └──────┴──────────────────────────┴────┘
   │ File Scan                │p │        │ Access Control             │
   │ Read                     │r │        │ Create                     │
   │                          │  │        │ Erase                      │
   │                          │= │        │ Modify                     │
   │                          │  │        │ Supervisory                │
   │                          │  │        │ Write                      │
```

To add rights, use the F5 key to tag each right you want to grant. When you have finished tagging rights, press the Enter key. As you do, you'll notice that the lists of rights moves to the left. Now when you press the Escape (ESC) key, those rights will appear under the trustee assignment summary as follows:

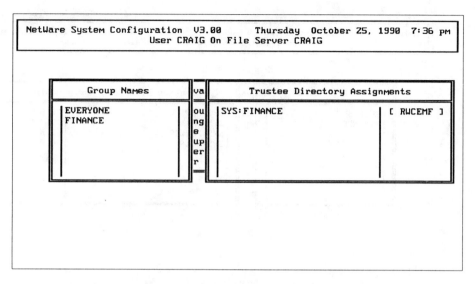

```
NetWare System Configuration  V3.00     Thursday  October 25, 1990  7:36 PM
                   User CRAIG On File Server CRAIG
```

Group Names	va	Trustee Directory Assignments	
EVERYONE	ou	SYS: FINANCE	[RWCEMF]
FINANCE	ng		
	e		
	up		
	er		
	r		

The rights are identified by single letter codes. Here's a brief summary of the rights shown in the preceeding screen:

(R) May Read from File
(W) May Write to File
(C) May Create Subdirectories and Files
(E) May Erase Directory
(M) May Modify Directory
(F) May Scan for Files

As you add each application to the network, set up the groups that enjoy rights to it, assign directory trustee rights to that group, and then add members to the group.

In addition to granting rights with group trustee assignments, you can also limit rights for groups of users. In NetWare, when a new user ID is created, the new user automatically becomes a member of the group EVERYONE. This group is the ideal place in which to both grant and limit rights for everyone on the network. Scroll to the EVERYONE group and hit ENTER. As mentioned earlier, no access privileges should be granted for the "control" directory level for users' home directories. Hit the INS key, and add the directory USER to the group EVERYONE. By default (see screen below), you'll see that this group has been granted minimal rights—(R) Read and (F) File Scan, or (R) read, (O) open (S) search under NetWare 286. However, we want to revoke all rights at this directory level.

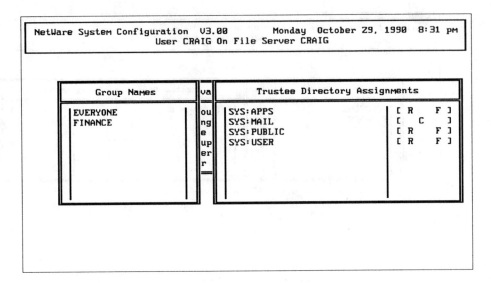

Because these rights, or lack thereof flow down, we'll delete both of these rights so that subdirectories below the USER directory will have no directory access rights until granted. Using the F5 key, tag the Read and File scan rights. Hit the Delete key, and answer Yes to the Revoke All Marked Trustee Rights prompt. It will look like this:

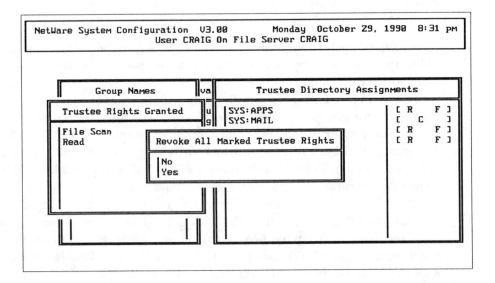

Now hit ESC and Enter, and you'll see that all rights at the directory level USER have been deleted.

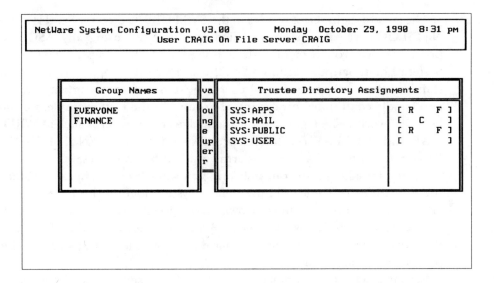

```
NetWare System Configuration  V3.00         Monday  October 29, 1990  8:31 pm
                        User CRAIG On File Server CRAIG
```

```
     Group Names           va     Trustee Directory Assignments

  EVERYONE                 ou   SYS:APPS               [ R     F ]
  FINANCE                  ng   SYS:MAIL               [   C     ]
                           e    SYS:PUBLIC             [ R     F ]
                           up   SYS:USER               [         ]
                           er
                           r
```

Setting the Environment

Fortunately, you do not have to create an operating environment for each individual user, a time-consuming and tedious task. NetWare has provided facilities for initializing environment variables, mapping network drives, and controlling users' program execution. These are the login scripts, and they come in two flavors—the system login script and the user login script.

As the name implies, the system login script is executed at the system level (on the file server), as part of the login procedure for all users. NetWare creates a default login script during installation. Novell recommends that it should be used only temporarily until you have a chance to develop a system login script for your environment. This default script is shown below.

```
WRITE "Good %GREETING_TIME, %LOGIN_NAME."
MAP DISPLAY OFF
MAP ERRORS OFF
Remark: Set 1st drive to most appropriate directory.
MAP *1:=SYS:;*1:=SYS:%LOGIN_NAME
If "%1"="SUPERVISOR" THEN MAP *1:SYS:SYSTEM
Remark: Set search drives (S2 machine-OS dependent).
MAP S1:=SYS:PUBLIC;
S2:=S1:%MACHINE/%OS/%OS_VERSION
Remark: Now display all the current drive settings.
MAP DISPLAY ON
MAP
```

The system login script resides in the SYS:PUBLIC directory and is named NET$LOG.DAT. It can be modified and updated using any ASCII text processor or through menu entries under SYSCON's Supervisor Options, System Login Script selections. You'll use the system login script to create standard drive mappings for all users, set standard environment variables, and handle conditional processing of groups. In the next example, we show how that works. The login scripting language contains verbs such as WRITE, MAP, and FDISPLAY, conditional processing using IF THEN . . . BEGIN . . . END statements, and a generous array of identifier variables.

On the initial login to your network, you will see errors, because some of the directories referenced in the default system login script have yet to be created. You should create your own system login script as soon as you can and tailor it to your network's needs. But remember, since SYS:PUBLIC is a directory in which users generally have at least read rights, never include passwords in the system login script.

Let's take a look at a sample login script. We'll use this example to explain some of the basic concepts of the scripting language. But for more detailed information, refer to your NetWare documentation.

```
WRITE "Good %GREETING_TIME, %FULL_NAME."
MAP DISPLAY OFF
MAP INS S1:=FS1/SYS:PUBLIC
MAP INS S2:=FS1/SYS:APPS
MAP INS S3:=FS1/SYS:\apps\util
MAP INS S4:=FS1/SYS:\APPS\BAT
MAP F:=FS1/SYS:USER\%LOGIN_NAME
DOS SET NAME = "%LOGIN_NAME"
DOS SET FULL = "%FULL_NAME"
DRIVE F:

MAP DISPLAY OFF

IF MEMBER OF "EXEC" THEN
  #CAPTURE Q=EXEC_HP3 L=2 NB TI=10 NFF
  #Capture q=exec_hp2 l=3 nb ti=10 nff
  DOS SET GROUP = "EXEC"
END

MAP DISPLAY ON

IF MEMBER OF "SALES" THEN
  MAP S5:=SYS:\APPS\NOTES
  MAP S6:=SYS:\USER\%LOGIN_NAME\DATA\NOTES
```

```
   #CAPTURE Q=SALES_QMS810 L=2 NB TI=3 NFF
   #CAPTURE Q=SALES_HP2    L=3 NB TI=3 NFF
   DOS SET GROUP = "SALES"
END

IF MEMBER OF "MARKET" THEN
   #CAPTURE Q=MARKET_HP2 L=1 TI=35 NB NT,NFF
   DOS SET GROUP = "MARKET"
END
```

The first line contains the verb WRITE as well as several of NetWare's identifier variables. The WRITE command, one of the more commonly used scripting verbs, enables you to send information to the user's screen while he or she is in the process of logging on. When you use the WRITE command, all text that is to appear on the user's screen must be enclosed in double quotation marks. This first line also contains the identifier variables %GREET-ING_TIME, %FULL_NAME. The variable %GREETING_TIME displays a message on the user's screen that says "Good Morning," "Good Afternoon," or "Good Evening," depending on the time of day recorded by the system clock. And the variable %FULL_NAME displays the full name of the user who's logging in as it is configured with SYSCON, which we discuss below. Identifier variables are always preceded by a % when used with the WRITE statement or in statements in the login script.

Some of the identifier variables you can use in a login script are listed below. Consult your NetWare installation manuals for a complete listing.

Variable Name	Description
Date Variables	
Month	Current Month Number
Month_name	Month Name—eg, January, February, etc.
Day	current day of month (1–31)
NDAY_OF_WEEK	Number of Weekday (1–7, Sunday=1)
Year	Year in four digit format (1990)
Short_year	Year in two digit format (90)
DAY_OF_WEEK	Weekday expressed in text (Monday, Tuesday, etc.)
User Variables	
FULL_NAME	User's full name as assigned in SYSCON
LOGIN_NAME	User's login ID (TJONES)
P_STATION	Node address of user's workstation
STATION	Station number

(continued)

Variable Name	Description
Time Variables	
GREETING_TIME	Morning, Afternoon, or Evening
HOUR	Hour (12-hour format)
HOUR24	HOUR (24-hour or military format)
MINUTE	Current minute (00–59)
SECOND	Current second (00–59)
AM_PM	AM or PM

The second line in the system login script, MAP DISPLAY OFF, prevents the login script from displaying the mappings that are set up in the four lines that follow it. These four lines create the search mappings for NetWare. Search mappings are similar to the DOS search path. They determine the order in which directories will be searched for .COM, .EXE, or .BAT files. Each of these search mappings is assigned a logical drive designation that proceeds in descending order starting from the end of the alphabet. Drive Z is the first search drive. Drive Y is the second search drive, and so forth. In NetWare 386 the DOS search paths that users have established in the AUTOEXEC.BAT files on their workstations are appended to the NetWare search mappings when users log into the network. In earlier versions of NetWare, including NetWare 286, the network search paths overwrote the DOS search path.

The seventh line in the script maps the network drive, F:, as the user's home directory. Notice how it makes use of the variable %LOGIN to name the user's home directory with that individual's user name. In the next two lines, the DOS environment variables NAME and FULL are set to the user's login ID and Full name, respectively.

Your workstations' default DOS environment of 160 bytes (DOS 3.30) is probably inadequate to set variables for future processing in batch files. If there is insufficient environment space, NetWare will be unable to complete its drive mappings as specified in the system and user login scripts. For this reason, you should increase the DOS environment at the workstations by using the following command in the CONFIG.SYS FILE:

```
SHELL=C:\COMMAND.COM /E:384 /P
```

where 384 is the number of bytes you wish to set aside for your environment. You may need to increase this to 512. Note that this format works only for DOS 3.2 and later versions. In earlier versions of DOS (though you really shouldn't be using them in a network), the number following the "E:" specified the number of 16-byte paragraphs, up to a maximum of 62 (992 bytes) rather than the actual size of the environment. DOS 3.2 and above support 32K environments.

The next line of the login script, DRIVE F:, logs the user to the network F drive previously mapped in the script in the same way that typing D: <CR> logs you to drive D on a local hard disk. In other words, it moves the person who is logged in to his or her home directory.

The first section of the system login script establishes universal environments and variables, ones that will be used for everyone who is logged in. The next three sections set conditional variables and commands that are to be invoked once the system determines which groups the person logged in belongs to. In these we get a glimpse of the conditional handling capability of the login scripting language. In each grouping of code, the login script tests for the membership in a group and executes appropriate lines of code if the user is a member of the group being tested for. Let's see how this is done by closely examining the first block of code:

```
IF MEMBER OF "EXEC" THEN
   #CAPTURE Q=EXEC_HP3 L=2 NB TI=10 NFF
   #Capture q=exec_hp2 l=3 nb ti=10 nff
   DOS SET GROUP = "EXEC"
END
```

In this sequence, *if* the user is a member of the group "EXEC", *then* he or she will be assigned to print queues that are serviced by EXEC department printers. Also, an environment variable GROUP is set to EXEC to ease batch file processing of any applications that are used by the entire group.

Another login script command that can be used with IF and THEN is DISPLAY. This causes the system to display the contents of a file on the user's screen if that user is deemed to be a member of a particular group. One example using the DISPLAY command would be:

```
IF MEMBER OF "FINANCE" THEN DISPLAY
Y:\SYS:\PUBLIC\FINANCE.TXT
```

In this case, only members of the FINANCE group would see the contents of the file, FINANCE.TXT, displayed when they login. A similar command to DISPLAY is FDISPLAY. It serves the same function but filters out non-ASCII characters.

The # sign gives you the ability to execute a command from within a login script. If you add a line such as:

```
#123
```

the script would launch the spreadsheet program, Lotus 1-2-3, immediately after the user logs in.

When using the # sign with any executable command, remember never to execute a TSR (terminate and stay resident) program from the login script. Doing so would leave memory "trapped" by login.exe that cannot be released. Instead, write the login script include batch files that will execute your TSRs upon EXITing the login script. The EXIT command is used to terminate the execution of the login script. Any lines of the login script that follow the EXIT command will not be executed. The EXIT command can also call .COM, .EXE, and .BAT files, but these file names must be enclosed in quotation marks. EXIT takes the information in quotes and puts it in the keyboard buffer as it terminates login. An example would be:

```
EXIT "C:\WP\WP"
```

After finishing the login script, you can use the INCLUDE command to chain the login to an external script file. INCLUDE will process a file containing valid login script commands. It will not, however, display text unless the INCLUDE file contains WRITE commands. INCLUDE files can call other files up to ten levels. This facility allows for very complex login scripts. (See LOGIN.INC included on disk and listed in chapter 10.)

In summary, the system login script should provide most of the mappings and establish the environment variables that all users on your network will use. You'll use the login scripting commands coupled with IF . . . THEN processing and an array of identifier variables to define the mappings and environments that are most suitable for your network configuration. The NetWare documentation contains a comprehensive listing of scripting commands for login processing capabilities. Remember, the more you can accomplish in the system login script, the less that you will have to set up in individual user login scripts.

User Login Scripts

The user login script is executed after the system login script. In the user login script, the network administrator can customize drive mappings and environment variables for individual users. You should create user login scripts after you write the system login script and establish universal mappings. In many cases, if the same mappings and variables will apply to all users, the system login script will be adequate and no user login script is required.

User login scripts are created from within SYSCON. Call up the SYSCON menu and select User Information, then select Login Script. If no user login script exists, NetWare will inform you that none exists and will prompt you to enter one. The screen will look like this:

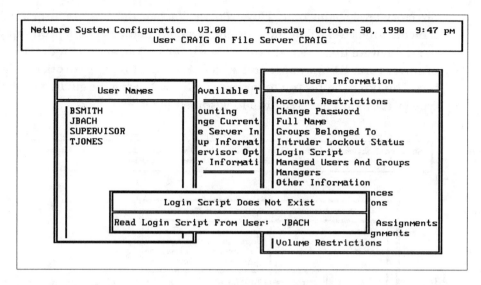

```
┌──────────────────────────────────────────────────────────────────────┐
│  NetWare System Configuration   V3.00      Tuesday  October 30, 1990  9:47 PM │
│                    User CRAIG On File Server CRAIG                     │
└──────────────────────────────────────────────────────────────────────┘
```

At this point, if you press Enter, you'll be given a blank screen into which to enter the user's login script. If, however, a login script exists for another user, NetWare will let you "borrow" it so that you don't have to type in all of the commands. To borrow another login script, press the Insert key, and a list of other Network login IDs will appear. Select the user whose login script is most similar to the one you want to create, and press Enter. That user's login script will be read into the new user's script. Now you can edit the script, customizing it to the new user's needs. When you're finished making modifications, press ESC and answer Yes to SAVE CHANGES?

Network Standards at the User Level

The first area in which to implement standards is in the creation of the user login IDs. On some smaller networks, the tendency is to assign a user's first name as the login ID. However, as the network grows, the likelihood increases that more than one user will share the same first name. A more standard convention for creating user IDs is to use the initial of a user's first name followed by up to seven characters of the last name. For electronic mail systems based on user IDs, you can see how it using first initials with complete last names gives you more flexibility. You'll likely find your organization has fewer persons with standard user names like BSMITH or BJONES than if you used first names and last initials, as in BOBS and BOBJ. By using first initials and last names, you can easily assign users' home directories to have the same name as the users' login IDs. Limiting the login ID to eight characters has the added advantage of being within the DOS file and directory naming scheme.

Now, let's now create a new user. As this new user automatically becomes a member of group EVERYONE, he or she has no rights at the SYS:USER directory level at this time. However, we'll assign rights to the user's home directory one level below the user directory. From the network prompt, type SYSCON, move the cursor down to User Information, and press Enter. A list of current user IDs will appear on the left. Press the Insert key to open a dialog box. This box prompts you for a new user ID. Following the guidelines above, type in TJONES. The screen will look something like:

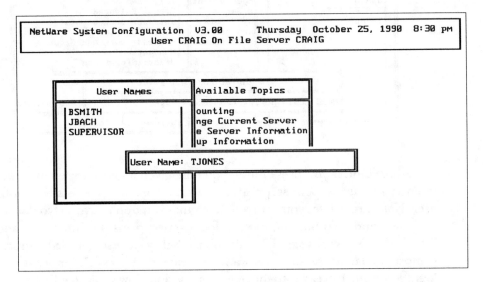

Now if you press the Enter key, you'll see the following User Information screen on the right-hand side of the screen. Move down to Full Name, press ENTER, and then enter the new user's full name. (You'll need the full name if you plan to use it in a user login script.) The screen will look like this:

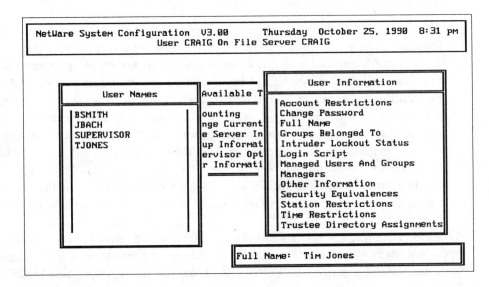

Assigning Passwords

The login IDs and the user passwords provide a two-level security mechanism at the file server level. But this security can be reinforced; customize the way in which users invoke their passwords by supplementing passwords with NetWare's many options.

Consider the security needs of your organization when you structure password control. What rule should you apply?

Netware's defaults offer some guidance. From any network prompt, type SYSCON, and choose Supervisor Options. From the submenu that appears, select Default Account Balance/Restrictions and you'll see a screen that looks like this:

```
┌─────────────────────────────────────────────────────┐
│   ┌───────────────────────────────────────────┐      │
│   │    Default Account Balance/Restrictions   │      │
│   ├───────────────────────────────────────────┤      │
│   │ Account Has Expiration Date:      No      │      │
│   │    Date Account Expires:                  │      │
│   │ Limit Concurrent Connections:     No      │      │
│   │    Maximum Connections:                   │      │
│   │ Require Password:                 Yes     │      │
│   │    Minimum Password Length:       5       │      │
│   │ Force Periodic Password Changes:  Yes     │      │
│   │    Days Between Forced Changes:   40      │      │
│   │    Limit Grace Logins:            Yes     │      │
│   │       Grace Logins Allowed:       6       │      │
│   │ Require Unique Passwords:         Yes     │      │
│   │ Account Balance:                  0       │      │
│   │ Allow Unlimited Credit:           No      │      │
│   │    Low Balance Limit:             0       │      │
│   └───────────────────────────────────────────┘      │
│                                                       │
└─────────────────────────────────────────────────────┘
```

The menu reveals NetWare's recommended guidelines for assigning passwords. The first line in the sample screen indicates that all users must have passwords. The minimum length for passwords is five characters. If users aren't familiar with using passwords—a common situation if you're installing a network for the first time—survey them before setting up the network and ask them what they prefer their first password to be. It should be something that's easy for them to remember, such as a color, the name of a favorite entertainer, or, perhaps, a sports team. It should not be something so obvious that an intruder can easily figure it out. Discourage users from using their first name, their initials, or simple words or items easily guessed by others.

On the other hand, users should avoid using obscure collections of letters. If passwords are too difficult for users to remember, they tend to write them down. So much for the security you thought an obscure password would promote.

As you continue down the list of the Account Balance Restrictions screen, you can see that NetWare provides you with an automatic facility for forcing users to change their passwords on a periodic basis. The NetWare default is forty days. After that time, users will be allowed to continue to log in using the old password, up to the number of times specified in the line labeled Grace Logins Allowed. In this example, the number of grace logins is six. After a password's time expires and the grace logins start being used, users will be informed that their passwords have expired each time they use a grace login. Each time, too, they'll be given an opportunity to change the password. After users exhaust the number of grace logins, their account is disabled and they will be unable to log in again until the supervisor permits access. If the grace logins are not limited, users will be able to log in after their passwords expire but they'll get error messages indicating that their password has expired until they change it.

The last password option on the Account Balance screen is Require Unique Passwords. This option forces users to choose a unique password each time they change it. This means they cannot use the same password twice. NetWare keeps track of all the passwords a person uses; it will not permit duplicates even if a person uses several different passwords before trying one again. This option prevents users from rotating through just two or three different passwords whenever it's time to change. You may find, however, that after eight to ten months, users will begin to complain that they can't come up with a new unique "meaningful" password.

Note that each of these system default options can be overridden at the user level under the User Information, Account Restrictions option. So while you may want the networkwide default to require five-character passwords, you can set individual parameters under Account Restrictions to allow some users to specify eight-character passwords. Or, for some users who work in departments that deal with sensitive data, you could increase the frequency for password changes to fifteen days.

Putting It All Together

Using the basic information just outlined, let's review the process you'll go through to authorize a person to use the network, make the user a member of a group, and assign rights to the user.

First, you'll enter a password for TJONES using the same procedure you used to create a password for the SUPERVISOR ID. For security purposes, when you type the user password, it will not appear on the screen. (Someone may be looking over your shoulder.) However, you will be asked to retype the password for verification. NetWare checks the retyped password against the original password. If they are the same, it accepts the password.

You will assign TJONES as a member of a group. In this example, we'll assign TJONES to the group FINANCE. Scroll down to Group Information and press ENTER. On the right-hand side of the screen, you'll see under Groups Belonged To that TJONES is now a member of EVERYONE. Press the Insert key to see what other groups he potentially could join. (See the following screen sample.)

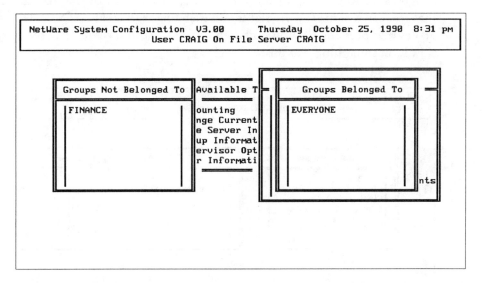

```
NetWare System Configuration  V3.00      Thursday  October 25, 1990  8:31 PM
                  User CRAIG On File Server CRAIG


     Groups Not Belonged To  Available T   Groups Belonged To

      FINANCE                ounting       EVERYONE
                             nge Current
                             e Server In
                             up Informat
                             ervisor Opt
                             r Informati

                                                                  nts
```

Move the cursor to highlight FINANCE and press ENTER. TJONES will now appear under Groups Belonged To.

Next you'll create a home directory for TJONES and assign trustee directory rights to it. Scroll down to Trustee Directory Assignments. As we're creating a new directory for this user, press the Insert key. An empty dialogue box will pop up. Fill it in so that it looks like this:

```
            Directory In Which Trustee Should Be Added

 SYS: USER\TJONES
```

In this case USER is the control directory. As this is a new directory, NetWare will ask you for verification to create the new directory. Highlight Yes and press Enter. The new directory will be created. Now hit ENTER again to see the default rights assigned to this directory. Just as you did above to assign rights to groups, press the Insert key to see additional available rights that you can assign. Tag the rights you wish to assign to TJONES by using the F5 key and pressing ENTER and then ESC to set those rights. The screen will now look something like this:

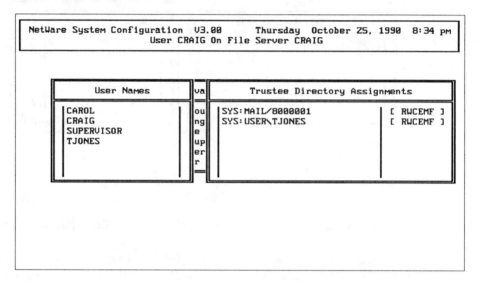

You have now created a user ID, TJONES, and made TJONES a member of a group, FINANCE. And you've assigned directory trustee rights to him.

Configuring a Printer Server

In a nonnetworked environment, users are used to having a printer attached to their printer port (LPT1:) or their serial port (COM1 or COM2). In a networking environment, this local printing function is intercepted by the CAPTURE command in the user login script and rerouted to a network printer that can service some or all of the network users. The printer may be attached to a local workstation, or it may be attached directly to the file server.

Starting with NetWare version 2.1X, Novell provided enhanced printer support through the use of printer queues. When printing on a network, all information is first passed through a queue, or holding area. Normally this holding area exists on the SYS volume of the file server. It can receive multiple print jobs and print them in the order they're received, while continuing to receive incoming print requests. Each print job is "spooled" to its own file.

Part of the magic of the NetWare's print queue system is that you can define multiple printers to service an individual queue, or multiple queues can be serviced by individual printers. Your printer queues will live on the file server, although you must work from the keyboard of a workstation to set them up.

When Novell introduced NetWare 386 in 1989, it changed NetWare 286's printing facilities to reflect the new printing facilities in 386. Now both versions give you, as a network administrator, several options for setting up network printing.

You can install PSERVER.NLM or the PSERVER VAP on the file server. PSERVER is a NetWare-loadable module (NLM, installed if you're using NetWare 386) or a value-added process (VAP, installed if you're using NetWare 286). PSERVER is a file server process that creates a print server that can support up to sixteen printers. This print server takes care of moving print jobs from the print queues and to individual printers. The TSR RPRIN-TER, which is installed at the workstations to which the printers are connected, accepts the print job from the print server and sends it through the printer. Both are discussed extensively in the Novell documentation.

The advantage of using PSERVER is that it can operate as a process on the file server and does not require the use of a dedicated print server. However, there is a disadvantage in configuring PSERVER on the file server. Once it is loaded on one file server, it cannot service print queues from other file servers. It also consumes file server resources and poses a risk to the network in general; should a printing process hang, it could also hang the file server. Under NetWare 386, the NLM can be unloaded to reconfigure printers without taking down the server; should PSERVER hang, the work session can usually be continued without interruption. However, under NetWare 286, the server must be "downed" and brought back up again to reinitialize printer configurations; users who are logged into the network at the time can lose the work they have onscreen.

You can also install PSERVER.EXE on a dedicated workstation as a separate printer server. In this situation, the "printer server" workstation can route jobs to printers across the network. Here, just as when the print server runs as a file server process (PSERVER.NLM loaded on a 386 server or PSERVER.VAP loaded on a 286 server), the remote printers are attached to workstations that run RPRINTER. The advantage of setting up a separate printer server is that, if the print server hangs, it can be rebooted without bringing down the file server. Under NetWare 386, there have been instances when the server hangs while unloading PSERVER.NLM. An independent printer server can service queues from up to eight different file servers. You'll also reduce the traffic on your file servers by running the process from a separate printer server. The disadvantage of this method is the expense associated with setting aside a dedicated computer to act as a print server.

Finally, you can install third-party print-server software. Numerous companies produce software, tightly integrated with NetWare's print queue structure, that allows you to use a nondedicated workstation as a print server. For that reason, and because these programs are easy to install and maintain, some network administrators prefer them to Novell's own printer server utilities. These third-party printer server utilities include Brightwork's PS PRINT, Lan Systems' LANSPOOL, and Fresh Technology's Print Assist.

As a rule of thumb, it's best to avoid file server printer processes. If they hang, you'll have a lot of unhappy users who didn't save their files just before the server went down.

5

Getting the Most from NetWare Commands

Like any good operating environment, NetWare offers users and managers a host of useful commands. In fact, NetWare offers so many commands that can do so many different worthwhile things that fully understanding and utilizing them all presents a major challenge. Here we show in a specific, step-by-step, hands-on way how both users and managers can take fullest advantage of the tools NetWare offers.

The ATTACH Command

ATTACH is a NetWare command that allows you to attach to other file servers after your initial login to your "home" file server. Using the ATTACH command, you remain logged into your "home" server, but you start the attachment process for another file server. The syntax for this command is:

```
ATTACH SERVER/USERNAME
```

In order for the attachment to be successful, you must have been established on the file server to which you are attempting to attach.

The ATTACH command does not execute any login script for the attached file server. You must create drive mappings for it.

Often the network administrator uses the user login script on the user's "home" file server to automatically attach and map drives on a second server. For example, let's assume that user TJONES had a "home" file server named FINANCE but needed access to resources on a server named SALES. The network administrator could accomplish this in the user login script for TJONES with the following commands:

```
ATTACH SALES/TJONES;MANAGER
MAP K:=SALES/SYS:\ACCTINFO
```

In this example, MANAGER is TJONES' password on the SALES file server.

Working on multiple file servers can become confusing. To check yourself, use the MAP and WHOAMI commands (discussed later in this chapter).

The CAPTURE Command

NetWare's CAPTURE command can be entered at the prompt or in user login scripts to redirect print jobs from a workstation's local printer to a network printer or from one network printer to another. Network managers typically use it when setting up login scripts to direct printing from a user's workstation to a specific printer on the network; users may also enter it at the network prompt if they want to direct their print job to a special printer. CAPTURE can also be used to redirect print jobs when a network printer is down.

Both users and system managers can change these specifications during a network session by entering the CAPTURE command at the DOS prompt, along with whatever switches are needed to set the new parameters desired. Type CAPTURE H at the DOS prompt (the H stands for Help) to see a list of the available switches and the syntax for using CAPTURE.

Before using CAPTURE to redirect printing, you first need to know which print queues and printers are available on the network. (See "The PCONSOLE Command" below.) And you also need to know how the CAPTURE setting on the workstation is currently defined. To find this out, type CAPTURE SH at the DOS prompt. This will return information on the configuration of each LPT port at the workstation you're typing from.

The changes you make by entering new CAPTURE parameters from the network prompt are only temporary. They remain in effect only until you log off the network. When you log back into the network, your login script defaults are restored. However, it is possible to make permanent changes in your user login script. System managers do so to customize the script permanently to the individual's printing needs.

Now, let's use an example to show how to use CAPTURE to change a few settings. Let's say the company sales force normally prints to a Hewlett-Packard (H-P) LaserJet II in the sales department and that printer is down for service. Linda, a secretary in sales, is preparing a mass mailing that must go out today. By using CAPTURE to print to another LaserJet on the network, work can continue.

From Linda's workstation, you would enter CAPTURE SH at the prompt (the SH stands for Show) to see which of her printer ports is directed to the down LaserJet. We get a message that looks like this:

```
CAPTURE L=3 Q=SALES_HP2
```

From this we see that the LaserJet II in the sales department (Q=SALES_HP2) is on LPT3 (L=#).

To redirect the print job to another printer—say, an H-P LaserJet III in the marketing department down the hall—you would change the LPT3 setting to different queue (one you identified after using PCONSOLE) by entering the following command at the prompt:

```
CAPTURE L=3 Q=MARKT_HP3
```

Additional parameters (such as L= and Q= in this example) can be used with CAPTURE to affect printer settings as well. For instance, users can add other switches to adjust how long it takes the network to print their documents, how many copies they produce, and to add title page banners.

By typing CAPTURE SH at the prompt, you can also see the time-out setting (TI=), which is the amount of time the network waits after a user sends a print job to it and before it releases the job to the user's specified printer. You might use this setting when a person who is not located near a printer wants to print a document on company letterhead, and needs some time to walk to the printer, find letterhead paper, and load it in the printer's paper tray. If the default timeout in the login script was set to, say, 10 seconds, the printer would probably print the job before the user could make the change. But the user could change the timeout to 60 seconds—enough time to get the letterhead in the paper tray.

Let's assume you want to print to the marketing department's LaserJet III, and the CAPTURE SH command shows you're "captured" to that printer on LPT2. To change the timeout, type:

```
CAPTURE L=2 Q=MARKT_HP3 TI=60
```

This increases the time delay to 60 seconds.

Another time when you might want to change the timeout is when you are running either a mail merge or a database report. NetWare has a specified default of 10 seconds—it assumes print jobs are complete and starts printing after that time. But in a database report or mail merge, there could be a greater delay as the applications prepare the documents by searching, sorting, and merging data. In these cases you might want to increase the timeout to 30 or 40 seconds to assure that the print job doesn't time out even before it begins to run.

You should also change the timeout setting when you print a large bit-mapped graphics file. Graphics application, such as Lotus's Freelance Plus, build a bit map in memory before dumping it to the printer for processing. When printing a graphic from a graphics application over the network, it's wise to increase the default timeout, TI, to about 60 seconds.

Another CAPTURE option is the banner switch, which inserts an individual sheet of paper at the front of each of your print jobs. It functions to separate users' print jobs as they stack up in the output tray. Information on a banner might include the name of the person who printed the job and when it was submitted for printing. While this is useful in large offices where many users share one printer, printing banners with every job wastes paper. Therefore, many system managers set login script defaults to No Banner.

Let's say a user named Larry wants to add a banner to a print job. He would enter the following at the prompt before printing the document:

```
CAPTURE L=3 Q=MARKT_HP3 TI=15 NAME=LARRY
```

This captures LPT3 to the marketing department's LaserJet III with a timeout of 15 seconds and prints a banner with the name LARRY at the beginning of the job. When Larry finishes with the print job, he could disable the banner by entering:

```
CAPTURE L=3 Q=MARKT_HP3 TI=15 NB
```

The NB in this command stands for NO BANNER.

Special note: Banner is a character-based function. Don't use a banner with a PostScript printer. It won't work!

The CAPTURE Copies option reduces traffic on the network when users print multiple copies of the same document. Unlike applications that send repeated print commands to network printers when multiple copies are selected, the network printing software sends the job to the printer only once and generates the additional copies at the printer. Copies is set with a C= switch, followed by the number of copies to be printed. As an example, a user in the sales department who needs ten copies of the same letter would type the following command at the network prompt:

```
CAPTURE L=1 Q=SALES_HP2 C=10
```

This command tells your application to send the letter to the print queue just once; NetWare handles the number of times the document is printed. Besides reducing traffic on the network, this frees the application software more quickly so that the user can continue with the next job.

The CASTOFF Command

CASTOFF is used to override the effects of the SEND command (see "The SEND Command" below). Messages sent via the NetWare SEND command will remain onscreen and freeze an application until someone depresses the CTRL key and strikes ENTER to clear them. But as there are times when users don't want that interruption, NetWare provides the CASTOFF utility to help them avoid it. You just need to type CASTOFF at the prompt to avoid receiving SEND messages from other users. You will, however, continue to receive messages from the file server console, but, unlike other user messages, which can often be frivolous, these should come through to alert you of network emergencies, such as "File Server goes down in 10 minutes."

To illustrate the CASTOFF command, let's take the example of Jill, a telemarketer in the sales department. Jill is a member of the network group called SALES. If she types CASTOFF at the network prompt, NetWare will return the following message to her screen.

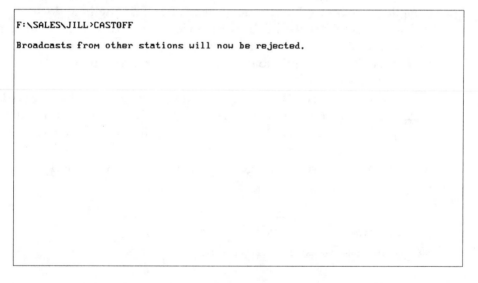

```
F:\SALES\JILL>CASTOFF

Broadcasts from other stations will now be rejected.
```

CASTOFF includes one option, the "A" switch, which also rejects messages from the file server console. It is best used at workstations that should never be interrupted, such as those set up as printer servers or communications servers. To invoke it, simply type:

CASTOFF A

You will receive the following message from NetWare:

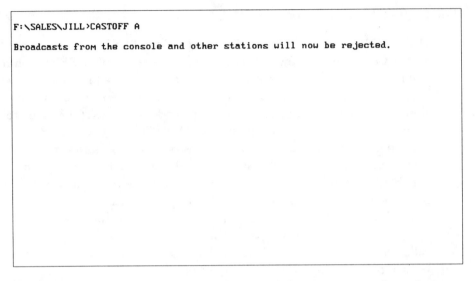

```
F:\SALES\JILL>CASTOFF A
Broadcasts from the console and other stations will now be rejected.
```

Network managers use CASTOFF to inhibit messages when they are compiling programs. Users inhibit them when printing long documents or mail merges, or when their PCs are set up for remote dial-in—times when they can't afford to have messages freezing the application onscreen until CTRL-ENTER is hit. CASTOFF should also be used on print spools to ensure that they continue printing.

When someone SENDs a message to a workstation that has invoked the CASTOFF command, he or she receives a NetWare message saying that the message was not delivered. If, for instance, Jill has used CASTOFF and Howard, another member of the sales group, tries to send her a message, he would get the following message back from NetWare (where FS1 is the name of the server):

```
F:\SALES\HOWARD>send "THIS IS A TEST MESSAGE" TO JILL
Message NOT sent to FS1/JILL (station 2).
```

The CASTON Command

When you want to start receiving messages after using the CASTOFF command, you would use CASTON, the companion utility. There are no options for CASTON. When you type CASTON, your screen will look like this:

```
F:\SALES\JILL>CASTON
Broadcast messages from the console and other stations will now be accepted.
```

The CHKVOL Command

NetWare's CHKVOL utility provides information about the network disk systems. Similar to the DOS command CHKDSK, CHKVOL shows the total volume size, the amount of space taken by files, the amount of space left on the volume, and the number of bytes available to you. If you type CHKVOL from any network prompt, you will see a status report that looks something like the following:

```
Statistics for fixed volume FS1/FINANCE:

Total volume space:                      150,588  K Bytes
Space used by files:                      75,984  K Bytes
Space in use by deleted files:            40,176  K Bytes
Space available from deleted files:       40,180  K Bytes
Space remaining on volume:                74,608  K Bytes
Space available to CRANE:                 74,608  K Bytes
```

When you use the command without any options, as we did, you will get a report on the current volume only. In this case, members of the finance group on File Server 1 (FS1/FINANCE) will see a report on the FINANCE volume only.

If you want a report on all of the volumes for the file server, you can type CHKVOL *, and you will get a report similar to the following:

```
Statistics for fixed volume FS1/SYS:

Total volume space:                      125,864  K Bytes
Space used by files:                      82,292  K Bytes
Space in use by deleted files:            37,164  K Bytes
Space available from deleted files:       37,164  K Bytes
Space remaining on volume:                43,572  K Bytes
Space available to CRANE:                 43,572  K Bytes


Statistics for fixed volume FS1/FINANCE:

Total volume space:                      150,588  K Bytes
Space used by files:                      75,988  K Bytes
Space in use by deleted files:            40,176  K Bytes
Space available from deleted files:       40,180  K Bytes
Space remaining on volume:                74,604  K Bytes
Space available to CRANE:                 74,604  K Bytes


Statistics for fixed volume FS1/EXTRA:

Total volume space:                      301,172  K Bytes
Space used by files:                     135,464  K Bytes
Space in use by deleted files:           156,300  K Bytes
Space available from deleted files:      156,380  K Bytes
Space remaining on volume:               165,788  K Bytes
Space available to CRANE:                165,788  K Bytes


Statistics for fixed volume FS1/SALES:

Total volume space:                      150,584  K Bytes
Space used by files:                      40,744  K Bytes
Space in use by deleted files:            20,176  K Bytes
Space available from deleted files:       20,176  K Bytes
Space remaining on volume:               109,840  K Bytes
Space available to CRANE:                109,840  K Bytes
```

In this case CHKVOL returned reports on all four volumes of our example network: SYS, FINANCE, EXTRA, and SALES. Because CHKVOL is not limited by NetWare security, users and system managers alike can see the same volume information for any disk for any file server that they're logged into.

In the preceeding example, you can see that the FS1 file server has four volumes. Finance and sales/marketing each have 150 megabytes (MB) of space on volumes named FINANCE and SALES, respectively.

If you use the CHKVOL * command and see you have no space available on some volumes, it is because there are volume restrictions on your groups. In our example members of the sales or marketing groups have no volume privileges on the FINANCE volume. Likewise, members of the finance group have no volume privileges on the SALES volume.

Volume restrictions take precedence over trustee and file rights. Even if you have been assigned trustee rights to a directory and are restricted from using the volume on which that directory resides, you will not be able to create or write a file to that volume.

The FILER Command

FILER is a NetWare menu-driven file management utility that gives you the ability to view directory contents, create, move or delete subdirectories, and change file attributes and the inherited rights masks. For the purposes of this discussion, the examples shown will be from NetWare 386. FILER features are similar under NetWare 2.15. To access FILER, type FILER at any NetWare prompt. The opening screen will look like this:

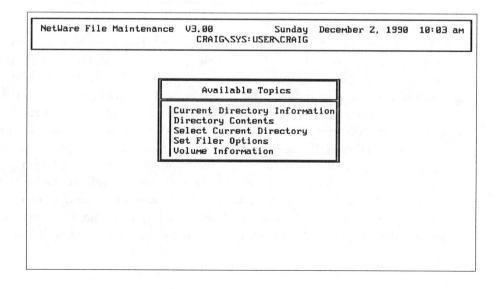

```
  NetWare File Maintenance   V3.00            Sunday  December 2, 1990  10:03 am
                             CRAIG\SYS:USER\CRAIG


                        ╔═══════════════════════════╗
                        ║     Available Topics      ║
                        ╠═══════════════════════════╣
                        ║ Current Directory Information
                        ║ Directory Contents
                        ║ Select Current Directory
                        ║ Set Filer Options
                        ║ Volume Information
                        ╚═══════════════════════════╝
```

Your current directory will be the default directory when you enter FILER and will be shown at the top of the screen. Let's move through the screen options and explore the major features of FILER.

The first option, Current Directory Information, lets you view and, with proper rights, change directory attributes and trustee assignments. Look at the next screen. You can see that this directory was created by the SUPERVISOR on May 12, 1990, at 4:35PM. If you highlight the Directory Attributes and hit ENTER, you'll see the current directory attributes. If you hit the INS key, you will be able to see the attributes that can be applied to the directory. Initially, unless specifically assigned, the box will be blank. The screen will look like this:

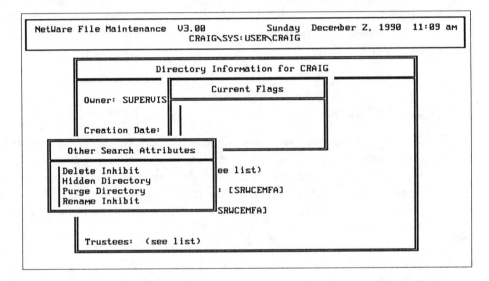

In addition to the four options shown here, a fifth option, System, comes into view when you hit the down arrow key. Delete Inhibit prevents the deletion of subdirectories even if users have been granted the Delete right. If Hidden Directory is applied, the directory will be hidden and won't be viewable to users when they use the DOS DIR command. With the Hidden attribute, the directory also cannot be deleted. However, the directory is viewable with the NDIR command (to be discussed later) if the user has File Scan (S) rights. If the Purge Directory attribute is set, files will be purged immediately after deletion and will not be recoverable with the SALVAGE command. If the Rename Inhibit directory attribute is set, the directory can not be renamed even if the user has Modify (M) rights in the directory. The System attribute flags the directory as used by the system and will not be viewable. However, the directory is viewable with the NDIR command (to be discussed later) if the user has File Scan (S) rights.

Note: In order to change the directory attributes, users must have Modify (M) rights in the directory. Users must have Erase rights (E) in order to set the Purge Directory option.

The next option on the Directory Information screen shows the current effective rights. (See "The RIGHTS Command" below.)

Next we come to the Inherited Rights Mask. Users cannot change this option unless they have at least ACCESS rights to the subdirectory. Hit the Enter key, and the Inherited Rights Mask for this directory will appear. In the next example, all rights have been granted. In cases where they haven't been granted, hitting the INS key will show a list of rights that can be granted. Hitting the DEL key will delete the highlighted or Marked rights (use the F5 key to mark multiple rights). If inherited rights are removed from a directory, they are removed for all users of that directory. The next screen shows the Inherited Rights Mask for the current directory; the DEL key has been hit to delete the Access Control right.

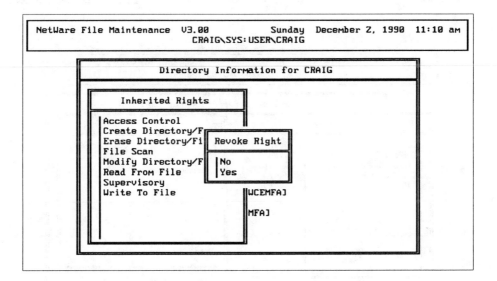

The last option on the Directory Information menu is Trustees. If a user has Access (A) privileges to a directory, he or she can grant directory access to others. To view the current trustee assignments, hit the Enter key. The list will appear as shown:

```
┌─────────────────────────────────────────────────────────────────────────┐
│ NetWare File Maintenance  V3.00          Sunday  December 2, 1990  10:22 am │
│                        CRAIG\SYS:USER\CRAIG                                │
└─────────────────────────────────────────────────────────────────────────┘
        ┌───────────────────────────────────────────────────────────┐
        │            Directory Information for CRAIG                  │
        │  ┌────────────────────────────────────────────────────────┐│
        │  │  Trustee Name        Type              Rights           ││
        │  │ ┌──────────────────┬──────────────────────────────────┐││
        │  │ │ CRAIG            │ (User)             [SRWCEMFA]     │││
        │  │ │                  │                                  │││
        │  │ │                  │                                  │││
        │  │ │                  │                                  │││
        │  │ └──────────────────┴──────────────────────────────────┘││
        │  │  Trustees:  (see list)                                  ││
        │  └────────────────────────────────────────────────────────┘│
        └───────────────────────────────────────────────────────────┘
```

To add trustees, hit the INS key. To delete trustees, hit the DEL key. When you hit the INS key, a list of potential other trustees appears. Other potential trustees can be either individual users or groups. The screen will look like this:

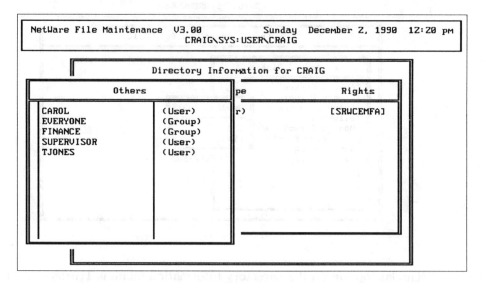

```
┌─────────────────────────────────────────────────────────────────────────┐
│ NetWare File Maintenance  V3.00          Sunday  December 2, 1990  12:20 pm │
│                        CRAIG\SYS:USER\CRAIG                                │
└─────────────────────────────────────────────────────────────────────────┘
        ┌───────────────────────────────────────────────────────────┐
        │            Directory Information for CRAIG                  │
        │  ┌──────────────────────────────┬─────────────────────────┐│
        │  │         Others               │pe         Rights        ││
        │  │ ┌──────────────┬────────────┐│r)         [SRWCEMFA]    ││
        │  │ │ CAROL        │ (User)     ││                         ││
        │  │ │ EVERYONE     │ (Group)    ││                         ││
        │  │ │ FINANCE      │ (Group)    ││                         ││
        │  │ │ SUPERVISOR   │ (User)     ││                         ││
        │  │ │ TJONES       │ (User)     ││                         ││
        │  │ │              │            ││                         ││
        │  │ └──────────────┴────────────┘│                         ││
        │  └──────────────────────────────┴─────────────────────────┘│
        └───────────────────────────────────────────────────────────┘
```

Highlight one or mark more than one with the F5 key and hit ENTER. In this example we've chosen TJONES. When we select him he will be added to the directory trustee list with minimal rights—Read (R) and File Scan (F)—as shown:

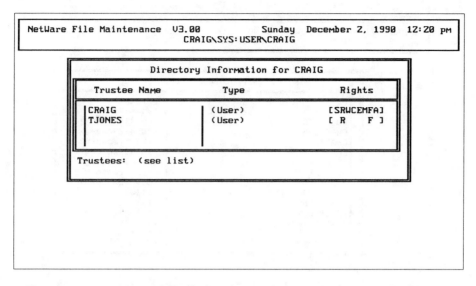

If you want to grant additional rights to the user (or group), highlight the name and hit ENTER. This will bring up a list of currently granted rights. To add rights, hit the INS key to see what other rights can be granted. Highlight the additional right to be granted (or tag multiple rights with the F5 key) and hit ENTER. The screen will look like this:

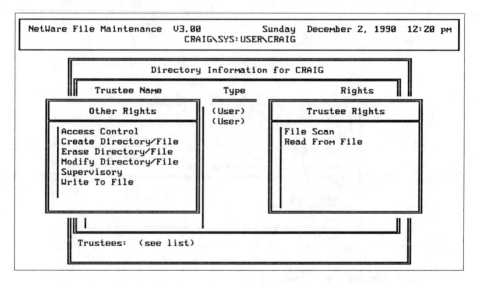

Returning to the main FILER menu, let's review the options under the Directory Contents menu. When you select this option and hit the Enter key, this screen will appear:

```
┌─────────────────────────────────────────────────────────────────────┐
│ NetWare File Maintenance   V3.00        Sunday  December 2, 1990  12:53 pm │
│                       CRAIG\SYS:USER\CRAIG                             │
└─────────────────────────────────────────────────────────────────────┘

        ┌───────────────────────────────────────────────────┐
        │                 Directory Contents                │
        ├───────────────────────────────────────────────────┤
        │ ..                          │ (parent)            │
        │ \                           │ (root)              │
        │ BUY_GUID                    │ (subdirectory)      │
        │ CHAPTER4                    │ (subdirectory)      │
        │ CHAPTER5                    │ (subdirectory)      │
        │ CHAPTER6                    │ (subdirectory)      │
        │ NETWARE!                    │ (subdirectory)      │
        │ NETWIRE                     │ (subdirectory)      │
        │ ZIP                         │ (subdirectory)      │
        │ !NETWARE.OUT                │ (file)              │
        │ ASSUR.DOC                   │ (file)              │
        │ ASSUR.OUT                   │ (file)              │
        │ CHAPT6.SCR                  │ (file)              │
        │ DOC.TXT                     │ (file)              │
        │ ELS1.BAK                    │ (file)              │
        └───────────────────────────────────────────────────┘
```

If you move the cursor to the ".." (parent) or the "\" (root) selection, you will be asked if you want to make that directory the current one. Otherwise, when you hit the Enter key, you will see a submenu that looks like this:

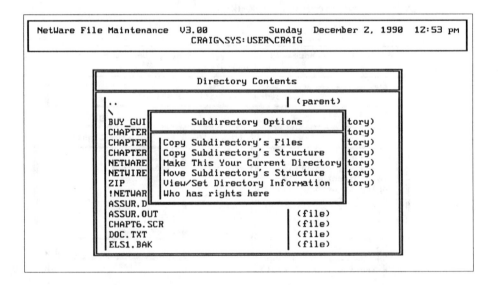

The options are as follows:

Copy Subdirectory's Files   This option copies all of the subdirectory's files to another location. You must have rights in the destination location for this to work.

Copy Subdirectory's Structure   This option makes a duplicate copy of the directory structure to a new location. If the location is other than the root of a volume, the new location must exist before the command is executed, and, of course, you must have rights in the new location.

Move Subdirectory's Structure   This is similar to Copy, except that it moves a subdirectory from one parent directory to another. This command is very useful when you have to reorganize directory structures. This is very similar to XTREE NET's "graft" function.

Make This Your Current Directory   This is the FILER equivalent of the DOS command "CD\directory name." It makes the currently highlighted directory the default file directory.

View/Set Directory Information   This option provides a submenu with the options of the Current Directory Information available for the current directory.

Who Has Rights Here   This is very useful to see which rights have been assigned to users for a particular directory. This option is available only to the network supervisor, or supervisor equivalent. The list looks something like this screen:

```
┌──────────────────────────────────────────────────────────────────────┐
│ NetWare File Maintenance    V3.00        Sunday  December 2, 1990  12:57 pm │
│                    CRAIG\SYS:USER\CRAIG                                  │
│                                                                          │
│   ┌──────────────────────────────────────────────────────────────┐     │
│   │   Trustee Name            Type              Rights            │     │
│   │  ┌─────────────────────────────────────────────────────────┐ │     │
│   │  │ CAROL              (User)         [         ]            │ │     │
│   │  │ CRAIG              (User)         [SRWCEMFA]             │ │     │
│   │  │ EVERYONE           (Group)        [         ]            │ │     │
│   │  │ SUPERVISOR         (User)         [SRWCEMFA]             │ │     │
│   │  │ TJONES             (User)         [ R    F ]             │ │     │
│   │  │                                                          │ │     │
│   │  │                                                          │ │     │
│   │  │                                                          │ │     │
│   │  └─────────────────────────────────────────────────────────┘ │     │
│   │  │ ELS1.BAK                      │ (file)                    │ │     │
│   └──────────────────────────────────────────────────────────────┘     │
└──────────────────────────────────────────────────────────────────────┘
```

Here you can see that TJONES has the (R) and (F) rights to this directory that we granted previously.

In addition to the menu options just described, you can also create or delete new directories or subdirectories from within FILER. To create a new subdirectory, hit the INS key, and you will be prompted for the new subdirectory name. It will be created under the current directory. You will see a pop-up box in the middle of the FILER screen like this:

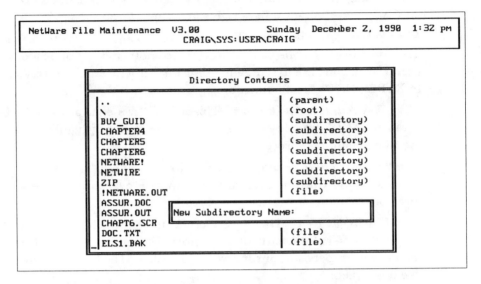

```
NetWare File Maintenance   V3.00        Sunday  December 2, 1990  1:32 PM
                          CRAIG\SYS:USER\CRAIG
```

```
                        Directory Contents

        ..                          (parent)
        \                           (root)
        BUY_GUID                    (subdirectory)
        CHAPTER4                    (subdirectory)
        CHAPTER5                    (subdirectory)
        CHAPTER6                    (subdirectory)
        NETWARE!                    (subdirectory)
        NETWIRE                     (subdirectory)
        ZIP                         (subdirectory)
        !NETWARE.OUT                (file)
        ASSUR.DOC
        ASSUR.OUT        New Subdirectory Name:
        CHAPT6.SCR
        DOC.TXT                     (file)
        ELS1.BAK                    (file)
```

You can also delete the current directory by hitting the DEL key. When you do, you will get an option box similar to this:

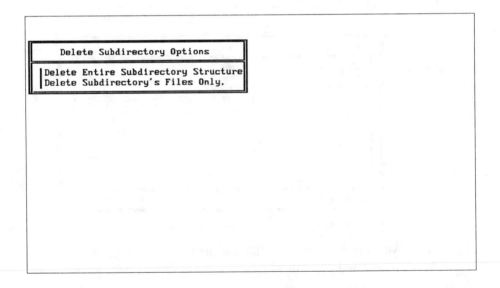

```
    Delete Subdirectory Options

   Delete Entire Subdirectory Structure
   Delete Subdirectory's Files Only.
```

If you select Delete Entire Subdirectory Structure, the subdirectories and all files will be deleted. This is similar to XTREE NET's PRUNE option. If you select Delete Subdirectory's Files Only, all files in the subdirectory will be deleted but the directory structure will remain intact.

Returning to the main menu, the next option is Select Current Directory. This option allows you to select a new current directory from the main menu without having to go into a submenu to change default directories.

The next FILER main menu option is Set Filer Options. When you select this option, the following submenu appears:

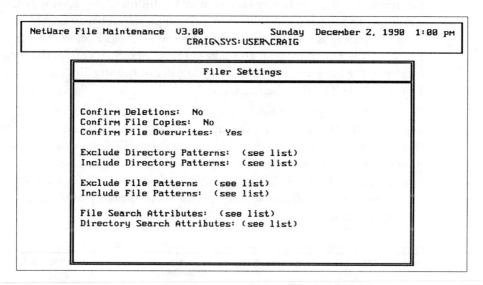

```
NetWare File Maintenance   V3.00           Sunday  December 2, 1990  1:00 pm
                           CRAIG\SYS:USER\CRAIG

                            Filer Settings


           Confirm Deletions:  No
           Confirm File Copies:  No
           Confirm File Overwrites:  Yes

           Exclude Directory Patterns:  (see list)
           Include Directory Patterns:  (see list)

           Exclude File Patterns  (see list)
           Include File Patterns:  (see list)

           File Search Attributes:  (see list)
           Directory Search Attributes: (see list)
```

The first three options determine how FILER will work during file copies and deletions.

Confirm Deletions   The default is No. With this option set, FILER will not prompt you before deleting individual files. If set to Yes, you will be prompted before each file deletion.

Confirm File Copies   The default is No. This option determines if you will be prompted when you copy multiple files to another directory.

Confirm File Overwrites   The default is Yes. You will be prompted for confirmation before FILER overwrites a file with a duplicate filename.

Exclude/Include Directory Patterns   These two options determine which directories FILER will show. The default for Include is "*" for all files, and the default for Exclude is blank.

Exclude/Include File Patterns   These options, which have the same defaults as the Exclude/Include Directory Patterns, give you control over which files FILER will display. This feature is much more useful than the directory pattern option.

Why would you use it? Say you have a directory full of word processing documents with the extension of DOC. Also in that directory are all of the automatic backups made by the word processor with the extension of BAK. If you wanted to view only the document files and not the backup files, you could either set the Include parameter for *.DOC or set the Exclude parameter for *.BAK. This command respects the DOS wildcards of ? and *. So, for example, if you wanted to search for all documents with a file name starting with any two characters followed by EXAM with the extension DOC, you could set your Include parameter to ??EXAM*.DOC.

Note: If there is a conflict between the Include and Exclude parameters specified, the Exclude parameter takes precedence. So if you set the Include to E* and the Exclude to ??TEST*.*, you will not see any files that start with E and include TEST in the file name.

File/Directory Search Attributes This option determines which directories and files FILER will display, but applies only to the attributes of Hidden (H) or System (S). FILER's default is not to show Hidden or System files or directories. To change either of these options, highlight it with the cursor and hit the ENTER key. To add either the System or Hidden attribute to either the file or directory search specification, hit the Insert key and this submenu will appear:

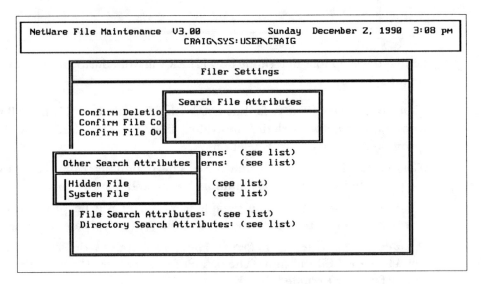

Select the option you desire, and hit the ENTER key.

Note: These FILER options are only temporary and are reset to the defaults each time you enter FILER. There is no way to save the FILER options you establish within a session.

The final option on the FILER main menu is merely an information summary for the current volume. It will look something like this:

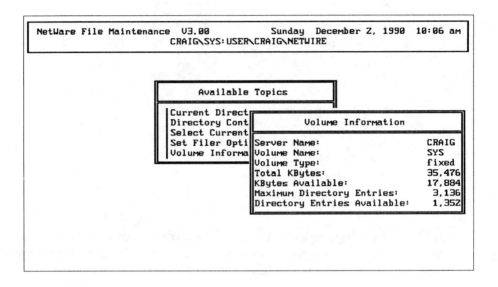

```
NetWare File Maintenance  V3.00         Sunday  December 2, 1990  10:06 am
                    CRAIG\SYS:USER\CRAIG\NETWIRE
```
```
                         Available Topics
                  Current Direct
                  Directory Cont         Volume Information
                  Select Current
                  Set Filer Opti  Server Name:                   CRAIG
                  Volume Informa  Volume Name:                   SYS
                                  Volume Type:                   fixed
                                  Total KBytes:                 35,476
                                  KBytes Available:             17,884
                                  Maximum Directory Entries:     3,136
                                  Directory Entries Available:   1,352
```

The FLAG Command

The FLAG command has to do with File Access Rights, the third class of NetWare's three basic security mechanisms. (The other two are permission to access the file server through the login/password sequence and permission to access a directory through the basic trustee rights.)

On an individual PC, where files reside on a local hard disk, a file can have any combination of four basic file attributes: H–Hidden, S–System, A–Archive Bit, and R–Read only.

On a network, quite a few additional file attributes can be assigned to files. The FLAG command can be used in conjunction with any of the DOS wildcards to display the current status of a user's files. For example, if users want to see the file attributes of all the .DOC files, they would type the following from their home directory network prompt:

```
FLAG *.DOC
```

A screen that looks something like this will appear:

```
PCONSOLE.DOC  [ Rw - A - - -- - - -- -- - - - ]
PUNCHDWN.DOC  [ Rw - A - - -- - - -- -- - - - ]
SONYRTN.DOC   [ Rw - A - - -- - - -- -- - - - ]
REQ.DOC       [ Rw - A - - -- - - -- -- - - - ]
PRICES.DOC    [ Rw - A - - -- - - -- -- - - - ]
HELP1.DOC     [ Rw - A - - -- - - -- -- - - - ]
NET0725.DOC   [ Rw - A - - -- - - -- -- - - - ]
PCC0727.DOC   [ Rw - A - - -- - - -- -- - - - ]
ZIFFNET.DOC   [ Rw - A - - -- - - -- -- - - - ]
RIGHTS.DOC    [ Rw - A - - -- - - -- -- - - - ]
0806.DOC      [ Rw - A - - -- - - -- -- - - - ]
```

Check the following list to interpret the attributes of these files. Note that the A attribute, the archive bit, is not included in the list. Except for the purposes of daily backups, it has no effect on users.

NetWare 386 File Attributes

RO	Read Only
RW	Read Write
S	Shareable
H	Hidden
Sy	System
T	Transactional
P	Purge
RA	Read Audit
WA	Write Audit
C	Copy Inhibit
D	Delete Inhibit
R	Rename Inhibit

From this list you can see that each of the .DOC files in our example has a Read/Write attribute. This means that the user can read the file and write (or overwrite) it.

In addition to checking the status of file attributes, people with adequate trustee rights can use the FLAG command to change the attributes of a file (or group of files). In order to change file attributes, they must have Read, Write, Scan, and Modify rights in a subdirectory.

When would you want to change file attributes? Let's assume that a worksheet, FORECAST.WKS, is a blank spreadsheet that one user keeps to use as a form. To prevent that user from accidentally overwriting the spreadsheet, you could FLAG it as Read Only.

To do so, you would type:

```
FLAG FORECAST.WKS RO
```

On the screen, you would see:

```
FORECAST.WKS   [ Ro - A - - -- - - -- -- - D R ]
```

Now the file is Read Only. Notice, in addition, that NetWare has added two related file attributes: D (delete inhibit) and R (rename inhibit). This file is now protected against being overwritten, deleted, or renamed.

With these additional attributes, if you try to delete this file by typing:

```
DEL FORECAST.WKS
```

you will get a message that says:

```
Access denied
```

If you want to return the file to its Normal status, you can type:

```
FLAG FORECAST.WKS N
```

and NetWare will return a message that says:

```
FORECAST.WKS   [ Rw - A - - -- - - -- -- - - - ]
```

The file attributes have been returned to the normal Read/Write status.

The GRANT Command

GRANT is a NetWare command-line utility that allows you to grant trustee assignments to other users and/or groups. Unlike other NetWare utilities, this is not menu-driven. However, these trustee assignments (directory assignments only for NetWare 286 and below, directory and file assignments for NetWare 386) can also be granted through either FILER or SYSCON, which are menu driven.

As with many NetWare commands, if you enter the command at the network prompt without options specified, a limited form of help will appear. For GRANT it looks like this:

```
J:\USER\CRAIG>grant

Command line arguments violate grammar defined for GRANT.

Usage:  GRANT rightslist* [FOR path] TO [USER | GROUP] name


286 Rights:            386 Rights:
---------------        --------------------
ALL = All              ALL = All
N   = No Rights        N   = No Rights
R   = Read             S   = Supervisor
W   = Write            R   = Read
O   = Open             W   = Write
C   = Create           C   = Create
D   = Delete           E   = Erase
P   = Parental         M   = Modify
S   = Search           F   = File Scan
M   = Modify           A   = Access Control

* Use abbreviations listed above, separated by spaces.
```

If we wanted to grant R (Read) and W (Write) trustee privileges to a user named TJONES, the command would be:

```
J:\USER\CRAIG>GRANT R W TO TJONES


CRAIG/SYS:USER\CRAIG
CRAIG                   Rights set to [ RW      ]
```

To verify that the rights had indeed been granted, use the TLIST command (discussed later in this chapter). As no path was specified in the command, the trustee rights were granted in the default directory. TLIST would yield a report like this:

```
J:\USER\CRAIG>TLIST


CRAIG\SYS:USER\CRAIG
User trustees:
    CRAIG               [SRWCEMFA]    Craig Ellison
    TJONES              [ RW     ]
No group trustees.
```

Note that no group trustees were assigned. If, however, we also wanted to grant rights to the group named EVERYONE, the command would be:

```
J:\USER\CRAIG>GRANT R W E C M F TO EVERYONE


CRAIG/SYS:USER\CRAIG
CRAIG                   Rights set to [ RWCEMF ]
```

Using TLIST again would confirm the new trustee assignments:

```
J:\USER\CRAIG>TLIST
CRAIG\SYS:USER\CRAIG


User trustees:


        CRAIG                   [SRWCEMFA]      Craig Ellison
        TJONES                  [ RW     ]
        - - - - -


Group trustees:


        EVERYONE                [ RWCEMF ]
```

Notes:

1. You must be attached to a server before you can grant trustee rights on that server.

2. Groups or users must exist on the server before you can grant them trustee rights.

3. You can grant trustee rights to only one user or one group with each command.

4. When you grant trustee rights to a user with the GRANT command, the user is enrolled in the directory's trustee list.

5. When you revoke rights for a user, the user remains a trustee until removed with the REMOVE command.

6. You must have appropriate rights in a directory or to a file (NetWare 386) before you can GRANT privileges to others—P (Parental) for NetWare 286 and below, A (Access) for NetWare 386.

The HELP Command

Novell offers on-line help in all versions of NetWare. To access on-line Help, type HELP at the home network prompt (typically F:), highlight NetWare, and hit ENTER.

To get help on any of these commands, highlight the command-menu option using the TAB key to move between menu selections and hit ENTER. Then tab over to the command that you want to learn more about and hit ENTER. A screen similar to the next one will appear. In this example, we accessed HELP to learn more about NetWare's NCOPY command.

```
┌─────────────────────────────────────────┐
│ NCOPY [path1] [[TO] path2] [option...]    │
└─────────────────────────────────────────┘

Format        Parameters. (Supports wildcard characters.
Purpose       Copies files between directories.
How to use    Type NCOPY [path1] [[TO] path2] [option...<Enter>
Examples      Copy to or from your default directory
              Copy between file servers
              Copy multiple files
              Change filename during copying
              Notes
```

To look at the parameters supported by the command, tab over to:

`^_Parameters. (Supports wildcard characters.`

Hit ENTER, and this screen will appear:

```
        NCOPY format parameters

[path1]                Directory path leading to and including
                       the file you want to copy.

[path2]                Directory path leading to and including
                       the volume, directory, or subdirectory
                       you want to copy the file to.

                       To rename the file, include the new
                       filename.

[option]               One or more of the following:

  /Subdirectories      Copies subdirectories.

  /Empty subdirectories  Copies empty subdirectories.
                         (Must be used with /S.)

  /Force sparse files  Forces the OS to write to sparse files.

  /Preserve file       Preserves existing file attributes
   attributes          when the file is copied.
```

The LOGIN Command

LOGIN is the NetWare command that you execute when you want access to a file server. After you execute IPX.COM and NETx on your workstation, the next most likely command you will issue is LOGIN. LOGIN.EXE is an executable file that resides in the SYS:LOGIN directory. Even though you are not logged into the network, you have access to this directory when you finish loading your NetWare shells (IPX and NETx).

The login directory is initially located on the first logical drive after your last local drive. If you just have diskette drives and a local hard drive with less than three partitions, the login directory will be on drive F:. If you have more than three local disk partitions, or the LASTDRIVE parameter was set in the CONFIG.SYS file, the network drive will be the next available drive letter. So, for example, if your CONFIG.SYS contained a command LASTDRIVE=G, the login directory would be H:.

The general syntax of the command is:

```
LOGIN [/option...] [fileserver/[name]] [script parameters]
```

If you just type LOGIN, you will be prompted for your user name and subsequently your password. The login process will attempt to log you into the file server to which you are currently attached. If your user name and password exist on the file server, you will begin the login process and will be given access to the resources that have been established for you.

Problems sometimes arise when there are multiple file servers on the same network. In such cases, your workstation may attach to a file server on which you are not an authorized user. In this case, you will be denied access. The login command format is one solution to this problem (see chapter 3). You can use the file server name option to specify which file server to use for your login.

For example, if your company has two file servers, one named FINANCE and one named SALES, and you can use only the FINANCE file server, you could enter the command:

```
LOGIN FINANCE/YOURNAME
```

Even if you were initially attached to the SALES file server, the login process would take place on the FINANCE file server.

NetWare 386 added three new login options:

/s (SCRIPT) With this option, you can specify a login script other than your default user login script. You must specify a path for the alternate script. This option is useful for supervisors who need to log in and test various startup options for different users.

/n (NoAttach) This option can be used to execute a login script while still logged into a file server. You will not be logged out. Without using this option, when you execute a login after your initial login, your previous login is automatically logged out.

/c (Clearscreen) This option is used to clear the workstation screen as soon as the login process completes.

You can use the Script Parameters option to pass parameters to your login script. These parameters are numbered and can be used in login scripts in conjunction with IF . . . . THEN commands. The file server is always %0, the first variable, and the user's name is always %1, the second variable. You could create a login script using parameter passing, for example, that would automatically execute PCONSOLE if the parameter passed were PCON. For this, the login syntax would be:

```
LOGIN FINANCE/USERNAME PCON
```

The LOGOUT Command

LOGOUT logs you out of the file server(s) to which you are currently attached. The syntax is:

```
LOGOUT [FILESERVER]
```

If you are attached to more than one file server, typing LOGOUT without a file server name specified will log you out of *all* file servers. (See "The ATTACH Command" above.) You can also log out of an individual file server by specifying the server's name. For example, if you were currently attached to file servers named SALES and FINANCE, you could log out of the SALES server by typing:

```
LOGOUT SALES
```

You would remain logged into FINANCE.

Important note: When you log out of a file server, all of the drive mappings (including search mappings) for that file server are deleted. Before you log out of a file server, use the MAP command and ensure that you have a drive mapped to the PUBLIC directory of the file server to which you intend to remain attached. If you log out of one file server and don't have access to the PUBLIC directory on the other server, you will be unable to map to the PUBLIC directory (since MAP.EXE resides in the PUBLIC directory), or even to log out.

The MAP Command

With the MAP command you can create and delete drive mappings across the network.

When would you want to create a drive mapping? If you were doing work in a directory or subdirectory, such as the SHARE directory for your department, it might be more convenient to create a logical drive than to type CD\EDIT\SHARE.

For example, let's start by looking at an individual's drive mappings as they might exist when he first logs in. From the F:\EDIT\CRAIG prompt he types MAP and gets the following listing:

```
Drive  A:     maps to a local disk.
Drive  B:     maps to a local disk.
Drive  C:     maps to a local disk.
Drive  D:     maps to a local disk.
Drive  E:     maps to a local disk.
Drive  F: = BAMBAM\EDIT:  \EDIT\CRAIG
Drive  G: = PRODUCTION\VOL1:  \COPYEDIT\NOV90
Drive  K: = BAMBAM\EXTRA:  \
       - - - - -
SEARCH1:   = Z:. [BAMBAM\SYS:  \PUBLIC]
SEARCH2:   = Y:. [BAMBAM\SYS:  \APPS]
SEARCH3:   = X:. [BAMBAM\SYS:  \APPS\UTIL]
SEARCH4:   = W:. [BAMBAM\SYS:  \APPS\BAT]
SEARCH5:   = C:
SEARCH6:   = C:\DOS
SEARCH7:   = C:\UTIL
SEARCH8:   = C:\WINDOWS
SEARCH9:   = C:\DATA\NOTES
```

Let's assume that our user wanted to create a drive mapping for the EDIT\SHARE directory. He can either create this logical drive using an existing drive letter, or he can choose an unused letter for the new mapping. In most cases you'll want to choose an unused letter for your new drive. If you choose a drive letter, such as F:, the previous mapping for F: will be overwritten. In this case, let's choose the letter I.

The format of the command is:

```
MAP [DRIVE:] = [SERVER] \ [VOLUME:] \ [DIRECTORY] \ [SUBDIRECTORY]
```

While this may look complicated, it's really not. Let's translate this format into something meaningful for our network. The command is:

```
MAP I:=EDIT:EDIT\SHARE
```

NetWare will confirm that the new mapping has been completed by showing:

```
Drive  I: = BAMBAM\EDIT:  \EDIT\SHARE
```

You may have noticed that we omitted the file server name from our command. If you are going to create a drive mapping on your current file server, you do not have to specifically name the file server. However, you must name the volume, or the drive mapping will fail. From our previous discussions on network layout, you may recall that the sales and marketing departments share a volume named SALES. For these departments, substitute the following command for the one in the previous example:

```
For sales:        MAP I:=SALES:SALES\SHARE
For marketing:    MAP I:=SALES:\MARKET\SHARE
```

Now let's check the results. From your home directory prompt, type I: and hit ENTER. You'll see something like:

```
F:\EDIT\CRAIG>I:
I:\EDIT\SHARE>
```

Alternatively, you could type MAP to see the entire drive mappings. You would see:

```
I:\EDIT\SHARE>MAP


Drive  A:    maps to a local disk.
Drive  B:    maps to a local disk.
Drive  C:    maps to a local disk.
Drive  D:    maps to a local disk.
Drive  E:    maps to a local disk.
Drive  F: = BAMBAM\EDIT:    \EDIT\CRAIG
Drive  G: = PRODUCTION\VOL1:    \COPYEDIT\NOV90
Drive  I: = BAMBAM\EDIT:    \EDIT\SHARE
Drive  K: = BAMBAM\EXTRA:    \
         ———
SEARCH1:   = Z:. [BAMBAM\SYS:    \PUBLIC]
SEARCH2:   = Y:. [BAMBAM\SYS:    \APPS]
SEARCH3:   = X:. [BAMBAM\SYS:    \APPS\UTIL]
SEARCH4:   = W:. [BAMBAM\SYS:    \APPS\BAT]
SEARCH5:   = C:
SEARCH6:   = C:\DOS
SEARCH7:   = C:\UTIL
SEARCH8:   = C:\WINDOWS
SEARCH9:   = C:\DATA\NOTES
```

Note that drive I: has been inserted into the drive map listing.
When you no longer need this drive mapping, you can delete it by typing:

```
F:\EDIT\CRAIG>MAP DEL I:
```

NetWare will confirm that the drive mapping has been deleted by showing:

```
The mapping for drive I: has been deleted.
F:\EDIT\CRAIG>
```

Drive mappings created by the MAP command stay in effect only for your current session on the network, or until you change them. When you log out, the logical drives that you created during your session are deleted. If you want an additional drive mapping, such as the SHARE directory mapped for you every time you log in, you can add the MAP command to your login script. (See "The SYSCON Command" below.)

Next let's investigate search drive mappings and changing existing ones.

First, as a reference point, here is the mapping we created for our test case's login.

```
F:\EDIT\CRAIG>map


Drive  A:    maps to a local disk.
Drive  B:    maps to a local disk.
Drive  C:    maps to a local disk.
Drive  D:    maps to a local disk.
Drive  E:    maps to a local disk.
Drive  F: = BAMBAM\EDIT:   \EDIT\CRAIG
Drive  G: = PRODUCTION\VOL1:   \COPYEDIT\NOV90
Drive  K: = BAMBAM\EXTRA:   \
          ----
SEARCH1:   = Z:. [BAMBAM\SYS:   \PUBLIC]
SEARCH2:   = Y:. [BAMBAM\SYS:   \APPS]
SEARCH3:   = X:. [BAMBAM\SYS:   \APPS\UTIL]
SEARCH4:   = W:. [BAMBAM\SYS:   \APPS\BAT]
SEARCH5:   = C:\DOS
SEARCH6:   = C:\MAYNARD1
SEARCH7:   = C:\NET
SEARCH8:   = C:\UTIL
```

Mapped drives can be changed merely by using the familiar DOS "CD" or CHDIR command. If, for example, you wanted to change to the EDIT\SHARE directory, from the F:\EDIT\CRAIG prompt you would type:

```
CD\EDIT\SHARE
```

You can determine that the change has been made in two ways:

1. The prompt for F: shows the new mapping (F:\EDIT\SHARE).

2. If you type MAP to see the listing after you make the change, you'll see something like:

```
F:\EDIT\SHARE>map


Drive  A:    maps to a local disk.
Drive  B:    maps to a local disk.
Drive  C:    maps to a local disk.
Drive  D:    maps to a local disk.
Drive  E:    maps to a local disk.
Drive  F: = BAMBAM\EDIT:   \EDIT\SHARE
Drive  G: = PRODUCTION\VOL1:   \COPYEDIT\NOV90
Drive  K: = BAMBAM\EXTRA:   \
       ——————
SEARCH1:   = Z:. [BAMBAM\SYS:   \PUBLIC]
SEARCH2:   = Y:. [BAMBAM\SYS:   \APPS]
SEARCH3:   = X:. [BAMBAM\SYS:   \APPS\UTIL]
SEARCH4:   = W:. [BAMBAM\SYS:   \APPS\BAT]
SEARCH5:   = C:\DOS
SEARCH6:   = C:\MAYNARD1
SEARCH7:   = C:\NET
SEARCH8:   = C:\UTIL

F:\EDIT\SHARE>
```

A listing of the search drives appears toward the bottom of the drive mappings. The search drives are logical drives where the operating system will look for commands that you enter at the network prompt and that it can't find in the current directory. The numbers indicate the order in which NetWare will search. As most NetWare commands, including MAP, reside in the SYS:PUBLIC directory, NetWare generally assigns the first search drive to SYS:PUBLIC. The system administrator sets up the order in which the additional drives are searched.

Notice how NetWare maps a logical drive starting from the end of the alphabet. SEARCH1: is "Z" and SEARCH2: is "Y", and so on. After the network search drives, the MAP command also shows the search path that had been stored in the DOS PATH environment. In this case, prior to logging into the network, C:\DOS was the first subdirectory on the search path. Appending the DOS path to the network search path is a new feature of NetWare 386. Under advanced NetWare 2.15, the operating system ignored the local search path.

As with the nonsearch drives, you can add and delete search drives. If you want to create a search drive that would be checked immediately after SEARCH1, use this command:

```
MAP INSERT S2:=Y:\APPS\WORD5
```

This command has inserted a new logical drive ("V") at the second location in the network search list. NetWare took the next available letter from the end of the alphabet and inserted it as the second search drive. NetWare confirms this by displaying:

```
SEARCH2:   = V:. [BAMBAM\SYS:   \APPS\WORD5]
```

Alternatively, you could type the MAP command again to see a revised listing, which would look like:

```
Drive   A:    maps to a local disk.
Drive   B:    maps to a local disk.
Drive   C:    maps to a local disk.
Drive   D:    maps to a local disk.
Drive   E:    maps to a local disk.
Drive   F: = BAMBAM\EDIT:   \EDIT\SHARE
Drive   G: = PRODUCTION\VOL1:   \COPYEDIT\NOV90
Drive   K: = BAMBAM\EXTRA:   \
        - - - - -
SEARCH1:   = Z:. [BAMBAM\SYS:   \PUBLIC]
SEARCH2:   = V:. [BAMBAM\SYS:   \APPS\WORD5]
SEARCH3:   = Y:. [BAMBAM\SYS:   \APPS]
SEARCH4:   = X:. [BAMBAM\SYS:   \APPS\UTIL]
SEARCH5:   = W:. [BAMBAM\SYS:   \APPS\BAT]
SEARCH6:   = C:\DOS
SEARCH7:   = C:\MAYNARD1
SEARCH8:   = C:\NET
SEARCH9:   = C:\UTIL
```

Notice that SEARCH2 now reflects the new logical drive V, and points to the SYS:\APPS\WORD5 directory.

Search drives can also be mapped without using the INSERT option. If you type MAP S1:=SYS: the mapping for SEARCH1 would become SYS: and the previous mapping of SYS:PUBLIC would be overwritten. Should you overwrite SYS:PUBLIC search mapping, you will be unable to execute any NetWare commands, including LOGOUT and MAP, unless your current directory is SYS:PUBLIC.

You can also delete a search drive in a manner similar to deleting nonsearch drives. To delete the second search drive, the command is:

```
MAP DEL S2:
```

NetWare will confirm by showing:

```
The search mapping for drive V: was deleted.
```

If you have a long path statement for your local drives, you may want to edit the list down. NetWare supports only sixteen search drives, so some of your local path will not be mapped to network search drives if the total exceeds sixteen.

Also, remember that any changes to drive mappings or search drive mappings are in effect only for your current session. When you log out, the changes you made during your session are lost.

The NCOPY Command

NCOPY is the network equivalent to the DOS XCOPY command. It is a powerful command that will copy all files from one directory to another and, if used with the /S option, will also copy all subdirectories below the directory being copied.

As an example, let's assume you want to copy all your manuscript document files (*.DOC) from your local C: drive to your home directory on network drive F:. Do the following:

1. Type C: to change the default drive to C.

2. Type CD\MS to change to the manuscript directory.

3. Type NCOPY *.DOC F:.

After using the NCOPY command, you'll see something similar to the following:

```
C:\MS>NCOPY *.DOC F:
From C:\MS
To    FS1/SYS:SYS/MANAGER
        SONYRTN1.DOC   to SONYRTN1.DOC
        PUNCHDWN.DOC   to PUNCHDWN.DOC
        SONYRTN.DOC    to SONYRTN.DOC
        REQ.DOC        to REQ.DOC
        PRICES.DOC     to PRICES.DOC
        HELP1.DOC      to HELP1.DOC
        NET07Z5.DOC    to NET07Z5.DOC

        7 files copied.
```

NCOPY shows where it's copying from (C:\MS) and the full path to which it is copying (FS1/SYS:SYS/MANAGER). If, in this example, you typed:

```
NCOPY *.DOC F: /S
```

NCOPY would have copied to the network drive all of the .DOC files in the MS directory as well as any .DOC files in any subdirectories below MS.

An obvious but important note: NCOPY works only if you're logged into the network. It is strictly a NetWare command. DOS will not recognize it.

As you copy files to other directories on the network, you'll need to be sensitive to those where you enjoy rights (see "The RIGHTS Command" below). Unlike your home directory on the network, where no one but you has access rights (Example F:\EDIT\CRAIG), all members of your network group have access to shared directories. Often, every group on a network will have a shared directory; many systems managers identify those directories by naming them SHARE (example: F:\FINANCE\SHARE). Security clearances won't allow you to copy files to the home directories of other users, but you can write files to a shared directory. And other users cannot retrieve files from your home directory, but they can retrieve files from the shared directories. Whenever you have files to share with all members of your group, store them in these shared directories.

Assume you had a file named TEST.DOC in your network directory and wanted to copy it to your group's shared directory. You would go to the prompt of your home directory and type:

```
NCOPY TEST.DOC \GROUP\SHARE
```

To view or access files in shared directories, you use the basic DOS navigation commands. Now, if you change to the SHARE directory and do a DOS DIR file listing, you should see the name of the file, TEST.DOC. At this point, you could send a message to your fellow group members via electronic mail or circulate a memo to alert them that the file is available.

The NDIR Command

NDIR is a NetWare command-line utility that is similar to the DOS command DIR but has an extensive array of command-line options. Using NDIR, you can generate sorted listings of directories and files based on specifications you define. Additionally, using some of the options, you can exclude files created, archived, or accessed before or after a specified date, files belonging to a specific user, or files with specific file attributes.

The general form of the NDIR command is:

```
NDIR path/filename options
```

If you type NDIR without any options, you will get NDIR's menu, which looks like this:

```
                              NDIR Options

                ┌─────────────────────────────────────────────┐
                │    To highlight options, use arrow keys.     │
                │    To select options, press Enter.           │
                │    To start processing, press End.           │
                └─────────────────────────────────────────────┘

        SORT BY          Filename Owner Size Update Create Access Archive
        RESTRICTIONS     None Flags Owner Size Update Create Access Archive
        PATH/FILE        Default Specify
        SCREEN FORMAT    Normal Dates Rights Macintosh
        DIRECTORIES      Current All
```

By using these options, you can generate a list, for example, of all files that belong to user CAROL in all directories. To do this, highlight the option of Sort By Filename. Under the Restrictions option, move the cursor over to Owner and hit ENTER. A submenu of operators will appear. Choose "=" and hit ENTER. Now type in the name CAROL. Accept the default path and screen formats, but change the directory option to All and hit ENTER. For this command, the following will appear:

```
CRAIG/SYS:USER/CAROL

Files:                   Size      Last Modified        Flags               Owner
───────────────────   ───────────  ─────────────────  ───────────────────  ─────────
4A          EDT         57,344  10-25-90 11:25p [Rw-A---------------] CAROL
BCHAP       DOC         36,352   8-07-90  6:36a [Rw-A---------------] CAROL
CHAPTER6    DOC        104,448  12-02-90  1:39p [Rw-A---------------] CAROL
GOOOZ       BAT              0  12-02-90  1:39p [Rw----------------] CAROL
LAWYER      MAR          9,022  12-02-90 11:58a [Rw-A---------------] CAROL
MW          INI            251  12-02-90  1:39p [Rw-A---------------] CAROL
RESTART     002              0  12-02-90  2:18p [Rw-A---------------] CAROL
S           DOC         45,056   7-28-90  4:31p [Rw-A---------------] CAROL
SCREEN      VID         14,283   8-04-89  8:52a [Rw-A---------------] CAROL
UPSTUFF     DOC          6,144   7-24-90  6:54a [Rw-A---------------] CAROL
USERNET     OUT          4,096   5-20-90  7:48p [Rw-A---------------] CAROL
WORKSTA     DOC         35,328   8-07-90  9:12a [Rw-A---------------] CAROL

                      Inherited    Effective
Directories:          Rights       Rights       Owner      Created
───────────────────   ──────────   ──────────   ──────     ──────────────
TOMNCAT               [SRWCEMFA]   [SRWCEMFA]    CAROL      5-20-90   4:00p

         469,587 bytes in   17 files
         495,616 bytes in  121 blocks
```

```
CRAIG/SYS:USER/CAROL/BOOK

Files:            Size      Last Modified          Flags             Owner
--------------  ----------  ----------------  --------------------  ----------
4A        EDT     57,344  10-25-90 11:25p  [Rw-A---------------]  CAROL
INTRO1    EDT     45,056  7-28-90   4:31p  [Rw-A---------------]  CAROL
INTRO2    EDT     40,448  8-07-90   5:00a  [Rw-A---------------]  CAROL
UPSTUFF   DOC      6,144  7-24-90   6:54a  [Rw-A---------------]  CAROL

       148,992 bytes in      4 files
       151,552 bytes in     37 blocks

       618,579 total bytes in     21 files
       647,168 total bytes in    158 blocks


_
```

This format displays the file name, file size, the last modified date and time,
file attribute flags, and the owner's name. In this case, as we specified that the
owner was to be CAROL and all other files should be excluded, it comes as
no surprise that all files in this listing belong to CAROL.

NDIR can also be used directly from the command line. If you are uncertain
of the options available to you, you can type NDIR HELP and a list of options
will appear. They look like this:

```
usage:          NDIR [path*] [option...]
options:        sortspec, format, flag, restriction, FilesOnly,

sortspec:       [REVERSE] SORT sortkey
sortkey:        OWNER, SIZE, UPDATE, CREATE, ACCESS, ARCHIVE

format:         DATES, RIGHTS, MAC [INTOSH]
flag:           [NOT] RW, RO, S, A, X, H, SY, T, I, P, RA, WA, C, D, R

restriction:    OWNER operator    name

SIZE            operator          number
UPDATE          operator          date
CREATE          operator          date
ACCESS          operator          date
ARCHIVE         operator          date

operator:       [NOT] LE, GR, =, #, BEFORE, AFTER

*path:          path [chain]
chain:          filename [,filename...] (up to 16 in chain)
```

To search filenames equivalent to NDIR KEYWORDS, the filename must be preceded by a drive letter or path.

Though this list might look intimidating, it's not really too bad. Following the usage and option line shown in the help screen, let's create an NDIR command line:

```
NDIR SORT OWNER SIZE GR 50000
```

This command would display files sorted by directory and owner, and show files only larger than 50,000 bytes. Options shown in brackets, such as [NOT] and [REVERSE], can be used in conjunction with the options they precede. For example,

```
NDIR\*.* NOT A
```

would show all files without the Archive attribute. The usefulness of this command is limited only by your imagination.

The NPRINT Command

The NPRINT command enables you to print any files you may have saved as text files to a network printer. These ASCII files generally have been saved from within an application and "printed to file" rather than to a printer. As with the CAPTURE command, quite a few command-line options are available, but you generally need to specify only one or two.

If you enter a NetWare command without any options, most will provide a brief listing of options. To see the available options for NPRINT, type NPRINT at any network prompt, and you'll see something like this:

```
F:\EDIT\CRAIG>NPRINT

Missing path/file specification in the file list.

Usage: NPRINT path flaglist

flaglist: /Banner=bannername /NAme=name /No Banner

          /[No] FormFeed /[No] NOTIfy

          /Tabs=n /No Tabs

          /Copies=n /Delete /Form=form or n

          /Job=jobconfiguration

          /PrintServer=printserver

          /Queue=queuename /Server=fileserver
```

Let's examine each of these options. For each of the command-line options, only the letters shown in capitals above need to be specified. However, you can use the full description if you prefer. Here we'll use the filename TUTOR.TXT.

The first line is the option for a banner, a page of paper that precedes the print job. You can specify the banner name, or let it default to the name set up by the network supervisor with the PRINTCON utility. The banner name specified can be up to twelve characters long and cannot contain spaces. So let's build the first part of our NPRINT command and let's give the banner a name of NET TIMES. Remember, because the banner cannot contain spaces, we'll have to use something else. Generally, the "_" underscore is used to separate words. Our command will start out looking like this:

```
NPRINT TUTOR.TXT B=NET_TIMES
```

or, if you prefer to spell it out:

```
NPRINT TUTOR.TXT BANNER=NET_TIMES
```

If you also wanted your name to appear on the banner, you could use the NAme option. In this example, if you wanted to add a name, the command would look like:

```
NPRINT TUTOR.TXT B=NET_TIMES NA=CRAIG
```

or

```
NPRINT TUTOR.TXT BANNER=NET_TIMES NAME=CRAIG
```

If you prefer no banner (which is the default specified here), you can leave out the banner reference or, to be sure, you could type

```
NPRINT TUTOR.TXT NB
```

or

```
NPRINT TUTOR.TXT NO BANNER
```

The next option is Form Feed. This option allows you to specify if you want your print job to start at the top of the next page. As most applications generate a form feed at the end of the print job, let's leave the default on the network as NO FORM FEED. However, if the job you're going to print with

NPRINT doesn't generate a form feed, you'll have to take the printer off line and force a form feed to get the last partial page out of the printer. Also, if there's another job in the print queue after yours and your job ends halfway through the page, the next job will start on the same page as your job ends. To add form feeds to your NPRINT job, the command would look like:

```
NPRINT TUTOR.TXT NB FF
```

You can spell out form feed, if desired.

Other NPRINT options include:

NOTI or NOTIfy—A switch that instructs NPRINT to notify you when your print job has been completed. However, with the third-party printing package we're using, NOTIFY does not function.

Tabs—The range for Tab expansion is 1 to 18. When you are printing an ASCII file with no special formatting code, the TAB option instructs NPRINT on how many spaces to substitute when it encounters the TAB character. However, most application packages do this tab conversion for you, and you should set this option to NO TABS, or use the shorthand method, NT. The networkwide default for this option is NO TABS, so if you don't specify it, it will default to NT.

COpies—Perhaps one of the more useful options of NPRINT is the COpies command. If you need multiple copies of the same print job, you can specify how many copies NPRINT should make. For example, if you wanted ten copies of a letter, you could instruct your word processor to send ten copies to the network print queue. But a far more efficient way to get those copies would be to set the COpies option to ten. With the COpy option set, your application will create only one copy of your letter and place it in the print queue. NPRINT will then use that one copy and generate the additional copies for you from that one. Your advantage is that your application has to generate only one copy, and your machine is freed up more quickly for your next task. The format for printing ten copies of the file TUTOR.TXT would be:

```
NPRINT TUTOR.TXT COPIES=10
```

or

```
NPRINT TUTOR.TXT CO=10
```

The networkwide default for this option is COPIES=1, so if you don't specify it, it will default to 1.

The next option is the Delete option. If this option is specified, then the text file that NPRINT is printing for you will be deleted when the print job has been completed. The format for this would be:

```
NPRINT TUTOR.TXT D
```

or

```
NPRINT TUTOR.TXT DELETE
```

FORM—NetWare gives your network administrator the flexibility to create up to 255 different forms. If the FORM option is not specified, the default that has been created for you with the PRINTDEF utility will be used; the default form is a standard 8 1/2 by 11 inch page in portrait mode; generally you won't need to specify this option.

Up to this point, we have not told NetWare where to print the job. The next three options provide this information.

The Print Server option needs to be used if your network administrator hasn't specified it by PRINTDEF. This tells NetWare which print server should service your print job. If you don't use the NetWare Print Server software, then this is not normally specified.

QUEUE—This option is identical to specifying the queue name in the CAPTURE command. For example, the print queues in the sales department are:

```
SALES_HP2 (HP LASERJET) AND SALES_QMS810 (POSTSCRIPT PRINTER)
```

If you need to see the available print queues, type PCONSOLE at any NetWare prompt to examine the queues available to you.

SERVER—This is the last option of NPRINT. Normally you will be printing on your default or "HOME" file server. However, with NetWare you can use printers on other file servers. If you had NetWare printers on the PRODUCTION file server, you could print to them.

So let's build a complete NPRINT command. It would look something like this:

```
NPRINT TUTOR.TXT TI=10 BANNER=NET_TIMES NAME=CRAIG FORMFEED
NO TABS QUEUE=SALES_HP2
```

or the shorthand version

```
NPRINT TUTOR.TXT TI=10 B=NET_TIMES NA=CRAIG FF NT Q=SALES_HP2
```

By now you've probably said to yourself, "There sure are a lot of options—isn't there an easier way?" Well, fortunately, there is. Your network administrator can set up default print "JOBS" that contain the majority of these options.

JOB—If your network administrator has created different print jobs using the PRINTCON utility, you can quickly change all of your options to match the print job specifications by using the JOB= option. You can create several standard print jobs to automate some of these options. Here is the description of the "SALES" print job:

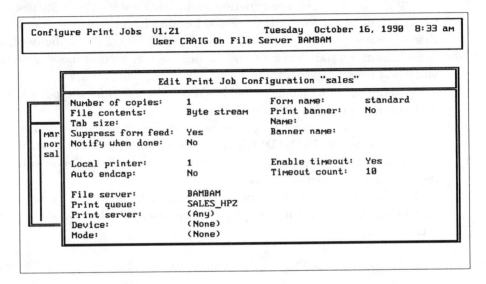

```
Configure Print Jobs  V1.21              Tuesday  October 16, 1990  8:33 am
                      User CRAIG On File Server BAMBAM

                         Edit Print Job Configuration "sales"

          Number of copies:     1            Form name:        standard
          File contents:        Byte stream  Print banner:     No
          Tab size:                          Name:
   mar    Suppress form feed:   Yes          Banner name:
   nor    Notify when done:     No
   sal
          Local printer:        1            Enable timeout:   Yes
          Auto endcap:          No           Timeout count:    10

          File server:          BAMBAM
          Print queue:          SALES_HP2
          Print server:         (Any)
          Device:               (None)
          Mode:                 (None)
```

This print job configuration contains many of the options previously described.

If we used the NPRINT command in conjunction with this predefined set of parameters, the command would look like this:

```
NPRINT TUTOR.TXT JOB=SALES
```

or

```
NPRINT TUTOR.TXT J=SALES
```

This would be equivalent to:

```
NPRINT TUTOR.TXT NO BANNER NO TABS NO FORM FEED TIMEOUT=10
COPIES=1 SERVER=BAMBAM QUEUE=SALES_HP2
```

or

```
NPRINT TUTOR.TXT NB NT NFF TI=10 CO=1 S=BAMBAM Q=SALES_HP2
```

As you can see, the JOB= option can save a tremendous amount of time.

The PCONSOLE Command

PCONSOLE, like CAPTURE, controls print jobs submitted to the network printers. It is a powerful command that allows you to delete a print job, change its order in the print queue, or put a job on hold.

Let's assume you sent a print job to an H-P LaserJet II but didn't realize until later that you loaded the wrong printer driver. Not wanting the result of that error—a lot of blank pages or pages with strange-looking control characters printed all over them—you want to kill the print job. By using PCONSOLE, you can determine if the job is still in the print queue at the time you catch the error and, if so, remove it before it prints.

To invoke the printer console (PCONSOLE) command, type PCONSOLE at any network prompt. After a brief pause, you will see PSONSOLE's opening menu. Cursor down to the first menu selection, PRINT QUEUE INFORMA-TION, and press ENTER. You'll see the following screen:

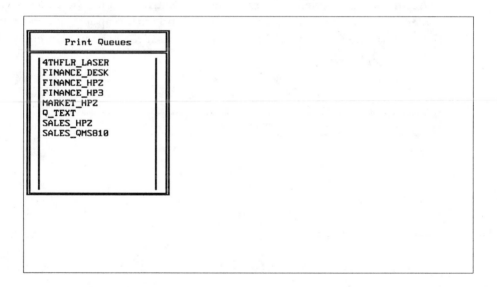

The next menu box will display all of the available print queues on the file server. Using the arrow keys, cursor down to the queue you want to see, and hit the Enter key. The following screen will appear with Print Queue Information in a pop-up menu:

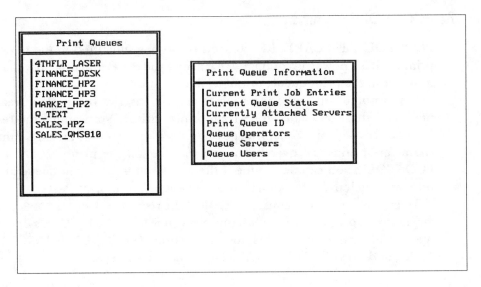

At this point, highlight Current Print Job Entries and hit the Enter key. A screen similar to the following will appear (if no entries appear, it means that the print queue is empty, and the job either has already been printed, or it's in another queue):

Seq Banner Name	Description	Form Status
1 JUDY	LPT2 Catch	0 Active

Each job submitted to the queue has the submitting user's name attached. If you see your job and want to delete it, simply hit the Delete key to remove the job from the queue. If you want to change some of the printing parameters, such as the sequence in which the job will be serviced, highlight the job and hit the Enter key. The following screen will appear, showing detailed information about the job:

```
┌──────────────────────────────────────────────────────────────┐
│  ┌──────────────────────────────────────────────────────┐    │
│  │            Print Queue Entry Information               │    │
│  ├──────────────────────────────────────────────────────│    │
│  │ Print job:       272          File size:      2559     │    │
│  │ Client:          JUDY[3]                                │    │
│  │ Description:     LPT2 Catch                             │    │
│  │ Status:          Being serviced by print server FINANCE_PRINT │
│  │                                                         │    │
│  │ User Hold:       No           Job Entry Date:  July 30, 1990 │
│  │ Operator Hold:   No           Job Entry Time:  8:05:00 am │  │
│  │ Service Sequence:                                       │    │
│  │                                                         │    │
│  │ Number of copies: 1           Form:            standard │    │
│  │ File contents:   Byte stream  Print banner:    No       │    │
│  │ Tab size:                     Name:                     │    │
│  │ Suppress form feed: Yes       Banner name:              │    │
│  │ Notify when done:  No                                   │    │
│  │                               Defer printing:  No       │    │
│  │ Target server:   (Any Server) Target date:              │    │
│  │                               Target time:              │    │
│  └──────────────────────────────────────────────────────┘    │
│                                                                │
└──────────────────────────────────────────────────────────────┘
```

By changing the parameters on this screen, you can put a job on hold, change the number of copies that will print, defer the printing until a later time and date, or change the order in which the job is printed.

The PRINTCON Command

With PRINTCON you can merge all your network printer parameter configurations into one print job. Once these parameters are defined as a print job, you merely have to specify the job to activate the defined parameters. PRINTCON automatically puts all the changes into effect in the other NetWare printing utilities that are affected (NPRINT, CAPTURE, and PCONSOLE).

When you run PRINTCON, you're presented with a main menu that looks like this:

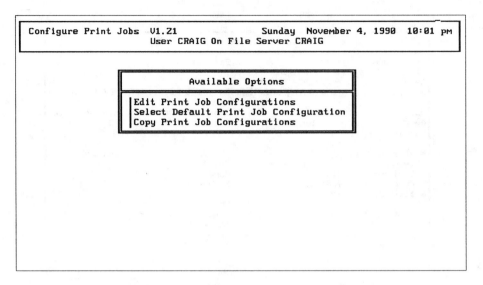

To create a job configuration, select Edit Print Job Configurations. If this is your first printer job configuration, there will be no jobs to edit. To create one, press INS and enter a configuration name, such as FINANCE. You'll see a screen like this:

```
Configure Print Jobs  V1.21              Sunday  November 4, 1990  10:01 pm
                        User CRAIG On File Server CRAIG

                    Edit Print Job Configuration "Finance"

        Number of copies:      1          Form name:        Normal
        File contents:         Text       Print banner:     Yes
        Tab size:              8          Name:             CRAIG
 CRA    Suppress form feed:    No          Banner name:
        Notify when done:      No

        Local printer:         1          Enable timeout:   No
        Auto endcap:           Yes        Timeout count:

        File server:           CRAIG
        Print queue:           FINANCE
        Print server:          (Any)
        Device:                (None)
        Mode:                  (None)
```

This is where you set your options. (See "The CAPTURE Command" above for more on printing options.)

Number of Copies lets you specify how many copies of each print job will be printed; you'll relieve traffic on the network by setting the number of copies in this menu instead of in the application. The application will send the job to the file server only once, and NetWare will make the additional copies. This saves time if you need to print more than one copy. The range for copies is 1 to 65,000.

File contents is where you specify the type of file you're printing. Highlight it and press the Enter key to see your choices:

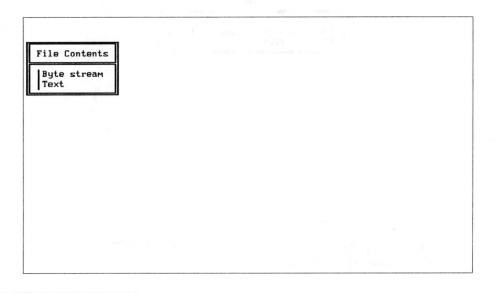

If you are printing text files, choose Text. If you are printing from within an application and you want that application to handle the formatting commands, choose Byte stream.

Tab size has no affect if you chose Byte stream in the preceding option. But if you chose Text mode, you'll need to specify the number of spaces to replace a tab character in the print jobs.

Select No at Suppress form feed if you don't want the printer to produce a form feed at the end of each print job. And answer Yes to Notify when done if you want to be notified when the job has been printed.

Local printer specifies which local printer port from which to capture the output. For example, you would enter 1 to capture print jobs being sent from the workstation's LPT1 ports.

If you select Yes at Auto endcap, print jobs will be executed when you exit an application or when the application closes the print job. If you select No, the job will print only if you enter ENDCAP from a NetWare prompt.

At File server, enter the name of the file server being used. At Print queue, name the print queue that will receive the print job. You can select only a queue that exists on the file server specified above.

To see a list of potential print servers authorized to service jobs in the queue, press ENTER at Print server. And press ENTER at Device to select a device as defined in PRINTDEF (described above). The device selection menu looks something like this:

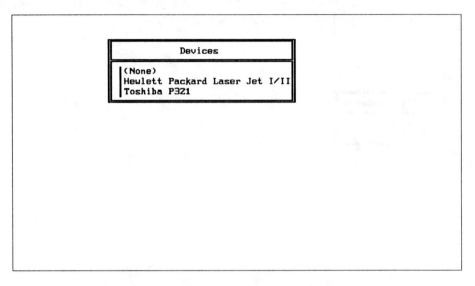

At Mode, press ENTER to select from the list as defined in PRINTDEF. It will look something like this:

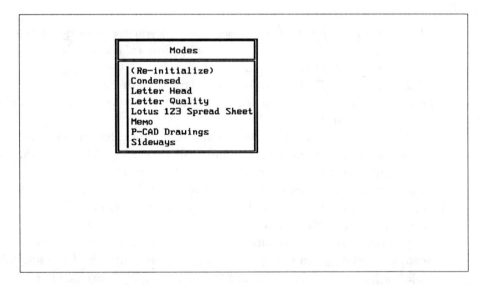

In the second column of the PRINTCON configuration screen, the Form name option lets you select a form you previously created with PRINTDEF.

Print banner determines whether or not a banner will print. If you specify a banner, you can also specify a Name, in the following selection, to be printed on it.

Enable timeout sends data to a print queue. If you enter Yes at this selection, the print job will be sent to the queue after the number of seconds specified in Timeout count. If you enter No at Enable timeout, the job will print as specified in the auto endcap field.

The printer timeout default is 5 seconds, although you can change that time to any number of seconds, ranging from 1 to 1000. The timeout affects how long the system waits before queueing a print job to a queue. You would set a longer timeout if you were printing a report from a database and the period between record output exceeded five seconds.

After selecting printer configuration options, press ESC to save your changes. Your final screen will look something like this:

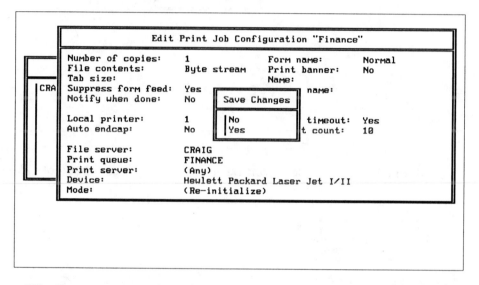

When you return to the main menu, the second option is Select Default Print Job Configuration. Highlight this option and hit ENTER. A listing of available print job configurations will appear. Select one and hit ENTER. This establishes the default that the system will use whenever a job is printed.

The PRINTDEF Command

PRINTDEF enables you to define printer devices and print forms that will be used on the network. With it you can specify the control codes that force your printers to initialize or print special characters, such as bold or condensed type. Additionally, you can specify standard forms, such as 8 1/2 by 11 inch, legal size page length, and columns per page. Novell provides a number of standard printer definitions. You won't need the special configuration capabilities of PRINTDEF if you're fortunate enough to be using a supported printer. However, if you're not, you'll use this utility with information in your printer reference manual to create your own definitions.

To configure your printer devices, enter PRINTDEF at the network prompt. You'll see the following screen:

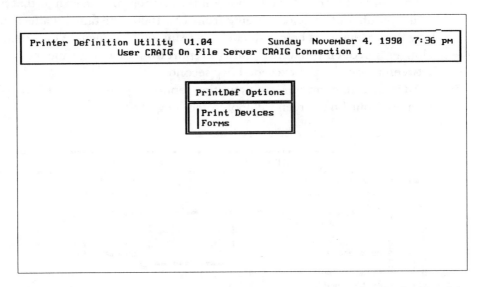

From this screen, select Print Devices to reach a menu that looks like this:

Here the Import Print Device selection will reveal the list of printers that Novell supports directly. With luck, you'll find one that matches your printer. After selecting your printer, you'll be prompted for a path that contains the NetWare-supplied printer definition files. By default, NetWare places the

*.PDF printer definition files in the PUBLIC directory upon installation. So, unless you changed the default, enter SYS:PUBLIC. Your screen will look like this:

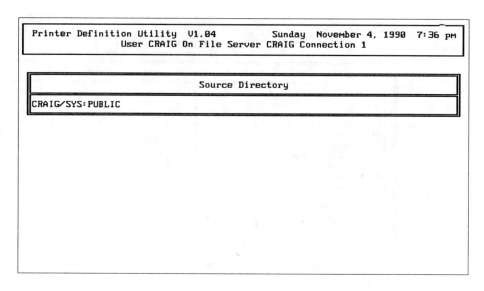

```
Printer Definition Utility  V1.04          Sunday  November 4, 1990  7:36 PM
                    User CRAIG On File Server CRAIG Connection 1


                              Source Directory
CRAIG/SYS:PUBLIC
```

After entering the source directory, press the INS key to see a list of available options. It will look like this:

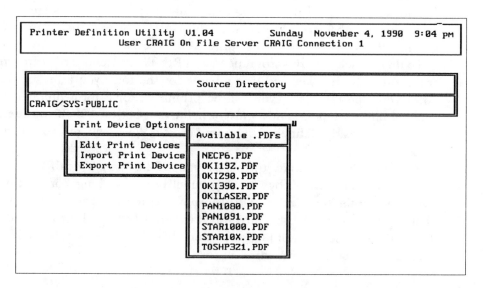

```
Printer Definition Utility  V1.04          Sunday  November 4, 1990  9:04 PM
                    User CRAIG On File Server CRAIG Connection 1


                              Source Directory
CRAIG/SYS:PUBLIC

        Print Device Options
                             Available .PDFs
        Edit Print Devices
        Import Print Device   NECP6.PDF
        Export Print Device   OKI192.PDF
                              OKI290.PDF
                              OKI390.PDF
                              OKILASER.PDF
                              PAN1080.PDF
                              PAN1091.PDF
                              STAR1000.PDF
                              STAR10X.PDF
                              TOSHP321.PDF
```

Select your printer, press ENTER, and then ESC.

If you need to edit,or want to check the configuration of the printer you just selected, highlight Edit Print Devices and press ENTER. Then select the printer you just defined. A listing of control codes will appear. In the next example, the codes are for an H-P LaserJet:

```
┌──────────────────────────────────────────────────────────────────┐
│ Printer Definition Utility   V1.04        Sunday  November 4, 1990  7:37 PM │
│                  User CRAIG On File Server CRAIG Connection 1      │
└──────────────────────────────────────────────────────────────────┘
        ┌───────────────────────────────────────────────────────┐
        │        Hewlett Packard Laser Jet I/II Functions       │
   ┌──┐ ├───────────────────────────────┬───────────────────────┤
   │  │ │ Big Font                      │ < ESC >%$3g           │
   │  │ │ Character Set - Line Draw     │ < ESC >( 0B           │
   │  │ │ Character Set - Roman Extension│ < ESC >( 0E          │
 │Hew│ │ Character Set - Roman-8       │ < ESC >( 8U           │
   │  │ │ Character Set - USASCII       │ < ESC >( 0U           │
   │  │ │ End-of-Line Wrap - Disable    │ < ESC >&s1C           │
   │  │ │ End-of-Line Wrap - Enable     │ < ESC >&s0C           │
   │  │ │ Font - Courier                │ < ESC >( s3T          │
   │  │ │ Font - HelvZ                  │ < ESC >( s4T          │
   │  │ │ Font - Letter Gothic          │ < ESC >( s6T          │
   │  │ │ Font - Linedraw               │ < ESC >( s0T          │
   │  │ │ Font - Lineprinter            │ < ESC >( s0T          │
   │  │ │ Font - Tms Rmn                │ < ESC >( s5T          │
   │  │ │ Orientation - Landscape       │ < ESC >&l1O           │
   │  │ │ Orientation - Portrait        │ < ESC >&l0O           │
   │  │ │ Paper Source - Lower Tray     │ < ESC >&l4H           │
   │  │ │ Pitch -  6                    │ < ESC >( s6H          │
        └───────────────────────────────┴───────────────────────┘
```

If you want to change the codes, you can do so from this screen by highlighting the selection and making the changes at that line.

You can also use PRINTDEF to define standard forms and assign them a form number that can be used with the CAPTURE and the PRINTCOM command to control the type of output you'll receive.

To do this, select Forms from the main PRINTDEF menu. To create a new form, press the INS key and type a name for the form you want to create. After you type the name, you will be prompted for a form number. The number must be unique, and it must be in the range of 1 to 999. If you attempt to use an already defined form number, NetWare will return an error message.

Next you will be asked for the page length of the form. Note that there are six lines per inch; an 8 1/2 by 11-inch page will be 66 lines long. For a standard-size form, enter 66. Next you'll be prompted for the page width. At 10 characters per inch, the standard width for an 8 1/2 by 11-inch page is 80. The completed screen will look something like the one that follows. In this example we used the form name Normal.

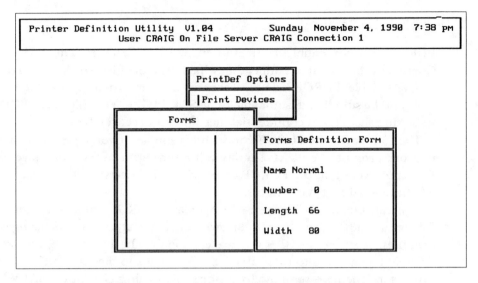

Because we were creating forms, no names appear in the Forms menu in this sample screen. But after you create forms, you can edit them by highlighting the name on the Forms menu and pressing ENTER. The Forms Definition Form will pop up just as it did in the preceding example. But this time you'll be changing values that are already there. When you finish, press ESC. NetWare will prompt you with a screen that looks like:

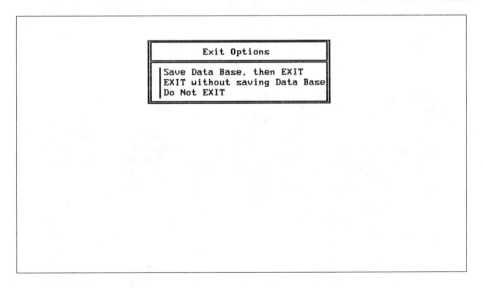

Select Save Data Base, then EXIT to save your changes.

The PURGE Command

PURGE is a compatible command to SALVAGE. (See "The SALVAGE Command" below.) It is a utility that wipes clean the files which are currently SALVAGEable. PURGE is a useful security measure when you want to delete a file and be sure that it is not able to be SALVAGEd. You might use PURGE to be sure that erased confidential files were not recoverable.

The format for the PURGE command is simple. If you type PURGE at the network prompt, the PURGE utility will return a list of files that have been PURGEd. Note that the PURGE command only affects the files over which you have Read and Write rights.

You can practice both the SALVAGE and PURGE commands with the following sample scenario on your own network. But, as you'll be using your own files, be sure to use files that are expendable. In this sample, we use the DOS DEL command to erase all of the .BAK backup files created by a word processor. Then we see how to restore them using NetWare's SALVAGE command. Next, we run PURGE and use DOS commands once again to see the files that have been purged. Finally we run SALVAGE once more to ensure that the files really were purged.

First, to identify the files to delete, go to the network directory that contains the files and use standard DOS commands to obtain a directory listing of the files you wish to erase. In our example, we would type:

```
DIR *.BAK /W
```

The system returns the following:

```
DIR *.BAK /W
Volume in drive F is SYS
Directory of  F:\SYS\MANAGER\DOC

0806     BAK    CASTOFF  BAK    CHAPTER5 BAK    DEADDELL BAK    HELP1     BAK
NET0725 BAK    NOTEWORK BAK    PCONSOLE BAK    PRICES   BAK    PUNCHDUN BAK
REQ      BAK    RIGHTS   BAK    SONYRTN  BAK    SONYRTN1 BAK    USERLIST BAK
WEND     BAK    DIFFNET  BAK    SALVAGE  BAK    PCC07Z7  BAK    PCC07Z7E BAK
5        BAK
         21 File(s)   76320768 bytes free
```

Delete the files, again using standard DOS commands:

```
DEL *.BAK
```

Now all of the .BAK files have been deleted. By typing SALVAGE at the prompt and selecting Recover files from the menu that appears, we can see a screen such as the one below, which shows that the twenty-one files we just deleted are SALVAGEable:

```
┌──────────────────────────────────────────────────────────────┐
│                                                                │
│  ┌──────────────────────────────────────────────────────┐     │
│  │                  21 Salvageable Files                 │     │
│  ├──────────────────────────────────────────────────────┤     │
│  │ 0806.BAK     │ 8-14-90  9:07:50am    6656 MANAGER      │     │
│  │ 5.BAK        │ 8-14-90  9:07:50am    2048 MANAGER      │     │
│  │ CASTOFF.BAK  │ 8-14-90  9:07:50am    4096 MANAGER      │     │
│  │ CHAPTERS.BAK │ 8-14-90  9:07:50am    4096 MANAGER      │     │
│  │ DEADDELL.BAK │ 8-14-90  9:07:50am    3072 MANAGER      │     │
│  │ HELP1.BAK    │ 8-14-90  9:07:50am    3072 MANAGER      │     │
│  │ NET0725.BAK  │ 8-14-90  9:07:50am    7168 MANAGER      │     │
│  │ NOTEWORK.BAK │ 8-14-90  9:07:50am    6144 MANAGER      │     │
│  │ PCC0727.BAK  │ 8-14-90  9:07:50am    4096 MANAGER      │     │
│  │ PCC0727E.BAK │ 8-14-90  9:07:50am    2575 MANAGER      │     │
│  │ PCONSOLE.BAK │ 8-14-90  9:07:50am   11264 MANAGER      │     │
│  │ PRICES.BAK   │ 8-14-90  9:07:50am     461 MANAGER      │     │
│  │ PUNCHDWN.BAK │ 8-14-90  9:07:50am    2560 MANAGER      │     │
│  │ REQ.BAK      │ 8-14-90  9:07:50am    2560 MANAGER      │     │
│  │ RIGHTS.BAK   │ 8-14-90  9:07:50am    4608 MANAGER      │     │
│  │ SALVAGE.BAK  │ 8-14-90  9:07:50am   11264 MANAGER      │     │
│  │ SONYRTN.BAK  │ 8-14-90  9:07:50am    2048 MANAGER      │     │
│  └──────────────────────────────────────────────────────┘     │
│                                                                │
└──────────────────────────────────────────────────────────────┘
```

Next we execute PURGE. The PURGE command will recognize DOS wildcards. In this case, we will purge all .BAK files. To do this, type:

```
PURGE *.BAK
```

and you will see the listing of files that PURGE has acted upon. Your screen will look something like this:

```
PURGE *.BAK

0806.BAK      CASTOFF.BAK   CATERS.BAK    DEADDELL.BAK   HELP1.BAK
NET0725.BAK   NOTEWORK.BAK  PCONSOLE.BAK  PRICES.BAK     PUNCHDWN.BAK
REQ.BAK       RIGHTS.BAK    SONYRTN.BAK   SONYRTN1.BAK   USERLIST.BAK
WEND.BAK      DIFFNET.BAK   SALVAGE.BAK   PCC0727.BAK    PCC0727E.BAK
5.BAK
```

Only specified files on file server FS1 have been purged from the current directory. This is an important note. When used without parameters, the PURGE command will PURGE files only in the current directory. PURGE can also be used with the /ALL command (PURGE/ALL); then all SALVAGEable files in the current directory, as well as subdirectories, will be purged.

Now, if we try to SALVAGE these files, we'll see the following screen:

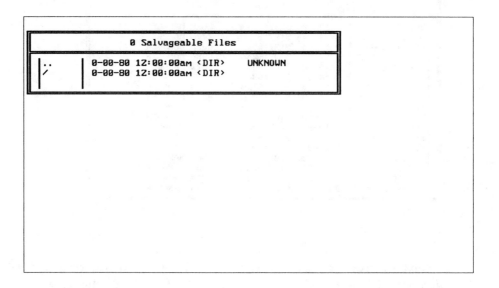

PURGE did indeed make these twenty-one files no longer SALVAGEable.

The REMOVE Command

REMOVE is a NetWare command-line utility that deletes a user or group trustee from either a directory or a file (NetWare 386 only). The syntax of the command is:

```
REMOVE [USER|GROUP] FROM DIRECTORY PATH|FILENAME
```

To illustrate, let's take a user directory in which TJONES has had rights revoked. (See "The REVOKE Command" below.) When rights are granted, the user or group becomes a trustee. When rights are revoked, the user or group still remains a trustee. To remove a trustee assignment, follow along with the example.

First we'll check the trustee assignment with TLIST and see that TJONES is a trustee with no rights to the directory J:\USER\CRAIG.

```
J:\USER\CRAIG>TLIST

CRAIG\SYS:USER\CRAIG
User trustees:

CRAIG               [SRWCEMFA]     Craig Ellison
TJONES              [        ]

No group trustees.

J:\USER\CRAIG>REMOVE TJONES

CRAIG/SYS:USER/CRAIG
User "TJONES" no longer a trustee to the specified directory.

Trustee "TJONES" removed from 1 directories.

J:\USER\CRAIG>TLIST

CRAIG\SYS:USER\CRAIG
User trustees:

CRAIG               [SRWCEMFA]     Craig Ellison

No group trustees.
```

After removing TJONES as a trustee, TLIST confirms that the trustee rights have been removed.

Note: Under NetWare 286 and below, you must have Parental (P) rights to a directory to remove a trustee assignment. Under NetWare 386, you must have Access (A) rights.

The RENDIR command

RENDIR is a NetWare command-line utility that will rename a directory. The syntax of the command is:

```
RENDIR oldname TO newname
```

where oldname is the complete path of the directory to be renamed and newname is the new directory name. It is not necessary to specify the full pathname for the new directory name.

In order to rename a directory, a user must have M (Modify) rights to a directory. To rename the directory USER\CRAIG to USER\GEORGE, the command would be:

```
J:\USER\CRAIG>rendir j:\user\craig george
Directory renamed to GEORGE


J:\USER\GEORGE>
```

A useful shorthand method is to use the "." for the current directory. For example, to rename the directory back to the original name of USER\CRAIG, the command would be:

```
J:\USER\GEORGE>rendir . craig
Directory renamed to CRAIG

J:\USER\CRAIG>
```

Notes:

1. The TO in the syntax is optional.

2. Login scripts for mappings to the changed directories will have to be changed manually.

3. Trustee rights remain unchanged even though the directory name has been changed.

4. Note that since the current directory was renamed in this example, the DOS prompt also changed to reflect the changed directory name.

The REVOKE Command

REVOKE is the NetWare command-line utility that is used to delete directory trustee rights (or file trustee rights for NetWare 386) from users or groups. It REVOKEs and removes rights that were granted under SYSCON or FILER. These other utilities can also be used to remove rights.

As with many NetWare commands, if you enter the command at the network prompt without options specified, a limited form of help will appear. For REVOKE, it looks like this:

```
J:\USER\CRAIG>REVOKE
Usage:            REVOKE rightslist* [FOR path] FROM [USER|GROUP] name
                  [options]
Options:          -SubDirectories | -Files

286 Rights:            386 Rights:
---------------        ---------------------
ALL = All              ALL = All
R   = Read             S   = Supervisor
W   = Write            R   = Read
O   = Open             W   = Write
C   = Create           C   = Create
D   = Delete           E   = Erase
P   = Parental         M   = Modify
S   = Search           F   = File Scan
M   = Modify           A   = Access Control

* Use abbreviations listed above, separated by spaces.
```

If we wanted to revoke the rights for user TJONES in directory USER/CRAIG that were created with filer, the command would be:

```
J:\USER\CRAIG>REVOKE ALL FOR TJONES

CRAIG/SYS:USER/CRAIG

Trustee's access rights set to [        ]

        Has NO RIGHTS to this Directory Area.

Rights for 1 directories were changed for TJONES.

J:\USER\CRAIG>TLIST

CRAIG\SYS:USER\CRAIG

User trustees:

        CRAIG           [SRWCEMFA]    Craig Ellison

        TJONES          [        ]
```

Here TLIST confirms that the trustee directory rights previously granted to TJONES have been deleted. As no path was specified in the command, the trustee rights were revoked from the default directory. Note, however, that TJONES still remains a trustee of this directory, but without rights. The trustee assignment will have to be removed with the REMOVE command.

The RIGHTS Command

NetWare has three basic security mechanisms—permission to access the file server through the login/password sequence; permission to access a directory through the basic trustee rights; and permission to access files based on file flags. The NetWare command RIGHTS addresses the second.

It shows you the rights you enjoy in a directory. You can see your effective rights in your "Home" directory (such as Controller Thomas Crane's home directory, F:\FINANCE\CRANE). By typing RIGHTS at the prompt, Crane will see something similar to the following:

```
F:\FINANCE\CRANE>rights

FS1\FINANCE: FINANCE\CRANE

Your Effective Rights for this directory are [ RWCEMF ]
          × May Read from File.                      (R)
          × May Write to File.                       (W)
            May Create Subdirectories and Files.     (C)
            May Erase Directory.                      (E)
            May Modify Directory.                     (M)
            May Scan for Files.                       (F)
          × Has no effect in directory.

            Entries in Directory May Inherit [ RWCEMF ] rights.
```

What's all this mean? It means that Crane has the ability to read from and write to files, create subdirectories, make modifications to files in his directory, and finally, type DIR and see a listing of his files. The rights shown in this example reflect NetWare's default rights for each user in their "home" directory.

Tip: If users are in an application and get a DIRECTORY WRITE PROTECTED error, chances are they are not in their home directory. When this happens, users should exit the application and type RIGHTS at the prompt. If they don't have (W) and (C) rights to a directory, the application cannot create the temporary working files it needs. Users can fix the problem themselves by changing back to their home directory and running the application again.

On many networks, various applications have different directory rights. Often applications are installed in directories to which users can read and scan but have no other rights. Users with limited rights can execute applications and get a DIR listing of the applications subdirectory, but they cannot create, write, or delete files from the subdirectory.

The next example shows how a user can see the rights in an application directory. In this example, applications are installed in the Y drive. Our user, Crane, can type Y: and hit the Enter key, then enter RIGHTS to see something like the following screen:

```
Y:\APPS>rights

FS1\SYS:APPS

      Your Effective Rights for this directory are [ R     F ]
        * May Read from File.                          (R)
          May Scan for Files.                          (F)
        * Has no effect in directory.

          Entries in Directory May Inherit [ R     F ] rights.
```

Unless Crane specifies a path, RIGHTS will just examine his current directory, but he can write a path to examine his rights in any directory.

The SALVAGE Command

The SALVAGE utility allows you to undelete files that you have erased with the DOS ERASE or DEL command. (See "The Purge Command" above.) It is a powerful command but it has some limitations:

1. You can't salvage files if you have created or deleted other files since you deleted the file you wish to recover.

2. If you delete a file and log out, you can log back in and recover files deleted in a previous session if you haven't created or deleted other files in the interim.

3. You must execute the SALVAGE utility from the same workstation from which you erased your file.

4. Files can't be SALVAGEd after running the PURGE command.

In the following exercise, we delete a file using standard DOS commands, run SALVAGE to recover the file, and then perform a directory listing to show that the file, in fact, was recovered.

First, type DIR at the network prompt. You will see a screen such as the following:

```
Volume in drive F is FINANCE
Directory of   F:\FINANCE\CRANE\WIN

NETWARE  DRV     45936   5-01-90   3:00a
VNETWARE 386     10013   5-01-90   3:00a
VIPX     386     14084   5-01-90   3:00a
VPICDA   386     11063   7-31-90   3:08p
SYSTEM   INI      1253   7-31-90   3:08p
         5 File(s)  74211328 bytes free
```

Next delete a file using the DOS DEL command:

```
F:\FINANCE\CRANE\WIN>DEL VIPX.386
```

and run the DOS DIR command again to be sure it is gone. The screen should look something like this:

```
F:\EDIT\CRAIG\WIN>DIR

Volume in drive F is EDIT
Directory of   F:\EDIT\CRANE\WIN

NETWARE  DRV     45936   5-01-90   3:00a
VNETWARE 386     10013   5-01-90   3:00a
VPICDA   386     11063   7-31-90   3:08p
SYSTEM   INI      1253   7-31-90   3:08p
         4 File(s)  74211328 bytes free
```

You can see that VIPX.386 has been deleted. To recover this file, type SALVAGE at the network prompt. Now the screen looks something like this:

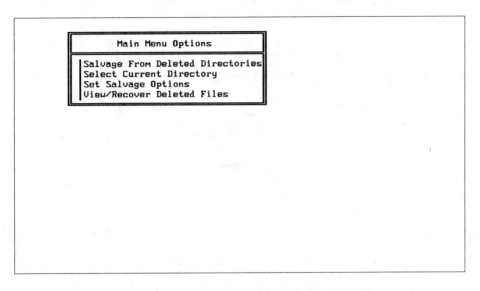

```
┌──────────────────────────────────┐
│         Main Menu Options        │
├──────────────────────────────────┤
│Salvage From Deleted Directories│
│Select Current Directory        │
│Set Salvage Options             │
│View/Recover Deleted Files      │
└──────────────────────────────────┘
```

Now highlight View/Recover Deleted Files and hit ENTER to see a screen pop up on top of the previous screen. It will prompt you for a Name pattern to match. It will default to *. Finish the files specification so that it reads *.*. This will give you a complete list of SALVAGEable files.

```
┌────────────────────────────────────────┐
│  Erased File Name Pattern To Match    │
├────────────────────────────────────────┤
│*.*                                     │
└────────────────────────────────────────┘
```

Move the highlight down to the file you want to recover, and hit the Enter key. Salvage will pop a screen of data showing the last modification date, the deletion date, who owned the file, and who deleted the file. This screen will look something like this:

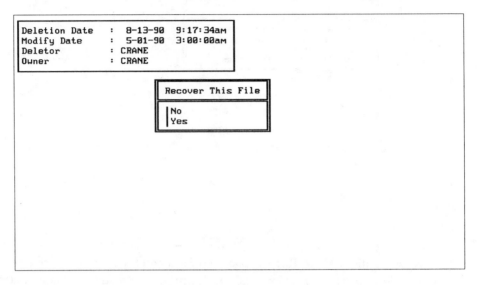

```
Deletion Date  :  8-13-90  9:17:34am
Modify Date    :  5-01-90  3:00:00am
Deletor        :  CRANE
Owner          :  CRANE


                      Recover This File

                     No
                     Yes
```

Postion the cursor over the Yes prompt and hit the Enter key to recover the file. To exit the SALVAGE utility, hit ESCAPE, and answer Yes to the Exit prompt. When you return to your network directory, type DIR to see if the file was successfully restored. When you do, you should see the original file in the directory listing. It will be restored to your default directory. In our example, the screen would display:

```
F:\FINANCE\CRANE\WIN>DIR

Volume in drive F is FINANCE
Directory of  F:\FINANCE\CRANE\WIN

NETWARE   DRV    45936   5-01-90   3:00a
WNETWARE  386    10013   5-01-90   3:00a
VIPX      386    14084   5-01-90   3:00a
WPICDA    386    11063   7-31-90   3:08p
SYSTEM    INI     1253   7-31-90   3:08p
        5 File(s)  74215424 bytes free
```

The SEND Command

It's no substitute for electronic-mail, but NetWare's SEND command lets users send messages of approximately thirty-six characters to other users who are logged into the network. (See "The CASTOFF Command" above.)

To do it, first type USERLIST (see "The USERLIST Command") at the prompt to see who is logged in. NetWare will display the user names and workstation numbers of everyone logged in, including the workstations of public devices such as the printer server.

Then type SEND at the prompt. NetWare will display the usage syntax for the SEND command. The following response from NetWare appears at the prompt:

```
F:\EDIT\CRANE>SEND

Usage:

SEND "message" [TO] [[USER | GROUP] [server/] name [, server/] name ...]
                    [server/] CONSOLE
                    [server/] EVERYBODY
                    [STATION] [server/] n[,n...]
```

If your message is only for other users on your server, you can omit the server name. NetWare assumes the default server name for you. Be sure to enclose your message in quotation marks.

For instance, say Jill, who works in the sales department and thus is a member of SALES, wants to send a message to Howard, who is also in the sales department and works at station 26. Jill would enter the following command at the network prompt:

```
SEND "This is a test" to Howard
```

After sending the message, NetWare would return the following confirmation to her:

```
Message sent to ASERVER/HOWARD (station 26)
```

NetWare notifies Jill that the message has been delivered and informs her of the connection number of the delivery. But note that she does not need to know the recipient's station number to send the message, only his name and, if he is on a different server, the name of the server he's attached to.

Recipients see the message displayed on the 25th line of their screen. They will have to hit CNTL-ENTER to resume their application. The bottom line of Howard's screen, in our example, will look like this:

```
>> From JILL[26]: This is a test    (CTRL-ENTER to clear)
```

NetWare won't wrap the message onto a second line. So anyone sending a message has to leave room for the user name and the (CTRL-ENTER to clear). The rule here is to keep your messages short. Also, remember there are no anonymous messages on a NetWare network. The operating system displays the sender's user name and workstation number alongside the message when it pops up on other people's screens.

Anyone who wants to send a message to everyone in the user group should substitute the group name (SALES, MARKET) for the user name in the command. By substituting EVERYONE, a message would be sent to everyone logged into the network. But note that frivolous messages can drive system managers and other users wild. Before educating your users on the SEND command, ask them to consider their professional image. The group they're in could include their (not to mention your) boss's boss, the CEO, and others who may not appreciate having their work interrupted with random messages that pop up across the bottom of their screens. And if they don't, they'll call the system manager.

The SESSION Command

The SESSION comand provides a menu-driven interface through which you can accomplish many of the same things you can with other command-line utilities: view, create, and delete drive mappings and send messages to others on the network.

When you type SESSION, the main SESSION menu appears onscreen. The first option on the menu is Change Server. This allows you to change to a different file server if there is more than one on the network. However, SESSION only shows drive mappings for the servers you're currently logged into.

The second option, Drive Mapping, gives you the ability to "map" a new drive through the menu instead of the command line. You could, for example, create a separate logical drive mapping to a directory called "SHARE," as we've done below. When you select Drive Mappings from the main menu, the following menu will appear:

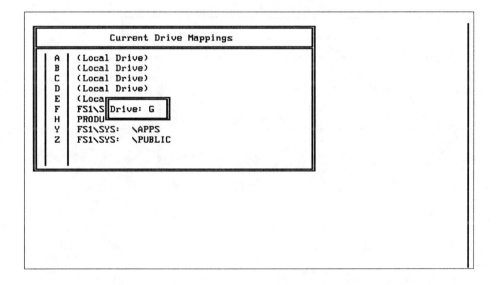

The screen displays the mappings for this particular user. SESSION shows users just their own mappings, not those of others.

To insert a new drive in this map, you would press INS to pop up a menu box onscreen. NetWare will look for the first unassigned drive, the G drive in this case, and display it in the pop-up box, as in the sample screen below:

Press ENTER to confirm you want to use G: as the new drive mapping, or, if you prefer, enter a different drive. Next NetWare will prompt you for a directory and another box appears:

```
┌──────────────────────────────────────┐
│   File Servers/Local Drives           │
├──────────────────┬───────────────────┤
│ FS1              │ CRANE             │
│ PRODUCTION       │ EXECUTIVE         │
│                  │                   │
│                  │                   │
└──────────────────┴───────────────────┘
```

To choose a server, press INS and select either FS1 or PRODUCTION. Another box appears. This one asks you to select a volume. We selected the volume EXEC in the screen below.

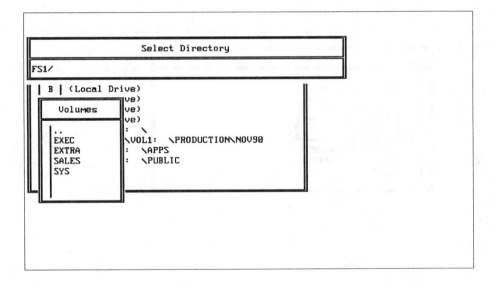

```
┌────────────────────────────────────────┐
│            Select Directory             │
├────────────────────────────────────────┤
│ FS1/                                     │
├────────────────────────────────────────┤
│ │ B │ (Local Drive)                      │
│ ┌────────────┐ve)                        │
│ │  Volumes   │ve)                         │
│ │            │ve)                         │
│ │            │ :    \                    │
│ │ ..         │\VOL1: \PRODUCTION\NOV90   │
│ │ EXEC       │ :    \APPS                │
│ │ EXTRA      │ :    \PUBLIC              │
│ │ SALES      │                          │
│ │ SYS        │                          │
│ └────────────┘                          │
└────────────────────────────────────────┘
```

Next a list of available network directories on the EXEC drive appears:

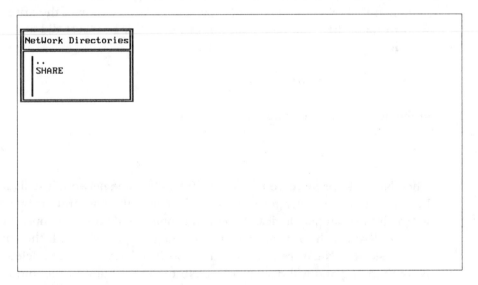

```
┌─────────────────────────────────────────────────────────────────┐
│ ╔═══════════════════════════════════════════════════╗            │
│ ║                  Select Directory                  ║            │
│ ╠═══════════════════════════════════════════════════╣            │
│ ║FS1/EXEC:                                           ║            │
│ ╚═══════════════════════════════════════════════════╝            │
│ ┌──────────────────────┐                                         │
│ │NetWork Directories   │                                         │
│ ├──────────────────────┤                                         │
│ │ │..                   │                                         │
│ │ │DESKTOP              │                                         │
│ │ │EXEC                 │                                         │
│ │ │                     │                                         │
│ │ │                     │                                         │
│ └──────────────────────┘                                         │
│                                                                   │
│                                                                   │
└─────────────────────────────────────────────────────────────────┘
```

Again we select EXEC. Finally, the SHARE directory appears:

```
┌─────────────────────────────────────────────────────────────────┐
│ ┌──────────────────────┐                                         │
│ │NetWork Directories   │                                         │
│ ├──────────────────────┤                                         │
│ │ │..                   │                                         │
│ │ │SHARE                │                                         │
│ │ │                     │                                         │
│ └──────────────────────┘                                         │
│                                                                   │
│                                                                   │
│                                                                   │
│                                                                   │
│                                                                   │
│                                                                   │
└─────────────────────────────────────────────────────────────────┘
```

Press ENTER, ESC, and ENTER again. If you are using the new NetWare 3.01 Client shells, you will see a message asking if you want to "MAP ROOT" this drive. In this practice session, answer No, and the new path will appear in the drive map listing. It will remain in effect until you log out. Your screen will now display the new drive mappings in a window that looks like this:

```
┌────────────────────────────────────────────────┐
│  ┌──────────────────────────────────────────┐  │
│  │           Current Drive Mappings          │  │
│  ├──┬───────────────────────────────────────┤  │
│  │A │ (Local Drive)                          │  │
│  │B │ (Local Drive)                          │  │
│  │C │ (Local Drive)                          │  │
│  │D │ (Local Drive)                          │  │
│  │E │ (Local Drive)                          │  │
│  │F │ FS1\SYS:    \                          │  │
│  │G │ FS1\EDIT:   \EXEC\SHARE                 │  │
│  │H │ PRODUCTION\VOL1:   \FACTORY\NOV90       │  │
│  │Y │ FS1\SYS:    \APPS                       │  │
│  │Z │ FS1\SYS:    \PUBLIC                     │  │
│  └──┴───────────────────────────────────────┘  │
│                                                  │
│                                                  │
│                                                  │
│                                                  │
└────────────────────────────────────────────────┘
```

While it is more work to create a new drive map through SESSION's menus than by using the MAP command at the network prompt, with SESSION, the available options are always presented to you. MAP (see "The MAP Command" above) would be easier if you knew the location of the drive you wish to map; then you could accomplish everything we just did above by entering:

```
MAP G:=EXEC:EXEC\SHARE
```

at the network prompt, and then:

```
EXEC:EXEC\SHARE
```

when NetWare prompts you for a directory. On some network installations, however, users are never given access to the command line, and the only way in which they can map logical drives is through the SESSION menus.

Should you wish to delete a drive mapping, highlight it with the cursor and press DEL. NetWare will ask you to confirm that you want to delete the drive mapping and will display a Yes/No menu selection in the middle of the screen.

You can also use SESSION to determine your effective rights to a mapped drive. To see your rights in a directory, highlight the directory entry and press ENTER. You should see something like this:

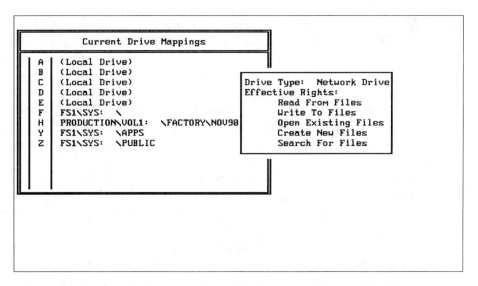

You can receive an effective rights report only for network drives.

SESSION also provides a convenient menu-driven method to SEND a message to groups on the network. To use it, highlight Group List at the main menu and press ENTER. A list of network group names appears. To SEND a message to all group members, move the cursor to that group name and hit ENTER.

A message window similar to the one below appears onscreen. This is where you type your message. As with the command-line version of SEND, the number of characters you can use is limited (see "The SEND Command" above).

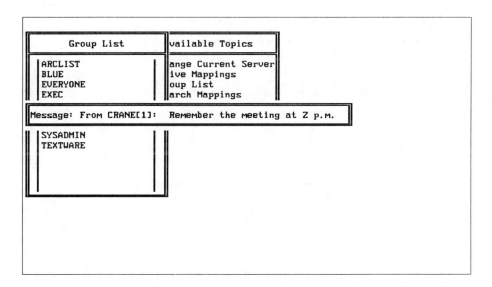

In this example the message would be sent to one group, EXEC, but you could also send the message to multiple groups. To do it, highlight the first group, press F5 to tag it, move to the next group, press F5 again, and continue tagging until you've identified all the groups to which you wish to send the message.

Recipients will see the message displayed on the 25th line of their screen, just as they would if you used the SEND command. And, like SEND, they will have to press CNTL-ENTER to resume their application after reading the message.

Other selections on the SESSION menu include Search Mappings, Select Default Drive, and User List.

Search Mappings are a new feature in NetWare 386. They are similar to Drive Mappings but they behave differently. When you load an application from your workstation, NetWare first looks for it in the current directory. If the application isn't there, it follows the search path to find the application. In some ways, the NetWare search path behaves like the DOS PATH command. In fact, if you had set a DOS path, that path would be appended to the network search path and NetWare would extend its search to the drives and directories listed in the DOS path.

Novell allows you as many as twenty-six logical drive mappings, of which sixteen can be search drives. When NetWare lists search mappings in the SESSION screens, it begins at the end of the alphabet, with the letter Z, and works to the front. You can see this backward-to-forward display by selecting Search Mappings on SESSION's main menu. A screen, similar to the one below, should appear:

```
                      Current Search Mappings
     1   Z:=FS1\SYS:      \PUBLIC
     2   Y:=FS1\SYS:      \APPS
     3   X:=FS1\SYS:      \APPS\UTIL
     4   W:=FS1\SYS:      \APPS\BAT
     5   V:=FS1\SYS:      \APPS\UTIL
     6   C:/DOS
     7   C:/UTIL
     8   C:/WINDOWS
```

As with drive mappings, you can add additional search drives to this list by pressing INS. SESSION will present you with a suggested drive letter, and you follow the same procedure you did to insert or delete drive mappings.

SESSION also gives you the ability to change your default drive. To do so, highlight Select Default Drive at the main menu and press ENTER. You will see a screen like this:

```
┌──────────────────────────────────────────────────────────────────┐
│   ┌──────────────────────────────────────────────┐                │
│   │         Select Default Drive                  │                │
│   ├──────────────────────────────────────────────┤                │
│   │ A │ (Local Drive)                             │                │
│   │ B │ (Local Drive)                             │                │
│   │ C │ (Local Drive)                             │                │
│   │ D │ (Local Drive)                             │                │
│   │ E │ (Local Drive)                             │                │
│   │ F │ FS1\EXEC:     \EXEC\CRANE                  │                │
│   │ G │ PRODUCTION\VOL1:    \FACTORY\NOV90         │                │
│   │ S │ FS1\SYS:      \SYSTEM                      │                │
│   │ V │ FS1\SYS:      \APPS\UTIL                   │                │
│   │ W │ FS1\SYS:      \APPS\BAT                    │                │
│   │ X │ FS1\SYS:      \APPS\UTIL                   │                │
│   │ Y │ FS1\SYS:      \APPS                        │                │
│   │ Z │ FS1\SYS:      \PUBLIC                      │                │
│   └──────────────────────────────────────────────┘                │
│                                                                    │
└──────────────────────────────────────────────────────────────────┘
```

Here all of your mappings are displayed, drive mappings as well as search mappings. To change your default drive to another drive, highlight the desired drive and press ENTER. When you leave SESSION, this becomes your default drive.

If, for example, your default drive was F:\EXEC\CRANE, and you selected drive Z as the new default, your prompt would show Z:\PUBLIC when you exit SESSION. Users who prefer the command-line interface could accomplish the same thing by typing Z: <CR> at any network prompt.

The last selection on the SESSION menu is User List. Through the User List, you can see some information about other network users and you can SEND a message to one or more users (see "The SEND Command" and "The USERLIST Command"). It is important to note, however, that you can only see information about and send messages to current users, users who are actually logged into the file server. Highlight User List, press ENTER, and windows similar to the ones below appear onscreen.

```
┌──────────────────────────┐        ┌──────────────────────┐
│ Current Users   Station  │        │ Available Options    │
├──────────────────────────┤        ├──────────────────────┤
│ ABOLL           011      │        │ Display User Info    │
│ ACLEO           030      │        │ Send Message         │
│ ADRONE          064      │        └──────────────────────┘
│ AGONNER         040      │
│ BLUELASER       032      │
│ BPANTONE        039      │
│ CCONNELL        017      │
│ CDONATTA        003      │
│ CDUNSTED        012      │
│ CELMONT         009      │
│ CPONTE          049      │
│ CRANE           001      │
│ CSHORE          056      │
└──────────────────────────┘
```

If you highlight a user and press ENTER, you'll be presented with an option box that looks like this:

```
┌──────────────────────┐
│ Available Options    │
├──────────────────────┤
│ Display User Info    │
│ Send Message         │
└──────────────────────┘
```

If you press Display User Info, you'll see a screen of information about that user. In the following example, we selected the user CSHORE:

```
Full Name:         Charles Shore
Object Type:       User
Login Time:        Thursday  September 6, 1990  1:09 pm
Network Address:   00000001
Network Node:      10005a605f1b
```

To send a message to CSHORE, you would select Send Message at the previous menu to see a text box like the one under the Send Message option in Group Info (see Group Information, discussed previously in this section).

The SETPASS Command

By allowing users to change their passwords, SETPASS addresses one of NetWare's three basic security mechanisms: permission to access the file server through the login/password sequence, permission to access a directory through the basic trustee rights, and permission to access files based on file flags. NetWare provides mainframelike security through the login procedure, which requires users to enter their user names and passwords.

NetWare 386 makes it easy to change passwords frequently. It's a good idea for users to do so—not only to protect their own files but also to protect the network. By regularly changing passwords, users minimize the possibility that uninvited users will install unwanted and potentially dangerous files in their directories and on the network.

Users can change their password simply by typing SETPASS at any network prompt. NetWare will return a message that says:

```
Changing password for FS1\KEVIN
Enter your old password:
```

In this case FS1 is the file server and KEVIN is the user's username. NetWare's request for the current password is a security feature. This protects against people changing users' passwords while they're away from their computers for a few minutes.

After entering the current password, NetWare will answer the user with the message:

```
Enter your new password:
```

Now the user enters the new one, which does not appear onscreen. All passwords must be at least five characters long and may contain numbers or letters, but no spaces. Passwords are not case sensitive. The password YEL-LOW, for instance, is interpreted the same as yellow or YeLlOw.

Now NetWare prompts the user to:

```
Retype your new password:
```

This request for verification is also a security feature. As users don't see their password as they type it in, Netware asks them to retype it. It checks the second entry against the first entry. If they are different, it will inform users of the mismatch. If that happens, the password will not be changed, and they'll have to start over. If the two entries match, users will get a message that says:

```
Your password has been changed.
```

Users in offices where two networks have been bridged are often attached to both networks. They will see the following message, identifying the names of groups on both servers:

```
FS1/FS2
Synchronize passwords on these file servers with
FS3/USERNAME? (Y/N)
```

Unless you have access to both (often only the system manager does) answer No.

An additional security tip: All users should log out of the network when they leave for lunch or to go home at the end of the day. Leaving a workstation logged in allows access to anyone who sits down at that workstation's keyboard.

The SLIST Command

SLIST reports information on each of the available file servers (see also "The CHKVOL Command" above). To use it, type SLIST at any network prompt. You will see a report similar to the following. This one assumes you're attached:

```
Known NetWare File Servers          Network     Node Address
- - - - - - - - - - - - - - - - - - - - - - - -     - - - - - - -     - - - - - - - - - - - - -
FS1                                 [    40258] [              1] Default
FS2                                 [     A01] [ 2608C1B7934] Attached
Total of 2 file servers found
```

In addition to listing the file servers, SLIST also reports on the network address and the node address. It also lists which file server you're logged onto and any other file servers to which you are attached.

SLIST offers a useful way of determining if a file server is available. When you load the network shell and change to F:\LOGIN> (assuming F: is your default network drive), you can run SLIST to check for server availability even before you login.

The SYSCON Command

SYSCON, which stands for system configuration, is a key utility for network administrators and for users. As a network administrator, you use SYSCON to add new users to the network, grant access to network resources, assign printer queues, and passwords, and set account restrictions. While users lack sufficient network rights to make such changes, they can use SYSCON to gain some control over their own account. Even if users can't change the configuration, they may be able to see how their own set of rights and privileges has been set up.

From any network prompt, type SYSCON, and you'll see SYSCON's master menu, a screen like this:

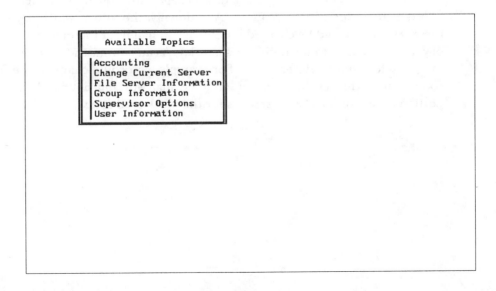

```
  Available Topics
 Accounting
 Change Current Server
 File Server Information
 Group Information
 Supervisor Options
 User Information
```

Accounting

The first topic on the SYSCON menu is Accounting. NetWare can track the times users log on to the network and how much use they make of it. Accounting is the facility through which network administrators can monitor usage and, if desired, bill back various departments for their employees' use of network resources. When you highlight the Accounting menu selection and press ENTER, you'll see a screen that looks like the following:

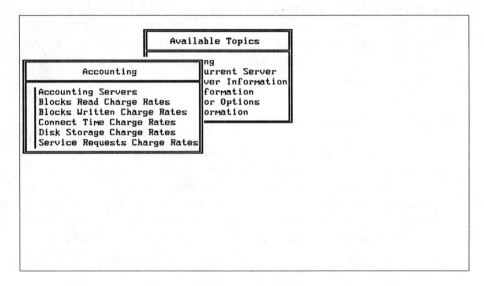

From this screen you can see that resources can be charged based on the number of data blocks that are read and written, the amount of connect time (how long the users are logged in), disk storage (how much of the network disk they use), and service requests. Additionally, the rate at which each of these resources could be charged is definable in half-hour increments, seven days per week and twenty-four hours per day. As an administrator you could assign up to twenty different rates. For example, you could charge more for connect time during the day than after normal working hours. Here is a portion of one of the charge screens for the block read rate:

```
                                        Sun Mon Tue Wed Thu Fri Sat
     Blocks Read Charge Rates    8:00am  1   1   1   1   1   1   1
                                 8:30am  1   1   1   1   1   1   1
                                 9:00am  1   1   1   1   1   1   1
 Sunday                          9:30am  1   1   1   1   1   1   1
 8:00 am To 8:29 am             10:00am  1   1   1   1   1   1   1
                                10:30am  1   1   1   1   1   1   1
 Rate  Charge      Rate  Charge 11:00am  1   1   1   1   1   1   1
  1   No Charge     11           11:30am  1   1   1   1   1   1   1
  2                 12          12:00pm  1   1   1   1   1   1   1
  3                 13          12:30pm  1   1   1   1   1   1   1
  4                 14           1:00pm  1   1   1   1   1   1   1
  5                 15           1:30pm  1   1   1   1   1   1   1
  6                 16           2:00pm  1   1   1   1   1   1   1
  7                 17           2:30pm  1   1   1   1   1   1   1
  8                 18           3:00pm  1   1   1   1   1   1   1
  9                 19           3:30pm  1   1   1   1   1   1   1
 10                 20           4:00pm  1   1   1   1   1   1   1
        (Charge is per block)    4:30pm  1   1   1   1   1   1   1
```

In this network, there are no charges. You can see that Rate 1 has been set to No Charge and is used for all time slots throughout the day.

File Server Information

The File Server Information selection on the SYSCON menu is strictly information-only for users. But, as a user, you can access it to learn a little more about the file servers on your network.

At SYSCON's main menu, move the cursor down to the File Server Information entry and hit ENTER to see the following screen.

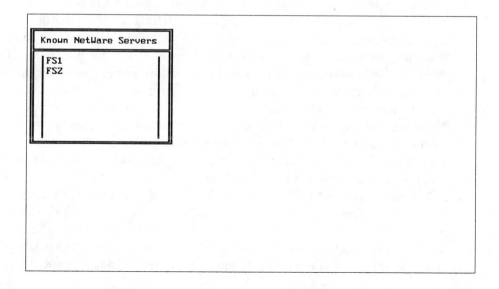

```
 Known NetWare Servers
 FS1
 FS2
```

As you can see, there are two servers on this network, FS1 and FS2. By highlighting FS1 and pressing the Enter key, you'll see a screen that looks much like the one below.

```
┌────────────────────────────────────────────────────────────────┐
│      ┌─────────────────────────────────────────────────┐        │
│      │            File Server Information              │        │
│      ├─────────────────────────────────────────────────┤        │
│      │ Server Name:           FS1                       │        │
│      │ NetWare Version:       Novell NetWare 386 V3.00 Rev. A│    │
│      │ OS Revision:           8/17/89                   │        │
│      │ System Fault Tolerance: Level II                 │        │
│      │ Transaction Tracking:  Yes                       │        │
│      │ Connections Supported: 250                       │        │
│      │ Connections In Use:    29                        │        │
│      │ Volumes Supported:     32                        │        │
│      │ Network Address:       00040258                  │        │
│      │ Node Address:          000000000001              │        │
│      │ Serial Number:         01814483                  │        │
│      │ Application Number:    4482                       │        │
│      └─────────────────────────────────────────────────┘        │
│                                                                  │
│                                                                  │
│                                                                  │
└────────────────────────────────────────────────────────────────┘
```

The first three lines are self-explanatory. System Fault Tolerance indicates that the operating system can take advantage of hardware-based Fault Tolerant data protection schemes. These might include such things as duplicate disks in which the data on one mirrors the data on the other.

The next item, Transaction Tracking (called TTS or Transaction Tracking System), is available only in Advanced NetWare 286SFT (installed on FS2, in this example) and in NetWare 386 (installed on FS1 in this example). This feature helps prevent databases from being corrupted if the power goes out or hardware fails as a database is being updated. Data corruption could occur during a power outage if the file server is not protected by battery backup or if it hangs while database information is being written to its disk. With TTS, NetWare looks at a block of data as a transaction. Either everything in the transaction is written to disk or, if there is a failure, the transaction is aborted.

The next information item on the menu is Connections Supported. NetWare 386 supports 250 simultaneous users, or connections. In other words, 250 people can be logged in at one time. (NetWare 286 supports 100 users.) You can see in the preceding screen that 29 people are logged into the FS1 file server, which is running NetWare 386.

Volumes Supported refers to the number of hard disks the operating system can support. The next two items listed on the menu, the Network Address and Node Address, refer to the network card installed in the file server. The serial number shown is the number of the network operating system, and it must be unique. The operating system is designed to look for, and protect against, duplicate serial numbers. If duplicate serial numbers show up on the same network, one of the two copies is an illegal copy. When NetWare files duplicates it automatically sends a message to all users who are logged in, notifying them of a licensing violation. The message freezes the workstations. Users must press the CTRL-ENTER combination to clear the message from their screens and continue their work. But NetWare resends the message every 30 to 60 seconds. Each time it does, users must press CTRL-ENTER to continue working.

Group Information

The SYSCON Group Information menu option provides network administrators with a convenient way of assigning and restricting network rights to groups of individuals with similar network needs. Users automatically receive the trustee rights that have been associated with a group when they are made members of that group. As a user, your effective rights on the network are the combination of your individual user rights (see "The RIGHTS Command" above) and the rights that have been assigned to the network groups of which you are a member.

Users can receive information about their groups by highlighting the Group Information selection on the SYSCON menu and pressing ENTER. That brings up a screen similar to the one below.

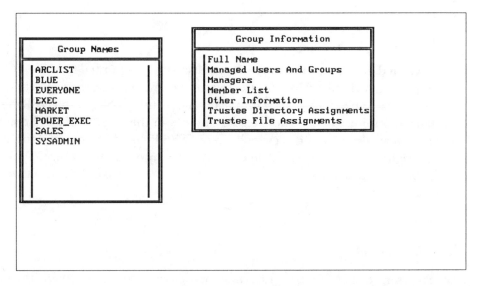

As a user, you can call up this screen and highlight the various menu options for each group to learn the group name, the managers in that group, and the members in the group (Member List). This is an information-only screen; you can't change the settings but you may want to check the screen occasionally to see who else is in your group.

In this menu, the Trustee Directory Assignments option is important. This selection displays the directory rights that have been assigned to members of the group you are reviewing. In this screen, we are reviewing the group named EVERYONE. (By default all network users are automatically members of EVERYONE when their user IDs are created.) As you might suspect, any changes to the trustee rights of the EVERYONE group affect all users on the network. If you highlight Trustee Directory Assignments and press ENTER, you'll see a screen that is similar to the one below.

```
    Group Names                Trustee Directory Assignments
  ARCLIST            SYS:APPS              [ R      F ]
  BLUE              SYS:APPS/CCDATA        [ RW     F ]
  EVERYONE          SYS:APPS/CCMAIL        [ RW     F ]
  EXEC              SYS:APPS/MENU          [ R      F ]
  MARKET            SYS:APPS/WP            [ RWCEMF ]
  POWER_EXEC        SYS:MAIL               [   C M  ]
  SALES             SYS:MHS                [        F ]
  SYSADMIN          SYS:MHS/EXE            [ R      F ]
                    SYS:MHS/SW             [ RWCEMF ]
                    SYS:MHS/SYS            [ R      F ]
                    SYS:PUBLIC             [ R      F ]
                    SYS:SHARE              [ RWCEMF ]
```

From this screen, you can see the rights that were granted to EVERYONE. For example, in the PUBLIC directory of the SYS volume, the rights granted are (R)ead, and (F)ile scan. This means the members of group EVERYONE have the right to read and execute any file in the SYS:PUBLIC directory. They may also view a directory listing of SYS:PUBLIC, but they don't have the rights to create, write, delete, or modify any of the files there. Typically SYS:PUBLIC is the directory that contains the NetWare utilities discussed in this chapter.

User Information

For users, SYSCON's User Information menu selection is probably the most important. With it you have some control over your workspace on the network. NetWare security, however, prevents you from making changes that affect other users.

To access User Information from the SYSCON main menu, move the cursor down to highlight the User Information selection and press the Enter key. You'll be presented with a list of User Names. If you highlight a name not your own and press ENTER, you'll see a screen similar to the following:

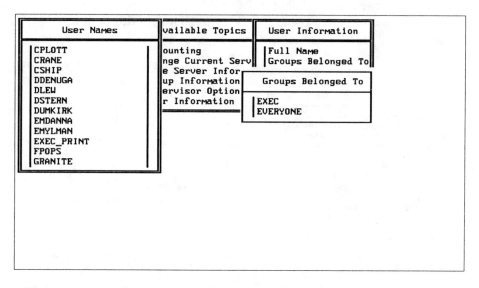

Unless you are the system administrator, if you highlight any name other than your own login name (EMYLMAN in this example), the only information you'll be able to see is what groups others belong to and their full names. In this example, we highlighted DDENUGA. By selecting Groups Belonged To, we can see only that she belongs to group EVERYONE and EXEC.

However, if you highlight your own name and press enter, you'll see a much more extensive list of options, similar to:

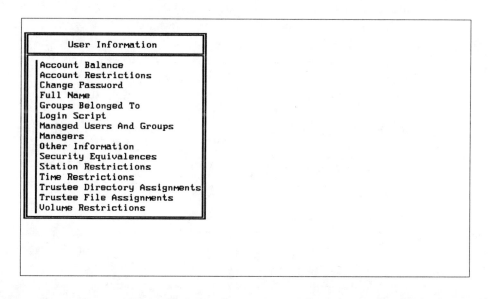

As a system administrator, you would see all of this information on any name you highlighted. Individual users, however, see this screen only when they highlight their own name. The first item is the user (your) Account Balance. This particular network has not implemented accounting on this file server so the account balance shows 0.

The next item is Account Restrictions. Highlight this option, press ENTER, and you'll see an information window like this.

```
        Account Restrictions For User EMYLMAN

Account Disabled:                        No
Account Has Expiration Date:             No
  Date Account Expires:
Limit Concurrent Connections:           No
  Maximum Connections:
Allow User To Change Password:           Yes
Require Password:                        Yes
  Minimum Password Length:               5
Force Periodic Password Changes:         No
  Days Between Forced Changes:
  Date Password Expires:
  Limit Grace Logins:
    Grace Logins Allowed:
    Remaining Grace Logins:
Require Unique Passwords:                Yes
```

This screen shows a lot about your restrictions on the network. As a user, you cannot change these restrictions, only a network administrator can. By using Account Disabled, a network administrator can temporarily suspend an account without deleting a user. This is handy when an account must be disabled for security reasons while a person is traveling or is on vacation.

The Account Has Expiration Date selection makes the account expire at a future date. This is useful when a temporary account is opened for an outside consultant or seasonal worker who needs the resources on the network but is scheduled to leave the company after a specific date. If the option is set to Yes, the date when the account expires will be shown on the next line. After that date, the user can no longer login.

The Limit Concurrent Connections option could be used to limit the number of times a user logs in simultaneously from different workstations. If this option is set to Yes, the number of connections will show on the next line.

If the Allow User To Change Password selection is set to Yes for all users, everyone on the network will be able to change their password by either using the Change Password option on the SYSCON menu or by using the SETPASS command utility (see "The SETPASS Command" above). The Require Password setting indicates that passwords are required to login and that each user's password must be at least five characters long.

Force Periodic Password Changes allows the network administrator to require users to change their passwords on a periodic basis. It isn't enabled on this network. But if this option were set to Yes, the network administrator would enter a number of days between changes and decide whether to allow the users "grace" logins after their password expires. If forced passwords are set and grace logins are limited, users can view how many remaining grace logins they have before they can no longer login.

The last option on this menu is Require Unique Passwords. If this option is invoked, NetWare will keep track of all passwords a user previously used and will not let old passwords be reused. For example, with this option invoked, a user couldn't use GREEN one month, switch to YELLOW the next month, and then switch back to GREEN. A unique password, one not used before, such as VIOLET, would have to be selected.

It's important to note that the menu options shown on the screen we just reviewed are "information only" to users. As a user you cannot change these settings; you can only view them. Only a system administrator can make the changes.

Users, however, can perform some activities using options under the User Information menu. There they'll find the Change Password option. If you are not restricted from doing so under Account Restrictions, you can select this option to change your password. As with the command-line utility SETPASS, you will be required to type in your new password twice, once to identify the new password and the second time to verify the spelling. Should you make a typo on either the first or the second entry, NetWare will not change your password. The new passwords you assign must fall within the Account Restrictions, which, on our example network, specify a word with a minimum of five letters.

Also under the User Information menu, you'll find the Full Name selection. This displays your Full Name as it was assigned on the network by the network administrator. In our example for user EMYLMAN, highlighting the Full Name option and hitting ENTER will bring up an information window similar to the following:

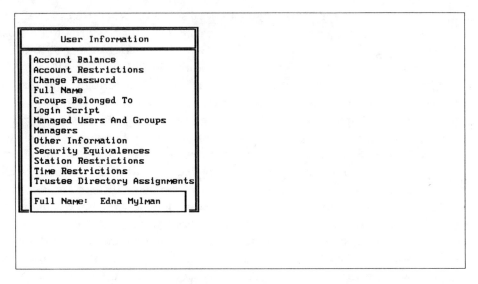

Many electronic mail packages allow you to use Full Names, as stored by NetWare, to identify users of the E-mail system. Because these systems use names already stored by NetWare, users don't have to type in their full names when starting them.

The menu selection Groups Belonged To predictably shows the groups to which you belong. Once you determine which group you belong to, you can check that group's privileges from the Group Information menu selection on SYSCON's main menu. In our sample session, selecting Groups Belonged To for user, EMYLMAN, will display the following:

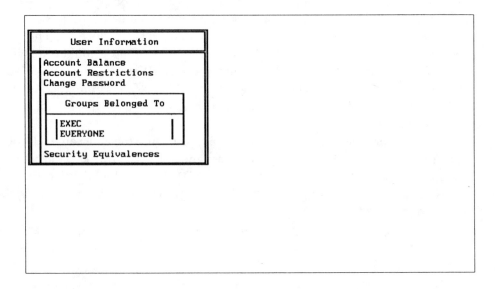

The Group Belonged To selection under SYSCON's User Information menu lets you access the Login Script. On many networks this selection is not information only. If the network administrator allows them rights to do so, users can go through it to actually make changes that will affect their work on the network.

The user login script is one of two scripts NetWare automatically executes when you login to the network. The other script is the system login script (see "The System Login"). Users typically have some control over their user login script, but they cannot make changes in the system login script, nor can they see it when they select it on the menu. Network administrators use the system login script to set up network parameters that affect everyone on the network and use the user login script to set up parameters for individual users.

To see your user login script, highlight User Information on SYSCON's main menu. Press ENTER and scroll down to your own name or, if you're a system administrator, the name of the user whose individual login script you wish to change. Press ENTER and scroll to the selection called Login Script. Press ENTER again and a screen similar to the following will appear:

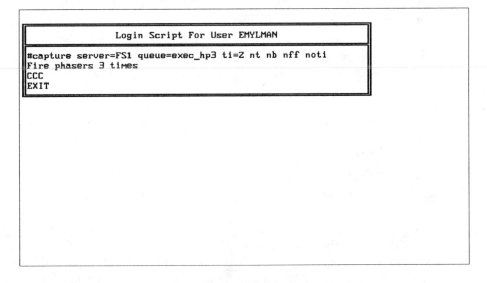

In this example we see a short login script in which the user has used the CAPTURE command (see "The CAPTURE Command" above) to individualize the way in which printed output is received and has used the FIRE PHASERS command, which we'll discuss in a minute, to individualize the way in which his or her PC boots up. The first line of this user login script will capture LPT1 to the queue exec_hp3. Note that the first character is a #. This tells NetWare to execute the program CAPTURE. The FIRE PHASERS command in the second line is a NetWare utility that will cause the workstation to emit a "phaserlike" sound, in this case, nine times. The "phasers" do no more than make noise, but some folks like to add it to their logins.

In this case, a batch file named CCC is executed from the login script. Here, CCC.BAT is a file that checks for messages on the network's electronic mail system when the user first logs in. Any batch file that's appropriate to the user's login can be executed from the login script. Simply include the name of the file and be sure the batch file is located somewhere on the user's search path.

The last line of this sample login script is the EXIT command. The line containing the EXIT statement should be the last line of the user login script, as no line following the EXIT statement will be executed.

Other useful commands can be included in the login script. For instance, if you want to see a listing of all of the network drives when you login as well as directories on the search path, you can insert a line with the NetWare command MAP (See "The MAP Command" above). You can also use the login script to have the network remind you of regular occurrences, such as a weekly report. To remind yourself of a task due every Monday, for instance, you would add the following three lines to the login script.

```
IF DAY_OF_WEEK = "MONDAY" THEN BEGIN
WRITE "MONDAY IS HERE. YOUR WEEKLY REPORT IS DUE TODAY"
END
```

Now every time you login the network will see the DAY_OF_WEEK variable and check to see if the system date variable is MONDAY. If it is, it will write any message between the quotation marks to the workstation screen.

After making changes to the login script, press ESCAPE and answer Yes to save the changes. Then, to see the impact of the changes, log off the network and log in again.

The next option on SYSCON's User Information menu is Other Information. This is another information-only selection. Users cannot modify the settings but they can view them. Administrators can make modifications.

Other Information shows users the last time they logged in, whether they have been granted file server console privileges, and any limitations the network administrator applied to how much disk space they can use on the file server. It also shows how much disk space the user has consumed. As a user, you can highlight Other Information and press ENTER to see the following information:

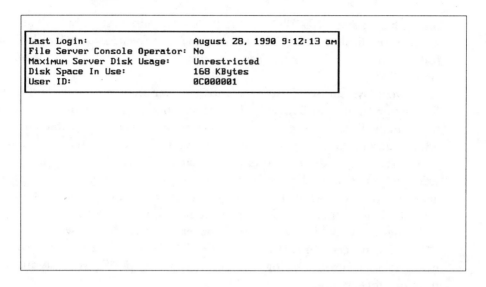

```
Last Login:                      August 28, 1990 9:12:13 am
File Server Console Operator:    No
Maximum Server Disk Usage:       Unrestricted
Disk Space In Use:               168 KBytes
User ID:                         0C000001
```

Here we see this user has 168K of file server space in use. The last item, User ID, is a number NetWare assigns to you when you are created as a user.

The next item on the User Information menu is Security Equivalences. These can include the individual rights you are assigned as a user and the rights you gain from being a member of groups.

```
          Security Equivalences
ARCLIST                (Group)
EVERYONE               (Group)
SALES                  (Group)
```

This screen could also show whether the user has been assigned another user's security equivalence. For example, if BPAMTIN needed access to the files of his assistant, KELWOOD, the network administrator could grant him a security equivalence to KELWOOD. In that case, the user name KELWOOD followed by the description (User) would appear in the status window on the right.

Network system administrators can use Station Restrictions and Time Restrictions under the SYSCON User Information menu to limit users' access to the network to specific workstations by specifying the acceptable network address and node id address of the network interface card in the workstation.

In certain cases, these features can add an additional level of security. For example, a network administrator may wish to limit the payroll manager's access to the network to the manager's own workstation. Then, when the manager leaves and locks the door, no one at another workstation can access his or her network files even if the manager's password is known.

In some offices, this feature is enabled for print servers to ensure, for example, that they can be logged in only from the specific workstations that have printers attached.

For the print servers, the screen would look something like this:

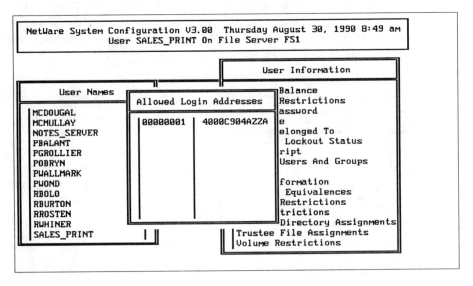

As with most of the SYSCON user information commands, users will be able to view only their own station restrictions. If the network manager has implemented station restrictions just for the print servers, the allowed login addresses screen will be blank.

With the time restriction feature, the network administrator can restrict access to the network by half-hour increments, seven days per week, twenty-four hours per day. The following sample screen shows time restrictions on a printer server called SALES_PRINT. The screen shows that the server can be logged in anytime.

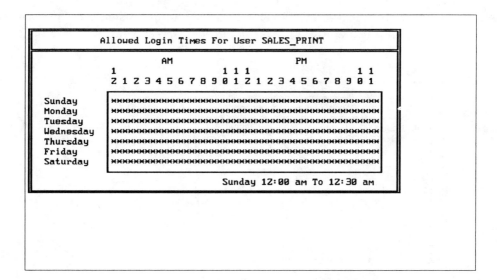

If time-restricted users are logged on when their time expires, the network will log them out automatically, severing the connection to the file server. If this happens to you, you will have to reboot your PC and log into the network during nonrestricted hours to complete your work. The message you get when this happens will look like this:

```
>> FS1 Connection Time Expired.  Please Log Out.  (CTRL-ENTER
to clear)
```

If you attempt to login during a restricted period, you will get a message similar to:

```
FS1/CRANE: Attempting to login during an unauthorized time
period.
The supervisor has limited the times that you can login to
this server.
You are attached to server FS1.
```

Other items you will find under SYSCON include Trustee Directory Assignments, Trustee File Assignments, and Volume Restrictions.

Trustee Directory Assignments are the network rights given to users as individuals (see "The RIGHTS Commands" above). Here the network administrator grants users the rights to their home directories. These directory assignments affect not only the named directory, but also all subdirectories that follow, down to a level where the network administrator changes the assignment.

As with most of the other SYSCON commands, users can view only the information that pertains to them. In the following example, we'll investigate trustee rights for user LBURTON. By highlighting Trustee Directory Assignments and pressing ENTER, you would see a screen similar to this:

```
┌─────────────────────────────────────────────────────────────────┐
│   ┌───────────────────────────────────────────────┐              │
│   │        Trustee Directory Assignments           │              │
│   ├───────────────────────────┬───────────────────┤              │
│   │ SALES:SALES/LBURTONN       │  [ RWCEMF ]       │              │
│   │ SYS:MAIL/ZA000001          │  [ RWCEMF ]       │              │
│   │                            │                   │              │
│   │                            │                   │              │
│   │                            │                   │              │
│   │                            │                   │              │
│   │                            │                   │              │
│   │                            │                   │              │
│   │                            │                   │              │
│   └───────────────────────────┴───────────────────┘              │
│                                                                   │
│                                                                   │
└───────────────────────────────────────────────────────────────────┘
```

Here we can see that LBURTONN has been assigned rights in his home SALES:SALES\LBURTONN directory. The second set of directory trustee assignments is set up automatically for every user when they are added as users to the network. The SYS:MAIL subdirectory is where individual user login scripts are stored. If the network administrator restricts rights in this directory, the user will be unable to change his or her login script.

Trustee File Assignments are similar to directory assignments, but they give the network administrator the ability to assign rights at the "file level" rather than at the directory level. This feature was introduced in NetWare 386 and is not available in earlier versions.

Volume Restrictions were also introduced with NetWare 386. With this feature, the network administrator can limit disk space for each user as well as which disks the user can write to. Volume Restrictions take precedence over trustee assignments. For example, the network administrator may have granted a user rights to create and write files on a volume, but users restricted from using that volume under Volume Restrictions, will be unable to write to that volume. If users switch to a volume to which they have been restricted and type DIR, they will see that 0 bytes are available.

Users can view their individual volume restrictions by highlighting Volume Restrictions and pressing ENTER. Then by highlighting the volume name that reflects the group they are in, they would see a message such as:

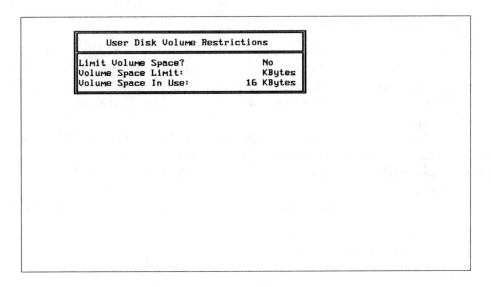

Here we see that there are no volume restrictions and that LBURTON has 16K of files.

However, if users highlighted a different volume, one where they did not enjoy access rights, they would see a message such as the following:

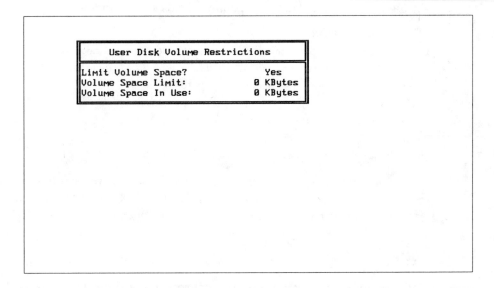

This shows that LBURTON is completely restricted.

The SYSTIME Command

A fairly simple command, SYSTIME's purpose is to synchronize your computer's time and date with that of the file server. On NetWare 386, this command is executed automatically when a user logs in. Under NetWare 286, users have to run this command explicitly or execute it as part of the login script.

In some environments, it's important that all workstations have the current time and date, as backups are performed based on the dates of a file or a range of dates for files. However, all files should be backed up daily regardless of the file date.

From any network prompt, type SYSTIME, and you'll see something like this:

```
F:\EDIT\CRAIG>SYSTIME
Current System Time:   Tuesday  September  18, 1990  8:01 am
```

If you then type date <ENTER> or time <ENTER>, you'll see that your local computer's time and date have been set to the file server's.

You can run SYSTIME only on a file server or servers to which you are attached.

So, to begin, let's use the command WHOAMI (explained more fully later in this chapter) to find out which file servers you are attached to.

Typing WHOAMI at the network prompt yields something like this:

```
F:\EDIT\CRAIG>WHOAMI
You are user CRAIG attached to server PRODUCTION, connection 20.
Server PRODUCTION is running SFT NetWare 286 V2.15 Rev. C.
Login time: Tuesday  September  18, 1990  7:24 am


You are user CRAIG attached to server BAMBAM, connection 1.
Server BAMBAM is running NetWare 386 V3.00 Rev. A.
Login time: Tuesday  September  18, 1990  7:23 am
```

As you are attached to the PRODUCTION file server, you could synchronize your password to the clock in the PRODUCTION server by typing SYSTIME PRODUCTION. It would generate the following result:

```
F:\EDIT\CRAIG>SYSTIME PRODUCTION
Current System Time:   Tuesday  September  18, 1990  8:01 am
```

Unfortunately, there is no way to synchronize the times between the file servers. The network administrator has to perform that manually.

The USERLIST Command

USERLIST is a utility that lists all users currently logged into the file server as well as their connection number, network and node address, and the time each person logged in.

The syntax for this command is:

```
USERLIST /A
```

When you type this command at any network prompt, you'll see something similar to the following screen:

```
User Information for Server FSA
Connection  User Name      Network      Node Address    Login Time
----------  ---------      -------      ------------    ----------
     1      MARKET_PRINT [       1] [10005A1E1D96]   7-24-1990  8:04 am
     3      JHOMMAN      [       1] [4000C904A0F0]   8-07-1990  9:08 am
     4      JDYKMAN      [       1] [4000C905AEB6]   8-07-1990  7:56 am
     6      EXEC_PRINT   [       1] [10005A602B68]   8-06-1990  4:00 pm
     7      BLUELASER    [       1] [4000C904D934]   7-11-1990 11:46 am
     8      RWHINER      [       1] [4000C904A0F1]   8-03-1990 11:56 am
     9      JWAMY        [       1] [10005A607C9B]   8-07-1990  7:57 am
    10      MJEREMY      [       1] [10005A607CF1]   8-07-1990  8:51 am
    11      JPRINCE      [       1] [4000C904ABAB]   8-07-1990  9:09 am
    12      LWALTER      [       1] [4000C904A3B0]   8-07-1990  9:03 am
    13      SCRONYN      [       1] [4000C904AA36]   8-03-1990  1:48 pm
    14      SALES_PRINT  [       1] [4000C904AZZA]   8-03-1990  3:40 pm
    15      SDENCY       [       1] [10005A6060F0]   8-07-1990  8:41 am
    17      SFINNAN      [       1] [10005A1CZA4E]   8-07-1990  8:39 am
    18      PWARDER      [       1] [10005A60373F]   8-06-1990  6:00 pm
    20      SPALS        [       1] [4000C905AD17]   8-06-1990 10:51 am
    21      KENWOOD      [       1] [4000C904AZZ1]   8-07-1990  8:46 am
    22      PBANE        [       1] [4000C904A30F]   8-06-1990  5:23 pm
    23      ACLIFTY      [       1] [10005A601E81]   8-07-1990  8:42 am
    24      *CRANE       [       1] [10005A603D82]   8-07-1990  9:12 am
    25      WTAYMAY      [       1] [4000C904AE28]   8-07-1990  9:13 am
```

The asterisk appears next to the name of the user who executed USERLIST.

The Network address is the address of the physical cabling for the network. In the office in our example, the server FSA has only one physical segment, or cabling scheme, and its number is 1. The Node Address is the address of the network card for each station. Notice that each card number is unique. These numbers are assigned by the manufacturer and are programmed or, "burned," into the network card. In this token-ring network, node addresses starting with 1000 are IBM Token-Ring cards. Node addresses starting with 4000 are Proteon token-ring boards.

The VOLINFO Command

VOLINFO lists information on each disk on the file server and shows how large it is, how many directory entries are available, the amount of free space and the directory entries. (See also "The CHKVOL Command" and "The SLIST Command" above.) From any network prompt, type VOLINFO, and you'll see something similar to the following:

```
┌─────────────────────────────────────────────────────────────────────┐
│ Page 1/1       Total     Free      Total     Free      Total     Free │
│ Volume name  ┌──────SYS──────┐ ┌─────EXEC─────^^┐ ┌─────EXTRA─────┐    │
│ KiloBytes    │ 125,864  43,484 │ 150,588  72,436 │ 301,172  165,464 │  │
│ Directories  │  21,344  17,178 │  16,736  10,859 │  25,792   13,633 │  │
│              └────────────────┘ └───────────────┘ └─────────────────┘ │
│ Volume name  ┌─────SALES─────┐                                        │
│ KiloBytes    │ 150,584 109,748 │                                      │
│ Directories  │   6,560   1,824 │                                      │
│              └────────────────┘                                       │
└─────────────────────────────────────────────────────────────────────┘

              ┌─────────────────────┐
              │ Available Options    │
              ├─────────────────────┤
              │ Change Servers       │
              │ Update Interval      │
              └─────────────────────┘
```

When this screen appears, you will notice that approximately every five seconds the word CHECKING appears between the page number and the Volume name. This indicates that VOLINFO is checking to see if the information on any of the disks has changed. In our example, the ^^ next to the free space on the EXEC volume indicates that someone deleted a file or directory during the previous scan interval, and the free space increased. A down delta symbol would indicate that someone created a file or directory, thereby reducing the free space on the volume.

The only options available to you on VOLINFO are to change the scan interval that determines how frequently VOLINFO updates its information and to change to other file servers.

The WHOAMI Command

WHOAMI is useful when you need to check the identity of a workstation logged into the network or determine whether the workstation is logged on.

It is especially useful to system managers who need to know more about the workstations they're servicing, but it is also useful to users who want some basic information about their network connection.

From any network prompt, simply type WHOAMI and hit the Return key to see a message listing the names of the server(s) to which you are attached, the version(s) of NetWare they are running, and your user name(s), connection number(s) on each, and the time you logged in.

A workstation in a sales or marketing department that's being used by someone in the SALES group would see something like the following:

```
F:\SALES\USERNAME>WHOAMI
You are user USERNAME attached to server FS1, connection 27.
Server FS1 is running NetWare 386 V3.00 Rev. A.
Login time: Thursday  August  2, 1990  7:12 am
```

A user who is attached to more than one file server via a bridge would see a screen similar to the following one:

```
F:\SALES\USERNAME>WHOAMI
You are user USERNAME attached to server FS1, connection 27.
Server FS1 is running NetWare 386 V3.00 Rev. A.
Login time: Thursday  August  2, 1990  7:12 am


You are user SALES attached to server FS2, connection 17.
Server FS2 is running SFT NetWare 286 V2.15 Rev. C.
Login time: Thursday  August  2, 1990  7:12 am
```

Members of the sales department group would see the additional file server information because they automatically attach to the FS2 server as a user named SALES when they login to FS1. This allows them to pass files to directories on the FS2 file server.

WHOAMI is also useful to check to see whether your workstation is logged on to the network. This network command is available only to users who are logged in. If you try to execute WHOAMI and you're not on the network, you'll get the following message:

```
Bad command or file name
```

Chances are, anyone who sees this message is not logged on.

WHOAMI also offers additional information, such as group membership, security equivalences, and trustee rights. You can also get this information by using the SYSCON command. But with WHOAMI you can neatly summarize the information by using the command with its command-line switches.

Like each of the NetWare command-line utilities, WHOAMI has a limited form of help that will assist with syntax when using the command with switches. You may enter WHOAMI with any switch to bring up a syntax help message. For instance, if you were to enter the following command from the network prompt:

```
whoami /z
```

NetWare would return a message that said:

```
Usage:
WHOAMI [Server] [/Security] [/Groups] [/Rights] [/System]
[/Object] [/All]
```

This is because WHOAMI does not understand the /z switch. Instead of acting on the command, it displays a list of the available command-line switches that it does recognize.

If you type WHOAMI without any switches, you'll get something similar to:

```
You are user CRANE attached to server FS1, connection 1.
Server FS1 is running NetWare 386 V3.00 Rev. A.
Login time: Monday  September  17, 1990  1:17 pm
```

If you apply the /S switch, NetWare will show you your security equivalences. In this example, for instance, it might tell CRANE that he is a member of the group EVERYONE and FINANCE.

The /G switch shows the groups to which you belong and will return information that looks something like this:

```
You are user CRANE attached to server FS1, connection 1.
Server FS1 is running NetWare 386 V3.00 Rev. A.
Login time: Monday  September  17, 1990  1:17 pm
You are a member of the following groups:

    EVERYONE
    FINANCE
    SALES_PRINT
```

If you want to see all the information WHOAMI can provide, type WHOAMI /A. NetWare will display a screen similar to the following:

```
You are user CRANE attached to server FS1, connection 1.
Server CRANE is running NetWare 386 V3.00 Rev. A.
Login time: Monday  September  17, 1990  1:17 pm
You are security equivalent to the following:
    EVERYONE (Group)
```

```
      FINANCE (Group)
      SALES_PRINT (User)
You are a member of the following groups:
      EVERYONE
      FINANCE
[          ]  SYS:
[ R     F ]  SYS:LOGIN
[ R     F ]  SYS:PUBLIC
[   C M   ]  SYS:MAIL
[ RWCEMF ]  SYS:MAIL/12000002
[ RWCEMF ]  SYS:MAIL/4F000004
[ RWCEMF ]  SYS:SHARE
[ R     F ]  SYS:APPS
[ RWCEMF ]  SYS:APPS/WP
[ R     F ]  SYS:APPS/MENU
[ RW    F ]  SYS:APPS/CCMAIL
[ RW    F ]  SYS:APPS/CCDATA
[       F ]  SYS:MHS
[ R     F ]  SYS:MHS/EXE
[ R     F ]  SYS:MHS/SYS
[ RWCEMF ]  SYS:MHS/SW
   [        ]   FINANCE:
[ RWCEMF ]  FINANCE:FINANCE/SHARE
[ RWCEMF ]  FINANCE:FINANCE/CRANE
   [        ]   EXTRA:
   [        ]   SALES:
```

The rights shown are the user's access rights (see "The RIGHTS Command" above). Their meanings are as follows:

May Read from File	(R)
May Write to File	(W)
May Create Subdirectories and Files	(C)
May Erase Directory	(E)
May Modify Directory	(M)
May Scan for Files	(F)

6

LAN Software

Once you have your LAN set up, you're ready to make it work. That means installing application software: word processing, spreadsheet, database, accounting, tax, CAD, whatever. Installing the LAN operating system may seem simple compared to installing LAN software.

Your first task in putting application software on a Novell server is to decide how you want to support that software. You must determine the directory structure you want to use and the type of search paths you need.

Application Setup

Directories

Should you install all your software in one directory? Put each product in its own directory? What criteria should you use in making your decision?

First, consider the number of files that comprise the application. If it has more than four or five, put the application in its own directory. And if it consists of only a few files but you want to limit access to a subset of your users, put it in its own directory.

As we suggested in chapter 4, these directories should be subdirectories off a primary root directory:

    \APPL\123R22

or

    \APPS\WP51

Remember, because you want to keep your root directory as small as possible, you should not create individual root directories for each product.

If the application consists of just one to three files and you either have no reason to limit access or want to make the product available to everyone, put it in what you might think of as a "grab-bag" program directory:

    \PUBLIC\VDR

or

    \PUBLIC\PGM

(VDR is shorthand for vendor, as opposed to USR for user-written programs; PGM is shorthand for programs.)

Search Paths

A search path tells DOS where to look for executable files (.com or .exe). NetWare, being smarter than DOS, can also find overlay and data files in a search path.

Why are search paths important? Because if you want to execute programs from a directory other than the program directory, that directory must be in a search path for DOS/NetWare to be able to execute it. On a LAN, you should always execute programs from a personal directory, not from a program directory. The reasons are several, some of which are aesthetic. Primarily, though, your users should have a stable work area, and the easiest way to provide one is to give each network user a personal directory from which all programs are invoked.

Search paths can be either dynamic or static. A dynamic search path is one that exists only while the application is in use. A static search path exists whether or not the application is in use.

On a stand-alone PC, a static search path would be the one set up in the AUTOEXEC.BAT. A dynamic search path would be one set up in a BAT file or menu option used to invoke an application.

On a NetWare LAN, the concept is similar. The static search path is the path set up in the login script. A dynamic search path is the one set up in a BAT file or menu option used to invoke the application.

Note: Static search paths can, of course, be changed after they have been established in either an AUTOEXEC.BAT or LOGIN script, but, generally, static search paths should be permanent.

Why shouldn't you just put all the search paths you will need into the login script? There are a number of reasons. First, NetWare supports only sixteen search paths. That may seem like a lot, but over time it is not difficult to exceed that limit, especially if you are supporting applications on local drives as well as on LAN drives.

Second, if you are running Advanced NetWare 2.1x, search paths consume a special type of memory at the server called D-Group. This is a 16K block of memory that cannot be expanded. The more users you have and the more permanently mapped search paths each has, the greater the likelihood that you will exceed that memory limit and crash your server.

Third, a search path is just that: an instruction to NetWare on where to look whenever a user types a command. If the application you want is on the sixteenth drive, it will take even NetWare awhile to locate and execute it.

Fourth, some programs search all mapped drives for executables (and don't have the sense to stop as soon as they locate the program). The more drives mapped, the longer it takes to execute the program.

Fifth, the more permanent search paths you have, the greater the likelihood of a program name conflict. This is especially true of word processing programs: Many (if not most) users use WP as the name of the primary program. If you are supporting two word processors and both are in permanent search paths, you must switch the search path order to ensure that the program you want is executed. Similar conflicts with other programs are not as likely, but why take the chance if you don't need to?

Static Search Paths

How should you decide which search paths should be dynamic and which should be static? Generally, static search paths should be limited to those directories that should always be accessible. A typical login script might, for example, contain the following:

```
MAP S1:=SYS:\PUBLIC
MAP S2:=SYS:\PUBLIC\BAT
MAP S3:=SYS:\PUBLIC\USR
MAP S4:=SYS:\PUBLIC\PGM
MAP S5:=SYS:\PUBLIC\DOS
MAP S6:=SYS:\APPS
MAP S7:=SYS1:\APPL
```

The PGM subdirectory would contain a variety of one-three file applications. The USR subdirectory is similar to the PGM subdirectory but contains public domain or locally written programs. ("USR" is the name given to the directory on Unix systems where such programs are stored.) The BAT directory contains all the BAT programs used to support the LAN. Search drives S6 and S7 establish permanent drive letters for two different application directories. They are useful if you choose a particular dynamic path technique we discuss further on.

Some LAN installers and administrators recommend that the user's home directory be placed in the search path. We choose not to do so for two reasons: (1) If all programs are invoked from the home directory, it's not necessary. (2) If programs are invoked from other directories, it may not be wise to include the user's home directory because programs may exist in that directory that will prevent your application setups from working properly.

Dynamic Search Paths

Dynamic search paths by definition exist only during the life of an application. You add the path to the application when you invoke the application and remove it when you exit the application.

Under NetWare, you can use several variations of the MAP Sn command (see chapter 5) to establish the application's path:

```
MAP Sn - - -
MAP INS Sn
MAP DEL Sn
```

Unfortunately, none of them provides much control over the drive letter assigned, and that can be critical for some applications.

If you map to an existing search path number, you will displace the program assigned to that drive. Using MAP INS S1, you can ensure that the application will be the first in the search path, but you will get the next available drive letter (working back from Z). Thus the drive letter assigned to a particular program will vary with the number of search paths in existence when the command is executed.

If you choose MAP S16, as some recommend, you won't displace another program only if you don't already have sixteen search paths. And you still can't guarantee what drive letter will be assigned. Moreover, if you standardize on a particular technique and, for one reason or another, are not able to release the path properly (for example, you use MAP INS S1, do not do a MAP DEL S1, and issue the MAP INS S1 command again), when you do a MAP DEL S1 you will be deleting only the last drive, not the prior one.

In fact, one major problem with Novell's search paths is that, in a way, they are too intelligent for dynamic pathing. Many programs have configuration files that require both a drive letter and a directory path. But Novell will do whatever it must to establish a search path, and that involves, first and foremost, ignoring drive letter integrity.

You can use these commands reliably if you have a stable LAN environment in which you can ensure no user environments may cause your dynamic paths to produce unexpected results, but we recommend against it.

(You may want to investigate the various alternatives to prove to yourself the "dynamic" nature of dynamic search paths. Try building a table of directories and various search path setups and deletions. The table will become complex rather rapidly. An exercise with such a table some years back convinced us that we did not want to use this technique in our BAT files.)

Is there an alternative? Yes. Use a combination of MAP commands and standard DOS commands rather than just NetWare commands. Several alternative techniques will work.

Technique 1

```
DEMO.BAT
    SET OP = %PATH%                      |saves existing path
    MAP P:=SYS:\APPL\DEMO  > NUL: |map drive P to prog
    PATH %OP%;P:\APPL\DEMO               |add drive to path
    program                              |run program
    PATH %OP%                            |restore orig path
    SET OP=                              |clear variable
    MAP DEL P:              > NUL: |clear drive
```

Note: If you try to delete the drive before you reset the path, NetWare will issue a warning.

This technique gives you complete control over the drive letter assigned to the application, but does not always work. For reasons we've never quite figured out, it is sometimes necessary to add the following code after the first PATH statement and before invoking the application to fully establish the NetWare search path.

```
MAP > NUL:
```

This command runs NetWare's MAP program but does not display the result (the NUL). Because it establishes an environment variable, you may need to increase your environment space.

When you can't guarantee that the drive letter you've chosen is available, you may want to use the following in place of line 2:

```
ECHO Y|MAP P:\SYS:\APPL\DEMO > NUL:
```

If P is already assigned to a search path, MAP will ask if you are sure you want to reassign it. The ECHO Y responds to that prompt. (With the NUL parameter in place, Novell's question will not be displayed and the BAT file will appear to be hung.)

Technique 2

An alternative technique is to use a program such as ADDPATH.EXE (a public domain utility) to add and remove directories.

The path:

```
DEMO.BAT
    MAP P:=SYS:\APPL\DEMO   > NUL: |map drive P to prog
    ADDPATH P:\APPL\DEMO           |add drive to path
    program                        |run program
    ADDPATH P:\APPL\DEMO -D         |restore orig path
    MAP DEL P:               > NUL: |clear drive
```

Technique 3[*]

You can use the following technique if you have established a generic search path (such as MAP S6:=SYS:\APPS) in your login scripts:

```
DEMO.BAT
    CD U:\APPS\program              |*see note
    program
    CD U:\APPS
```

The CD U: assumes that U is the drive letter assigned to the S6: drive in the login script. The CD command makes the current directory for that drive the program directory.

This technique has several advantages: It uses neither Novell's MAP command (so the BAT file does not need to load and execute that program) nor environment variables (which consume environment space). It will not work if you run into an application that insists on a particular drive letter.

BAT Files/Menus

You will probably want or need to invoke all applications from either a BAT file or menu system (or combination thereof). On a LAN, application support may require a variety of actions that aren't necessary on a stand-alone computer. You may want to audit use, control concurrent access, invoke the application from a particular directory, or test for the existence of certain files.

Application Issues

Don't be mislead by software advertisements that say a product will run on all NETBIOS LANS or that list a number of the major LANS on which the product will run, or even that indicate special support for NetWare. Some

---

*We are indebted to Richard Retin of Wells Fargo Bank for the idea.

products written and designed for a stand-alone PC can be installed and supported more easily on a LAN than products specifically designed for it. Most administrators need a bag of tricks to make software work the way they want it to on their LANs.

LANability

A product's LANability is a function of the interaction of the structure of your LAN, the product's design, and your ability to overcome flaws in the product to make it work with your LAN. Software that one person may extol for its LANability may be derided by another person for its unLANability.

In the next two sections, we identify the LAN characteristics that affect software LANability and then the software features that affect LANability. Because they are closely intertwined, we raise issues in the first section that we explore more fully in the second.

LAN Characteristics

The following areas can affect an application's LANability, from the network's side:

    user experience—high/low
    person/computer ratio—high/low
    support/staff ratio—high/low
    hardware configurations—single/varied
    local hard disks—many/none
    software variety—low/high
    data storage—central/local
    LAN size—small/large
    LAN structure—loose/controlled
    LAN management philosophy

Software Characteristics

Here are the potential hangups on the application's side:

    installation
       programs
          install drive/directory
       copy protection
          hardware
          software

                    name
                    user setups
            path support
            data directory support
            resource constraints
                memory
                    conventional
                    expanded/extended
                disk space
                    temporary
                    permanent
            configurations
                executables
                single, central location
                hardware
                personal
                central
            printing
            file locking
            pricing
                workstation
                user
                concurrent user
                server

Now let's look at all these problems in more detail.

LAN Characteristics

Remember the decisions we asked you to make in chapter 2 about implementing your LAN? Many of them will affect the ease with which you can select, install, and support software.

User Experience

Are your users computer experts? Novices? Do they understand specific products but not hardware or technical issues? If you want to "hide" the "hard stuff" (knowledge about a particular computer's configuration or how to set up a particular product) from your users, you need software that is smart enough to let you do that.

Person / Computer Ratio

Does each person have a computer? Are some computers public? Are there any circumstances under which a person may work on two or more different kinds of computers? The single most common design flaw in software today is the lack of distinction in setup and configuration between the person who invokes the software and the machine on which it is invoked.

Support / Staff Ratio

What's your ratio of support staff to users? High? Low? The better the ratio of staff to users, the greater your ability to handle both a variety of software packages and the various support problems some programs may create. If your ratio is low, as it is on many networks (a ratio of one support person to every 80 to 100 computers is not uncommon), you will want to install software in such a way that it minimizes support calls.

Hardware Configurations

How many computers and how many different kinds of computers are on your network? Are you supporting different brands and models? Different processors, video cards, monitors, keyboards, amount and type of memory? Although we tend to take hardware compatibility for granted today, much software is still (even increasingly) dependent on the type of machine on which it is run. If all of your machines are identically configured, hardware support will not be an issue.

Local Hard Disks

Do all your computers have hard disks? Some? None? Or do you plan to install all software only on the server? Generally it is much easier to install a product once on the server than many times on local hard disks. Similarly, if the software is on the server, you can prevent it from being erased or accidentally modified. But what if the product won't run from the server? Could you, or would you, if need be, install software on those local hard disks rather than on the server?

Software Variety

Are you planning to support just your spreadsheet, your word processor, your graphics package? Or do you expect to support multiple products in a variety of product categories? Do you need or want to use terminate and stay resident programs? The more products you want to support, the more problems you will run into, and the more important LANability may be to you. TSR problems (conflicts between them or with other packages) increase exponentially as you add other products or TSRs. If you are supporting a large variety of products, you may choose not to support any TSRs, simply to minimize the potential support issues.

Data Storage

Will your users store all of their data on local media (diskettes, local hard disks) or on the server? If they store it on the server, do you want to give each individual personal storage, or do you want to keep all the data in one location? Some products make the former easy and the latter difficult to implement or the reverse.

LAN Size

How large is your network? A few PCs in one room? Dozens, hundreds, thousands? Are they spread throughout one floor, a building, a city, the country, the world? If it's small now, do you expect the network to grow? On a small, centrally located LAN, it is relatively easy to treat each PC or each person differently. On a large, dispersed network, the ability to create generic setups for all users and machines becomes much more important.

LAN Structure

Do you insist on a distinction between data directories and program directories on the server? Does each of your users have a personal directory on the server for data files? Do some, or all, of your users share data in a single directory? With some products, you can support either type of setup; others make one or the other difficult to implement.

LAN Management Philosophy

Is this an anything-goes type LAN where any user can install any software and expect it to be supported? Or do your users expect you to handle such details? Are you willing to install software that will require users to know technical details about their computers (type of video card, type of memory, and so on)? Is it okay for a package to bomb if it is run on the wrong type of computer? If you are willing to limit what your users can do with a product, or accept occasional errors generated by their lack of technical knowledge, you can be less particular about how, for example, software products support different kinds of hardware.

Many of these features are interrelated. The more your LAN resembles a collection of stand-alone computers, all with local hard disks (on which users install the software) and local printers, which happen to be connected by a wire to share perhaps just one or two peripherals or a gateway, the less you must be concerned about a product's LANability. (You will still run into problems, but they will not be much different from those experienced by any microcomputer manager.) The more your LAN resembles a minicomputer or mainframe environment in which all software and data are stored on the server, the less technical your users (that is, the less they understand about hardware or software installation), the more you must be concerned about a product's design.

Software Characteristics

Installation Issues

None of the following issues is a show stopper, but you should be on the alert for them all when you evaluate network software.

The Manual

We all hate to read manuals, and vendor installation documentation can be mind-numbing, with page after page of instructions on how to copy files and what an AUTOEXEC.BAT is. Worse, some of the documentation on how to install software on a LAN is downright misleading. Read any such sections with skepticism. Very few software vendors know how to set up LAN software. Many still write manuals as if users will be installing the software themselves on local C: drives. Do not worry. In most instances, one of the techniques we discuss in this chapter will work, no matter what the documentation says.

Still, bite the bullet and skim the manual. You may find one or two useful pieces of information. See Environment Variables at the end of this chapter for a listing of the types of information you should look for.

Installation Programs

In the old days, you installed software by copying it from your floppy to your hard disk. Then vendors started including BAT programs that did the copying for you. Now they use .EXE programs, which often not only copy the files but decompress them or combine several into one.

Before you type INSTALL, read the manual and any "readme" files on the diskettes. If it's a BAT program, look at what it does. We've run into software products that not only change your AUTOEXEC.BAT and CONFIG.SYS files but also change your login scripts. Other products may start creating a bunch of user subdirectories and can wipe out all your free directory entries (on NetWare versions prior to 386) before you know what's happening. Others insist on being run from the same drive/directory to which they are installed. If the documentation doesn't tell you anything and the program is not a BAT file, call the vendor and find out what it does before you run it.

Drives/Directories

Some products insist on being installed in your root directory with a particular directory name. If you're using a NetWare shell and utilities prior to the 3.01 shell, there's nothing you can do about this. If you are using the 3.01 shell, try the MAP ROOT function. You may be able to install the software in a subdirectory rather than the root. Not only does installing products in the root directory clutter up your root, but upgrade testing becomes difficult with any product that must be installed with a particular name. (See "Software Upgrades" below for more detail.)

Other products must be installed on a particular drive letter, for example M: and must be run from that same drive letter. If you use dynamic pathing for your applications, this may or may not create problems, depending on the technique you are using. If you use static search paths and your users have become accustomed to M: for another product, this will be a problem. If the product wants an E: or F: and your first LAN drive is H: but your users rarely, if ever, use a local E: or F: drive, try mapping the drive letter to the required directory with the following command:

```
ECHO Y|MAP E:=SYS:\APPL\SOFTW1 > NUL:
```

The ECHO Y responds to the NetWare prompt warning you that the letter is mapped to a local drive. The NUL prevents the command from being displayed. (Don't add the NUL: until you've tested your application.) This won't always work. Software products that demand a C: or D: drive often address the hardware directly and can't be tricked by logical remapping. If the product wants drive letter C:, you may not want to fool with it at all.

Some products don't care what drive they're installed on but do specify a particular directory name. As mentioned, this can be troublesome when you want to test an upgrade. (See "Software Upgrades" below.)

If you are adventurous, check the executable for the drive and/or directory name and try to modify it with DEBUG or a HEX editor. We don't recommend this. Programs that insist on a particular installation drive/directory often hard-code the location in multiple programs or deep inside the program code. And even if you are successful, you must then make the same modifications every time you update the software.

Copy Protection

Copy protection is alive and well in several forms: hardware devices, serialization, and "name" serialization.

Hardware Devices

Some programs require you to attach a hardware device to a computer's parallel or serial port. Such protective devices make no sense on a LAN on which software licensing based on servers or concurrent usage is possible. They limit usage not only to particular users or numbers of users but to particular physical machines. If you must buy such a product, test the devices carefully to ensure that they do not interfere with either serial or parallel communications. But complain vehemently to the manufacturer. These products are, at worst, incompatible with something and are, at best, an annoyance. (And what happens if you buy two applications that require these devices?)

Serialization

Many LAN-specific products that are licensed per server require you to enter a serial number. Find out what the vendor is doing. If the serialization is in any way connected with a particular hard disk, server name, or NetWare serial number, you may run into problems when you replace the hard disk, rename the server, or install a copy of NetWare with a different serial number. As these tasks are normally done after working hours when the vendors aren't available, this type of copy protection can be very dangerous. Avoid such products if you can.

"Name" Serialization

This is the least offensive and dangerous type of copy protection but it can, nevertheless, be troublesome. When you install the software, it asks you to enter your name (or a server name) and your company's name. We strongly recommend that you enter your company's name in both fields. People move, department names change, server names change (and, besides, if you have several servers, you probably copy files from one server to the others rather than reinstall the software). Obviously company names can also change, but usually less frequently than other names.

If you really want to put in a meaningful name, try making a DISKCOPY of the original installation diskette. With some software (not Lotus products), you can do the installation from the copy and save the original diskette for future name changes. The worst part about this practice is that you must write to the installation diskette. As the first thing you should do with original diskettes is write-protect them (if they are not already write-protected) to protect them from a virus attack, the vendor is forcing you to take a risk you should not be required to take. These diskettes will be your last resort if your LAN is attacked by a virus; you want to be sure that they are not infected at your site.

User Setups

Many vendors of LAN software assume your users will be responsible for part of the installation process. Generally speaking, however, users usually don't have to do anything if you know how to set up the software. Sometimes the vendor gives you a program to run for each user. If it's a good one, it will let you put the commands in a BAT file so you can run it automatically for all users. Most programs, unfortunately, only work interactively. Don't despair. The functions these programs are designed to accomplish can often be handled in other ways.

Path Support

It should be possible to run all LAN software from a path, because you don't want your users to execute software from the program directory. Why not? Two reasons. First, data files should be stored in personal directories. Users invoking applications from the program directory may try to write files to that directory, even if they lack write rights to it. If they must have write rights, the directory will contain personal data files as well as program files; if they don't have write rights, a save may fail. Second, many programs can display the current directory. The display of ten or twenty program files would overwhelm naive users.

Data Directories

The software should not require you to create a particular data directory in a particular location unless, of course, it is a database-type application. If you give all users personal directories, you shouldn't need to duplicate those directories under a program directory. To increase directory entries under NetWare 286, you must down the server and run the install program—a task not to be undertaken lightly. To trick programs such as these, you may need to write your own software. On the other hand, with some products it can be difficult for multiple users to share data in one directory either because of personal configuration files or the lack of file locking. (See "Configuration File Directory" and "File Locking" below.)

Resource Constraints

Conventional Memories

How much conventional memory does the software require to run? After you've loaded DOS and the NetWare shell, you'll have about 530K available (depending on the DOS and shell version). If you must load NETBIOS, you'll be down to about 510K. If the software won't run in 510K—and some products won't—you're in trouble. If you rely on some TSRs or device drivers, you will have even less memory available. (If you must use a TSR, try to find one that can be unloaded from memory from the command line. You could then unload it before invoking a memory-hungry application and reload it thereafter.) Even if the software runs, it may not be fully functional. If, for example, a word processor loads the entire document into memory, the less memory available, the smaller the document you can create. This is not a fatal condition, because you can always split a document into smaller components, but you must understand the limits of your product and the workarounds available.

There are a couple of possible solutions that may or may not be practical on your network. If your computers have expanded or extended memory, you can use the EMS and XMS memory shells from Novell, which will load the shell into high-DOS memory. But do all your computers have such memory? Can you control which computers the software will run on? If you are not using these shells, how much effort will be required to update your computers to use them? (Remember, any time you upgrade your shells, you'll need to test them with all your software and hardware configurations.) These are management as well as technical issues, and you must decide what's practical on your network.

Extended/expanded memory managers such as 386 MAX or QEMM will let you load TSRs and device drivers into high memory on 386 computers. If you are not currently using these products, can you justify the cost of purchasing them? Are they worth the testing and support involved? You will have to test these products with all your hardware and software, and all subsequent changes to it, and you might be tied into a series of software upgrades.

Hardware devices are available that will give you the same functions on 286 machines. The same questions apply: Do you have available slots? Can you justify the installation and support costs? Do you get enough additional memory to make it worthwhile? Products such as these increase conventional memory by loading TSRs and device drivers into unallocated "high" memory, that space between 640K and 1M of memory. Use of this area is not well regulated. If you have some NICs and VGA cards in place, this area has very little address space.

Expanded/Extended Memory

What about software that takes advantage of or requires either expanded or extended memory? The major issue here is one of support. The product's LANability depends primarily on your network configuration. Do all your machines have the requisite type/amount of memory? If so, you're set. If not, can you easily control the machines that are used? What do you do if many of your users share computers, only some of which can run the software?

Imagine this scenario: John has a computer with extended memory and can, therefore, run LOTUS 3.0. Mary has a computer with expanded memory and can, therefore, run Lotus 2.01 or 2.2 but not 3.1. You install both products. How do Mary and John know which products they can run? How can you make sure Mary doesn't try to run 3.1? How do you make sure John doesn't try to run 3.0 on Mary's computer? What happens if Mary is using John's machine?

You need a way to test for the type of memory each machine has. One method is to set up an environment variable that can be interrogated in the BAT file you use to invoke the program. For example:

SET MEM=EMS for expanded memory
SET MEM=XMS for extended memory
SET MEM=EX for expanded and extended memory

In your BAT file for accessing 3.0, you enter the following test before you run the program:

```
IF .%MEM==      GOTO badmem
IF .%MEM==.EMS GOTO badmem
:badmem
ECHO  Your machine cannot run LOTUS 3.0.
      Select LOTUS 2.2
```

An alternative is to find a program that can identify the type and amount of memory installed and return an error level.

Disk Space

An increasing number of TSR programs are advertised as being low memory users, 8K or even 2K. Although this appears to be a welcome change from the 40K to 60K of yore, all is not always what it seems. Check your disk space. Some programs save conventional memory by swapping either to EMS or to disk. The file they create on disk may be temporary or permanent. In either case, estimate how much disk space might be consumed at once if all your users run the program. If they can execute a program from any directory, and the file is created in the current directory, the difference between a temporary file and a permanent file may be critical. You may have enough disk space to support, say, 10M of temporary space (1M per user). But you may not have enough to support, say, 30M of permanent space (the number of different directories from which the program could be invoked times the size of the temporary file).

Some programs let you specify where temporary files should be placed. As this is becoming more common, we recommend setting up a root directory called TEMP and directing all such programs to store their files in that directory. You can then easily check on and erase these temporary files.

Check the size of the program's configuration file. Although most are only a few hundred bytes in size, Quattro Pro's is over 100K. This is a permanent file. If you want to give your users the choice between a Lotus menu and a Quattro menu, you're talking about 250K of space per user (minimum) to run the software. If you let your users invoke the program from any directory and store these configuration files in all directories, space usage can grow dramatically.

Is there any way to limit the growth of these permanent files? Yes, but only if you are willing to accept a constraint on the product's usage. The trick here is to force your users to invoke the software from a particular directory. For example:

```
cd \home\%userid%
```

or

```
cd \home\%userid%\pgm
```

Configurations

Most software products allow a certain amount of customization for either hardware or personal options. How they do this and whether or not they distinguish between hardware options and personal options present the single most common setup issue for LAN managers.

SAVING TO .EXE/.COM FILES

It is still, unfortunately, possible to buy software that saves configuration information to its executable. (Some programs are even worse and install configuration information into three or four different executables.) You can't share such software on a network unless you are willing to accept one of the following situations:

1. You flag the file ROS (see FLAG command, chapter 5). Your users make changes that don't take effect, because they don't have such rights. The software may or may not inform the user that the file can't be written to. It may generate an error message. Your users can't understand the error message or why their configuration changes don't "stick," and you must constantly explain why.

2. You flag the file writable. Your users make changes. But each person overwrites the last person's changes. Nobody understands why his or her changes seem to disappear. If two people try to write a change at the same time, the software bombs. The file is, obviously, also vulnerable to being erased or invaded by a virus.

3. You copy the executable to the person's current directory. This may work, although products like these often expect all program files to be in the same directory as the executable. If you copy the executable to the person's current directory, you could end up with a bundle of them (one for each directory). If you force the user to execute the program from a particular directory, you can reduce the number of copies but are still giving up more disk space than you should. When you upgrade the software, you must remember to replace all these copies.

4. You give each person a complete set of the program files, a solution that defeats one of the primary reasons for installing a LAN.

Configuration File Directory

Only marginally better than the preceding are products that save configuration information to a particular file name in a particular directory.

EASYFLOW (Haventree) saves its configuration information to a file called EASYFLOW.CFG in the Easyflow directory. Personal options, including the name of the last file used, are stored in this file. (Haventree sells the product for stand-alone computers and makes no claim to its being installable on a LAN.)

ALLWAYS (Funk) must be installed in a directory called ALLWAYS below the Lotus directory. Video card information is saved in ALLWAYS.ASD, which must be in the ALLWAYS subdirectory. This is fine if all your machines have the same hardware configuration. If they don't, you've got a problem. If you can install the configuration file in a different directory or give it a different name, you can handle such a program with a minimum of effort. We'll show you how a bit further on.

Hardware Versus Personal Options

Many vendors believe each person who uses a computer has a personal computer and never works on any other. In Corporate America, however, many people still share computers. And even those who have their own may occasionally work on someone else's.

Thus, software products that combine personal and hardware information in a single file make LAN management difficult. But if the products make any kind of reasonable distinction, you can set things up fairly transparently for your users.

Hardware Option Files

Let's look first at hardware configuration files. The most common hardware options relate to the video card, monitor, and keyboard. To keep matters simple, we'll focus on the video card and monitor. You can expand the technique, within limits, to other hardware components.

First, you need a way to identify the hardware item in question. You need either a program that can return an error level, or you must create an environment variable for the hardware item. Then you must create a configuration file for each type of hardware. Last, you must pass the information to the application when you invoke it.

To create an environment variable, you issue a DOS SET command with a name and a value. For example, SET GM=EGAC, where GM is the variable (graphics monitor) and EGAC is the value (short for EGA card with color monitor). It's a good idea to make the variable name and the values short because you have a limited amount of environment space and can increase it only by modifying your CONFIG.SYS file (or patching COMMAND.COM).

As this variable contains hardware information, you should not create it in a user's login script, even if each user has a personal computer. Sooner or later, for one reason or another, person A will sit down at person B's computer and try to run the software. Put the variable in the AUTOEXEC.BAT file on your boot diskette or hard disk. See "Environment Variables" at the end of this chapter for a more detailed explanation of environment variables and techniques for setting them up.

Then you create multiple configuration files, one for each system. In Lotus, for example, run INSTALL to create a .SET (2.x) or .DCF (3.x) file. Lotus defaults to the name 123.SET (123.DCF) but will let you give the file a different name. So you would name your EGA/COLOR .SET file EGAC.SET. Once you have created the basic configuration, you can create multiple variations by changing just the video parameter and saving the settings to a new file name (such as EGAM for an EGA card and a monochrome monitor, CGAM for a CGA card and monochrome monitor, CGAC for a CGA card and color monitor, and so on). You can store these files in the program directory.

Last, you put the application's command in a BAT file and pass it a parameter telling it the name of the configuration file. Your Lotus BAT file would, for example, contain the following line:

```
123 %GM%
```

Lotus will look for a .SET file with the same name as your GM environment variable.

But what do you do if your software expects to find a configuration file called VIDEO.CFG? If it looks for that file in the current directory, and your users invoke the software from their personal directories rather than the program directory, all is not lost. In your BAT file do the following:

```
COPY P:%GM%.cfg VIDEO.CFG > NUL:
program
ERASE VIDEO.CFG
```

The first line copies your named configuration file (EGAC.CFG) from the drive on which it is located (P:) to a file called VIDEO.CFG in the current directory. The NUL keeps the copy from being echoed to the screen. (NCOPY ignores the NUL, which is why COPY is better here.) The second line executes the program. The third line erases the video file from the current directory. It's usually not necessary to do this, but it is generally a good idea to clean up.

Are there any drawbacks to this technique? Yes, as mentioned earlier, your environment space is limited. Also, when you put environment variables onto boot diskettes, you create machine-specific boot diskettes that can be difficult to change or update. (See "Environment Variables" at the end of this chapter for a discussion of your alternatives.)

Last, as mentioned earlier, some software products (such as EASYFLOW and ALLWAYS) not only insist on a configuration file with a specific name but insist that that file exist in the program directory. With ALLWAYS, you could copy, for example, your EGAC.ASD file to ALLWAYS.ASD in the ALLWAYS directory, but your users would need write rights to the directory, and you'll have to hope that people with different video cards don't open the ALLWAYS.ASD file when it's in the wrong mode. You can also copy the ALLWAYS.ASD file to the current directory, but then you must copy over the appropriate .ASP files, because ALLWAYS will look for them in the same directory where it finds the .ASD file. And if you have many different printers on your LAN, you'll have to copy over many files (unless you know which printers the person invoking the software needs) whenever the program is invoked.

Is there an alternative to using environment variables for hardware options? Some programs can detect hardware information, but even with them, the answers must be converted into environment variables. (See "Environment Variables" at the end of this chapter for a complete discussion of environment variables.)

LANSMITH (805-687-1271) makes a product called NETAWARE that can make dumb software such as ALLWAYS act like smart software. It is a small TSR that redirects a program's OPEN calls from one file or directory to another. First you set up a configuration file that identifies the program and the file it is seeking. Then you tell NETAWARE the filename or directory to substitute. Before you invoke the application, you run NETAWARE. It will intercept the program's OPEN call and redirect it to the file/directory you specify. NETAWARE ships with a program called MONITOR that shows you the files the program is seeking. Such a product shouldn't be needed (Lotus, in particular, should know better). But we're glad it exists.

Personal Option Files

A "personal" configuration file is a file containing those options that tend to be unique to an individual rather than a machine: favorite colors, document formats, autosave intervals, and so on. Lotus's spreadsheet and print graph personal configuration files are called PGRAPH.CNF and 123.CNF. Harvard Graphics uses HG.CFG. Org Plus uses ORG.BIN.

How you handle these files will depend on how you set up your LAN and how the software works. Do your users have personal directories? Do you run applications from a search path? Does the software create a blank configuration file automatically or bomb out if it doesn't find one? Does it look for the configuration in the current working directory or in the program directory? How does it react if the configuration file it finds is not writable? You need answers to all these questions before you can decide how best to set up a particular application. In most instances, one or more of the following techniques (or variations thereof) should work.

The easiest way to take advantage of these configuration files is to store them in your users' personal directories. And, generally speaking, this is not at all difficult because most products look for such a file in the current working directory.

But there are some tricks you may need to use. The most common issue is how to handle the initial use of the software. If an application doesn't find a configuration file in the current directory, it may create one there, look for it in the program directory, or bomb out. In the first case, you may need to do nothing. In the other cases, you usually do (because you don't want the software to bomb, and you don't want your users to share a "personal" configuration file even if it is technically possible to do so, which it usually isn't).

So, how do you handle this first-time use? Create such a file for each application for each new user you set up? That's much too much trouble. Instead, create a standard configuration file and store it in the program directory. Then, in the BAT file you use to invoke the application, check if the user has such a file. The command should be similar to the following:

```
IF NOT EXIST H:123.CNF COPY P:123.CNF H:123.CNF > NUL:
```

where 123.CNF is the configuration file, H: is the standard drive letter for your users' directories, and P: is the drive letter assigned to your application software. The > NUL: keeps the DOS message "1 file copied" from being displayed.

This is the easiest solution and one that often works with little effort on your part, but there are variations and several different issues you must consider.

First, this code obviously assumes that you have established a standard drive letter for your users' personal directories (which is a pretty good idea). And it assumes that you know the drive letter assigned to your application directory. If neither is true, however, the IF NOT EXIST will check the current working directory for the named file. You can provide a full path name for the application directory if you have only one volume.

This code can also generate multiple configuration files, one for each directory from which a user invokes the program. Sometimes this is a good idea; sometimes it isn't. It will lead to a proliferation of configuration files, one for each user subdirectory. Your users may want a different set of options for each subdirectory. On the other hand, they may want to use the same options regardless of the particular subdirectory in which they are working.

You can, therefore, modify this code in two different ways. First, if you want to limit the number of individual configuration files, you can always start your users in their home directories by adding to your BAT file a command similar to the following:

```
cd H:\USER\%ID\
```

where %ID% is an environment variable you have created to store the logon ID. (You can add a DOS SET ID=%LOGIN_NAME% in the login script.)

Should you do this? There's no right answer. Some LAN managers believe users should always start applications from their home directories and then change directories within their applications. Others believe users should be able to invoke applications from the current working directory, whatever it is. If you always move users to their home directories first, you can run into trouble if, for example, the person invoking the application is not logged on (a situation that may occur when one person is trying to show something to someone else and changes to his or her own directory before accessing the application). If you don't, your users must modify the standard configuration file each time they invoke the application from a different subdirectory.

If you think your users should be able to start their applications from whatever subdirectory they are in, but think they may want the same configuration file in each subdirectory, you can add a command similar to the following to your BAT file:

```
IF EXIST H:\USER\%ID%\FILE.CFG COPY H:\USER\%ID%\FILE.CFG
H:FILE.CFG > NUL:
```

This command should be placed prior to the IF NOT EXIST command described earlier. Beware, however. This solution will also create problems if John sits down at Mary's machine while Mary is logged on, moves to a subdirectory under his ID that does not have a configuration file (and to which Mary, for one reason or another, has rights), and runs the program. The configuration file copied to his directory will be Mary's, not his.

Creating a Standard Configuration File

To make life easier for both yourself and your users, you may want to create a standard configuration file with default parameters (program directory name, working directory, printer options, etc.). The trickiest problem here tends to be the current working directory (CWD). Again, if you have standardized on a drive letter, you can often indicate the CWD by entering the following for the data directory entry in many configuration files:

```
H:.
```

The "." stands for the current working directory. Unfortunately, some products automatically convert that entry into the full path of the directory in which you create the file. Lotus's PGRAPH.CNF is such a file. To overcome that obstacle, change the full pathname back to H:. by using a HEX editor.

Some software products, also unfortunately, search the program directory first for a configuration file. If yours do, rename the configuration file in the program directory from, for example, 123.CNF to 123.STD and in your BAT file copy the renamed file:

```
IF NOT EXIST H:123.CNF COPY P:123.STD H:123.CNF > NUL:
```

Software Upgrades

When you get a software update, test how it handles the existing configuration files. Many programs change the form and content of the configuration file but not the name. If the new software encounters an old configuration file, it blows up. (Lotus uses the .CNF extension for all of its various versions, but no version can use another version's file.)

Vendors never supply configuration file update programs that can be run automatically against the existing configuration files. At best, they supply interactive programs that force you to enter, one by one, the directory in which the old configuration files are located. If your vender does offer an automatic program, you are lucky. If it doesn't, often your only choice is to wipe out the existing configuration files and replace them with the new ones.

To do so, use a utility such as PC Magazine's free SWEEP.COM (available on CompuServe, type GO PC MAGNET).to rename all the old configuration files first, so you can keep them around until you're sure the upgrade works. (Even after the best testing, unforeseen critical errors can develop when you go "live.") Once the conversion is complete, use SWEEP to erase all the old configuration files.

```
SWEEP RENAME 123.cnf 123old.cnf
```

Multiple Software Versions

But what if you must support multiple versions of the software and think your users may, for one reason or another, use more than one version? Is there hope? Yes. But it's not nice. Let's use Lotus as an example.

It took us awhile to upgrade all our 1A copies to 2.0. Because of some incompatibilities in 2.0, some people used 1A for some spreadsheets and 2.0 for others. To accommodate them, we used one BAT file for the 1A version, another for the 2.0 version, and three configuration files: the base 123.CNF, a 123A.CNF, and a 1232.CNF file.

In the 1A BAT file we used the following code:

```
IF EXIST H:123A.CNF COPY H:123A.CNF H:123.CNF > NUL:
IF NOT EXIST H:123.CNF COPY P:123.CNF H:123.CNF > NUL:
123
COPY H:123.CNF H:123A.CNF > NUL:
```

The first line checks to see if the user has a 123A.CNF file (which could have been created only if the person had previously used 1A). The second line is the standard check for a .CNF file. It will not be executed if the previous test found a 123A.CNF file. The third line invokes Lotus. The last line copies the existing .CNF file to 123A.CNF, thus preserving any configuration changes the user made during the Lotus session.

In the 2.0 BAT file we used the following code:

```
IF EXIST H:1232.CNF COPY H:1232.CNF H:123.CNF > NUL:
IF NOT EXIST H:123.CNF COPY P:123.CNF H:123.CNF > NUL:
123
COPY H:123.CNF H:1232.CNF > NUL:
```

As this is the 2.0 BAT file, the first line checks for a 1232.CNF file rather than a 123A file. The next two lines are identical to those in the 1A BAT file. (We can use the same drive letter for both versions because we set the appropriate path earlier in the BAT file.) The last line copies the existing .CNF file to 1232.CNF rather than 123A.CNF. It's not particularly pretty, but it works.

If the vendor has combined hardware and personal options, and your users sometimes, or often, work on different platforms, transparent support is difficult. If, on the other hand, the vendor has not placed machine-specific options (such as type of video card) in the same configuration file as the more personal options, you can usually, with a minimum amount of effort, use the preceding techniques (with your own twists) to give users their own configuration files.

Ideally, vendors should write smart software that can sense the various hardware components. And if they can't, they should design their configuration files to separate hardware from personal options. Lotus's .SET file contains, in addition to hardware options, a collating sequence, which, more properly, should be a spreadsheet option. Some hardware options also contain a personal element. EGA and VGA cards can often display 20 lines or 43 lines. The type of video (EGA, VGA) is a hardware option. The LAN administrator should be able to control the former; the user should be able to control the latter.

Organizational Versus Personal Options

In addition to hardware and personal options, some programs may have features that ideally should be centrally supported. The most obvious example is printer support. Users shouldn't have to set up or define printers. Network administrators should be able to set up and maintain a central printer file so that users always get the most current printer and font definitions. Unfortunately, if software is not designed properly, there is usually little you can do about this.

Dictionaries are another prime candidate for central support. Most word processors support a central dictionary. Some also support a personal dictionary. But an organization might want a third or fourth dictionary (for example, the company and the division). Again, only the vendor can provide this kind of option.

If personal dictionaries are supported, treat a personal dictionary as if it were a personal configuration file. You can use the same techniques we discussed earlier to ensure that each person has a startup personal dictionary. Some of the same issues also apply, such as whether to set up one personal dictionary in the home directory or set one up in each working directory. The former usually makes the most sense, but much depends on how your users set up their working environments.

Multiple Personal Files

Some software, particularly such products as personal information managers, mail systems, and so on, may create a number of special-purpose files similar to but not exactly configuration files. If these files contain information (calendars, appointments, etc.), you want to make certain each person has one set and only one set. How can you do this?

You could simply borrow one of the preceding techniques and ensure that these products are executed only from the person's home directory. But then you run the risk that the user might accidentally erase them. More important, perhaps, the program's performance might deteriorate if it must search through 50 or 100 files to find the ones it is looking for. Your alternative is to create for each user of the product a special directory below the home directory just to hold these files:

```
subdir h:\user\%ID%\pim
if errorlevel 1 goto program
md h:\user\%ID%\pim
copy p:\appl\pim\*.pim h:\user\%id%\pim > nul:
:program
```

Subdir is a program that checks for the existence of a subdirectory. %ID% is an environment variable that contains the person's logon ID. Subdir checks to see if a subdirectory called pim exists under that person's home directory. If it doesn't, the next line (md . . .) will create it. If it does, you can execute the program.

The biggest risk with either of these techniques is that the person running the program is logged on to somebody else's ID. If the runner has no rights to the logged-on person's directory, the program may bomb. To avoid this, you could add a line to the above BAT file that would check for the existence of one of the files in the pim directory. If it exists, you know the person has rights to the directory (this is no guarantee that the invoker and the ID owner are identical, but it does eliminate most other possibilities):

```
subdir h:\user\%ID%\pim
if errorlevel 1 goto testid
md h:\user\%ID%\pim
copy p:\appl\pim\*.pim h:\user\%id%\pim  nul:
goto program
:testid
if exist h:\user\%id%\pim\file.pim goto program
:bad
echo you are not authorized to run this program
goto exit
:program
pim
:exit
```

Printing

What can you do if you have twenty different kinds of printers on your network and the software will let you set up only four printers for each user? If many of those printer types are variations on a theme (different models of Epsons or Epson compatibles) and if you can create your own printer definitions, try building a generic Epson driver that will work, at the lowest common denominator, on all the Epsons you've got. Your users may lose some of the top-end functions, but you'll be able to use the other three options for completely different problems. Then complain to the vendor. Users should be able to print to any type of printer supported by the software without running an installation or setup program.

Make sure your software can print to DOS devices such as LPT1 (or LPT2 or LPT3 if you are using those). Some products insist on talking to the hardware and can't spool across a network. Some can print only to LPT1. (This is true primarily of older public domain products.)

A few products can now support NetWare queues directly. This support can be both a boon and a bane for LAN administrators. If you are using a third-party pop-up utility for printing, does the software's implementation work with or against the pop-up? Can you disable it? If only one product on the LAN can access the queues directly, you may prefer to rely on a standard third-party utility for everything.

File Locking

Record locking is not necessary for products other than databases or similar applications. But all software sold for LANs should support file locking for both data files and configuration files. The locking need not be sophisticated—a simple message ("file is in use") would be sufficient—but it should exist.

Does It Run?

After you have installed the software on your server, you must still determine if it will actually run on your LAN. Move into the program directory and execute the software. Your objective is simple: to find out if the software will run on your LAN (even if the box says it will, it may not for any of a variety of reasons.) If the program executes properly, test all its major features. In one software package we installed, three major functions worked but two didn't.

Some single-user products know when they are being run on a LAN and refuse to run. Others will execute properly but won't let more than one person at a time use them. (The single-user version of Lotus 2.01 can be shared by multiple people on a LAN; the single-user version of 2.2 or 3.1 can't.)

Many public domain file management utilities won't work on a network. Other utilities may have problems with open files. The error messages they generate will vary greatly, but you can generally guess the cause. Smarter programs will recognize they are on a server, know they can't work on a server, and tell you.

If the program fails completely and you don't know why, don't panic. The problem may be with your hardware/software configuration and not with the LAN. LAN software, even when installed on a server, still runs on a local computer—yours. If your machine has a local hard disk, reinstall the software on the local hard disk and boot the machine in local mode. Remove all TSRs and special device drivers. If the software still doesn't run, the problem is with your computer (video card, memory—something) and not with the LAN. If the software does run, load the NetWare shell but stay on your local drive. Try it again. If it fails, you've got a conflict of some kind with the NetWare shell. You may want to try different versions of the shell (and you should if you are supporting more than one revision level on your LAN(s)).

If it runs from a local hard disk under a NetWare shell, try to execute it again from your server disk. The original failure may have been due to a conflict with one of your TSRs or device drivers. If it runs okay, you know there is no inherent conflict with the LAN. You should then load, one by one, the device drivers and TSRs you removed to determine which one (or ones) created the problem. Be sure to test each one individually, then in combination (if no problem occurs with each one individually). Once you've found the offender, you'll have to do some detective work with both products and may need to call the vendor. Don't mention the LAN. It isn't a LAN problem. You installed a product on a computer and it didn't work with a TSR (or device driver).

After you've established that the software will run on a server, you need to determine if it will run from a search path. Map a search drive to the program directory. Execute it from another directory. If it doesn't run, check your rights. At this stage, you should be logged on with supervisor privileges and all the files in the directory should be writable. If it works, go on to the next step. Flag all the files SRO. Does it still work? If not, which files must be writable? If it does, your last test is to run the software from a path, as an ordinary user (with only SRO rights). Now you've got an idea of your software's basic LANability, but there are lots of potential problems still out there, as we have seen.

Software Pricing

Several different pricing strategies are available for software on LANs. The most common are per workstation, per user, per server, and per concurrent user.

If the product is priced per workstation, you must buy a copy for each PC attached to your LAN, even if, for example, only five of the PCs are capable of running the software. Such pricing is, generally, completely unreasonable unless the product is DOS or you will be running it simultaneously on every station.

Per-user pricing may appear in two variations. The first is almost the same as per-workstation pricing: It requires you to buy a copy for each user on the network, whether or not each will be accessing the software. The second requires you to buy a copy for each person who will ever use the software. Thus if, for example, John Smith needs to use the product only once a year and then only for an hour, you must still buy a copy specifically for him. Both kinds of pricing present administrative problems. In the former case, you must buy an additional copy whenever you add a user to the LAN (you get no rebate if the number of users decreases). In the latter case, you will generally need to put the application in a directory to which only designated users have access and not only buy additional copies for additional users, but keep the access rights to that directory up to date.

Concurrent user licensing is the most sensible strategy for typical LAN applications (word processing, spreadsheet, graphics, and so on). It most closely imitates the classic stand-alone, two-diskette-drive PC pricing requirements that permitted you to buy a single copy of the product and run it on any machine as long as you used only the original diskettes and only on one machine at a time. Implementation of this strategy varies widely. Some vendors rely on the honor system. Others, increasingly, are adding "counter" programs to their products to control LAN access. (The stand-alone copies of Lotus 2.2 and 3.1 can be installed on a server but can be used by only one person at a time. You must buy and install a LAN version to support concurrent access.) Some products (such as the LAN versions of Lotus 2.2 and 3.1) allow you to run a simple program to increment the number of users. You are then honor-bound to buy the additional copies. Some vendors require you to purchase a "bump" diskette in some incremental number (usually five). Not only can this be irritating, it can also be expensive—especially if you need only one more copy.

Per-server software pricing makes the most sense for products that are designed to support central functions: menu systems, directory management utilities, performance monitoring products, LAN administration utilities. Multiple-server discounts are sometimes available.

If you like a product but find the pricing unacceptable in your environment, object. Talk to the marketing manager, your account representative, or the president. Some vendors are willing to negotiate; others are not. If the number-one product on your list is priced inappropriately for your environment, and alternative, fairly competitive products are available that do offer acceptable pricing, buy one of those. And make sure the other vendor knows you have done so and why.

The software market has reached no consensus on pricing software for LANs. Your actions can help establish some de facto standards.

Application Problems: Product by Product

Now that we've identified product problems, we'll visit the issue from a slightly different angle and show you how to set up several different applications. Between these applications and the techniques we presented earlier, you should be able to handle almost any product that comes your way.

These examples all assume that your users have personal directories and run all applications from those personal directories. They also assume that the home drive is F: and the server has only one volume. The techniques will work in other environments with modest changes.

Lotus 2.01

Lotus 2.01 has three configuration files: .SET files, which contain hardware information; 123.CNF files, which contain personal configuration information for the spreadsheet; and PGRAPH.CNF files, which contain personal information for Lotus graphs.

To create the .SET files, run the INSTALL program from the Lotus directory. Select a video card and monitor. As you can set up only four printers, select the most common ones in your environment. Most Epson printers will work with an FX80 definition. You can select almost as many graphics printers as you want. Save the file with a name that corresponds to the video card and monitor and your environment variables. Use the MODIFY option in the INSTALL program to change the video card and monitor and save it with a new name. Continue until you have a unique .SET file for each video card and monitor you must support.

Now you must create a default 123.CNF file. This is easy. Make all the selections you think appropriate for a startup file. Be sure to select a DOS device for the printer interface, even if some computers may have local printers. Enter F:. for the default directory. The period indicates the current directory. Lotus will pick up the full directory name for whatever directory the .CNF file is in. Update the 123.CNF file. Name it something like 123.STD.

Use the same technique to create a standard PGRAPH.CNF file. The F:. will be converted into a full path name. To convert it back to F:., use a HEX editor. Name the corrected file something like PGRAPH.STD.

Your Lotus batch file should look something like this:

```
:setpath
  MAP L:= SYS:APPL\LOT2    NUL:
  SET OP=%PATH%
  PATH %PATH%;L:\APPL\LOT2
  IF NOT EXIST F:123.CNF COPY L:123.STD F:123.CNF  NUL:
:program
  ECHO Loading 1-2-3 Release 2.01...
  L:123 %GM%
  GOTO WRAPUP
rem
:WRAPUP
  PATH %OP%
  SET OP=
  MAP DEL L:   NUL:
  GOTO EXIT
:exit
  MENU
```

But what if you must be able to support more than four printers? You can, but only if you can figure out some way to differentiate one set of multiple printers from another. Let's say, for example, that different groups have different printer requirements. If you keep a group variable in your login script, you can use it to identify your .SET files. The process is essentially the same as just described, but your .SET file names will be more complex:

```
ACCTEGAC.SET
PERSEGAC.SET
```

Now each name contains information about both the video card and monitor and the department. Your batch file might look like the following:

```
:setpath
  MAP L:= SYS:APPL\LOT2  > NUL:
  SET OP=%PATH%
  PATH %PATH%;L:\APPL\LOT2
  IF NOT EXIST F:123.CNF COPY L:123.CNF F:123.CNF > NUL:
  GOTO lotus
rem
:lotus
  ECHO Loading 1-2-3 Release 2.01...
  IF NOT EXIST H:123.SET SET DRV=%GRP%%GM%
  L:123 %DRV%
  GOTO WRAPUP
rem
:WRAPUP
  PATH %OP%
  SET OP=
  SET DRV=
  MAP DEL L: > NUL:
  GOTO EXIT
:exit
  MENU
```

%DRV% is a temporary environment value that combines the values of your GM and GRP variables. The test for F:123.SET file illustrates how you could also support a personal .SET file if, for example, you need a really special one for one or more of your users.

Lotus 2.2

First, ignore the Lotus documentation regarding LAN installation. It is extremely misleading. You can create .SET and .CNF files just as you do for Lotus 2.01. The tricky part about 2.2 is ALLWAYS.

ALLWAYS stores video card information in a file called ALLWAYS.ASD. This file must be located in the ALLWAYS directory and must be called ALLWAYS.ASD. If all your video cards are the same, this is fine. If they are not, you will have some problems.

You can create multiple .ASD files, but not nearly as easily as with the Lotus install program. ALLWAYS does not give you a chance to rename the .ASD file. So you must create the file, exit the INSTALL program, rename the file, go back in, and start all over. Once you have a series of .ASD files (egac.asd, egam.asd, and so on), you have several alternatives.

One way to deal with the problem is to copy the video .ASD file in your BAT file to ALLWAYS.ASD:

```
COPY P:%GM%.ASD P:ALLWAYS.ASD > NUL:
```

where P: is the drive assigned to Lotus and ALLWAYS. This technique is very risky. First, you must give your users write rights to the ALLWAYS subdirectory, which makes the programs subject to accidental or purposeful erasure and to viruses. Second, even if your users load ALLWAYS as soon as they load Lotus, they can subsequently remove it from memory and then try to load it later. If they load it later and the ALLWAYS.ASD file no longer matches their video card, it will bomb. In addition, Lotus staffers have advised us that ALLWAYS may try to read in that file even after it has been loaded.

A second solution is to copy the video .ASD file and all relevant .ASP files in your BAT file to the current working directory:

```
:setpath
  MAP L:= SYS:APPL\LOT2  > NUL:
  MAP P:= SYS:\APPL\LOT2\ALLWAYS > NUL:
  SET OP=%PATH%
  PATH %PATH%;L:\APPL\LOT2;P:\APPL\LOT2\ALLWAYS
  IF NOT EXIST F:123.CNF COPY L:123.STD F:123.CNF > NUL:
  IF NOT EXIST F:ALLWAYS.CNF COPY P:ALLWAYS.STD
F:ALLWAYS.CNF >
NUL:
      COPY P:%GM%.ASD ALLWAYS.ASD > NUL:
      COPY P:*.ASP > NUL:
  GOTO lotus
:lotus
  ECHO Loading 1-2-3 Release 2.01...
  L:123 %gm%
  GOTO WRAPUP
rem
:WRAPUP
  PATH %OP%
  SET OP=
  MAP DEL L: > NUL:
  MAP DEL P: > NUL:
GOTO EXIT
:exit
  MENU
```

If you are supporting a variety of printers, the copy will take awhile. Please note the different technique in the ALLWAYS copy. If you don't specify a drive letter, the DOS copy will still copy to the current working directory.

The third solution is to buy Lansmith's NETAWARE and trick ALLWAYS into looking for a different .ASD file. If you must use ALLWAYS, this is the cleanest alternative.

Lotus insists that metering information be installed under a root directory called LOTSHARE, in a subdirectory called 123v22. As the counter program provides no useful information, you may want to continue using a third-party utility.

Lotus 3.1

In Lotus 3.1, the .SET file is now a .DCF file. The .cnf file has, finally, a release-specific name: 123r31.cnf. In addition, there is a LAYOUT3.cnf file and a LTSADDIN.CNF file. Lotus will create the .cnf files if they do not exist, but you should still set up default 123r31.cnf and ltsaddin.cnf files so your users will have certain defaults, especially the home directory and addin directory, correctly specified.

The .DCF file now supports sixteen printers, and the collating sequence is no longer a component.

The worst part about the 3.1 .DCF installation—and it's pretty irritating—is font generation. Even if all your .DCF files are identical except for the video card and monitor, you must generate fonts for all printers selected. If you select the extended font generation and sixteen printers, it will take a very long time to generate the video-specific .DCF files. The two files you want to copy to the current directory, if they don't exist, are the 123r31.cnf and ltsaddin.cnf files. Lotus will automatically create the others.

You can use essentially the same BAT file techniques as you would for 2.01 or 2.2. Luckily, IMPRESS, unlike ALLWAYS, does not have its own video card setup file.

The ADDINS directory does not need to be part of the search path.

In this version, Lotus has relented a bit regarding metering. The actual counter directory must still have a specific name, but it can be located in the root or under any root directory. As an increasing number of programs are shipping with their own metering functions, you may want to establish a root directory, such as CONTROL, under which you can install the individual programs.

Harvard Graphics

Harvard has historically been one of the easiest programs to support on a network. The latest versions are both easier and harder to use.

When you install Harvard, it will ask for a data directory. Simply press the Enter key and it will create a configuration file with a current directory indicator.

The program seems quite adept at identifying the appropriate video card. When you set up the default HG.CGF file, select DEFAULT for the video card. You can also specify the location of the SYMBOL and GALLERY directories.

And you can specify the current directory with a period. Once you have created a default configuration file, give it a name such as HG.STD. In your BAT file, you would have something such as:

```
IF NOT EXIST F:HG.CFG COPY P:HG.STD F:HG.CFG
```

That's about it.

Harvard, too, now uses metering. You can choose the directory location you want to use. As with Lotus, the information it provides is pretty useless. To increment the counter, you must buy a one-node or five-node pack and run the counter utility with the non-write-protected node disk in your A: drive.

WordPerfect

WordPerfect (WP) has a reputation for being very NetWare aware. But it is also rather dictatorial about telling you how to set it up. Some LAN administrators have actually created three-character LAN ids to deal with WP's predilection for three-character passwords and setup files. You can, however, avoid the whole sorry mess with a BAT file similar to the following:

```
echo off
f:
cd v:\apps\wp51
:setup
  subdir f:\home\%ID%\wpdata
  if errorlevel 1 goto program
  MD f:\home\%ID%\wpdata
:program
  cd \home\%ID%\wpdata
  if not exist wpwp5}.set set macro=newuser
  wp %1 /ps=f:\home\%id%\wpdata /U=wp5
/D=f:\home\%ID%\wpdata /m-%macro%
  :wrapup
  set macro=
  cd v:\apps
```

This BAT file illustrates several different techniques. The command cd v:\apps\wp51 assumes that a permanent V: search path has been set to \APPS. SUBDIR checks for the existence of a directory. If it doesn't exist, we create one. Thus, the setup for WP here assumes that each person will store his or her data files in a subdirectory called WPDATA. Instead of a three-character user id, a single set of three characters (WP%) is used and a macro has been created to set up the default settings, including the location for temporary files. If the user's WP directory does not contain a .SET file, it will be created.

Easyflow

Easyflow is a flow-charting package from Haventree and is not designed to work on a LAN. It is so difficult to handle properly, however, that it is an excellent example of how to handle almost impossible programs.

Easyflow stores configuration information in a file called EASYFLOW.CFG. This file must be in its program directory. (You can use an environment variable to tell EASYFLOW the name of the directory in which it is installed.)

The .CFG file contains personal options and the name of the last file worked on. None of the techniques just used will work. You can't give it a different name. You can't copy it to the current working directory (Easyflow will look only in its own directory).

The only solution appears to be limiting it to a single user at a time.

First, use a program such as SITELOCK or Turnstyle to allow only one person at a time to use it. The primary trick here is to copy a person's personal configuration file to the program directory for execution before proceeding to the person's home directory.

```
    :lock
   SLOCK eflow
   IF ERRORLEVEL=100 GOTO setpath
   IF ERRORLEVEL=  0 GOTO tryagain
 :setpath
   MAP P:= SYS:\APPL\EFLOW  > NUL:
   SET OP=%PATH%
   PATH %PATH%;P:\APPL\EFLOW
   IF EXIST F:easyflow.cfg COPY F:easyflow.cfg
P:easyflow.cfg>
NUL:
   IF NOT EXIST F:EASYFLOW.CFG COPY P:EASYFLOW.STD
P:EASYFLOW.CFG
> NUL:
   GOTO eflow
 :tryagain
   ECHO All copies of EASYFLOW are in use. Please try
again later.
   PAUSE
   GOTO exit
rem
 :eflow
   SET EASYFLOW=P:\APPL\EFLOW
   P:easyflow
```

```
    GOTO WRAPUP
  rem
  :WRAPUP
    COPY P:easyflow.cfg F:EASYFLOW.CFG > NUL:
    PATH %OP%
    SET OP=
    MAP DEL P: > NUL:
    SUNLOCK EFLOW
    GOTO EXIT
  :exit
    MENU
```

SLOCK is the SITELOCK program that locks an application. The BAT file checks the working directory for a .CFG file. One will exist if the person has used the program before from the current working directory. If it does exist, the BAT file copies it over to the program directory. If it doesn't exist, the BAT file copies a standard configuration file to EASYFLOW.CFG (this is the standard startup file, created just as other configuration files are created). EASYFLOW requires the SET EASYFLOW parameter. At the end of the BAT file, we copy the .CFG file from the program directory to the working directory, retaining all the changes made during the current session.

This BAT file does not make EASYFLOW a LAN application because, no matter how many copies you may purchase, only one person can use it at a time.

Its font handling is also extremely difficult to manage on a LAN, but that is another issue.

The best solution to the configuration file problem is Lansmith's NETAWARE. It can force EASYFLOW to look for a different file or in a different directory.

Environment Variables

What They Are

If you are using DOS 3.1 or above (and you really shouldn't be using any earlier version of DOS), you can create and use ENVIRONMENT (or ENVIRONMENTAL variables.) In fact, these variables are so critical a tool for a LAN manager, they are reason enough to upgrade to a newer version of DOS if yours doesn't support them.

DOS sets aside a special space in memory to store variables. The default space is 160 bytes, usually much too small for a LAN because your path and COMSPEC information is stored there.

To find out what variables you have in memory, type SET at the prompt.

To add a variable, you must assign a name and a variable. At the prompt, type

```
SET varname=varvalue
```

where varname is the name of the varible and varvalue is the value you want to assign. For example:

```
SET GM=EGAC
```

To clear the variable and value, type:

```
SET GM=
```

Once you have created an environment variable, you can use it in BAT files to select an action or pass information to a program.

Hardware Environment Variables

In chapter 5, we discussed how to use environment variables to identify hardware characteristics. If you rely solely on environment variables to identify hardware, you must set them up in each machine's AUTOEXEC.BAT, either on the C: disk or on a boot diskette.

On a large network, this leads to a multiplicity of boot diskettes and unique AUTOEXECs, with multiple variables in each AUTOEXEC. It then becomes difficult both to add additional environment variables and to automate boot diskette updates. Alternatives are available.

The first reduces the number of unique variables to one but still requires unique AUTOEXECs. First you assign your own workstation numbers (or use the last six digits of the workstation address if you are using EtherNet or a token-ring network and have cards from only one vendor). Then, in the AUTOEXEC.BAT, set you environment variable:

```
SET WSBAT=wsnumber
```

When a station logs in, it will run the login script and then a BAT file, the name of which is the workstation number:

```
login script:
    exit "start"
start.bat
    CD WS
    call %WSBAT%
```

This code runs a BAT file on exiting the login script that, among other actions, changes to a directory (WS) containing a BAT file for each workstation. It then executes a BAT file with the name corresponding to the workstation number. If you have fewer than 100 workstations, this will work reasonably well. We don't recommend it for larger networks, because performance can deteriorate when a program must search through a large number of files.

Several programs exist (as public domain, shareware, and standard products) that can detect hardware options. They return various error levels that can be tested in BAT files. Unfortunately, they are generally unable to detect several odd but common combinations: CGA cards and monochrome monitors (still common in organizations with large numbers of old 8088 computers) or EGA cards and monochrome monitors. In addition, error-level checking takes more time than environment variable substitution. On the other hand, these programs don't depend on machine-specific boot diskettes. If you decide to try one, test it thoroughly on all of your computers to ensure that its results are correct.

If, however, you can't find programs that will work reliably in your environment or can find programs for some features but not others, another alternative is to find a program that will store hardware variables in a server-based file.

If you are using the SABER menu system, you can create a file on your server that will hold environment variables for each physical workstation address. When you run the SABER menu system, it will interrogate the network for the workstation address and execute the appropriate environment variables. MARX Menu will also let you set up environment variables and assign them to particular workstation addresses.

Last, you can, of course, write a program to accomplish the same task.

The goal, always, is to find a way to get hardware-specific information out of the AUTOEXEC.BAT file and onto the server where it can be added to and modified easily.

Reading Documentation

In skimming a software product's documentation, look for answers to the following questions:

1. Must the installation program be used or can the files be copied to a directory? If it must be used, why? What does it do? Can the program be stored in any directory on any disk?

2. How much available RAM does the software require? "Runs in 640K" is a meaningless phrase. The best you can get on a NetWare LAN without using an EMS or XMS shell is about 510K.

3. Does the software create any files in the program directory during execution, or is data written to the executable?

4. Is it LAN-aware? Will the stand-alone version run on a LAN, or must you install the LAN version? If it uses a counter for concurrent access, where is the information maintained and what rights do users need?

5. How does the software support video cards? Does it auto-sense them, or does it need a configuration file?

6. If the program uses configuration files, what are their names and what information do they contain? Where does the software expect to find them? In the program directory? In the current directory? Can you tell the program where to look (with a command-line parameter or environment variable)?

7. Will the software run from a path, or must it be run from the program directory?

8. Does the executable accept command-line parameters?

9. Can environment variables be used to set defaults? Must they be used? (Two very different issues.)

10. If the software has printer drivers, where and how are they maintained? Can you build your own? Can you store them centrally, or must each user have a personal copy?

11. If this is an upgrade, what are the major changes or enhancements? Must data or configuration files be converted?

12. Are all the files on the program diskettes required? Look for a complete listing, by diskette, with a brief description of each one's function.

13. Are there any "gotchas"? For example, must you use the original non-write-protected diskette to do the installation? Or must you run program X before you can run program Y?

A few paragraphs describing the environment for which the vendor has designed the program would be helpful for complex or unusual products—especially for programs written to take advantage of LANs. If the software has multiple modules, you want to know how the pieces fit together, what choices, if any, you must make about the configuration, and what the tradeoffs are for different setups.

But read any sections on how to install the software on a LAN with skepticism. Most vendors don't know how to do it properly.

7

Backup and Maintenance

It's been said there are two types of PC users: those who have lost data due to poor or infrequent backups, and those who are going to lose data due to poor or infrequent backups. The importance of backing up data cannot be overstressed. Data files are as important as any other company asset. And they are company assets. Companies pay, in salaries and wages, for the many man-hours invested in the creation of the letters, spreadsheets, databases, analyses, business plans, financial statements, and project plans entrusted to the network. Even in nonnetworked organizations, failure to perform regular backups is often treated as negligence, and employees who lose data due to hard disk failures are subjected to disciplinary action. But in a networked environment, the threat of hard disk failure on a file server underlines the importance of backups.

The data, like the file server itself, represent an asset to the organization, and often the data are more difficult to replace. A server can be repaired or replaced, but data that are critical to the company's mission must be reconstructed. Business operations are seriously crippled until the data are re-created. The process may take days, or weeks, or even prove impossible.

Backups

It's easier to ensure regular backups of corporate data files that are stored on a network with a single network manager in charge than it is on a collection of PCs where backups are done at the discretion of individual users. Centralized backups are a key benefit of installing a network.

On a network installation, backup options range from standard tape backups that utilize standard DC100 or DC600 streaming tape technology to high-capacity 8mm cassettes, digital audio cassettes, or optical disk drives. One company, Vortex, even offers a product called RetroChron that makes automatic continuous backup to any SCSI or optical device. Whichever device you choose, the backup system's function is essentially the same. A backup enables you to restore completely the data files on your network if catastrophic hard disk failure does occur. And that's what is really important—your ability to restore those data files, not the device that allows you to do it.

To maximize the usefulness of your backup device, you need to devise a strategy for corporate backups that ensures the integrity of the data and offers an efficient means of restoration if hard disk failures occur.

If you're installing a network for the first time, it's best to determine your firm's specific needs before you select a backup system. The company's needs for timely backups, the type of network being installed, and the kind of backup strategy you employ all have an impact on the type and size of backup device you choose and on how it is installed.

Choosing a Backup System

Your options in a tape drive range from 40M systems to 80M, 150M, and 300M on an individual tape cartridge. Beyond tape systems, backup options take a quantum leap to the high-capacity 8mm tapes and the Digital Audio Tapes (DAT), which boast a whopping capacity of 2.2 gigabytes.

How large of a unit should you buy? Here's a rule of thumb. If you know that your network will grow, and you know how many file servers you're likely to add, purchase a backup system with sufficient capacity to back up all current and future volumes on the network. If you select a tape drive, aim for a system that will allow you to back up all files to one tape.

If you don't know how large your network is likely to grow, it's a good idea to purchase a system that can at least double the capacity of your current network. Don't try to save money on a network backup device. Buy the largest one that makes sense for your company and that you can afford. Remember that the backup is your network's safety net. The quality of hard disks is improving, and many provide a high level of fault tolerance. But, at some point, you'll be called upon to restore data from the backup system, and you'll need to be sure that the system can do it.

Installation Considerations

In a dedicated NetWare server environment, there is no provision to back up files directly from the file server. Backups must be done from a workstation attached to the network. Besides RetroChron, no Value-added processes (VAPs) for NetWare 286 or NetWare Loadable Modules (NLMs) for NetWare 386 are available to perform server-based backups. You don't necessarily need to purchase an additional workstation to facilitate backup, but you will need to consider the backup device when you configure the particular workstation that will host it.

Most backup devices require that an interface card be installed in the workstation that will contain the backup system. And, as with any interface card, you'll have to set a configuration that allows the backup device to interact with the network. Here there is no typical default configuration. The configurations vary from manufacturer to manufacturer. But as you install the card in the workstation, you must find a configuration that does not conflict with the hardware settings of the workstation's other interface cards (the network interface card, disk controller card, and so on). Generally, you expect to set an Interrupt (IRQ), a port address, and a DMA channel on the interface card of your backup device. If conflicts do occur, they will most likely be with the network interface card. However, if you know the configuration of your NIC—and you will, if you use the spreadsheet database offered in chapter 3—configuring the backup interface card to avoid conflicts should be fairly straightforward.

If you're adding a backup device to an installed network and don't know how the NIC was previously configured, it's easy enough to find out by requesting the information from the command line. Before installing the backup card, move to the directory in which the network shell files are located, usually C:\NET, type IPX I and press ENTER. NetWare will return information on the current settings. On a token-ring network, the information on your screen should look like this:

```
C:\NET>ipx i
Novell IPX/SPX V2.15
(C) Copyright 1985, 1988 Novell Inc. All Rights Reserved.

LAN Option: Proteon ProNET-4 p134X/p1840 Vers 3.00
Hardware Configuration: ProNET-4/AT p1344, IRQ=12, IO=A20,
DMA=5
```

The screen information varys according to the type of network you're running. On an ArcNet network, it would look something like this:

```
C:NET>ipx
Novell IPX/SPX v3.01 Rev. A (900507)
(C) Copyright 1985, 1990 Novell Inc. All Rights Reserved.
```

```
LAN Option: NetWare RX-Net V1.00 (881010)
Hardware Configuration: IRQ = 3, I/O Base = 300h, RAM Buffer
at CC00:0
```

On an EtherNet network, it would look something like this:

```
C:\NET\NET>IPX
Novell IPX/SPX v3.01 Rev. A (900507)
(C) Copyright 1985, 1990 Novell Inc. All Rights Reserved.

LAN Option: NetWare Ethernet NE2000 V1.03EC (891227)
Hardware Configuration: IRQ = 3, I/O Base = 300h, no DMA or RAM
```

Devising a Backup Strategy

Developing a sound strategy for backing up your network files is as important as choosing an appropriate backup device. Possibilities include full or incremental backups, and they can be attended or unattended. Each approach has its own advantages and disadvantages.

Full Backups

Of the various types of backups you can perform, full backups are the most convenient. In a full backup you'll back up virtually all the files on the file server's hard disks. A full backup takes a snapshot of the contents of the hard disk and stores the files and file structure off to tape or a backup device. The chief advantage of a full backup is the ease with which you can restore the files and directories if the file server's hard disk fails completely. Often backups can be done from a single tape within a relatively short period of time and with little inconvenience to the users. Should a system fail, down time is limited and data loss is usually confined to updated information in the files that were open at the time of the failure.

The disadvantage of doing full backups is the cost and, often, the inconvenience. The size of the backup system's capacity becomes even more important if you plan to run unattended backups. If a tape fills up completely during the process, the device will wait until someone physically changes tapes.

Incremental Backups

In an incremental backup, you back up only the files that have changed since the last backup was done. With most backup software, there are two ways to perform an incremental backup. The first is to use the date range feature of the tape backup software and set the range to start the backup at the last backup date and end it at the current date. But you generally have to reset the date range each day, a disadvantage. It's more convenient to do an incremental backup by specifying that the system back up only the files that have the archive bit "set." When a file is created or modified, the archive attribute is set. The set bit signals to the system that this is a new or changed file. Virtually all backup software can back up only the files that have this bit set. However, be sure to instruct the backup software to reset the archive bits after backing up the files, so that the same files are not picked up again when you do the next incremental backup.

Incremental backups allow you to back up only data that has changed. This offers two obvious advantages: (1) You use less backup media (tape, optical drive, and so on), and (2) the backup process is more efficient. The backup takes less time because it doesn't have to record everything on the hard disk, only the changed files.

The savings, both in cost and time, is attractive. In order to avoid having files scattered across the backup tape or drive, however, you'll also have to perform periodic full backups. For instance, you might perform a full backup once a week, along with daily incremental backups. There are, however, two disadvantages to a strategy that employs incremental backups.

First, if the hard disk fails completely and you need to restore the directory structure of the volume and all files stored on the network, you'll need to restore the last "full" backup you performed on the system and then individually restore the subsequent incremental backups. For example, let's say your backup schedule calls for a full backup each Monday with incremental backups on all other weekdays. If the disk fails on a Saturday, you'll need first to restore the files and directory structure from Monday's full backup, and then restore each incremental backup done from Tuesday through Friday to ensure that all active files on the disk were properly restored.

The other disadvantage of incremental backups becomes evident when a user asks that you restore a particular file but can't remember the last time it was modified. If your backup strategy calls for a weekly full backup and daily incremental ones, you may have to search through several days' worth of tapes to find the latest copy of the user's file. However, most tape systems offer catalog utilities that can help you find the file.

Storage Considerations

If you're using tape backup, you'll also need to consider how you want the backups stored. Most tape software gives you the option of overwriting or appending a backup to the current tape. This lets you mix full and incremental backups on a single tape. But it is not always wise to append subsequent backups until the tape fills up. Sometimes it is better to keep individual backups on separate tapes.

It's clearly more economical to fill each tape completely before installing another. But there's a trade-off. Say you have a 2.2-gigabyte tape system and each day you perform a full backup that consumes 400M. You could easily fit five days' worth of data on one tape. But if you need to restore data from the fifth day's backup, the tape drive will have to read through the first four days' backups (1.6 gigabytes) until it comes to the beginning of the fifth day's "save set." The savings in the cost of media can be offset by the time to restore the needed files. Depending on the speed of your tape, the best approach may be to do a full backup to separate tapes each day.

Attended Versus Unattended Backups

Who should be present when the backup is done? Does anyone really need to be there? Those are the questions you'll have to ask yourself to determine whether to schedule attended or unattended backups. In an attended backup, someone is there to start the process and change tapes if the amount of data being backed up exceeds the capacity of the first tape. This generally means that someone must be on-site to monitor the process as the entire backup takes place. There are two advantages of attended backups: (1) You can purchase a smaller tape unit, because someone will be available to change tapes during the backup process. (2) If a problem occurs during the backup process—if the tape is bad or if there is a hardware failure—the attendant can correct the problem and restart the process. The problem doesn't wait to be discovered until the staff shows up for work.

The chief disadvantage of attended backups is that they require personnel. Either you'll have to schedule someone to attend the backup after normal working hours, or you'll have to conduct the backup during the working day when there is traffic on the network. Conducting backups when the network is busy adds to the traffic on the cabling system and can diminish network performance.

Unattended backups are automated processes that are scheduled to begin at a given time and run to completion. Unattended backups have two chief advantages: (1) They can be run in off-hours when network traffic is very low and no users are actively logged in. (2) Unattended backups demand backup devices that are large enough to accommodate the entire contents of your network volumes on a single unit of media. Consequently, with a tape drive system, you have fewer tapes to catalog and store.

There are three chief disadvantages to unattended backups:

1. If hardware or media failure occurs during an unattended backup, the problem will not be detected until someone comes in and actually checks the system. If the backup is run during the night, the failure will

not be discovered until the following morning. By that time your options are to run an attended backup during the day, which will tie up the backup workstation and put traffic on the network, or to skip the backup scheduled for the previous day and try again at the next scheduled unattended backup, a dangerous option because it leaves company data files at risk.

2. Under NetWare, virtually all backup software requires the workstation performing the backup to be logged in as supervisor or a supervisor equivalent to ensure full access to all files and all volumes on the file server(s). This also ensures that archive bits can be reset as needed. If the workstation is in an area that can't be physically secured, this presents a major security problem.

3. If you do not configure your NetWare system properly, some files may not be recorded in an unattended backup, because backup systems will not back up files that are open and in use. This creates a problem on networks where users fail to log off before leaving the office and on networks with round-the-clock usage.

Preparing for Unattended Backups

Fortunately, two of these disadvantages—keeping the supervisor logged in and the difficulty of open files—can be addressed.

There are several things you can do to address the security risk of having an unattended workstation logged in as supervisor. The problem is minimized if the workstation can be kept in a locked room where only the network administrator has access. But say the network administrator sits in a partitioned cubicle and does not have an office that can be locked.

The first option is simply to lock the keyboard. If this is not adequate security, consider physically securing the workstation case so that it cannot be opened or moved without an additional key. You could also minimize the time that the workstation is logged in by using an event-scheduling software program, such as the shareware product CRONJR, which is on the disk included with this book. CRONJR automatically logs you in, permits you to launch a program at a predefined time, and logs you out after the program has run. Several commercial programs, such as Complimentary Solutions' Automate/Anytime or Brightwork's PS-Batch, also perform this service.

Constructing a Login Sequence

No matter which program you use, the key to security is in the login sequence. The following seven-step strategy will help you go about constructing a secure login.

Step 1. Create a user on the file server(s) that you'll be backing up and assign supervisory privileges to this user. You might, for the sake of simplicity, name the user BACKUP.

Step 2. Create special mappings for this user. The root of each volume to be backed up should be mapped to a drive. For example, the mapping in the backup user's login script might look something like this:

```
Map G:=SYS:
Map H:=VOL1:
Map I:=Vol2:
```

This step is especially important because some software will only back up mapped drives that are specified and the subdirectories below them. Other software automatically recognizes the logical volumes and backs up all subdirectories, but it is still a good idea to prepare for the first possibility.

Step 3. Create a batch file in the BACKUP login script that will invoke the tape backup routine. The last line of this batch file should be either LOGOUT or WARMBOOT, a public domain utility that's available on the IBM CompuServe forum that will reboot the workstation. Either one will ensure that the supervisor-equivalent workstation will be logged out as soon as the backup is completed. The following two-line batch file, called BACKUP.BAT, can be used with a Maynard Systems backup unit:

```
C:\MAYNARD1\TBACKUP G:\/S/AU:1 H:\/S/AU:1 I:\/S/AU
LOGOUT
```

The syntax for your batch file will vary according to the backup software being used, but the concept is the same. The batch file shown above, for example, would back up drives G, H, and I, and all subdirectories beneath them. It would automatically verify each backup and then log out the workstation.

Step 4. Place the batch file on the BACKUP user's search path. You'll invoke the batch file by calling it from the BACKUP user's login script. So, in addition to the drive mappings you've assigned to the BACKUP user login script, you'll need to add the following line to call the batch file:

```
EXIT "BACKUP.BAT"
```

Step 5. On the BACKUP user's workstation, you'll have to create a batch file that will be "launched" by the scheduling software. This file must be written to load the network shells automatically and login to the network as user BACKUP. The batch file should look something like this:

```
C:
CD\NET
IPX
```

```
NET4
F:
LOGIN FS1/BACKUP <PASSWORD.DAT
```

The last line logs in the user, BACKUP, to a file server named FS1 and supplies the user's password from a file named PASSWORD.DAT that you will create in the next step. Once BACKUP is logged in, the user login script you developed in Step 4 will take care of the backup.

Step 6. Load your favorite word processor and create the PASS-WORD.DAT file in flat ASCII format. The file should contain only one word, the password you assigned to user BACKUP. For security reasons, it's important to hide this file. After all, it contains a supervisor-equivalent's password. You can use the DOS ATTRIB command to hide the file. At the DOS prompt, simply type:

```
ATTRIB PASSWORD.DAT +H.
```

Step 7. Use the commands and syntax of your scheduling software to schedule the "launching" of the batch file you created in Step 3.

Perform a full unattended backup on schedule every weekday, e.g., at 11:00 p.m. Back up multiple file servers onto tape, such as a 2.2-gigabyte tape, and use a new tape each day. This will provide you with the ability to restore the contents of any of your file servers quickly, without searching through multiple tape backups.

Depending on your organization and the size of your backup hardware, other options may be more appropriate for you. In a small office, for instance, you could perform a full, attended backup once a week and unattended incremental daily backups the balance of the week. If you don't have many data files that change every day, you'll probably be able to append your incremental backups to a single tape.

Verifying the Backup

The software that comes with backup systems gives you utilities to verify that what has been written to tape is really what was stored on your file server(s). If you fail to run the verify procedure, you'll never know if your backup reflects exactly the information on the disk or, worse, if a media defect prevented the files from being backed up at all. Murphy's Law would predict that any media errors that do occur would happen right in the middle of a mission-critical database.

Typically, you restore data from your backup only when there's a problem. Either a user has erased the data, or you've had a file server problem and you're reinstalling virtually everything. Any backup that hasn't been verified is not a good backup. It's more like a safety net with "just a few holes" in it. Why risk having a faulty backup? Run the verify procedure as part of the backup procedure.

The verification can take longer than the actual backup. In our office, the backup takes one and one-half hours and the verification takes approximately two hours. But because we run an unattended backup and all data are on the same tape, no operator intervention is required to do the verification. Ease of verification (keeping it on the same tape) is another argument for purchasing a storage device large enough to back up all of your data on one piece of media.

Testing the Backup

After you've performed your backup and verification, you should test the tape's restoration capabilities. This will raise your level of confidence in the data, should you have to restore it. You really won't know the backup works unless you test it, and the time to find out is not when you have to do the restoration. Testing will also help you learn how to use the restoration software. You need to be familiar with how to restore individual files, subdirectores, volumes, and Novell's bindery files. Each manufacturer's software is different, and you don't want to go through the learning curve during a have-to situation.

Nevertheless, it's best to practice on files that are expendable. For practice, create a few test subdirectories and copy some files to them. Back up and verify those subdirectores. (This exercise will also show you how to back up individual files and directories.) Delete the files and subdirectories, and practice the restoration capabilities of your backup software.

Tape Rotation and Cataloging

Housekeeping should be an incidental item in your backup strategy. Nevertheless, you should consider it. Cataloging tapes can become a problem. How do you keep track of them as they accumulate? Where should you keep them and for how long? Should you reuse the tapes? You should have a plan for archiving and cataloging your tapes. Many manufacturers of tape hardware and software include a section in their instruction manuals that suggests methods for archiving tapes. Review them and see if they meet your needs. You may prefer to devise your own.

You should keep old tapes. They'll allow you to respond to users' requests that you recover files that they accidentally deleted days ago but didn't realize until now. If the files have been purged and are no longer available for recovery with NetWare's SALVAGE command (that should be your first recourse; see "The SALVAGE Command," chapter 5), you're going to have to recover the files from your backup. Sometimes your users won't want the most recent version of their files; they'll want a previous version of a document or spreadsheet that can only be gotten off a backup. Most backup software today either includes a cataloging program or offers one as a companion product. These programs keep an itemized catalog of the files on the backup tape and their locations and will spare you headaches if you need to look for specific files. But they often consume a fair amount of disk space, as much as 8 to 10M depending on the amount of detail you choose to catalog. So if you plan to use them, be sure to have plenty of space available for the catalog files on the backup tape as well as on the hard disk.

How long you should keep the tapes depends on your organization's needs. At PC/Computing we work on a four-week rotation schedule, perform full daily backups of all file servers on 2.2-gigabyte tapes, and keep twenty tapes in the rotation. To catalog the tapes, we label each by date and color-code them by week: Week 1, red; Week 2, green; Week 3, yellow; Week 4, blue. If Week 1 started on July 30, 1990, the tape bears a red label marked Monday, July 30. Each Monday, the previous Friday's tape is removed to an off-site location and remains there until it is needed in the rotation.

Off-site storage is important. So far we've discussed backup plans aimed at recovering data due to network file server failure. But what happens if there's a fire at the office? All of your well-planned and executed backups could go up in smoke along with the hardware. You can purchase new hardware, but critical records would have to be reentered, and it's likely that any paper copies of the files were also destroyed in the disaster. You'll doubly protect your company's data by keeping duplicate off-site backups. If one tape is destroyed you'll have the other. It doesn't really matter where you keep the off-site backup. Some companies specialize in off-site backup storage, but you could also send the duplicates to a branch office or, in a small business, take them home or keep them in a safety deposit box at your bank. What's important is that you have duplicate off-site backups.

Backup Plan Checksheet

As we said earlier, your backup strategy should reflect the needs of your own organization and users. But as you purchase the system and implement the strategy, there are three key points to keep in mind:

1. Before purchasing tape hardware/software, ensure that it is certified to work with the version of NetWare you're planning to use. This is especially important if you're using NetWare 386 because, as of this writing, not all manufacturers' hardware was certified to work with it.

2.   Determine if you need to back up specific hard disks of workstations on the network in addition to those on the file server(s). Some tape hardware manufacturers include this capability with their product. Others offer it in a companion product. This capability allows users to "publish" their disks on the network or make them available to the backup system, so that the tape software includes the contents of their individual hard disks as it backs up the network volumes. If you plan to back up the hard disks on individual workstations, make note of the sizes of those hard disks as you choose your backup system and the amount of storage media you plan to back up to. These factors will significantly impact the amount of storage media you need.

3.   Do not rotate all your tapes. Keep some as permanent records. Once a month, generally on the first of the month, make two full monthly backups. Keep one in house and one off-site as a permanent "monthly archive."

Cleaning Up the LAN

Some users are pack rats. Given a chance, they'll keep every file they ever created on the network disk for "on-line" access even if they haven't used it for the past twelve months. Such practices unnecessarily consume storage on the file server. To compound the problem, many applications make automatic backup files each time a file is resaved.

As a network manager, you may have little control over a user's personal files, but you can eliminate unnecessary backup files from the system. Only rarely do users use the automatic backups beyond the date on which they were created; yet many applications do not automatically delete the backup files. Even if they do, you'll have the files on your backup media if you make daily network backups. Novell's own menu system can contribute to cramped conditions; it creates two control files for each user—RESTART.XXX and GOXXX.BAT files (XXX designates the connection number)—which ensure that users will be returned to the menu when they exit the application. But if users reboot their workstation or turn off their computer without logging out, those files are left on the system to take up directory entry and disk space. These files will never be used again and may never be copied over, as users will most probably get a different connection number when they login again. As a network manager, you'll need a method of weeding out excess files and keeping the network clean. A good file maintenance utility will do this for you.

Executive Systems' XTNET version 2.0 is the file manager utility we use at PC/Computing. For that reason, we'll use it in our examples. But many such utilities on the market work similarly. As we move through this discussion, focus more on the methods we discuss than the utilities used in our examples.

Weeding Out Unnecessary Files

Before putting any utility to work, look at the popular applications in use on your network and determine those that make automatic backups and the backup extensions they use. Microsoft Word, for example, makes automatic backups and assigns them name extensions of ".BAK" for backup files. To delete all of Word's .BAK files prior to July 1, 1990, you would follow this procedure:

1. Map a search drive to the volume that contains the ".BAK" files you want to delete

2. Switch to the directory that contains your file maintenance utility. In this case, it is XTREE Net.

3. Start XTREE Net and log to the drive which you mapped in step 1, the one that contains the backup files.

4. Issue the command, or make the menu selection, within the utility that will delete the files. With XTREE Net, you would press F (for file specification) and type * .bak. This will filter out all files except those with the .BAK extension.

5. Press S (for Show All). This will show all files that match the specification defined in step 4 in all subdirectories on this disk. If you're using XTREE Net, your screen will look something like this:

```
5.BAK            27,648 .a..   8-25-90 12:51 PM     FILE: *.BAK
SYSCON5 .BAK      7,168 .a..   8-24-90  3:35 PM
PF1.BAK           2,048 .a..   8-24-90  8:32 am    |DISK: F:EXEC
PF2.BAK             780 .a..   8-24-90  7:47 am    |Available  ª
PFDEC.BAK         4,726 .a..   8-23-90  3:38 PM    |Bytes: 73,273,344
SYSCON4 .BAK     12,288 .a..   8-23-90  1:59 PM
386UPGRD.BAK      4,096 .a..   8-22-90  1:04 PM    SHOW ALL Statistics
SYSCON3 .BAK      8,704 .a..   8-22-90 12:36 PM    Total
SYSCON2 .BAK     10,752 .a..   8-21-90  8:09 am      Files:        3,880
ERTHOT  .BAK      2,048 .a..   8-20-90  2:34 PM      Bytes: 67,011,408
SYSCON1 .BAK      9,216 .a..   8-20-90  7:43 am    Matching
VOLINFO .BAK      8,704 .a..   8-16-90  7:55 am      Files:           80
EMAIL   .BAK     14,349 .a..   8-15-90 10:59 am      Bytes:      711,869
PUBLIC  .BAK      7,560 .a..   8-15-90 10:59 am    Tagged
PRIVATE .BAK      6,840 .a..   8-15-90 10:59 am      Files:            0
UD1     .BAK      1,836 .a..   8-15-90 10:59 am      Bytes:            0
UD3     .BAK      4,896 .a..   8-15-90 10:59 am    Current File
SENT    .BAK     13,260 .a..   8-15-90 10:59 am    5          .BAK
UNSENT  .BAK          0 ....   8-15-90 10:59 am      Bytes:       27,648
```

In this case, there are 80 backup files consuming over 700K of the network disk. To be sure you're not deleting backups that may not be on your network backup tape, you could sort the files by creation date. To to this in XTREE Net, you should sort the files by date by pressing Alt S (Sort) and choosing D (Date). Then press Alt S and choose O (Order) to change to a descending sort order. The .BAK files will be sorted in descending date order, making it easy to scroll down to find the files older than 7/1/90. As you scroll, you would press T at each entry you want to delete in order to tag each file. Your screen will look something like this:

```
NET      .BAK_  25,472 ....  6-18-90  8:37 am      FILE: *.BAK
INFIX    .BAK_   8,269 ....  6-13-90 10:31 am
INFOR    .BAK_  26,191 ....  6-12-90  1:35 pm      DISK: F:EXEC
486BEN   .BAK_  25,445 ....  6-06-90 10:34 pm      Available
486BEN3  .BAK_  16,565 ....  6-06-90 10:14 pm        Bytes: 73,273,344
MENU     .BAK_   1,391 ....  5-23-90  4:36 pm
MENU     .BAK_   1,391 ....  5-23-90  4:36 pm      SHOW ALL Statistics
FINMENU  .BAK_   1,213 ....  5-23-90  2:59 pm      Total
FINMENU  .BAK_   1,213 ....  5-23-90  2:59 pm        Files:        3,880
NETOUT   .BAK_   5,632 ....  5-23-90 11:21 am        Bytes: 67,011,408
SHELL    .BAK_   7,168 ....  5-20-90  8:56 am      Matching
5-11-90  .BAK_   1,550 ....  5-11-90 11:16 am        Files:           80
CMENET   .BAK_  19,456 ....  5-07-90  5:38 pm        Bytes:      711,869
NOVELL   .BAK_  19,456 ....  5-07-90  3:41 pm      Tagged
NOVELL   .BAK_  19,456 ....  5-07-90  3:41 pm        Files:           22
!BUDGEN  .BAK_   1,266 ....  5-04-90  7:20 am        Bytes:      225,508
430NEWS  .BAK_  15,484 ....  4-30-90  7:23 am      Current File
COVER    .BAK_   5,130 ....  4-04-90 10:23 am        NCSTIX   .BAK
NCSTIX   .BAK_   2,256 .a..  2-23-90  6:27 pm        Bytes:        2,256
```

At this point, press CTRL D to delete all tagged files. In our example, 22 files consuming 225K were deleted. You would follow the same process to erase .TMP files created by some programs as well as the RESTART.XXX and GOXXX.BAT files left over by Novell's menu system.

It's a good idea to perform this kind of cleanup at least once a month. And, if you plan your monthly cleanup for the day after you performed your monthly archive backup, you'll be able to recover the files in the unlikely event that a user wants an old backup. Daily incremental backups, as we noted, will also do the trick if a user needs an old file.

You may want to grant users access to the file management utility and encourage them to keep their own directories clean. The XTREE file management utilities respect Novell's security, so users will be able to use them only to the extent of their network privileges. In other words, they'll be able to view files in directories where they enjoy Read rights but they can delete files only in directories where they enjoy Delete rights.

Assuring User Support

In many organizations, the person responsible for maintaining the network, generally the network administrator, is also the person responsible for providing user support. On large local area networks, campuswide networks, or wide area networks (WANs), the distance between the user and the support person can be more of a problem than the problems the support person is there to correct. Users have to wait until the support person shows up. Depending on the situation and the distances involved, that can take hours. User telephone support is generally not too successful. Actually seeing what's on the user's screen often leads to better results. Fortunately, one solution gives the user instantaneous access to the support person and allows him or her to see what is on the user's screen.

Supporting Users Across the LAN

Remote support software enables a network administrator to connect to a user's workstation across a LAN or WAN, take control of the user's computer, and pass commands to that computer as if he or she were sitting at the keyboard. All the while, the information on the user's screen appears simultaneously on the network administrator's screen. Some of the more popular programs that perform this function are Lan Assist + by Fresh Technology, Co/Session Lan by Triton, and Net Remote by Brightwork.

The programs allow access through a small (5–10K) "shell" or TSR program loaded on the workstation. It is through this shell that the support person accesses the workstation being supported. Generally, the shell can be loaded in a batch file and invoked by exiting to the batch file from the user login script.

Remote support programs can save the network administrator a tremendous amount of time. For example, if a user calls with a problem, you as the administrator could merely invoke the support side (sometimes called the "remote" side) of the software, identify the user's name on the software's own screen, then bring up the image of the user's screen onto your own, and issue the sequence of commands yourself to solve the problem. You could have the problem resolved in less time than it would take you to get an elevator and go to the user's office, see what is onscreen, and fix the problem.

This sort of software is also ideal for supporting print servers. Print servers generally are stand-alone machines that automatically log in to the network when booted. If the print server were to hang, you could use one of the LAN support packages remotely to reboot it without leaving your desk.

Using Fresh Technologies Lan Assist +, for instance, you could reboot a print server named SALES_PRINT that had hung, as long as the shell remained loaded. On accessing the print server through the shell, your screen would look something like this:

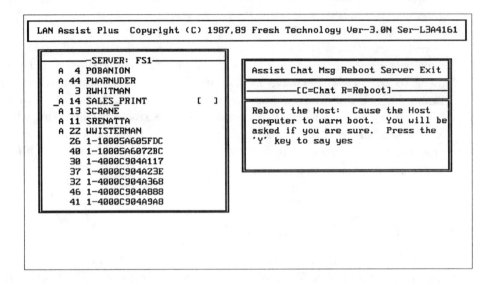

```
LAN Assist Plus  Copyright (C) 1987,89 Fresh Technology Ver-3.0N Ser-L3A4161

    ---------SERVER: FS1---------          Assist Chat Msg Reboot Server Exit
    A  4 POBANION
    A 44 PWARNUDER                         ----------[C=Chat R=Reboot]----------
    A  3 RWHITMAN
   _A 14 SALES_PRINT        [   ]          Reboot the Host:  Cause the Host
    A 13 SCRANE                            computer to warm boot.  You will be
    A 11 SRENATTA                          asked if you are sure.  Press the
    A 22 WWISTERMAN                        'Y' key to say yes
      26 1-10005A605FDC
      40 1-10005A6072BC
      30 1-4000C904A117
      37 1-4000C904A23E
      32 1-4000C904A368
      46 1-4000C904A888
      41 1-4000C904A9A8
```

Note, in the window at the top right, that you are given six action options from which to choose. In our example, choose R to reboot the server. If you chose Assist instead, anything that was showing on the SALES_PRINT screen would appear on your screen.

As useful as remote support software is, it also poses security risks, and for this reason there are many times when you would not want to use it. The financial officers of most organizations, for instance, will not want to load an assist shell that allows access to confidential information on their screens, particularly because this software can often be configured to keep the person whose screen is being viewed from knowing that someone is looking in. Fortunately, most such software provides a facility that brings the name of the viewer onto the user's screen when someone attempts access. Some packages also require that the remote user grant access to the person providing assistance. From a security standpoint, this is the preferred way to configure such software.

As the remote access shells are TSRs that should be loaded onto the users' individual workstations, they should not be loaded from within NetWare's login scripts using the # command (example: #Y:\APPS\LA\LA+). Instead, load them from a batch file to which the login script exits.

For security reasons, do not install remote assist shells on all machines in the organization. Use Novell's Groups to identify those users whose machines you will equip with support shells and automatically load the shells in only those users' machines. Here's how you do it:

1. Use the Novell command SYSCON to create a group named ASSIST.

2. To this group assign the users who should have the Assist shell loaded in their workstations.

3. Modify the system login script with the following line:

```
IF MEMBER OF "ASSIST" THE DOS SET ASSIST = "Y"
```

4. Use your favorite text processor to create the following batch file named START.BAT:

```
cls
@echo off
IF "%ASSIST%"=="Y" GOTO LOAD
goto end
:LOAD
Y:\APPS\LA\LA+
:END
```

5. In the user login script, enter the last line as:

```
EXIT "START.BAT"
```

When a user who is a member of the group named ASSIST logs onto the network, a DOS environment variable named ASSIST will be set to Y. The START.BAT file tests to see if the variable being set is actually set to Y. If it is, it loads the Assist shell. In this case, the syntax of the batch file indicates the shell being used is Fresh Technologies Lan Assist +, which was located in Y:\APPS\LA.

Providing Remote Support

LAN remote support software will not help your support problems if you, as the network administrator, happen to be away from the office or at a PC that is not connected to your network when a problem occurs. But similar software packages are available that allow you to dial in via modem and take control of a workstation on your LAN. As with the LAN remote support packages, these programs essentially put you at the workstation's keyboard. By logging in as supervisor, you'll be able to access and control central processes on the LAN. With this type of software, all of the processing takes place in the LAN workstation and only the screen display is sent down the phone line. Examples of such software include Triton Technology's Co-Session, DCA's Remote/2, Norton-Lambert's Close Up, or DMA's PC/Anywhere.

With this type of software, the speed of your operations is limited to the speed of your modem and how fast it can refresh the screen on the remote end. If you are working at 2400 baud, it could take several seconds for a screen to refresh. But this is a minor trade-off for being able to access and service your LAN off-site. Often the types of problems that you can solve remotely involve granting users additional access privileges, resetting intruder detection counts (if the user tried too many times to log in with the wrong password), and so on.

For the sake of security, plan to do the following:

1. On the workstation set up to receive the problem calls, load the remote application software from the AUTOEXEC.BAT file.

2. Reboot the workstation. This way the remote software will be loaded but the workstation will not be attached to the network.

3. Use the PASSWORD security features of the support software package to limit access to the remote machine. This ensures that persons dialing in will gain access only if they issue the correct password on the call-in software as well as the correct Novell username/password login sequence.

4. The dial-in software includes a "dial back" feature. Use it. The feature links the caller's telephone number to a particular password. When someone calls in from a remote location and gains entrance with the password, the workstation will immediately hang up and call the person back at the number assigned to the password when the software was configured. This works especially well if you're going to be dialing into the remote machine from locations where you know the phone number. And any long-distance or toll charges incurred for the call will be charged to the office rather than to the off-site location.

5. Configure the software to reboot when the remote session is finished. That way the machine will no longer be attached to the file server. If you loaded the communication software in the AUTOEXEC.BAT file as we recommended in step 1, the remote workstation will reinitialize after you hang up.

If you use this type of software in conjunction with the LAN remote software discussed earlier, you'll be able to dial in from any off-site location and support users as if you were in the office.

Accessing On-line Support

If you don't have a CompuServe account, get one. This is not a plug. It is good, solid advice. NetWire, CompuServe's network forum, is the on-line service through which Novell distributes patches and fixes. NetWire has three user forums. Novell users from across the United States use all three to post problems and engage in discussions. Novell support personnel frequent the forums and answer questions; they forward specialized problems to Novell's engineering department where the problems can be tested, duplicated, and, often, resolved.

Periodically, Novell support personnel host conferences that focus on specific topics of general interest, such as using Windows 3.0 with Novell products. To give you a sampling of the kinds of things you'll find on NetWire, let's take a look at the kinds of things you'll find in the "A" forum. The Novell Forum A is divided into three basic areas: The Message Board, The Library, and The Conference Area. You can go direct to the library you're looking for by using CompuServe's "go" command with the library numbers listed beside the library names below. Note that libraries 10 and 15 are not in use.

Message Board Sections
   (1) ELS NetWare
   (2) NetWare 2.0a & below
   (3) NetWare 2.1x
   (4) NetWare 386(v3.x)
   (5) NetWare Macintosh
   (6) NetWare VMS
   (7) Portable NetWare
   (8) NetWare NFS

Libraries
   (1) Product/Gen'rl Info
   (2) Tech Bulletins
   (3) Novell Educ'tn Info
   (4) NETWIRE Information
   (5) Btrieve/XQL/Xtrieve
   (6) NetWare Utilities
   (7) NetWare 386
   (8) Novell Patch/Drv'r
   (9) Communic'tns Product
   (11) Other Ptchs/Drvs
   (12) Independent Devl'mt
   (13) User Groups
   (14) Public Domain/Demo
   (16) Novell NEW UPLOADS
   (17) Other NEW UPLOADS

The contents of the itemized subsections in the other two areas reflect the "theme" of the section. For instance, NetWare Utilities are stored in Library

6, and all the messages relating to Installations and Upgrades are found in message section 11.

The conference offers a forum for interactive exchanges among the NetWire members. Through it, you can use electronic mail to have a private conversation with one particular person, or conference interactively with many people at once. Forum conferencing is used for quick, informal chats among members and for scheduled presentations by guest speakers.

Documenting Your LAN Plan

In setting up a network, it may seem that policies, procedures, and documentation are the last things you need to be concerned about. Well, you're partially right, but you should document your network setup as you install the network.

Things never go according to plan, and there are little deviations from the documentation that you made just to get things working. Document these changes as you go along. If you ever need to re-create the setup, you'll have good notes. Several months later you may be installing another network and you may wish that you had taken notes. Even if you just need to maintain, upgrade, and expand one network, it's easier to create the documentation as you go rather than to try to go back and re-create it.

One of the best scenarios to illustrate the need for good documentation is in the wiring closet. Most buildings have block numbers on the data jacks in individual offices. These correspond either to punchdown block numbers or patch panel numbers in the wiring closet. As you add each user, simply note the block number or patch panel number and the port # (and MAU# or Hub# or Concentrator#) as you plug in the cables. Once your network is up and running, it will be difficult to trace back through the maze of wires to re-create this information. But if you ever have a wiring problem, this map will be indispensable.

Also, as you install the network interface cards in each computer, take a few minutes to document the settings for the card. This is especially critical in ArcNet environments where you must assign a unique node address to each interface card. Duplicate addresses in an ArcNet network will cause serious problems and can crash the network. Having a record of each workstation's settings is also helpful when you have to upgrade network shells. A simple spreadsheet, such as the one provided in the worksheet, will make a difference.

It's also a good idea to purchase a third-party utility to help you document information on user and group rights. Although NetWare provides excellent security features, it's ability to report them is virtually nonexistent. Fortunately, third-party utilities will provide you with a number of consolidated reports that will detail user trustee information, disk usage by user, group rights, security equivalences, and so on. Fresh Technologies publishes a product named Fresh Utilities, and Frye publishes Frye Utilities for NetWare. Both packages will generate these reports. Run the reports periodically (perhaps the same day you perform your monthly backup). It may help you to spot a security loophole or help track disk usage trends on your network.

Disaster Planning

Although you don't like to think that disasters will (or even, can) occur on your network, at some point in time they will. After you've done all of your backups and ensured a comfortable level of hardware fault tolerance for your organization, take one additional step. Identify mission-critical applications and create a plan by which you can immediately recover them from a hardware failure.

For example, if your organization prepares its payroll on the network and transmits data once a week to a service bureau, what happens if there's a disk crash on the day the data have to be transmitted? Do you install a new network disk? Do you even have time to install one? This scenario is taken from a real-life situation. To prepare for such an occurrence, the organization's network administrator came up with a two-part plan that was placed in a procedure book:

1. The administrator listed a step-by-step procedure for installing a new hard disk, reinstalling NetWare, and restoring data from tape. This included purchasing a spare network disk that he Compsurfed and left on the shelf ready to install. By having the prepared disk available, all he would have to do is transfer files from a backup tape onto the new disk. Recovery would take about ninety minutes. Without the prepared disk, recovery could have taken twenty-four hours or more if a new hard disk had to be purchased and compsurfed, (unless you're using NetWare 386).

2. He created a duplicate environment for the payroll department on a second file server that was bridged to the first file server. Payroll user IDs along with appropriate security and drive mappings were set up on the secondary server. This enabled the payroll department to restore files and continue operations in no longer than it would take to restore data from the previous day's backup if the first file server's problem was related to a component that wasn't "on the shelf." This part of the plan also included step-by-step documentation of the procedures needed to restore files to the bridged server. The documentation

included enough detail so that anyone who was familiar with the basics of DOS and NetWare could perform the restoration.

The clear advantage of having a plan that documents restoration procedures so that they can be reviewed and followed by persons other than the network manager is that systems do not always fail when there's someone around to fix them. With a disaster plan in place, company operations are not vulnerable if a network administrator attends an off-site conference, gets sick, or takes a vacation.

Beware of Viruses

Computer viruses can wreak as much, if not more, havoc on your network as hardware failures. Hardware failure is something you can fix, and then you return to normal operation. But computer viruses are becoming increasingly sophisticated and difficult to isolate. Once they are on the network, they can erase files and destroy directory tables. Some viruses act instantly; others, such as the Jerusalem B virus, are time bombs that are set to cause their destruction on a specific date. Others sleep on the system, remaining undetected for long periods of time, and can be backed up along with data files, only to wreak havoc again when the backup is restored. The extent of the damage they cause is limited only to the imagination of the programmer who creates them.

Viruses typically creep onto a network in one of two ways: when you load a program that is already infected with a virus onto the network, or when an unauthorized user gains access to the network and plants the virus. You can diminish the possibility of a virus attack and protect your LAN by adopting a few practical procedures. These include:

1. Before loading a new program onto your network, particularly public domain software, test it in a stand-alone computer that is not connected to the LAN. As you run the program, watch for changes in the size of executable files previously installed on the PC and for changes in the amount of memory the programs consume. Viruses will often implant themselves as additional code in executable files such as COM-MAND.COM. To do this, you'll need to keep a record of the file sizes of the executables installed on the machine and of the amount of memory the programs there consume. The Norton or Mace utility programs can help you with this task. Also change the system date on the stand-alone PC to known "trigger" dates of particular viruses and see if they take effect.

2. Write-protect all original diskettes before installing new programs. If a virus does attack your system, restore the applications from the

original disks and not from a backup tape where the programs may have been corrupted by the virus.

3. Never install a program that a user has downloaded onto the network unless you know its origin. Many software vendors have forums on CompuServe, Genie, or their own bulletin board services that you can assume contain virus-free program patches or updates. However, if you don't know a program author or company that markets it, attempt to contact the person or company before downloading its software from a bulletin board and installing it on your network. If you can't make contact other than through a bulletin board or user ID, be wary.

4. Educate your network users on the dangers of virus infection. You cannot protect a network from infection if users casually install public domain programs in their personal or shared directories.

5. Flag executables as Read Only. This will keep some viruses from replicating themselves, especially if the applications reside in a directory where users don't have Modify rights.

6. Networks with dial-in capabilities are particularly vulnerable to hackers. Implement the dialback feature of your communications program to help prevent hackers from gaining access to your network.

7. One part of recovering from a virus attack is to have good, reliable backups in place. By archiving executable files as programs are installed, you'll be able to compare file sizes over time. This can help you isolate the virus, remove the threatening file, and restore your data with some degree of confidence that the virus won't be resurrected.

8. Notify users to contact the network administrator immediately if the applications they're running start behaving in suspicious ways or if mysterious activities begin occurring at their workstations.

It may also be a good idea to buy one of the many virus detection and scanning programs on the market. However, new viruses continue to be developed, and the programs constantly change in an effort to keep up with them. Do not assume that a detection program you purchased last year will be able to ferret out threats to your system today.

Service Contracts

Even if you choose to do much of your own maintenance, you may want to purchase service contracts on your network equipment. Consider what level of support you'll require. One of your main considerations should be your in-house level of expertise to repair equipment. If someone on staff can repair virtually all equipment, your next challenge is to figure out what level of spare parts inventory you should stock. If, on the other hand, in-house expertise is limited and you elect to enter into a service contract with an outside contractor, you should be aware of the various levels of service available to you. Different vendors offer different service options. In general, the levels of service contracts include:

1. *Time and materials.* This arrangement typically works well in environments where response time is not critical. Most computer repair companies service their contract customers before they service customers who are billed on a time-and-material basis. If you don't have a history of equipment failures, don't want to place each piece of equipment on a service contract, and are willing to live with as-available responses to your service needs, this may be the option for you. You're essentially gambling that your equipment won't fail or that the failure won't severely interrupt business operations.

2. *Depot service.* This level of service is similar to time and material, except that you must take the equipment to the service contractor's location. This is not a viable option for most companies because of the amount of time the LAN will remain down.

3. *Retainer contract.* With this type of arrangement, you pay an upfront retainer to the service company. When you require service, you are billed as if it were a time-and-material contract, except that the billing is "drawn" against the retainer fee. The advantage in this plan is that you get the same guaranteed response time as customers with guaranteed-response-time contracts but your costs are limited to the amount of the retainer. After the retainer is used up, you pay for service calls as you require them but you continue to receive guaranteed response.

4. *Guaranteed response time.* With this type of contract, the service vendor guarantees that a service technician will arrive at your site and begin working on the hardware failure within a given amount of time, typically either four or eight hours. It doesn't mean that the problem will be fixed within that time period, only that a service technician will show up. All costs for parts and labor are usually included in this type of contract as well. This type of contract is advantageous if you require many service calls. Unfortunately, you can rarely predict that need.

5. *Guaranteed resolution time.* This is usually the most expensive type of service contract, but it is recommended for mission-critical situations. It guarantees that hardware failure will be fixed within the resolution time specified in the contract. All parts and labor are typically included in the contract price.

Another consideration, and one that can be a point of negotiation in your service contract, is your requirements for loaner equipment when your own LAN hardware fails. Items such as monitors typically cannot be fixed at your worksite and must be returned to a repair shop. Your users will not be inconvenienced if your service contract specifies loaner equipment must be provided as required.

It's often wise to mix and match various types of service contracts. This will help you achieve the level of service that's optimum for various LAN configurations in your office and, at the same time, limit your expense. For example, you may wish to have response-time contracts on file servers and specific mission-critical computers while you maintain a retainer contract on workstations and other equipment.

Assembling Your LAN Maintenance Toolkit

The tools and utilities you put into your LAN maintenance toolkit will vary depending on your budget, your level of technical proficiency, and your degree of involvement in maintaining both the physical LAN and the files located on it. At a minimum, the toolkit should contain a file maintenance utility and the phone number of the value-added reseller who installed the network. But if you prefer not to rely on a VAR for routine backup and maintenance, here are some items that will enable a network administrator to deal with most of the day-to-day problems that arise. In addition to the utilities for file maintenance, remote access, virus detection and scanning, a CompuServe account for on-line access to NetWire, and an appropriate mix of service contracts, your LAN maintenance toolkit should include as many of the following tools as you need to deal with the problems you wish to handle yourself:

1. Spare cabling, connectors, and tools for the type of wiring (twisted pair, coaxial, or fiber optic) used on your LAN. If your network uses unshielded twisted pair wiring, stock a supply of RJ-11 and/or RJ-45 connectors and the cable strippers and crimpers you'll need to assemble new cables. If it runs over coaxial cable, have some lengths of spare coax on hand, along with some crimp-on BNC connectors, a coax stripper, and a BNC crimping tool to build your own cables with connectors.

2. A good multimeter to measure voltage, resistance, and current on the line. This will be valuable in tracing cable shorts and for checking cable continuity.

3. 1/2-watt resistors of the value required by your LAN. Use 50-ohm resistors for EtherNet and 100-ohm resistors for ArcNet. (Token-ring

cards are not terminated so you will not need resisters for them.) For unshielded twisted pair networks, it's a lot easier and cheaper to make terminators from a resistor and an RJ-11 plug (at a cost of about 50 cents each) than it is to order them from the manufacturer.

4. Tone generator. One of the more difficult tasks on a twisted pair network is tracing out a cable that runs from an office to the telephone closet (or wherever your Hub/MAU is located). A tone generator, such as the FOX and HOUND from Triplett, can cut the job down to size by helping you find where the wiring terminates. When you plug a tone generator into the data jack in the office, the generator puts a tone on the line that the pickup unit can find. The pickup unit is an inductive device; when positioned near the line in the telephone closet, it will "hear" the tone. The tone is loudest when you're near the pair you're trying to trace. This device can cut the time involved in tracing wiring from hours to minutes. Without a tone generator, you would spend hours trying to trace the problem using a multimeter; first you'd have to creat a short on one end of the cable and then examine all cables in your phone room until you found the short at the other end.

5. Cable Scanner or Pair Scanner from Microtest. These devices, when attached to a cable, tell you exactly where a cable is shorted or open. The LCD display on the Cable Scanner will return a message such as "Short at 170 feet." The more sophisticated Pair Scanner also evaluates the twisted pair line and reports on its suitability for 16 MBIT token-ring or 10Base-T EtherNet installations. Both devices work on coaxial cable as well.

6. Spare network interface cards and cables that are preconfigured to your network standards. If cards go bad—and they will—you can change cards in a workstation and get the user up and running in a matter of minutes.

7. L-COMM's RJ-11 or RJ-45 twisted pair cable checker. When you plug both ends of a cable into this device, its colored LEDs show you if the cable is wired "straight through," open, or if the pairs are reversed. Most RJ-11 cables used on networks are straight-through wiring. You can bring down an ArcNet network if you accidentally use a cable, such as a telephone cable, with reversed pairs.

8. Persons with a large budget should also consider a protocol analyzer. These devices, costing from $2,000 to $15,000, analyze all network traffic in detail and generate reports. Some of the units also let you set a number of alarms that will notify you when the preset alarm levels are exceeded. We recommend these devices only for persons with a fair degree of technical background. Although they can provide a

wealth of information about what's happening on the network, they'll only produce information overload for individuals who are not trained to use them.

9. Disk Manager -N from Ontrack Systems. If you're running NetWare 286, this utility can save you a lot of time. It prepares a hard disk for NetWare installation in a fraction of the time required for Novell's own Compsurf utility. (Compsurfing is not required in NetWare 386 installations.)

10. Computer repair toolkit containing an assortment of screwdrivers, pliers, Torx screwdrivers (required if you have Compaq equipment), and so on.

11. Disk and tape cleaning kits. These items are especially important. You will encounter read errors if the heads of the disk drive or, more important, the tape drive are not cleaned periodically. A dirty tape head can also keep your tape backup from verifying properly.

8

Troubleshooting NetWare

The fact is that, no matter how proficient you are with NetWare, things will still go wrong. Networks are inherently complicated, and like anything complex, they are prone to Murphy's Law: If it can go wrong, it will.

All you can do is be prepared. That's what this chapter is all about. Here we present a compendium of things that have been known to go wrong in NetWare installations and the workarounds that can help you fix them. It won't catch every problem, and each specific solution may not be right for your setup. But you should be able to find something close here. Use it as a jumping-off point in your own search for solutions.

Problems at the Workstation

THE PROBLEM: Workstation search paths overwrite the local drive path in AUTOEXEC.BAT files.

NetWare version: Any.

When it happens: When users login.

Why it happens: NetWare's MAP S16: and MAP INS S1: are sensitive to the syntax of local path statement. They will overwrite the following statement in an AUTOEXEC.BAT file:

```
SET PATH=[paths]
```

Possible solution: To keep this from happening, the local path statement in the AUTOEXEC.BAT should be written as:

```
PATH=[paths]
```

THE PROBLEM: When generating shells for the workstation, the system returns an error message that says "Nlink has disappeared from SHGEN volume". The message "DCONFIG has disappeared from SHGEN volume" appears if you then press ESC. And if you press ESC again, the system is halted and you get a message that says "Invalid COMMAND.COM, System halted".

NetWare version: Any.

When it happens: This occurs when you run SHGEN to generate shells for Thomas-Conrad 16-bit ArcNet cards, but only if a file called TCCARC.LAN appears on the LAN_DRV_XXX diskette.

Possible solution: Delete TCCARC.LAN. and run SHGEN again.

THE PROBLEM: Workstations can't login after token-ring source routing drivers are upgraded.

NetWare version: NetWare 286, version 2.15c.

When it happens: After upgrading to new Token-Ring 050 drivers on file servers and workstations and loading the SR VAP.

Why it happens: The old SR shells will not work with the new drivers.

Possible solution: LAN Support and IPX will run with no problem, but you'll get "File Server not found" when NET3 is loaded. You'll need to upgrade the workstation shell.

THE PROBLEM: Users remap their local drives when they do a directory search on a network volume.

NetWare version: Any.

When it happens: This occurs on workstations running DOS3.x.

Why it happens: Unlike DOS 4.x, the 3.x versions do not use File Control Blocks to handle directory requests. The system must change to the directory being searched in order to execute the command. When it does, the drive is remapped. The command:

```
C:>DIR SYS:
```

will display the directory in SYS: but will remap the C drive to SYS:.

Possible solution: Users on workstations that do not have DOS 4.x should perform the search from network drives only.

THE PROBLEM: The workstation mouse won't work with Windows 3.0's enhanced mode when the EtherNet card in the workstation is set at INT3. It will, however, work in real mode.

NetWare version: Any.

When it happens: When the mouse is installed on COM1.

Possible solution: Change to another interrupt. INT5 may work.

THE PROBLEM: Users cannot print files from Windows 3.0 applications running in enhanced 386 mode.

NetWare version: Any.

When it happens: When printing a file from a Windows application.

Why it happens: This is apparently due to a bug that occurs when running in enhanced mode. Although the file isn't printed, you will find it stuck in the print queue waiting to be printed if you exit Windows and check PCONSOLE.

Possible solution: Edit the WIN.INI file Insert:

```
RPT1.PRN=
```

below the LPT1= line. Save the file. Reload Windows, go into the configuration, and redirect the print output to RPT1.PRN instead of LPT1. This will print the file from DOS instead of through Windows.

To print the file to disk instead of to a printer, enter the above command with a colon following the statement, as in:

```
RPT1.PRN:=
```

THE PROBLEM: Windows 3.0 conflicts with network interface cards.

NetWare version: Any.

When it happens: When users load Windows.

Why it happens: Windows conflicts will occur if the network cards use interrupts 2 or 9 or have a base memory address of D000.

Possible solution: The quick fix to the interrupt problem is to use another interrupt and use the INSTALL program in the DOS 3.01 shells to replace the VPIC.386 file with the VPICDA.386 file. To fix the base memory problem, call up SYSTEM.INI in a text editor and, under the file's 386ENH section, add an EMMExclude setting that specifies a range of memory addresses from D000.0 to DFFF:F, such as:

```
EMMExclude-D000-DFFF
```

Save the file and exit and restart Windows.

THE PROBLEM: Workstations hang when applications are loaded.

NetWare version: NetWare 286, version 2.15, Revision C, NetWare 386 version 3.0.

When it happens: When the application is loaded.

Why it happens: Workstation shells will conflict with applications that use IRQ3. This can occur when users run devices, such as a mouse, or applications that use the interrupt, such as Microsoft Quick C or Microsoft Basic.

Possible solution: Configure devices to use different interrupt settings.

THE PROBLEM: Windows 3.0 users can't load the network shell in extended memory.

When it happens: When logging onto the network through the Windows desktop.

Why it happens: The wrong network shell was installed or memory is improperly configured.

Possible solution: Use the 3.01 expanded memory network shell using Windows' HIMEM.SYS and Microsoft's EMM386.SYS high-memory drivers. However, this will not work unless you assign some value behind HIMEM.SYS in the CONFIG.SYS file and indicate behind EMM386.SYS how much extended memory you want to allocate as expanded memory.

The user's CONFIG.SYS should look like this:

```
DEVICE=C:\HIMEM.SYS 1
DEVICE-EMM386.SYS 64
device=C:\WINDOWS\smartdrv.sys 1024 512
```

THE PROBLEM: When using the ATTACH command, users get an error message that says "Can't Get Connection Status".

NetWare version: NetWare 286, version 2.15C, NetWare 386, version 3.0.

When it happens: During login.

Why it happens: This is due to a bug in the ATTACH command in these versions.

Possible solution: Whenever possible, use the LOGIN command in login scripts instead of ATTACH.

THE PROBLEM: Users cannot load NETBIOS applications.

NetWare version: Any.

Why it happens: The number of users authorized to use NETBIOS applications exceeds the number of names supported by NETBIOS.

Possible solution: Check the revision of NETBIOS that you are using and update to a version that supports the number you need. Although NETBIOS originally allowed only sixteen names to be used in a Local Name Table,

Revision C can accommodate up to twenty-six users. The size of the local name table is expected to be user-configurable in future versions of NETBIOS.

THE PROBLEM: Users cannot copy files larger than 1K from their workstation to the file server.

NetWare version: NetWare 386, version 3.01 Rev B shell.

When it happens: On workstations using token 16/4 boards with the 3.1 token-ring drivers.

Why it happens: The problem is in the size of the data packets that the boards use. The 16/4 board uses a 4K data packet.

Possible solution: You can work around the problem by specifying the size of the data packet in the IPX as 2K.

Example:

```
A>   IPX o,tbz=2000
```

THE PROBLEM: Users who format floppy disks (FORMAT A:) report that the system does not take them back to the drive and directory they were formatting from when they press N to answer they do not want to format another disk. Instead they get a message that says "Insert disk with COMMAND.COM in drive A".

NetWare version: Any.

Possible solution: This happens on workstations using the older NET4.COM files to load the network shells. The 3.01 revision A NET4.COM will work correctly.

THE PROBLEM: IBM PS/2 machines do not work with IBM Token-Ring cards.

NetWare version: Any.

Why it happens: Because of conflicting RAM addresses. The default RAM address on the IBM SCSI adapter in the PS/2 machines is d800h, the same as the factory address for most of the Primary options on the Token-Ring card.

Possible solution: Change the address on either the adapter or the cards to avoid conflicts. Option 8 (CC00h) is the only Primary Token-Ring option that won't conflict with the IBM SCSI. Option 4 (DC00h) is the only Alternate Token-Ring option that won't conflict with the IBM SCSI.

THE PROBLEM: Token-ring workstations can't find the file server when they attempt to login.

NetWare version: Advanced NetWare 286, version 2.12 or version 2.14A.

When it happens: When workstations use the 2.21 or 2.50 Token-Ring drivers.

Why it happens: The drivers apparently interfere with the ability of the shells in versions 2.15 and 3.01 to find a file server when the IBM Token-Ring Adapter 16/4 is set for an 8KB RAM Size and Address Range.

Possible solution: The workstations will locate and attach to the server if the adapter is set to the normal 16KB RAM Size and Address Range.

THE PROBLEM: Users who edit files with EDLIN don't see the changes when they TYPE the file from the command prompt.

NetWare version: NetWare Entry Level System I, version 2.0A.

When it happens: After saving the new file.

Why it happens: EDLIN creates a backup copy whenever you change a file. If this file is flagged with SRO rights, EDLIN will not update your file. Instead, it writes the changes to a file called FILENAME.$$$.

Possible solution: Flag your files SRW before modifying them by using EDLIN.

THE PROBLEM: NetWare returns a File Creation Error message when batch files are run.

NetWare version: Any.

When it happens: This occurs on workstations using the NetWare 2.15C shells with DOS 3.3 if the batch files contain recursive nul operators.

Why it happens: The shell cannot handle nul operators correctly and will execute files, such as the following, only once or twice before returning the error message.

```
@echo off
set > nul
dir > nul
ver > nul
TEST
```

Possible solution: Use the 3.01 shells. They handle nul operators correctly.

THE PROBLEM: A "Bad command or file name" error message appears when workstation shells are generated.

NetWare version: NetWare Entry Level System I, version 2.12.

When it happens: On workstations running DOS 3.1x or 3.2x.

Why it happens: Only DOS 3.3 and above support the @ symbol. Novell's SHELL.BAT file uses the @ symbol to suppress the echo of the error message statement (which is a bug) when it calls the SHGEN command to generate the shells.

Possible solution: Edit the @ command out of the batch file or execute SHGEN from the DOS prompt.

THE PROBLEM: Menus don't appear on the workstation.

NetWare version: Advanced NetWare version 2.15, revision C shells.

When it happens: This occurs during login. Users are unable to login properly.

Why it happens: The shells are sensitive to the syntax used on the login. The following login, for instance, executes properly only if a user is a member of the MENU_USERS group. For all others, it just executes the INCLUDE statement.

```
IF MEMBER OF "MENU_USERS" THEN BEGIN
MAP F:=SYS:MAIL\%USER_ID
INCLUDE F:LOGIN
#MENUGEN
EXIT "MENU %LOGIN_NAME"
END
```

Possible solution: Replace the login with one that contains a MAP statement in the opening line. Such a login should execute properly for everyone. In the example above, a correct login would read:

```
MAP F:=SYS:MAIL\%USER_ID
IF MEMBER OF "MENU_USERS" THEN INCLUDE F:LOGIN
IF MEMBER OF "MENU_USERS" THEN BEGIN
#MENUGEN
EXIT "MENU %LOGIN_NAME"
END
```

THE PROBLEM: The network will not accept passwords or other keyboard input from the workstation.

NetWare version: NetWare version 3.0.

When it happens: When logging in from Compaq workstations: Deskpro models 386s, 386/20e, 386/20, 386/25e, 386/25, 386/33, 486/25, and the Systempro. It happens when SERVER.EXE is called from the AUTOEXEC.BAT on the workstation's drive C.

Why it happens: Compaq's Power-On Password and Network Server Mode features allow the PCs to boot from a hard disk but will not accept input from the keyboard until the password is entered. However, NetWare takes control of the keyboard before the password is entered; thus it becomes impossible for the user to enter the password or anything else from the keyboard. This effectively immobilizes the workstation.

Possible solution: Disable the keyboard and use either the key switch on the PC or the Console Lock in Monitor.NLM.

THE PROBLEM: Users who try to copy files larger than the disk space allocated to them are not only unable to copy the files, afterward they are told they have 0 bytes free when they do a DIR listing.

NetWare version: Advanced NetWare, version 2.1.

When it happens: On systems using the Disk Limitation Feature.

Why it happens: This is a bug in that version. The NCOPY utility looks for available space in the allocated limit before copying the file and returns the error message if it doesn't find enough. Until files are purged, the operating system shows space being consumed by deleted files just as if these incomplete files have not been deleted.

Possible solution: Users may still copy files that are smaller than the allocated limit. The only way to get a correct directory listing is to do a PURGE. Otherwise, ignore it.

THE PROBLEM: Is there any way to avoid doing a user-by-user file transfer with PRINTCON to copy one user's configuration files for use by others in the group?

NetWare version: Any.

When it happens: During installation and setup.

Possible solution: The utility GMCOPY.ZIP, available on NetWire Library 17, works with all versions of NetWare. It allows the user SUPERVISOR to copy print job configurations, personal login scripts, or other configuration files from a source user's mail directory to all users or specified users from a user list (on the default server).

THE PROBLEM: When mapping a search drive in a LOGIN script, the following line returns an 8998 error:

```
map s3:=*1:
```

NetWare version: NetWare 386, versions 3.0 and 3.1.

When it happens: During login.

Why it happens: The problem generally stems from the syntax being used.

Possible solution: Place a period at the end of the MAP command. The line in the example above should work if it is written:

```
map s3:=*1:.
```

THE PROBLEM: When one user works on a large file, the pending input/output causes other workstations to hang.

NetWare version: Any.

Why it happens: Any file cache size other than 4096 will cause this to happen.

Possible solution: To find out what the cache size is, run FCONSOLE and select Cache Statistics from the Statistics menu. This will show the current file cache size setting. To change the cache size to 4096, run DISKED and enter the following:

```
>r 15            { Read in sector 15     }
>c 0159          { Change location 0159 }
01F9 00->03      { from 00 to 03          }
01FA 34->.       { Exit Change function }
>w 15            { Write out sector 15   }
>q               { Quit                   }
```

Reboot the system and check the cache size in FCONSOLE again. It should now say 4096.

THE PROBLEM: Workstation performance decreases when expanded or extended memory is installed.

NetWare version: Any.

When it happens: When the Preferred Server Option in SHELL.CFG is used with 3.01 EMS and XMS shells.

Possible solution: Discontinue using the Preferred Server option or use the version 3.01 NET3 shell file instead of EMSNET or XMSNET.

Problems at the Printer

THE PROBLEM: Print jobs disappear from the print queues.

NetWare version: Any.

When it happens: At the time of printing. Users don't receive their print jobs after sending them from their applications.

Why it happens: Faulty printer hardware can cause this. So can loose connections.

Possible solution: Make sure the printer pinouts are correct and check to see if sheet feeders and hardware switches between the printer and printer port are correctly fitted and installed.

On a serial com port connection, the following pin settings should work with RPRINTER:

PC pin 2 to printer pin 3
PC pin 3 to printer pin 2
PC pin 4 to printer pin 5
PC pin 5 to printer pin 20
PC pin 6 to printer pin 4
PC pin 7 to printer pin 7
PC pin 8 jumpered on printer pin 4

Also be sure that the data terminal is ready (DTR) and that XOFF/XON is set to ON in PCONSOLE.

THE PROBLEM: Jobs sent to the printer are not printed even though RPRINTER shows that the printer is printing. Sometimes the print jobs do come out, but it takes an hour or more to get a single page.

NetWare version: Any.

When it happens: When users send print jobs from XT or 286 workstations.

Why it happens: For RPRINTER to work properly, the COM or LPT ports must be hardware-driven instead of poll-driven. Most PC or XT COM and LPT ports are poll-driven. And because DOS does the polling, RPRINTER will think the job is printing even though the printer will not work.

Possible solution: Replace PC and XT ports with hardware IRQ ports.

THE PROBLEM: NetWare version 2.1 won't support downloadable fonts.

NetWare version: NetWare version 2.1.

Why it happens: The problem is usually related to the way in which the fonts are sent to the printer.

Possible solution: You'll get full support from version 2.1's PRINTDEF and PRINTCON functions if downloadable fonts send control codes to the printer that let you define or download the font you want. However, if the application takes total control of the printer with a page language such as PostScript, you'll have to use third-party software. NetWare version 2.1 can't print PostScript-generated documents.

THE PROBLEM: PCONSOLE cannot find the server when used with a LaserWriter on an AppleTalk network.

NetWare version: Any.

When it happens: When print queues were created with MACSETUP.

Possible solution: PCONSOLE should be used only to view the jobs in Macintosh queues. Use MACSETUP for all other functions. Be sure you use the correct printer name when using MACSETUP and be sure you covered all options in the Install/Configure print services part of MACSETUP. Use the QLIST and PLIST Console commands to get information on the Mac printers and queues.

THE PROBLEM: Entire print queues disappear from the system.

NetWare version: Any.

When it happens: When users print from WordPerfect.

Possible solution: Users who are capturing print jobs directly from Word-Perfect should print instead to the LPT port and use CAPTURE to control printing to the network.

THE PROBLEM: PSERVER was not included in the NetWare software.
NetWare version: NetWare Entry Level System, versions I and II.
Possible solution: PSERVER is bundled with Advanced and SFT NetWare
286 as well as NetWare 386 but not with the Entry Level System. It is, however,
available to ELS clients as an option.

THE PROBLEM: Is there any way to avoid downing the file server and
unloading PSERVER to make changes in PCONSOLE?
NetWare version: NetWare 286.
When it happens: When making changes in PCONSOLE.
Possible solution: The file server needn't be taken down if you use the
PSERVER VAP and first run PSERVER STOP before making the change.
After running PSERVER STOP, make the change and run PSERVER START
to reactivate the printer server. This solution will unload PSERVER and will
not interfere with the VAP as the change is made. You could also use
PSERVER.EXE to down the print server from within PCONSOLE. If you use
this method, type PSERVER, then select:

```
Print Server
Printer Server Status/Control
Server Information
Printer Server Information/Status
Down
```

This will logout the print server. You can make your changes and log the
print server back on by running PSERVER.EXE.

THE PROBLEM: Users cannot print. RPRINTER returns an Error 776
when run from the batch file that loads it.
NetWare version: Any.
When it happens: RPRINTER returns this error when a printer connection
is not free at the print server. It happens most often when a workstation with
RPRINTER loaded has been rebooted; the SPX connection has not timed out
to let RPRINTER reattach so that other users may send jobs to the printer.
Possible solution: An alternative is to use the following batch file to load
RPRINTER:

```
Echo off
:loop
rprinter printserver printer#
if errorlevel 1 goto :loop
Echo Rprinter loaded Successfully !!!
```

Problems at the File Server

THE PROBLEM: COMPSURF does not work.

NetWare version: NetWare Entry Level Systems I and II, Advanced NetWare, and Advanced NetWare SFT.

When it happens: When doing a low-level format on ESDI drives.

Why it happens: COMPSURF will not do a low-level format on ESDI drives in versions of ELS, Advanced, or SFT NetWare or in the Install NLM for NetWare 386.

Possible solution: Use other format programs such as those found on the IBM Advanced Diagnostics disk for ISA bus computers or the reference disk for PS/2s.

THE PROBLEM: A system login script that works in a NetWare 386 environment hangs in a 286 environment.

NetWare version: NetWare 286.

When it happens: This happens when the system login script includes the following command:

```
< set path = ";;" >.
```

Possible solution: Avoid hanging the workstation by using the ATTACH command to attach to the 286 server, then change directories to the PUBLIC directory and run SYSCON. Call up the login script and remove the < set path = ";;" > statement.

THE PROBLEM: Novell's menus cause problems at the workstations. They don't support search mappings and won't release memory or allow batch file logouts.

NetWare version: Any.

Possible solution: There are several versions of Novell menus. None support all of the functions, but version 1.02a and the 1.22/1.23 combination (when using MENU.EXE version 1.23 and MENUPARZ.EXE version 1.22) solve all but one. Use the following chart to see which functions are supported in which menu version.

MENU VERSION

	1.02a	1.22	1.23	1.22/1.23 [*]
Release Memory	Yes	NO	Yes	Yes
Batch File Logout	Yes	NO	NO	NO

(continued)

MENU VERSION

	1.02a	1.22	1.23	1.22/1.23 *
!LOGOUT	Yes	Yes	NO	Yes
Search Mappings from MENU	NO	Yes	Yes	Yes
Search Mappings from Batch file	NO	Yes	Yes	Yes

THE PROBLEM: How to install the IBM Enhanced 386 memory board expansion option in the file server.

NetWare version: NetWare 286.

Possible solution: The 2MB Kit j—PN 34F3077, FC 3077, and the 4MB Kit—PN 34F3011, FC 3011, will both support the IBM Enhanced 80386 Memory Expansion Option in a NetWare 286 server.

Use the device driver (DOSMEMDD.SYS) on the Option Diskette to initialize the Enhanced 80386 Memory Expansion Option. To do this, NetWare 286 must be run as a nondedicated server and the driver must be copied to the DOS partition and identified in the CONFIG.SYS file.

Now delete the INITPROG statement from the @FDDF.ADF file on the Reference Diskette. This is very important; if you don't delete the INITPROG statement, the boot record on drive C will be destroyed when SET CONFIG-URATION is executed.

Boot the system from the Option Diskette. A screen will appear that instructs you to insert the Operating System Diskette in drive A and press any key to continue. Remove the Option Diskette from the A drive. Press any key and the system will boot NetWare 286 from drive C.

Novell NetWare 386, unlike 286, is fully compatible with the IBM Enhanced 386 Memory Expansion Options and does not require any of these work-arounds.

THE PROBLEM: Reducing the number of directory entries on the file server causes the loss of data.

NetWare version: NetWare 286.

When it happens: Files vanish when you bring a file server back up after downing it to reduce the number of directory entries.

Why it happens: Because NetWare fills directory entries sequentially, you leave holes in the table when you remove some entries. The problem occurs if a volume has ever had more than the maximum number of directory entries defined in NETGEN. This includes files, directories, and trustee privileges.

NETGEN simply truncates the directory blocks at the end of the table; it does not check to see if they are in use.

Possible solution: VREPAIR can generally restore the files to the root, but it restores them with names such as VF000000.000, so you will have to examine and rename the files accordingly. It may be easier to restore the files from a backup tape.

THE PROBLEM: NetWare ignores the backslash when you use the DOS SET command in the login script.

NetWare version: NetWare version 2.1.

When it happens: During login.

Why it happens: A bug in the version.

Possible solution: This version of NetWare will ignore the backslash (\) when using the DOS SET command. In the following command:

```
DOS SET TEXTWARE="HART\SYS:TEXTWARE"
```

login will ignore the backslash and set your variable to:

```
HARTSYS:TEXTWARE
```

You can correct this problem by using the forward slash (/) instead. In this case, the following would work:

```
DOS SET TEXTWARE="HART/SYS:TEXTWARE"
```

THE PROBLEM: PSERVER and other NLMs return messages about not releasing resources in small memory and in large memory when they terminate.

NetWare version: NetWare 386.

When it happens: When NLMs are terminated.

Why it happens: This is a cosmetic bug.

Possible solution: This isn't really a problem. The resources are still available. If an NLM doesn't release resources, NetWare can recover them automatically through the operating system.

THE PROBLEM: Users can't run applications that require point-to-point communications.

NetWare version: Any.

When it happens: When the application is loaded.

Why it happens: Either NETBIOS or the OS/2 Communication Manager may be using the wrong files. The files required by communication manager, named NETOEM.DLL and NETAPI.DLL, are in the MUGLIB/DLL subdirectory. NETBIOS uses different files but they are found under the same name in the NetWare directory. Novell's NETBIOS requires the NetWare files. Communication Manager requires the MUGLIB files.

Possible solution: If your network runs NETBIOS, make sure the NetWare directory comes first in the Libpath statement. If you run Communication Manager, make sure you list the MUGLIB directory first.

THE PROBLEM: Users reveal hidden files when they use the FLAG command.

NetWare version: NetWare 386.

When it happens: When users invoke wildcards with the flag command, as in

```
FLAG *.* Normal
```

Why it happens: Only NetWare 286 version 2.15c or below allows you to change four of the eight options (Shareable, Read Only, Indexed, and Transactional) with the FLAG command. Beginning with NetWare 386 version 3.0 and up, users can change all of the attributes with FLAG. And persons who have modify rights can change all of the attriutes on the NetWare 286 server if they use the NetWare 386 flag command with NetWare 286.

Possible solution: You can control users' ability to use the FLAG command through their trustee assignments.

THE PROBLEM: The new Token-Ring TRN050 cards do not coexist well with the old drivers. File servers and workstations will lock up, and file servers can disappear on the network. IBM and Novell bridges also cannot coexist.

NetWare version: Any.

When it happens: When expanding and upgrading installations.

Why it happens: You cannot run both types of bridges with source routing; you must run either one or the other.

Possible solution: To avoid having to change over all cards at once, something that is almost impossible in a large network, you could update one ring at a time. The rings must be separated by Novell bridges, and the whole ring must use the new drivers. If the rings are connected by IBM bridges, do not run source routing and do not filter out IPX packets. Novell representatives can help you regenerate NetWare 286 software without downing the server and copy NET$OS to the system directory so that the next time you boot, the new drivers will be there.

THE PROBLEM: How to do a custom installation of Entry Level System I, version 2.12.

Possible solution: To use the custom options, you must first install the system by default. After the default installation is complete, type INSTALL -M at the

DOS prompt. The default printer port will be COM1. If COM1 does not exist, spool to LPT1 as printer 0.

THE PROBLEM: The server, an EISA-style 486 machine, asks that you verify the slot that the network adapter card is in each time it comes up.

NetWare version: NetWare 386, version 3.0.

When it happens: When the server comes up.

Why it happens: The operating system cannot find the adaptor card.

Possible solution: Try calling the file AUTOEXEC.NCF into your word processor and add a line that says:

```
slot=
```

along with the slot number. This is the same procedure that the documentation says can be used only in IBM MCA machines. However, it's been used successfully on a number of EISA machines as well.

THE PROBLEM: The operating system returns the following error message on the file server:

```
Problem with drive 00.
Error reading disk redirection information.
Error reading NetWare configuration information.
```

NetWare version: NetWare Entry Level System II, version 2.15.

When it happens: When a nondedicated file server is booted.

Why it happens: This occurs on older machines with BIOSs that are dated. Early BIOSs can typically support dedicated network operations but cannot deal with disk redirection in a nondedicated system.

Possible solution: The newer BIOSs will support nondedicated mode. Update the BIOS in the server, and the nondedicated network should work fine. It's a good idea to update the BIOSs in all PCs on the network as well. This will assure optimum performance and feature support.

THE PROBLEM: A user corrupted the fake root the system manager created.

NetWare version: Some versions of the 3.01 shells.

When it happens: When someone remaps directories to see the contents of the volume. For example, the command:

```
MAP ROOT G:=SYS:THIS/THAT
```

creates a fake root directory in the subdirectory, THAT. Now if you enter:

```
DIR SYS:
```

you'll see the contents of SYS: listed onscreen. But if you type:

```
MAP G:
```

SYS: is returned and the fake root to THIS/THAT is gone.
Why it happens: This is due to a function in the NET3 file.
Possible solution: For security reasons, users should not be assigned rights at the root directory. Users should not be able to do a DIR.

THE PROBLEM: The SYS: volume is slow to mount.
NetWare version: Any.
When it happens: When users login.
Why it happens: Deleted files have probably been building up in the directory.
Possible solution: You need to purge the deleted files. Login as supervisor and run the following commands from the root directory:

```
CHKVOL
```

This will show the space in use by deleted files.

```
PURGE ALL
```

This will purge all deleted files in the system.

```
CHKVOL
```

Compare the report to what you saw the first time you ran the command and you'll see how much space was freed. This should speed the volume mount.

THE PROBLEM: The upgraded NetWare 386 network will not accept old NLMs.
NetWare version: NetWare 386, version 3.1.
When it happens: When loading a version 3.0 INSTALL.MLM. The network returns the following errors:

```
Loader cannot find public symbol:  DosClose
Loader cannot find public symbol:  SaveMirrorList
Loader cannot find ................
      Many other similar errors occur
      referencing different public symbols
Load file referenced undefined public variable.
Module INSTALL.NLM not loaded.
```

Why it happens: The load will load off the mounted SYS: volume unless told to load from the DOS side. These errors occur if you try to load version 3.0

NLMS with a version 3.1 SERVER running or if you load the old SERVER.EXE when you try to do the upgrade.

Possible solution: Use the new SERVER.EXE file or load the NLMs before running SERVER.

THE PROBLEM: Users are mysteriously disconnected from the token-ring network and a beaconing error message appears on the file server.

NetWare version: Any.

When it happens: Anytime there is traffic on the network.

Why it happens: The following message appears on the file server when one workstation does not receive the token from its upstream neighbor:

```
Token ring status beaconing. Status=520 (or 420)
Alert condition has been corrected.
```

After a given period of time, the waiting workstation sends a "beacon packet." The first line of the error message appears on the screen of the server, or active monitor on the ring. The active monitor sees which workstation does not respond to the beacon, assumes it has a problem, and disconnects it to allow continued network activity.

Possible solution: You'll need to find the bad element. It may be a bad card in a workstation or a problem in the cable or in a MAU port.

THE PROBLEM: How to avoid loading Btrieve when upgrading from NetWare 386 version 3.0 to version 3.1.

NetWare version: NetWare 386.

Possible solution: The Btrieve disk is the last disk that you're prompted for when you upgrade the system. Just abort the installation after the print services and utilities disks are installed.

THE PROBLEM: File servers do not update their routing tables and workstations will not connect.

NetWare version: Any.

When it happens: This occurs as you update drivers on token-ring networks, when both old and new drivers are in use.

Why it happens: Old token-ring source routing drivers do not recognize data packets that lack RI fields. But the new drivers will not put in an RI field if the destination of the packet is on the same ring. Nodes (file servers, bridges, workstations, and so on) that have the old source routing drivers installed will not receive the field necessary to make appropriate connections.

Possible solution: Rings that are separated by IBM bridges can update one ring as long as you update every node on the ring at the same time. The process is more difficult if the rings are separated by Novell routers, because neither NETGEN nor BRGEN lets you mix old and new drivers. If you are using Novell routers, you should use the Novell nonoptimizing routers. That are available on CompuServe's NetWire in the private area named TEMPRT.ZIP.

THE PROBLEM: Plotters do not work well with PSERVER.

NetWare version: Any version earlier than NetWare 386, version 3.1.

When it happens: Plotters go off-line when a file is sent to them.

Why it happens: This apparently was due to a bug in earlier versions of NetWare.

Possible solution: The newest PSERVER printing files, those that ship with NetWare 386 version 3.1, should correct the problem.

THE PROBLEM: Finding a version of the DOS utilities that will work in the OS/2 version 1.2 DOS box.

NetWare version: Any.

Why it happens: The list of supported utilities in the NetWare Requester for OS/2 version 1.2 manual erroneously includes MENU, which is *not* supported.

Possible solution: The following utilities should work:

Name	Length	Method	Size	Ratio	Date	Time
ALLOW.EXE	20859	Implode	12896	39%	08-15-89	14:55
ATOTAL.EXE	18941	Implode	11957	37%	07-28-89	10:57
ATTACH.EXE	36885	Implode	19940	46%	05-10-90	11:10
CASTOFF.EXE	12633	Implode	8041	37%	07-20-89	14:11
CASTON.EXE	8209	Implode	5513	33%	07-18-89	11:14
CHKDIR.EXE	18053	Implode	11327	38%	07-18-89	11:15
CHKVOL.EXE	49407	Implode	28109	44%	07-20-89	15:02
CMPQ$RUN.OVL	2400	Implode	1327	45%	07-26-89	22:26
DSPACE.EXE	196585	Implode	96199	52%	04-27-90	09:02
DSPACE.HLP	5575	Implode	1900	66%	05-29-90	10:54
FILER.EXE	270781	Implode	141299	48%	05-11-90	16:23
FILER.HLP	65519	Implode	17678	74%	08-09-89	16:41
FLAG.EXE	29837	Implode	17327	42%	05-30-90	11:24
FLAGDIR.EXE	27093	Implode	16792	39%	03-23-90	11:06
GRANT.EXE	33369	Implode	19851	41%	03-27-90	16:04
IBM$RUN.OVL	2400	Implode	1357	44%	07-13-89	09:30
LISTDIR.EXE	26389	Implode	15628	41%	05-29-90	09:29
LOGIN.EXE	96171	Implode	51474	47%	05-29-90	13:52

(continued)

Name	Length	Method	Size	Ratio	Date	Time
LOGOUT.EXE	29255	Implode	18103	39%	05-31-90	08:16
MAKEUSER.EXE	133595	Implode	75799	44%	05-14-90	10:46
MAKEUSER.HLP	1845	Implode	884	53%	05-31-90	11:49
MAP.EXE	47463	Implode	28633	40%	04-26-90	15:56
NCOPY.EXE	56189	Implode	28970	49%	06-22-90	11:19
PAUDIT.EXE	27255	Implode	15624	43%	07-18-89	11:41
REMOVE.EXE	32333	Implode	19647	40%	05-31-90	12:21
RENDIR.EXE	20185	Implode	12186	40%	02-02-90	11:05
REVOKE.EXE	34621	Implode	20488	41%	02-06-90	14:20
RIGHTS.EXE	18761	Implode	11308	40%	04-25-90	10:46
SALVAGE.EXE	129787	Implode	73357	44%	05-02-90	19:05
SALVAGE.HLP	7053	Implode	2372	67%	08-17-89	12:37
SECURITY.EXE	22385	Implode	13572	40%	08-03-89	08:33
SEND.EXE	21109	Implode	12985	39%	03-01-90	15:25
SETPASS.EXE	31935	Implode	17149	47%	05-24-90	16:48
SETTTS.EXE	16855	Implode	10537	38%	05-18-90	08:41
SLIST.EXE	25143	Implode	16443	35%	05-10-90	11:11
SMODE.EXE	27573	Implode	15779	43%	06-06-90	12:27
SYS$ERR.DAT	6489	Implode	2961	55%	07-29-87	09:57
SYS$HELP.DAT	17343	Implode	4647	74%	08-11-87	10:06
SYS$MSG.DAT	22298	Implode	7412	67%	12-22-87	08:42
SYSCON.EXE	270103	Implode	148168	46%	05-29-90	13:23
SYSCON.HLP	142570	Implode	36687	75%	06-03-90	13:42
SYSTIME.EXE	16225	Implode	11112	32%	04-30-90	12:21
TLIST.EXE	29799	Implode	19061	37%	05-29-90	15:55
USERDEF.EXE	173837	Implode	88902	49%	04-27-90	14:21
USERDEF.HLP	24718	Implode	7242	71%	06-04-90	11:13
USERLIST.EXE	25413	Implode	16605	35%	07-18-89	12:00
VERSION.EXE	21551	Implode	14193	35%	03-28-90	10:09
VOLINFO.EXE	142235	Implode	71290	50%	04-26-90	15:39
VOLINFO.HLP	7442	Implode	2748	64%	05-29-90	14:11
WHOAMI.EXE	25723	Implode	15505	40%	05-18-90	11:05
50 files	2530194		1318984	48%		

THE PROBLEM: Finding NetWare-ready drives to use on the network.
Possible solution: Here's the list of NetWare-ready drives that support the NetWare Ready option in DISKSET for both versions. These should be used with the drive's DCBs (ADIC/Novell or Novell).

Drive	Model	Vendor
Wren III	155	ADIC
Wren IV	376	ADIC, Seagate
Wren VI	766	ADIC, Seagate
Wren VII		ADIC, Seagate
Micropolis	1674	ADIC
Micropolis	1578	ADIC

Note, too, that all NetWare-ready drives bear a red sticker that says "NETWARE READY", but not all vendors automatically include the DISKCHECKER utility with the drive. If you want NetWare-ready drives that include the utility, you should specify this in your order.

THE PROBLEM: The network runs out of dynamic memory, slows down, and eventually stops when users are using Windows applications installed on the file server.

NetWare version: NetWare 286, version 2.1.

When it happens: This occurs when many users run Windows 3.0 applications simultaneously from the network drives.

Why it happens: As more users load Windows from a network drive, memory consumption is increased.

Possible solution: Install and run Windows 3.0 applications from the local drives of workstations with sufficient hard disk space. For all others, add the following lines to the SYS.INI file file. Type them exactly as they appear here. The instructions are case sensitive:

```
[NETWARE]
NWShareHandles=True
```

THE PROBLEM: How do I install generic SCSI drives?

NetWare version: NetWare 286 and 386.

Possible solution: If you know how to set up SCSI drives, they shoud be easy to install using the DCB Generic SCSI Option. WREN drives will normally default to the correct settings. These are the ones you should use:

- No parity.
- Terminating power comes from the last drive in the chain, not the DCB.
- The drive should spin up when power comes on.
- The drive should not make synchronous transfer requests to the DCB.

If you are using large drives with NetWare 386, version 3.0, you should download and install the DCB driver that you'll find in CompuServe's NetWire file 386DCB.ZIP.

THE PROBLEM: Performance on the network drops as NetWare-loadable modules are added.

NetWare version: NetWare 386.

When it happens: The network will slow down as NLMs are added. How much it slows depends on the size of hard disks and the amount of memory on the file server. Performance degradation is most noticeable on file servers with limited available memory and disk capacity.

Possible solution: Upgrade the hardware.

THE PROBLEM: The network will not load DRVRDATA.DAT in NETGEN and returns an error code of -1.

NetWare version: NetWare 286, using shells higher than 2.15C.

When it happens: When generating the operating system. This error occurs in NETGEN when using a shell newer than version 2.15C. It occurs only if the system being generated is version 2.15a or older and the DRVRDATA.DAT file does not exist on the SUPPORT directory. You will see the error after choosing the option "Save Selections and Continue".

Why it happens: The return code in the shell is being interpreted incorrectly.

Possible solution: Look for the DRVRDATA.DAT file in the SUPPORT directory. If the file is there, it is probably corrupted. In that case, rename it as well as the backup file DRVRDATA.BAK, if one exists. Once you have renamed the file, or if the file is not there, use COPY.CON to create a new file. Now perform a NETGEN -N. (You must use the -N option or NETGEN will try to read DRVRDATA.DAT.)

Now a valid DRVRDATA.DAT will exist and the problem should no longer occur. Another solution is to use the version 2.15a shell, which does not return an error code when it tries to open the nonexistent file.

THE PROBLEM: The server crashes or hangs.

NetWare version: Any.

When it happens: On EtherNet networks in multiprotocol environments. Either there are various TCP and XNS packets from other systems on the same backbone, or there are 3C503 cards in workstations. This problem appears to be caused by various rogue packets being sucked into the servers.

Possible solution: Some LAN drivers are better at rejecting bad packets than others, but it's not really known which drivers are the best. In an environment of TCP and XNS protocol packets, there are two solutions. In some instances the problem can be corrected by replacing NP600s by NE2000s. You could also configure all server and bridge drivers on the backbone side to run on EtherNet II. The drivers will then reject all packets without the correct type number for NetWare. This may also speed up server performance, because the server will spend less time trying to figure out whether any given packet is meant for it.

If you have the 3C503 cards, try using the ODI workstation drivers shipped with version 3.1. This seems to help solve the problem on the backbone.

THE PROBLEM: Two MENU.EXE programs are currently being shipped with NetWare. Which is best?

NetWare version: Any.

Possible solution: These programs are updates that fix problems users reported in previous versions. There's no need to install either if you're not having problems with the older versions.

As with previous versions of MENU.EXE, no one version will satisfy all users. Certain features are mutually exclusive and cannot be provided in the same version.

Novell Menu System version 1.23 releases memory and successfully creates search mappings when made by a menu or batch file called from a menu. It does not use the !LOGOUT command and will not work correctly when called from a batch file. Novell Menu System version 1.02a successfully releases memory and creates search mappings made by a menu. Unlike version 1.23, it does not create search mappings made by a batch file called from Menu. When called from a batch file, NetWare 286 reports "Batchfile missing". NetWare 386 reports "Access Denied-X:\Path\Filename". In this version, the !LOGOUT command functions correctly only when MENU.EXE is not called from batch file.

THE PROBLEM: Users can't login. At the same time, "Fatal Dir Error" messages show up on the file server screen.

NetWare version: Any.

When it happens: As drives near their capacity.

Why it happens: As large SCSI drives near their capacity, users can't login unless the server is rebooted. Some large SCSI drives vary in the number of cylinders and heads that are actually on the drive. Therefore, drive types may not correctly match what is defined in the drive setup. When NetWare reaches the end of the drive, it cannot access sectors that are defined in the drive setup but are not actually there. This occurs most often when you mix and match controllers and drives.

Possible solution: You can avoid this by buying controllers and drives from the same manufacturer.

You can also get the correct drive-type information from the drive manufacturer and install it. Or you can back up the drive, reinitialize it, and define a smaller NetWare partition so that NetWare will not attempt to access sectors beyond the drive's maximum limit.

THE PROBLEM: The INSTALL disk does not include the CONSOLE.-COM file.

NetWare version: NetWare Entry Level System I, version 2.12.

Possible solution: The documentation in ELS I says to install CONSOLE.COM from the Install disk but, if you're using the 5 1/4-inch installation disks, you actually find CONSOLE.COM on the PUBLIC-3 disk. Look for it there.

THE PROBLEM: How to avoid downing the file server and unloading PSERVER to make changes in PCONSOLE.

NetWare version: NetWare 286.

When it happens: When making changes in PCONSOLE.

Why it happens: The file server needn't be taken down if you use the PSERVER VAP and first run PSERVER STOP before making the change.

Possible solution: After running PSERVER STOP, make the change and run PSERVER START to reactivate the printer server. This solution will unload PSERVER and will not interfere with the VAP as the change is made. You could also use PSERVER.EXE to down the print server from within PCONSOLE. If you use this method, type PSERVER, then select:

```
Print Server
Printer Server Status/Control
Server Information
Printer Server Information/Status
Down
```

This will logout the print server. You can make your changes and log the print server back on by running PSERVER.EXE.

THE PROBLEM: Compaq SystemPro file servers do not deliver the performance increase advertised.

NetWare version: NetWare 386.

When it happens: The performance differential is most noticeable when there is heavy traffic on the network.

Why it happens: This occurs if you are using the wrong disk driver. The SystemPro will work with the standard ISADISK.DSK driver but will not perform as well as if Compaq's own driver is used.

Possible solutions: Change drivers. The driver you need is CPQDA386.DSK. It is on the User Programs diskette that is shipped with the SystemPro.

THE PROBLEM: The Novell NE2000 and NE1000 EtherNet boards, which work fine in Compaq DeskPro servers, won't work at all in the SystemPros.

NetWare version: Any.

Why it happens: Although these EtherNet boards are not EISA boards, the SystemPros must think they are to resolve this problem.

Possible solutions: Copy the NE2000 configuration file from the SystemPro library. Indicate which slot the board is installed in and which I/O port and interrupt it uses. The NE2000 file will work whether you're installing an NE2000 board or an NE1000 board.

THE PROBLEM: The operating system refuses to address all of the memory on a Compaq SystemPro file server.

NetWare version: NetWare 386, version 3.0.

When it happens: When you boot the file server.

Why it happens: This version of NetWare 386 requires that you run the TSR utility CPQ16MB.EXE to recognize the 32M of RAM on the SystemPro.

Possible solution: The utility that allows version 3.0 to address more than 16M of RAM is available from Compaq.

THE PROBLEM: Garbage and error messages appear on screen when you cold boot the file server.

NetWare version: NetWare 286.

When it happens: When NetWare tries to read the Hot Fix redirection table during a reinstallation on systems using hard drives with more than 1024 cylinders.

Why it happens: Some sectors of the NET$OS.EXE file are written to cylinders higher than 1024.

Possible solution: To avoid the problem, back up the system and use DOS 4.0 to install a bootable DOS partition. You can copy the .EXE file to C: and use an AUTOEXEC.BAT to boot NetWare.

THE PROBLEM: Garbage characters show up in the volume names.

NetWare version: NetWare 286, version 2.15.

When it happens: When you run value-added processes.

Why it happens: A bug.

Possible solution: Before running any VAPs on the file server, install files in the VAPVOL.ZIP file, which is available in NetWire's Library 16. The patch not only fixes the problem of volume names getting corrupted, it should fix other VAP problems as well.

THE PROBLEM: The controllers in PS/2 file servers can't duplex.
NetWare version: Any.
Why it happens: The controllers cannot share interrupts. This is true when duplexing MFM eith ESDI, MFM with MFM, or ESDI with ESDI.
Possible solution: Change controllers. An IBM SCSI controller can be duplexed with another IBM SCSI controller.

THE PROBLEM: How to interpret the Track On information at the file server console. What do the "IN Get nearest server" and "OUT Give nearest server" mean?
NetWare version: Any.
When it happens: When performing diagnostics on the file server.
Why it happens: Track On is a diagnostic feature that helps determine if a workstation and file server are communicating.
Possible solution: If, when a workstation is not connecting after it loads the shell and requests a connection from the file server, the file server console displays these messages:

```
IN Get nearest server
OUT Give nearest server
```

this indicates a hardware or shell problem at the workstation. If the console displays only:

```
IN Get nearest server
```

it means the file is unable to respond to the request. The problem could be noisy lines caused by faulty network hardware. If the file server shows neither

```
IN Get nearest server
```

nor

```
OUT Give nearest server
```

it means the file server cannot see the workstation. This may be due to problems with the file server hardware, the shells being used, or noise in the hardware.

THE PROBLEM: IBM PS/2 machines will not work with IBM Token-Ring cards.
NetWare version: Any.

Why it happens: The default RAM address on the IBM SCSI adapter is d800h, the same as the factory address for most of the Primary options on the Token-Ring card.

Possible solution: You'll have to change the address on either the adapter or the cards so that they don't conflict. Option 8 (CC00h) is the Primary Token-Ring option that won't conflict with the IBM SCSI. Option 4 (DC00h) is the only Alternate Token-Ring option that doesn't conflict with the IBM SCSI.

THE PROBLEM: How do you select the DIX or Thick EtherNet option to use 3Com 3C503 Etherlink II with NetWare 386, version 3.0?

NetWare version: NetWare 386, version 3.0.

When it happens: At installation.

Possible solution: Type LOAD 3C503 DIX at the command line. The driver will prompt you for other parameters. These can all be entered in one command, and the driver prompt will display the syntax for it.

THE PROBLEM: The error message "Abend: Internal send packet got an ECD that was already sent" appears on the file server.

NetWare version: NetWare 386, version 3.0.

When it happens: When there is heavy traffic on the internet.

Why it happens: This can happen if you use the original Generic SCSI option with a DCB. However, the message could indicate other problems, because the error message also deals with low-level IPX.

Possible solution: If the error appears to be disk-related, load the new DCB.DSK driver, available on NetWire, after you reinitialize the drives.

THE PROBLEM: My Access Server does not support source routing.

NetWare version: NetWare 286 and 386.

Why it happens: You should use the new Lansup driver to generate the shell. However, the driver has a problem.

Possible solution: You can correct the problem by replacing all Ss in the driver's stack with 0s. To do this, load DEBUG by typing:

```
DEBUG IPXSPX.SYS
```

Debug comes up with a '-'prompt. Type:

```
D
```

to display the data. Note the address of the first S; the Ss start on the first or second page. Type:

```
E (address)
```

to change at least the first byte of Ss to zeroes. Type

W

to write out the changes. Then type:

Q

to quit. Finally, place ROUTE.COM in the AUTOEXEC.BAT file and load the Access Server.

THE PROBLEM: Users can't login and "`Fatal Dir Error`" messages show up on the file server screen.

NetWare version: Any.

When it happens: As large SCSI drives near their capacity, users can't login unless the server is rebooted.

Why it happens: Some large SCSI drives vary in the number of cylinders and heads that are actually on the drive. Therefore, drive types may not match what is defined in the drive setup. When NetWare reaches the end of the drive, it cannot access sectors that are defined in the drive setup but are not actually there. This occurs most often when you mix and match controllers and drives.

Possible solution: You can avoid this by buying controllers and drives from the same manufacturer.

You can also get the correct drive-type information from the drive manufacturer and install it. Or you can back up the drive, reinitialize it, and define a smaller NetWare partition so that NetWare will not attempt to access sectors beyond the drive's maximum limit.

THE PROBLEM: ELS cannot be properly installed on a dedicated file server. It only works with nondedicated servers.

NetWare version: Entry Level System I and II.

When it happens: At installation.

Why it happens: NetWare can be sensitive to the BIOS in the server.

Possible solution: Try updating the Phoenix BIOS, version 1.1003, with a more recent version such as version 1.1010.

THE PROBLEM: How can you change the order in which VAPs are loaded in NetWare 286, version 2.1x?

Possible solution: When the NetWare operating system comes up, it looks in the SYS:SYSTEM directory for the *.VP? and *.VAP files. NetWare first loads the *.VP? files in the order specified. For instance, it first loads *.VP0, then *.VP1, and so on. Next it loads the *.VAP files based on the order in which they are listed in the SYS:SYSTEM directory. You can change the numeric order of the file names to change the order in which NetWare loads your VAPs.

THE PROBLEM: Is there a way to restore NetWare 386 bindery files from one 386 server to another using NBACKUP command?

NetWare version: NetWare 386.

Possible solution: NBACKUP will return a message that says you cannot restore the binderies to a server with a different name. But this is only true of the binderies. You can back up only the data and restore them to another server with a different name. Then, by changing the name of the server from which you are backing up, you can restore the binderies. Use the AU-TOEXEC.NCF file to change the name.

You could also run BINDFIX on the server, copy the *.OLD files to the other server, and run BINDREST.

THE PROBLEM: GPI errors occur when you do a selective RESTORE from the tape backup software. This does not happen when you do full-system RESTOREs.

NetWare version: Any.

When it happens: When performing backups on systems that have two SYS volumes.

Possible solution: If you have only one SYS volume, you should experience no problem. To work around the problem, restore at least one file to one SYS volume before restoring other volumes.

THE PROBLEM: The IDE drive on the file server was destroyed during a COMPSURF format.

NetWare version: Any.

When it happens: When formatting an IDE drive using COMPSURF.

Why it happens: IDE drives were developed by Conner & Compaq for a 3.5-inch format and are popular in workstations because they don't require a separate disk controller. IDE stands for Integrated Device Electronics. Basically, it is a controller like the WD1003 that is integrated on the hard drive. A 40-pin cable connects it directly to the signals on the system board or to an adapter card that fits in a bus slot. So, be aware that you can ruin intelligent IDE drives if you format them using COMPSURF. This is true of some Miniscribe drives, though not Compaq or IBM. As IDE drives all have their own controller, a server that works with one might not work with another if a new one is swapped into place.

Possible solution: The IDE drive's built-in controller is theoretically ISA Western Digital compatible. So the ISA driver should work. Sometimes, however, it returns an error message from NETGEN or COMPSURF that will tell you the drive type number is out of range. If that happens, use the latest version of ISADISK available on NetWire. Novell has certified one such drive, Maxtor's LXT200A, for use with the ISADISK driver. Some of the so-called intelligent drives have HOT FIX built in and often come from the factory low-level preformatted.

THE PROBLEM: The INSTALL.BAT program returns an error message that says the installation disk is damaged when you install NASI applications on the server.

*NetWare version:*NetWare 386, version 3.0 or 3.01.

When it happens: During installation.

Possible solution: Don't use INSTALL.BAT. Instead, do the following:

- Log in as supervisor.
- Create SYS:NASIAPPS.
- Copy the installation disk files to NASIAPPS/.
- Run INSTAPPS and install applications and users as described in the manual or just follow the prompts.

THE PROBLEM: A NetWare bridge initializes LAN A but hangs after the "Initializing LAN B" message appears.

NetWare version: NetWare 286, version 2.12 or 2.15C bridge.

When it happens: When used with a WNIM card and a 2,400 bps modem.

Why it happens: This can happen with fast 80386 machines such as Compaq and AST. The bridge waits for the OK response from the modem after it is reset with the ATZ command. On a fast machine, it appears that the bridge timesout before the modem sends the OK response.

Possible solution: A modem with a faster command response will beat the timeout. Using a COM port may also solve the problem in many cases. So will slowing down the machines.

THE PROBLEM: After installing Windows 3.0 on the network and after running SETUP /N (Network), the following error message appeared:

```
Unknown copy failure
```

NetWare version: Any.

When it happens: During installation of Windows 3.0.

Why it happens: Windows evidently does some type of auto configuration to see what IRQs and base I/O addresses are being used. The default base I/O address of ArcNet cards (2E0h) can conflict with other addresses and cause the Windows auto configuration to return the error. But it can happen when any type of interrupt, base I/O, or memory address conflict occurs.

Possible solution: You can get around it by using the SETUP /I (ignore) /N (network), or you can change the conflicting address/interrupt of the interface card.

THE PROBLEM: The network sometimes returns error messages when loading two token-ring card drivers.
NetWare version: NetWare 386, versions 3.0 and 3.1.
When it happens: During installation and setup.
Why it happens: Improper hardware settings.
Possible solution: When using the 16/4 cards with version 3.0, you will get an error message that says:

```
Token-Ring adapter does not exist at port A24.
```

if you set the first card to option 0 and the second card to option 2. Instead, try the following setting:

```
Lan A:IRQ=2 ROM=CC00
```

This sets RAM at D800 switch #9 to off and selects the primary card.

```
Lan B:IRQ=3 ROM=C800
```

This sets ram at D400 switch #9 to on (alternate). Other combinations may work as well, but this one was tried and verified in Novell's own labs.

When loading two token-ring cards with version 3.1, you may get an error message that says:

```
ERROR: frame type is already loaded
```

This occurs when you enter LOAD TOKEN twice. The correct sequence of statements is

```
LOAD TOKEN PORT=A20
```

```
LOAD TOKEN PORT=A24
```

The first port assignment is assumed but the second must be specified.

Problems with Cards and Cabling

THE PROBLEM: The VGA address conflicts with ArcNet cards in PS/2 machines.
NetWare version: Any.
When it happens: During installation.
Why it happens: The IBM REFERENCE diskette will allow duplicate interrupt levels in a workstation, but NetWare won't. Nevertheless, there is nothing

on either to show that Int 2, or the memory range from A000 to C800, is being used. Consequently, the RX net/2s or SMC PS110s cannot be configured for Int 2 or these addresses.

Possible solution: Details on this problem are spelled out in the NetWare 386, version 3.1, Supplements Manual. Do not choose an interrupt level that conflicts with other boards in the station.

THE PROBLEM: It's difficult to adjust the speed of Western Digital's 16-bit EtherNet cards to optimize communications.

NetWare version: Any.

Possible solution: The card can be set to address no wait states, one wait state, or two wait states. If you cannot get the card to function correctly at zero wait states, try setting it for one or two wait states.

THE PROBLEM: The new Token-Ring TRN050 cards do not coexist well with the old drivers. File servers and workstations will lock up and file servers can disappear on the network.

NetWare version: Any.

When it happens: When you expand and upgrade installations.

Why it happens: If your network uses both IBM and Novell bridges, you may have problems. You cannot run both types of bridges with source routing; you must run either one or the other.

Possible solution: To avoid having to change over all cards at once, something that is almost impossible in a large network, you could update one ring at a time. The rings must be separated by Novell bridges and the whole ring must use the new drivers. If the rings are connected by IBM bridges, do not run source routing and do not filter out IPX packets. Novell representatives can help you regenerate NetWare 286 software without downing the server and copy NET$OS to the system directory so that the next time you boot, the new drivers will be there.

THE PROBLEM: The SNA gateway hangs in the local target loop.

NetWare version: Any.

When it happens: As workstations attach to the file server.

Why it happens: This occurs when several workstations attempt to attach simultaneously across a Novell bridge. It occurs among workstations using the 2.15 and 3.01a shells, or the NE1000 version 3.00 and NE2000 version 1.3 drivers.

Possible solutions: Use the new IPXSPX.OBJ or the new NE1000, version 1.4, and NE2000, version 3.01, drivers instead.

THE PROBLEM: IBM PS/2 machines will not work with IBM Token-Ring cards.

NetWare version: Any.

Why it happens: The default RAM address on the IBM SCSI adapter is d800h, the same as the factory address for most of the Primary options on the Token-Ring card.

Possible solution: You'll have to change the address on either the adapter or the cards so that they don't conflict. Option 8 (CC00h) is the only Primary Token-Ring option that won't conflict with the IBM SCSI. Option 4 (DC00h) is the only Alternate Token-Ring option that doesn't conflict with the IBM SCSI.

THE PROBLEM: The network sometimes returns error messages when loading two Token-Ring card drivers.

NetWare version: NetWare 386, versions 3.0 and 3.1.

When it happens: During installation and setup.

Why it happens: Improper hardware settings.

Possible solution: When using the 16/4 cards with version 3.0, you will get an error message that says:

```
Token-Ring adapter does not exist at port A24
```

if you set the first card to option 0 and the second card to option 2. Instead, try the following setting:

```
Lan A:IRQ=2 ROM=CC00
```

This sets RAM at D800 switch #9 to off and selects the primary card.

```
Lan B:IRQ=3 ROM=C800
```

This sets ram at D400 switch #9 to on (alternate). Other combinations may work as well, but this one was tried and verified in Novell's own labs.

When loading two Token-Ring cards with version 3.1, you may get an error message that says:

```
ERROR: frame type is already loaded
```

This occurs when you enter LOAD TOKEN twice. The correct sequence of statements is

```
LOAD TOKEN PORT=A20
LOAD TOKEN PORT=A24
```

The first port assignment is assumed but the second must be specified.

Other Problems

THE PROBLEM: Users who try to map drives after logging in get an error message that says "The following drive mapping operation could not be completed. "S1:=SYS:".

NetWare version: Any.

When it happens: During the login.

Why it happens: This often happens with workstations running DOS 3.2 and 3.3 and is usually due to a lack of environment space.

Possible solution: Use the DOS SHELL command in CONFIG.SYS to increase the amount of environment space on the workstation.

THE PROBLEM: A user who invoked the PURGE command managed to destroy other user's files.

NetWare version: Any.

When it happens: When users invoke PURGE in shared directories.

Why it happens: Although all NetWare manuals report PURGE will purge only files owned by the user who invokes the command, this is not true. The command will purge everything regardless of ownership.

Possible solution: Do not do a generic PURGE. Specify the files to delete according to filename.

THE PROBLEM: Users can't receive SEND broadcasts when they're running Windows.

NetWare version: Any.

When it happens: When the users have loaded Windows and haven't done anything on it.

Possible solution: Go to a DOS prompt from inside Windows, then exit back to Windows. You should start receiving broadcasts.

THE PROBLEM: The TREE command only displays every other subdirectory.

NetWare version: NetWare 386, version 3.0.

When it happens: This occurs when users on workstations running DOS 4.0 attempt to run the TREE command.

Possible solutions: If users insist on using the TREE command, install a lower version of DOS at those workstations.

THE PROBLEM: Users cannot make changes in a file even after they have been assigned all rights to it.

NetWare version: All.

When it happens: Users experience this problem whenever they call a file from a directory where they enjoys only Read and File Scan rights even though they are attempting to write to a directory where they enjoy Write rights.

Why it happens: Most applications attempt to create temporary work files in the directory from which the file is called. Users will get error messages when they try to edit the file because the application attempts to write the temporary file to a directory where the user does not enjoy Write privileges.

Possible solution: Copy the file to a directory where the user has Write privileges. The user can then call the file from that directory and edit it without problems.

9

How to Evaluate Gateways

Mainframe gateways are one of the most complex of LAN accessories. They're also one of the toughest things to buy. The dizzying number of issues involved in an educated gateway purchase—from hardware to software, from session management to keyboard support, from performance to link speed—is enough to try the patience of even the most determined LAN manager. The following list of fifty-three questions should make the process a bit easier.

These questions were compiled by a very determined LAN manager during her own search for a 3274-type mainframe gateway for a large NetWare LAN. While the questions are geared toward that situation, they are also appropriate for users looking for DFT-type or even 5250 gateways.

The questions are also appropriate for smaller networks, though their relative importance may vary with the size—and composition—of your LAN. If you support a small LAN with standardized workstations, you should have little difficulty finding an acceptable gateway. However, if your LAN covers several floors and consists of a variety of workstations (different brands, different video cards, different printers), your search will be more difficult.

Weigh gateway vendors' answers to the following fifty-three questions carefully. Remember, we didn't say it was going to be easy.

Session Management

1. Can you dedicate specific logical units (LUs) to specific PCs and maintain a pool of LUs for other PCs? A gateway's ability to share a pool of LUs among a number of PCs on a LAN is one of its chief

economic advantages over a setup with coax boards—such as DCA's IRMA—and a 3274 cluster controller. Under an IRMA-style setup, a separate card has to be dedicated to each PC, even if that PC accesses the mainframe only a few days a month.

A gateway that allows only static allocation of LUs, with certain LUs permanently assigned to certain PCs, has the same disadvantages. On the other hand, a gateway that allows dynamic allocation—with a pool of LUs that are doled out as PCs need them—is much more cost-effective in environments where users access the mainframe infrequently. A small pool of LUs can service the needs of a large number of intermittent users. Still, static allocation has its place: Security is tighter with a static setup, and users who need guaranteed access to the mainframe are assured of always having an LU available. Gateways that allow a combined static/dynamic scheme are the most flexible.

2. If an LU is not being used by a station on the LAN but goes inactive on the host side, will the gateway still offer it to a PC as an available LU? If the LU is part of a pool and it is offered to workstations regardless of its host status, an inactive LU can be handed out repeatedly. If the hunt sequence is sequential and, for example, LU 2 is hung, no one will be able to acquire an active LU until someone grabs and holds the inactive LU 2. This can be a major inconvenience.

3. Can a PC, on the fly, select a specific LU from a pool of LUs? This may be useful for troubleshooting or may be necessary as a workaround if the gateway offers inactive LUs to workstations (see number 2 above). It is also a very useful technique for acquiring printer sessions.

4. Is the LU number displayed on the bottom of the workstation's screen? Because a 3278-type terminal or PC with a coax board is physically attached to a specific port on a 3274-type controller, the device's LU number does not need to be displayed. An identification tag with the appropriate information (line ID, device name, and so on) may be attached to each device. But when PCs share a pool of LUs, tags won't work: A station may acquire LU 2 in the morning and LU 9 in the afternoon. Because your telecommunications or operations staff need to know the device ID of a workstation in trouble, the gateway should display the LU number at the workstation.

Alternative identification methods may be provided, but they are not as effective. You can't exit to DOS and run an identification program on your PC if your keyboard is locked. If someone must run a gateway status program on another station or at the gateway itself, troubleshooting will be tougher.

At a minimum, the display should consist of the last two digits of the LU name in hexadecimal format. If you plan to install multiple gateways on your LAN, the gateway should display the entire device name.

5. Are telecommunication error messages (such as "505") displayed at the workstation? The staff responsible for responding to network problems recognize IBM's "lightning bolt" numbers. A vendor's interpretation (for example, "LU inactive" or "33") will mean nothing to either your users or your support staff. Although it may be technically sufficient, under most circumstances it may not be practical in a large LAN to display the error message only at the gateway console.

6. If a user forgets to log off the 10 mainframe but terminates the session (from the gateway's perspective), will the gateway allow another user to access that session? This is the single most critical security problem with pooled LUs. If a user can terminate the session from the gateway's point of view (thus making it available to others) but has failed to log off the mainframe, the next user to acquire that LU will be logged on to the previous user's ID. That user will have the first user's security clearance and can get at his or her data. Serious security breaches may result.

7. How does a user terminate a session (that is, make it available to another user)? What happens to a session when a workstation is turned off or rebooted? Does the gateway think the session is available or unavailable? To reap the cost advantages promised by LU pooling, it must be possible to acquire and release sessions easily. If a user must reboot the PC or turn it off to return an LU to the pool, pooling isn't practical. Pooling will also fail if sessions are retained by a PC even after the PC is rebooted or turned off. The gateway should offer two simple exit sequences: one when you want to hot key between the mainframe and DOS, and one when you want to return to DOS permanently.

8. If you have a pool of terminal and printer LUs, will the gateway offer a printer LU to someone requesting a terminal LU just because the printer LU is the next available one in the sequence? Your VTAM programmers define which LUs support terminals (and the type of terminal) and which LUs support printers. In addition, you identify these LU types to your gateway software. The gateway should, therefore, be able to distinguish requests for the one from requests for the other and, in essence, maintain one pool for terminal LUs and one pool for printer LUs.

9. Can you monitor LU usage to determine which LUs are being used and which LUs are available? Can you find out which stations are using which LUs? If the function exists, can it be invoked from any station or only from the gateway console? To manage pooled LUs effectively, you must know who is using which LU (if only to kick off people who have acquired LUs but have gone out to lunch). You should be able to obtain this information from any workstation, not just the gateway console.

10. From the gateway console, can you monitor the status of LUs on the host? This is a useful troubleshooting tool.

11. Can you kill a session from the gateway console, making the LU available to another station? If you know that an LU is tied up but is not being used (for example, you know workstation 4 has LU 2, but no one is logged on to workstation 4), you should be able to terminate the session and make it available to someone else without physically going to the offending machine.

12. Can you disable an LU from the gateway console? You may want to remove an inactive LU from the pool.

13. What message does the gateway generate when all the LUs are being used? Look for a meaningful message, such as "all terminal sessions are in use, please try later." An error message is not acceptable.

Emulation Program

14. Must the user be in the same directory as the programs to invoke the emulation or file transfer? If you make a distinction between program and user directories, your users should, from their personal directories, be able to invoke gateway programs stored in a search path directory.

15. Is emulation accessed through a menu? If a menu facility is provided, can it be installed in a program directory and be run from a user directory? Can it be bypassed? Is there a command-line alternative? It should always be possible to invoke an emulation program from a batch file.

16. What rights must a user have to the directory in which the programs are stored? Users should need only read, open, and search rights to program directories. They should not need to—or be able to—create, delete, or write to files in a program directory.

17. When executed, does the gateway program place the user in the mainframe session, or must the user hot key from DOS to start the mainframe session? Some gateways leave you in DOS after you execute the emulation program on the assumption that the session is then available whenever you want to use it.

    If you have sufficient memory in your PC and you are using dedicated LUs, this may be a nice feature. But if you are using pooled LUs, you will want the LUs to be acquired and activated only when they are going to be used. You won't want them hanging around in the background, waiting to be used. Moreover, if your PC users are familiar with IRMA boards, they will expect to see the mainframe session when they execute the gateway program; they won't expect to find themselves still in DOS.

18. How much memory does the emulation software require at the workstation? A 640K workstation loses a considerable amount of memory to DOS, NETBIOS, and the network shell. If the gateway emulation program uses 150K or 200K, being able to hot key to DOS won't mean much because there won't be enough memory left to run any significant DOS programs.

19. Can the program be made memory-resident or nonresident? Once it has been made resident, can it be unloaded easily from memory, or must the user reboot? To perform file transfers, the mainframe session must remain "resident" so users can hot key between the mainframe and DOS. If you want to implement LU pooling, the gateway must offer an easy way to remove that mainframe session from memory and return it to the pool. The more complex the method, the less likely the user will be to use it—thus defeating the purpose of shared LUs.

20. What 3278-type terminal emulations are available? Which graphics cards are supported or required? Are mainframe graphics supported? Most gateways offer MC 2 emulation; some offer MOD 4. If your installation needs MOD 5 emulation, find out if your graphics cards are supported. Similarly, if you need support for mainframe graphics, find out if it is supported and what hardware is required.

21. Can you do screen prints to local and LAN printers? You should be able to do a screen print to any spooled printer.

22. Are multiple concurrent sessions supported? Must you preallocate them, or can they grabbed on the fly? If the session must be preallocated, you may need to buy more sessions than you actually need,

because each station will get two, three, or four sessions you select at the default each time it asks for one whether or not the additional sessions are required. If an additional session can be obtained on the fly from the pool, you may not have to buy "extra" LUs. In that case, the user should not have to specify an LU number but should need only to rerun the emulation request program to acquire a second or third session. In some cases, you may want the ability to assign multiple sessions either up front or on the fly.

Printer Management

Unless your LAN installation has only a few printer models and a very accommodating systems programming group, it may be impossible for a gateway to provide truly flexible printer support. On the mainframe side, printer definitions must, for example, be established in RSCSSNA or VPS tables. Few if any systems programmers will be willing to create eight or sixteen printer definitions just to support local PC printers.

If you do set up one or two printer LUs on a gateway, you must then decide how to make them available to individual users and how to accommodate different setup strings. If your installation has only two printer types, say a laser and a dot matrix, you could set up one LU for each. But true laser support is difficult even under these limited circumstances. If, for example, the laser is an H-P LaserJet 500*+ with two paper trays and multiple fonts, how does a user who has acquired a printer session tell the laser to print condensed from the lower, legal cassette?

Here are some more questions to consider.

23. Can a printer session and a 3270 session be maintained at the same time? If so, how? This is necessary if you want to disseminate printer access to users. If, however, you must attach a printer session to a terminal session, only the person who acquires that terminal session may use the printer session. Ideally, an individual should be able to acquire a printer session dynamically when it is needed.

24. Can a workstation establish a printer session without establishing a 3270 session? Given the problems inherent in sharing printer sessions, one solution is to establish a printer session at the gateway and dedicate it to a particular LAN printer. But you should not have to give up a 3270 session to do this.

25. Can setup strings be passed to a printer session? If you want to distribute printer sessions and allow users to control the setup strings,

and the gateway doesn't provide appropriate facilities, find out if it will work in concert with printer utilities such as Pacific Software's Network Assistant.

PC Configuration

26. If the gateway requires a PC configuration file, what information must be provided (type of PC, video card, keyboard, software interrupts)? If all the PCs on your LAN are identical, this is not a problem. But if the LAN has many different PCs, the more information about each that the program requires, the harder it will be to set up the gateway for shared LUs. If the gateway does require PC configuration information, it should store the information in a data file (not in its .EXE or .COM file) and it should not care what that file is called.

27. Are multiple graphics cards supported (CGA, EGA, Hercules, and so on)? If so, how? Ideally, the program should be able to sense a PC's video card. It must support the video card/monitor combinations you have installed. Will the workstation software work with a 64K EGA card and monochrome monitor?

28. Are there any known conflicts with various hardware/software configurations (such as the Microsoft Mouse)? Ask for a list of known conflicts or a list of supported configurations. You don't want to waste time installing a gateway that won't work with your equipment.

29. Must you add drivers to the workstation CONFIG.SYS files? On a large LAN, this is cumbersome and must be repeated whenever the driver is updated. Imagine having to update 100 CONFIG.SYS files each time a driver is changed, or just the testing required when a change is made. (Say, for example, that you test the new version on ten PCs, decide it's fine, change the 100 boot diskettes . . . and then discover a serious conflict. Not only does the program software have to be backed off, but each of those files must be changed back and then, presumably, changed again when a fix is available.) In addition, each time you add a driver to a CON FIG.SYS file, you increase the likelihood of a conflict now or in the future.

30. If a driver must be installed in the workstation CONFIG.SYS files, must any options be set to prevent conflicts with your LAN operating system or other drivers? The gateway company should maintain an up-to-date list of all known conflicts and workarounds and provide this list to all

new and existing customers. No one wants to spend ten hours trying to solve a problem only to learn that it is known and a fix exists.

Keyboard Support

31. Is it easy to change the default keyboard configuration? Can the "standard" be changed for all sessions? It should be possible to modify the gateway's 327 keyboard mapping (for example, identify which PC key does a reset) for all sessions. You should not have to define it for each session—and the friendlier the interface the better. Can you also change the gateway's hot key assignments?

32. Is the enhanced A keyboard supported? Do you need a special configuration fil to support it? The program doesn't have to take advantage of the new, extended keyboards (you could always tell your staff to use the cursor keys on the number pad), but you shouldn't have to set up different configuration files for different keyboards to make the emulation work.

33. How does the software manage the PC keyboard? If the software does not assume control of the keyboard, existing keyboard macros must be cleared before the program is used and must be restored when the emulation program ends. On the other hand, if the software does assume control of the keyboard, it may not be possible to, for example, clear Novell's messages or pop up a RAM-resident printer utility.

Gateway Hardware

34. Can the board run at 19.2K bits per second? At 56K? It should be possible to run the board, at a minimum, at either 9.6 or 19.2K without any special or additional requirements. In certain environments, 56K could be very useful.

35. Does the gateway support your communications protocol? Some boards support both BSC and SNA/SDLC links. Others support only one or the other.

36. Are any special VTAM settings required (for example, a logmode table with query bit on)? Will the software work properly if your logmode table differs from the vendor's recommended settings? The vendor's software should accommodate your installation's defaults. Systems programmers do not like to deviate from their standard VTAM settings.

37. Does the gateway support Novell's IPX as well as NETBIOS? If you are a Novell administrator and you don't currently load NETBIOS, IPX support is an advantage.

38. Does the gateway board derive any processing power from the PC in which it is housed? Do you really want to waste a '286 machine on a gateway? Wouldn't you rather put the gateway board in one of your old, clunky 8088s and give the '286 to a deserving employee? Some gateways won't work well—or at all—unless they are installed in '286 or even '386 machines.

39. What is the maximum number of LUs the board can support? If there are multiple configurations (for example, 8, 16, 32), can you upgrade without a penalty? Is the upgrade accomplished through software or hardware? Depending on the pricing, you may not want to pay for thirty-two LUs if you need only sixteen. Software upgrades are preferable to hardware upgrades, for obvious reasons.

40. Can individuals on a multiple-server network use a single gateway? Can a network support multiple gateways? Will the gateway work over bridged LANs? Consider both your current and future needs.

41. What interrupts and memory addresses does the gateway board use? Can they be changed? You should be able to set the gateway board's interrupt and memory addresses to avoid conflicts with your network shell (if it must be loaded in the gateway PC) or with other hardware you may have in your gateway PC. It is just not good manners for one vendor to assume that you will be able to resolve conflicts by relying on another vendor's good manners.

42. Is the software copy protected? Is an activator diskette required? Does the software use a "key file"? Gateway software doesn't need and should not employ copy protection. Two PCs cannot share a single LU. There is no way to violate a "one PC, one program" license.

43. How is the gateway priced? By LU, server, or number of PCs on the LAN? As a single LU cannot be used by two PCs at the same time and a gateway consists of hardware as well as software, it makes sense to price either the board as a whole or as groups of LUs (8, 16, 32). If you do not need an LU for each and every PC on your LAN, avoid gateways that charge by the workstation. Why pay for gateway software for a PC that may already have a coax board?

44. Does the gateway support an API (Application Program Interface)? Does the vendor offer an API? Will it meet your requirements? Does the vendor support IBM's HLLAPI?

45. Does the gateway have a file transfer program? If so, is it proprietary? It is easy to implement file transfer software that uses your mainframe's editor, but such software is inevitably very slow and limited. If you have some control over the software that goes onto your mainframe, you may be able to install the vendor's proprietary program. But if your company has standardized on IBM's IND$FILE (send/receive) software, your gateway should support that protocol.

46. How fast is the file transfer software? If it is two to three times slower than your coax board's program, your users will not be happy.

47. Can the file transfer be run from a menu? If so, must the user be in the program directory to execute it? Does it support directory paths? Is help available, and how good is it?

Vendor Support

48. Does the gateway have built-in diagnostics? Sooner or later, no matter how good the gateway, something is bound to go wrong. If the gateway offers diagnostic utilities, such as a trace facility, it will be easier to resolve these problesms.

49. Does the gateway vendor have your LAN (operating system and hardware) installed? Does the vendor have access to your mainframe operating system (for example, VM or MVS)? Is the file transfer software written in-house, or has it been contracted to a third party? How good is the technical staff? Can you talk directly to them?

    Much can go wrong when you try to install and support a gateway. Your vendor's technical support will be critical.

Performance

50. Can an evaluation be arranged? A gateway is a very visible, and rather expensive, addition to your LAN. Insist on a thirty-day evaluation period. Some functions cannot be evaluated through a questionnaire.

51. Is the gateway robust? Does it ever crash? How does it respond to companywide network problems? Can your telecommunications staff

resolve gateway problems with standard troubleshooting techniques? If you must reboot the gateway PC to activate an inactive LU, you are in trouble.

52. How fast is the gateway? From the user's perspective, speed is easy to measure: How long does it take to paint the screen after I press the Enter key? The gateway is not likely to match a 3278-type terminal running at the same line speed, but it should not be significantly slower either.

53. What effect does gateway usage have on LAN performance? Does LAN performance deteriorate when all the LUs are being used? If so, is the level of deterioration acceptable? What happens to LAN performance when several file transfers are being performed over the gateway?

Although gateways have been available for quite a while, they are still rather primitive. Many appear to have been developed by people who have never managed a large, complex LAN or have never had to support PCs in a large company's telecommunications environment. Gateways can be difficult to install and support and offer performance levels adequate only for casual mainframe users. Continue to give your mainframe programmers 3278-type terminals. Give your PC/mainframe programmers coax boards. For the moment, gateways can make economic sense, but only if you have a number of casual mainframe users on your LAN who can accept middling performance.

Meanwhile keep your eye out for that dream gateway that makes coax boards and even 3278s truly obsolete.

10

NetWare Power Tools

While NetWare is a full-featured operating environment, like any product it can be extended, altered, and improved in innumerable ways. NetWare's extraordinary popularity has attracted the attentions of gifted programmers and network managers of all stripes.

As a result, the NetWare environment has become home to some of the cleverest third-party utilities in PC networking. These range from complex, well-constructed batch files to complete system configuration and management routines.

We have scoured user groups, on-line forums, Novell's own support staff, and the experiences of dozens of NetWare managers to glean the most powerful and useful NetWare add-ons possible.

The following pages contain descriptions and brief documentation about these programs, all of which can be found in ready-to-use form on the enclosed Novell NetWare Power Tools disk.

All of the programs on the disk have been archived using LHarc archiving program. They are presented here in self-extracting forms. An "X" extension has been added at the end of each file name to differentiate it from the program's .EXE or .COM executable file. After the program is extracted, to avoid confusion, you may wish to store the one with an "X" extension in a separate directory.

Enjoy.

ADMIN.BAT

Benefit:

This one-line file saves keystrokes for a frequently used CC:Mail function. It starts the administration function of CC:Mail for adding/deleting users, changing passwords, and so on. It is perhaps the most frequently used of the CC:Mail batch files. Other related files included are:

```
DIAGS.BAT
DIRECTOR.BAT
RECLAIM.BAT
MSGS.BAT
USERS.BAT
```

Syntax: ADMIN

How to operate it:

Type ADMIN at the command line. ADMIN.BAT must be in the search path, which makes sense anyway, because the ADMIN function is one of the most frequently used CC:Mail utilities. Substitute the name of your mailbox for MBX_NAME and the location of the CC:Mail CCADMIN and CC:Mail CCDATA directories to match your directory structure. You will be prompted for the mail box administrator's password.

Listing:

```
Y:\APPS\CCADMIN\ADMIN MBX_NAME Y:\APPS\CCDATA COLOR
```

AGENDAB.BAT

Benefit:

This file was written to allow multiple users access to Lotus Agenda on a network. It provides a method for keeping the AGENDA.ENV configuration file for each user. First the user is placed in an AGENDA data directory. Next a drive for the Agenda application is dynamically mapped. Then the user's own AGENDA.ENV file is copied to Agenda's application subdirectory. Upon exiting Agenda, the AGENDA.ENV file is recopied to the user's AGENDA data to ensure that any changes to the ".ENV" file are recorded, and then the user is returned to his or her home directory. The last line deletes the mappings set up at the beginning of the batch file. The simple file locking concepts used in ALPHA.BAT (included on this diskette) could also be employed in this file.

Syntax: Type AGENDAB at the command line. AGENDAB.BAT must be in the search path.

Listing:

```
F:
CD AGENDA
MAP L:=SYS:APPS\AGENDA
COPY AGENDA.ENV L:
L:AGENDA
COPY L:AGENDA.ENV
CD ..
MAP DELETE L:
```

ALPHA.BAT

Benefit:

This batch file provides a rudimentary file locking capability. The version of Alpha4 used was a single-user version, and application locking was necessary to prevent multiple users from simultaneous access. This batch file changes the user into the application subdirectory. It then checks for the existence of a "dummy file" named FILE.LOC. If this file exists, it branches out to an IN USE message.

If the file does not exist, it copies the dummy file from the public directory and changes the printer timeout (to allow a longer timeout for printing database reports). Upon exiting the application, the printer is reestablished with a shorter timeout, the locking file is deleted, and the user is placed in his or her home directory again.

Syntax: Type ALPHA. ALPHA.BAT must be in the search path.

Notes:

User must have Create, Delete, and Modify rights in the application subdirectory in addition to standard ROS (NetWare 286) or RF (NetWare 386) rights. Mappings and subdirectories will have to be changed to match individual requirements. If the user normally reboots without exiting the application, FILE.LOC will remain in the application subdirectory and the application will remain locked until it is manually deleted. For applications that support more than one simultaneous use, use XMETER.

Listing:

```
@ECHO OFF
CLS
MAP K:=SYS:\APPS\ALPHA4
K:
IF EXIST FILE.LOC GOTO INUSE
NCOPY Y:\PUBLIC\FILE.LOC
CAPTURE QUEUE=PRINTQ_0 TI=15 NB NT NFF
A4
CAPTURE QUEUE=PRINTQ_0 TI=2 NB NT NFF
```

```
DEL K:\APPS\ALPHA4\FILE.LOC
GOTO END
:INUSE
ECHO ALPHA FOUR IN USE...
ECHO PLEASE TRY AGAIN LATER ...
:END
CD\
F:
MAP DEL K:
```

BINDARC

Benefit:

Creates archive of NetWare binderies. This program archives the bindery files for NetWare version 2.1x or 3.x to files that can be copied or backed up using normal procedures.

Where to find it:

On the Power Tools disk as BINDARC.COM or on CompuServe NOVA Public Domain/demo Library #14.

Syntax: BINDARC

How to operate it:

When you run this utility, the files that are archived are:

NetWare v2.1x	*NetWare v3.x*
NET$BIND.SYS	NET$VAL.SYS
NET$BVAL.SYS	NET$OBJ.SYS
NET$PROP.SYS	

The files are archived to files with the extension of "OLD". The files can be restored at any time using BINDREST.EXE (supplied with NetWare). BINDARC produces the same files that BINDFIX does but does no fixing or checking of the bindery files during the process.

CCC.BAT

Benefit:

Here's a simple batch file that will check for the existence of new mail for CC:Mail users. If it finds new mail, it will prompt the user to run CCM.BAT, to load the E-mail program.

This program makes use of the FULL environment variable that is set to the user's full name in the system login script. This batch file also provides users with a quick way of checking for new mail without loading the full program and typing their password.

Syntax: CCC

How to operate it:

Type CCC at the command line. CCC.BAT must be in the search path. Substitute the CC:Mail CCDATA directory to match your directory structure.

Examples of usage:

To check mail upon each login, the user's login script (under SYSCON) could contain the line:

```
EXIT "CCC"
```

Listing:

```
CLS
ECHO OFF
CLS
ECHO
ECHO
ECHO CHECKING YOUR MAIL...
ECHO
ECHO
ECHO
```

```
y:\apps\ccmail\NOTIFY %FULL% Y:\APPS\CCDATA CHKONLY
ECHO
IF ERRORLEVEL==1 ECHO Type CCM to load CC:Mail
ECHO
ECHO
PAUSE
CLS
```

CCM.BAT

Benefit:

This batch file is primarily a keystroke saver and will load CC:Mail. It utilizes the %FULL% environment variable, so users need only type in their passwords. By specifying FILES/F:, the administrator can specify the default directory for file attachments.

Syntax: CCM

How to operate it:

Type CCM. CCM.BAT must be in the search path. Substitute the name of your mailbox for MBX_NAME. The location of the CC:Mail CCMAIL and CC:Mail CCDATA directories may have to be changed to match your directory structure.

Notes:

The %FULL% environment variable must be set to the user's CC:Mail name. For ease of configuration, the Full Name stored in the NetWare bindery (under SYSCON) should be set the same as the CC:Mail name. The %FULL% environment variable can then be set in the system login script with the command DOS SET FULL=%FULL_NAME.

Listing:

```
CLS
ECHO OFF
CLS
ECHO
ECHO LOADING MAIL...
Y:\APPS\CCMAIL\MAIL %FULL% Y:\APPS\CCDATA %1 FILES/F:
```

CCMAIL.PIF

Benefit:

This Windows PIF file launches CC:Mail from within Windows 3.0.

Syntax: Mouse click on CC:Mail button.

Set up:

Copy CCMAIL.PIF to your Windows directory. Then select the Create New Program option in the Windows 3.0 Program Manager. Follow instructions there referencing CCMAIL.PIF as the program to be invoked. You will wind up with a button, named whatever you like, that will call CCMAIL.PIF whenever it is pushed.

Listing:

PIF files are in a format readable only within Windows or by the Windows PIF Editor program.

CHKMAIL

Benefit:

This batch file is used in conjunction with the Higgins mail system to check for new mail for a user.

Syntax: CHKMAIL

How to operate it:

This batch file maps a drive to the Higgins mail directory, changes into that directory, and then tests for the existence of a file named %name%.MLW where "name" is the registered user name for Higgins mail (usually the NetWare variable %full_name). If the file exists, it will inform the user that there is new mail. If it doesn't exist, it will inform the user that there is no new mail. Substitute the location of the Higgins HIGMAIL directory to match your directory structure.

Listing:

```
MAP H:=SYS:\APPS\HIGGINS\HIGDATA\HIGMAIL
CLS
@ECHO OFF
H:
IF EXIST %NAME%.MLW ECHO YOU HAVE UNREAD MAIL WAITING ...
IF NOT EXIST %NAME%.MLW ECHO YOU HAVE NO NEW MAIL
WAITING...
PAUSE
:END
MAP DEL H:
F:
```

CMD_ED

Benefit:

Allows recall and editing of previously entered DOS commands.
This 2.5K memory-resident (TSR) program is a command line editor
similar to those in the VAX VMS environment. With this program loaded,
you need only to hit the up arrow key on the keyboard to recall the last
several commands entered at the command line.
Press RETURN for more; type NO to stop.

Syntax: CMD_ED

Price:

Shareware - $15.00

Restrictions?

None

Available from:

Sub Systems
159 Main St. #8C
Stoneham, MA 02180
1-800-447-6819

How to operate it:

Up and down arrow keys scroll through previous commands. Left and
right arrow keys position the cursor on the recalled DOS command line.
The Insert key toggles between insert and overtype mode.

CONFMT

Benefit:

CONFMT is a 12K memory-resident (TSR) utility that lets you format floppy disks while you are doing something else.

Where to find it:

On the Power Tools Disk as CONFMT.COM or in CompuServe IBM Hardware Disk Utilities Library #1.

Syntax: CONFMT

Price:

Shareware, $15 ($50 for site license).

More information available from:

Sydex
153 North Murphy Avenue
Sunnyvale, CA 94086
(408) 739-4866

CRON_JR

Benefit:

CRON_JR is a batch scheduler; it is used to run standalone programs at specific times and intervals. CRON_JR requires an MS-DOS–based machine running MS-DOS 3.30 or higher. MS-DOS versions below 3.1 or 3.21 may be used but are not recommended, as they require CRON_JR to use more memory.

Where to find it:

CRON_JR and all of its accompanying documentation can be found on the Power Tools disk under the name CRON_JR.COM. It can also be found on CompuServe IBMSYS DOS utilities Library #1.

Syntax: See below.

Price:

Shareware, $45; $75 for next version of CRON_JR and other products as available.

More information available from:

Software Shorts
14101 Yorba Street, Suite 101
Tustin, CA 92680

Background:

CRON_JR was designed because nothing better existed in the MS-DOS world. Simple but powerful programs like CRON (part of AT&T's Unix) or Sleeper (public domain for H-P's MPE) are nonexistent for PCs.

With more and more companies moving from minicomputers to PC-based LANs, one of the many things that has been lost is the ability to schedule the nightly reporting and maintenance programs needed to keep a business working during the day.

Sure, it's possible to just write a large batch file that will run all your programs one after another. That solution is fine if it meets your needs. But if you need programs to run at specific times, and especially if your business revolves around a LAN, then this product is for you.

The solution:

There are three methods of scheduler implementation in a DOS environment:

1. Make a background RAM-resident program that will pop up when it is time to run the tasks.
2. Make a foreground program that loads the tasks as child processes.
3. Make a transient program that is in memory only when it is needed. Therefore, all memory is available for the task.

Faults for method 1:

The last thing the world needs is another RAM-resident program to eat up memory, steal clock cycles, and substitute custom interrupt vectors. Most LAN users already use 20 to 30K for their network shell, and even more if they are running a NETBIOS emulator.

The way most resident schedulers work is to stuff the keyboard when it is time to execute a task. This method, used in various automatic tape backup programs, is unreliable because it assumes that the DOS prompt is available, the command line is clear, and the path is set.

Faults for method 2:

This method requires too much memory. If you want to run a batch file, then you have to load another version of COMMAND.COM on top of the parent scheduler. If you want to run an .EXE or .COM file, then you lose the option of command-line parameters and must resort to running a batch file, which brings us back to the first problem of loading COMMAND.COM.

Why method 3 is so swell:

It is so simple. It relies heavily on two simple operating system–level batch files. It is not RAM resident so it uses no memory.

One caveat:

If you are using a DOS version below 3.3, then around 23K is lost because COMMAND.COM needs to be invoked a second time. It is strongly recommended that DOS 3.30 or above be used.

314 NOVELL NETWARE POWER TOOLS

How it works:

1. You create the schedule file CRONJR.SCH. It contains the timing parameters for the tasks to be executed.

2. The master batch file, CRONJR.BAT, is loaded from the command line. That is your last intervention.

3. The work file, CRONWK.BAT, is deleted by CRONJR.BAT.

4. The scheduler program, CRON.EXE, is loaded and the schedule file CRONJR.SCH is read.

5. When the time comes to execute a process, CRON.EXE dumps its scheduling information to CRONJR.JOB, writes the CRON-WK.BAT bat file, and unloads from memory to return control to CRONJR.BAT.

6. If CRONJR.BAT can find CRONWK.BAT, then the CRON-WK.BAT work file is called/executed.

7. Upon completion of CRONWK.BAT, control is returned to CRONJR.BAT, which then executes CRONJR.BAT (thus ending the original CRONJR.BAT execution) with the parameter RE-LOAD, which is passed to CRON.EXE in step 4, which causes the file CRONJR.JOB to be loaded rather than the file CRONJR.SCH.

Hard to follow? Try this one. It is the remedial version.

```
CRONJR.BAT -> CRON.EXE -> CRONWK.BAT (YOUR TASK) ->CRONJR.BAT
       A.           B.            C.                       A.
```

Installation:

Create a directory for CRON_JR (any name will do), and copy the CRON.EXE program into the new directory. If you are going to use CRON_JR on multiple machines in a LAN, then you must make a separate directory for each machine.

Examples:

```
F:\CRON\386
F:\BOB\CRON
F:\CRON\486
F:\ACCTNG\CRON
```

Each directory must contain its own CRONJR.SCH file and its own unique CRONJR.BAT file. A path may be set to point to the location of CRON.EXE.

For each CRON_JR directory created, type CRON START at their respective DOS prompt, such as:

```
F:\CRON\386>cron start
```

This will create the CRONJR.BAT file that is specific to its home directory. If you type out the CRONJR.BAT file, you will understand.

Create a flat ASCII file (no tabs) named CRONJR.SCH or edit the one on the distribution diskette. Enter one task per line using the following format.

```
minute hour day_of_month    month    day_of_week executable
```

Examples:

```
50    16    *    *    motuwethfr        f:\public\bin\killuser.exe
0     17    *    *    motuwethfr        f:\mtn_tape\databack.bat
0     5     *    *    mo                g:\acctng\weekly.bat
0     1     1    *    sumotuwethfrsa    g:\acctng\monthend.exe
0     1     1    1    sumotuwethfrsa    g:\acctng\yearly.exe
49    16    *    *    motuwethfr        f:\funny\gohome.exe
2i    *     *    *    motuwethfr        f:\stream\kevin.bat
```

Type CRON_JR at the DOS prompt and you are finished.

Field definitions:

Minute: the minute of the hour you want your schedule to execute, 0 through 59.

Hour: the hour of the day in military time, 0 through 23.

Day_of_month: the day of the month, 1 through 31.

Month: the month of the year, 1 through 12.

Day_of_week: the day of the week, SU MO TU WE TH FR SA.

Executable: a DOS executable string, .BAT, .EXE, and .COM files with a maximum combined path of 64 characters. EXTENTIONS MUST BE USED!

Wild cards and increments:

* *: execute on every occurrence; not used by day_of_week.
* i: execute in increments; only applies to minute and hour. The seventh line in the example shows 2i, which means execute in 2-minute increments. In theory this task could be executed 30 times an hour. Obviously * must be used for every level after the first i. Combinations of i in the minute and hour are not recommended. The expected outcome is that only the hour increment will be used.

Launch time:

Task checking and launching occur on the first second of the minute.

EXTREMELY IMPORTANT:

Be very careful when assigning launch times. A "feature" of CRON_JR is that it launches tasks only when CRON.EXE is resident. Example: You have two tasks set to execute at 19:00; each takes 45 minutes to run; and a few tasks are scheduled at 19:15. At 19:00 all 19:00 tasks are tagged for launching; the first task will be launched then. The second task will be launched when CRON.EXE is reloaded—thus it is effectively launched at 19:45.

Well, it is now 19:46 and all tasks scheduled from 19:01 through 19:46 have missed their launch window.

To prevent this from happening you should do the following. Schedule enough time between tasks. The 19:15 tasks in the example should have been set later, to 20:00, or earlier, to 19:00. Had they been scheduled at 19:00, then they would have run as part of the 19:00 launching. If you have an OS/2 version of CRON_JR, this problem can be completely avoided.

Proper scheduling:

The best way to debug a faulty schedule is to run CRON.EXE instead of CRONJR.BAT and use the F1 key to exit to DOS and change the time. Inspect the CRONWK.BAT file that is created.

There is no limit to the number of tasks you can put into the CRONJR.SCH file.

Anomalies and hints:

There are two known anomalies and one other point that you need to remember.

Anomaly 1. CRON_JR executes tasks only on the first second of the minute. Example: If you had three tasks that each take 5 seconds to complete, and they are all scheduled to launch at 19:00, then they will be effectively launched at 19:00, 19:01, and 19:02. This feature was designed into the product.

Anomaly 2. Anomaly 2 arises out of anomaly 1. Example: If you set up a schedule that has three jobs, each set to run in increments of 10 minutes (10i * * * ...), you would assume that they would execute at the 10-, 20-, 30-, 40-, 50-, 00-minute clock demarcations (assuming that the first launch minute was hh:00) and always launch one after the other. In reality this is not true.

The first launching schedule would look like this:

1a. Job #1 launches at the first available minute.

2a. Job #2 launches at the first available minute after job #1 completes.

3a. Job #3 launches at the first available minute after job #2 completes.

The second and subsequent launchings might look like this:

1b. Job #1 launches 10 minutes after its first launching or at the first available minute after job #3 finishes; or it may launch at the first available minute after job #3 if job #3 takes more than 10 minutes.

2b. and 3b. Who knows?

The best way to get around this confusion is to do one of three things:

1. Carefully plan and test your incremental launchings.

2. Rather than make your launchings incremental, make them minute-specific. This may involve multiple line entries into the CRONJR.SCH file for the same job at different times.

3. Make jobs 1, 2 and 3 one job.

One thing you must remember: The CRONJR.SCH file is loaded only at the initial load time. If you are running CRON_JR on a LAN, if

CRON_JR is running on a remote machine, and if you modify the remote machine's CRONJR.SCH file, the remote CRON_JR will not reflect any of the changes made in the new CRONJR.SCH file until the remote CRON_JR is aborted and reloaded.

Examples of usage:

To do a quick installation, type the following commands at the DOS prompt.

```
C:\> md cron
C:\> cd cron
C:\CRON> copy a:cron*.*
C:\CRON> cron start
C:\CRON> cronjr
```

DIAGS.BAT

Benefit:

Saves keystrokes for a frequently used CC:Mail function. This utility will perform diagnostics on the CC:Mail database. Other related files included are:

```
ADMIN.BAT
DIRECTOR.BAT
RECLAIM.BAT
MSGS.BAT
USERS.BAT
```

Syntax: DIAGS

How to operate it:

This batch file and the other CC:Mail administration files are placed in the CC:Mail CCADMIN directory and are run from there. Alternatively, they could be put in a batch subdirectory on the search path and invoked with the alternate listing shown below. Substitute the name of your mailbox for MBX_NAME and the location of the CC:Mail CCDATA directory to match your directory structure. The CC:Mail instruction manual cautions that the administrator must have exclusive use of the mail database while running the diagnostics. You will be prompted for the mail box administrator's password.

Listing:

```
CHKSTAT MBX_NAME Y:\APPS\CCDATA DIAGNOSTICS
```

Alternate listing:

```
Y:\APPS\CCADMIN\CHKSTAT MBX_NAME Y:\APPS\CCDATA DIAGNOSTICS
```

DIRECTOR.BAT

Benefit:

Saves keystrokes for a frequently used CC:Mail function. This batch file will provide a directory listing of CC:Mail users. Other related files included are:

```
ADMIN.BAT
DIAGS.BAT
RECLAIM.BAT
MSGS.BAT
USERS.BAT
```

Syntax: DIRECTOR

How to operate it:

This batch file and the other CC:Mail administration files are placed in the CC:Mail CCADMIN directory and are run from there. Substitute the name of your mailbox for MBX_NAME and the location of the CC:Mail CCDATA directory to match your directory structure. You will be prompted for the mail box administrator's password.

Listing:

```
CHKSTAT MBX_NAME Y:\APPS\CCDATA DIRECTORY
```

DOWNLOAD.BAT

Benefit:

This batch file does a binary DOS copy of a downloadable soft font file to a printer. The downloadable font file is created with Hewlett Packard's PCL-PAC. This batch file could be used as a menu entry for users to download fonts into H-P LaserJet IIs. Different versions of the file could download multiple font sets.

Syntax: DOWNLOAD

Examples of usage:

The font file referenced is a file that can be created with Hewlett Packard's PCL-PAK program. This program takes individual soft fonts and combines them into one file that can be downloaded into an H-P LaserJet as semipermanent soft fonts. The /b binary switch is essential, as the font file contains high-order data bits. Also, for this to work properly, the capture statement must include an NT (no tab expansion), NB (no banner), and NFF (no form feed). Otherwise the download will abort.

Listing:

```
CLS
@ECHO OFF
ECHO DOWNLOADING FONTS.....
COPY /B Y:\PUBLIC\FONTS.FNT > LPT1:
```

FTLIGHT

Benefit:

FTLIGHT is one utility of many that make up the Fresh Utilities package. FTLIGHT is a small, memory resident program that displays an arrow in the upper right-hand corner of your computer's display screen during disk reads from and disk writes to NetWare file server drives. The arrow points to the left when reading from a file server disk, and to the right when writing to a file server disk. The program is very small and efficient, requiring less than 800 bytes of conventional RAM.

Syntax: `FTLIGHT <CR>`

Price:

Commercial. This product is part of a larger package called the Fresh Utilities. FTLIGHT is one of 10 command-line utilities that are included in the package. The entire package sells for $179.

Restrictions?

This promotional version of FTLIGHT may be installed on a single file server for use by users logging into the single file server. This version of FTLIGHT may not be resold or otherwise distributed to any other party. Persons using the software bear all risk as to the software's quality and performance. Fresh Technology Group disclaims all warranties relating to this software, whether express or implied, including without limitation any implied warranties.

Available from:

Fresh Technology
1478 North Tech. Blvd, Suite 101
Gilbert, AZ 85234
(602) 497-4200 voice
(800) 545-8324 voice
(602) 497-4242 FAX

How to operate it:

Loading FTLIGHT Into Memory

FTLIGHT can be loaded either from the command line or from within a batch file. To load FTLIGHT into memory from the command line, type:

```
FTLIGHT
```

and press the <Enter> key. A screen will be displayed stating that the resident portion of FTLIGHT is loaded
UNLOADING FTLIGHT FROM MEMORY
Although FTLIGHT only takes around 750 bytes (that's less than 1K of memory), you may, at times, need to remove it from memory. To unload FTLIGHT from memory, type:

```
FTLIGHT -
```

and press the <Enter> key. A screen will be displayed stating that FTLIGHT has been removed from memory. Remember, memory resident programs must be unloaded in the reverse order they were loaded; the last one in must be the first one out.
FTLIGHT COMMAND LINE PARAMETERS
There are a total of three optional command line parameters that may be used with FTLIGHT. The parameter is enclosed in square brackets [] and performs the function described as listed below. When using the parameters, type FTLIGHT followed by the parameter itself. DO NOT TYPE THE SQUARE BRACKETS:

[-]   The minus parameter removes the resident portion of FTLIGHT from memory as described in the section UNLOADING FTLIGHT FROM MEMORY.

[I]   displays the Fresh Technology Group copyright notice and number to call for ordering information.

[?]   displays a help screen for using FTLIGHT that summarizes the available commands.

INIT.BAT

Benefit:

This file can be invoked using the EXIT command from a user login script. In this file, the environment variable named LP is tested and, if set to a specific value, branches to a section that loads the PS-PRINT (Brightworks) remote printing shell. The environment variable LP can be set in the AUTOEXEC.BAT of the workstation setup as the print server or can be set based on the node address of the workstation in the system login script. The line in the system login script would read:

```
IF P_STATION="XXXXXXXXXXXX" THEN DOS SET LP="YYYY"
```

Syntax:

```
INIT
```

or from a login script,

```
EXIT "INIT"
```

How to operate it:

This batch file can be run directly from a network prompt or can be invoked from either the system or user login script.

Listing:

```
cls
@echo off
IF "%LP%"=="FINANCE" GOTO FINANCE
GOTO END
:FINANCE
Z:\APPS\PSPRINT\PSP FINANCE -NOFORM
z:\APPS\psprint\psp-con -r
GOTO END
:END
F:
```

LOGIN.INC

Benefit:

This file can be used in place of a system login script.

How to operate it:

The system login script needs only to have the statement INCLUDE SYS:\PUBLIC\LOGIN.INC. LOGIN.INC, in this example, needs to be located in SYS:PUBLIC. LOGIN.INC can then invoke another script file, such as START.BAT. The INCLUDE feature of NetWare can support nesting up to ten levels deep.

Examples of usage:

This file shows examples of setting environment variables, the use of conditional statements, and the use of the WRITE and DISPLAY commands. This file can be modified to meet individual network requirements.

Listing:

```
rem LOGIN.INC
WRITE "Logging in to FIN1 ..."
MAP DISPLAY OFF
MAP *2:=SYS:\USER\%LOGIN_NAME
MAP S1:=SYS:\PUBLIC
MAP S2:=SYS:\PUBLIC\BAT
MAP S3:=SYS:\PUBLIC\DOS
MAP S4:=SYS:\PUBLIC\VDR
MAP S5:=SYS:\PUBLIC\USR
COMSPEC=S3:COMMAND.COM
DOS SET DD="%MONTH_NAME %DAY, %YEAR"
DOS SET DT="%SHORT_YEAR%MONTH%DAY"
DOS SET GRP=" "
DOS SET ID="%LOGIN_NAME"
DOS SET PSV="FIN1"
DOS SET ST="%STATION"
DOS SET VL=""
REM DOS SET WS="%P_STATION"
DRIVE *1:
DISPLAY Y:CLRSCRN.DAT
```

```
#SYSTIME.EXE
WRITE " "
IF MONTH = "12" AND DAY >= "21" AND DAY <= "25" THEN BEGIN
    DISPLAY Y:SANTA.DAT
    #PLAY SANTA.TUN/F
    END
IF MONTH = "12" AND DAY > "28" THEN BEGIN
    DISPLAY Y:NEWYEAR.DAT
    #PLAY NEWYEAR.TUN/F
    END
IF MONTH = "01" AND DAY <= "05" THEN DISPLAY Y:%YEAR.DAT
IF NEW_MAIL="YES"               THEN DISPLAY Y:NEWMAIL.DAT
WRITE
MAP DISPLAY ON
FIRE PHASERS %NDAY_OF_WEEK TIMES
DISPLAY Y:BLKSCRN.DAT
EXIT "Y:START %2"
```

LOTUSB.BAT

Benefit:

This file partially solves the problem of PCs with multiple video standards on a network using an application whose driver sets are configured for specific video standards.

Syntax: LOTUSB

How to operate it:

Lotus 1-2-3 can be loaded with alternate driver sets. In the absence of a specified set, it defaults to 123.SET. This batch file first maps a drive, then executes a program, also included on the disk, named NWHAT4. NWHAT4 passes a string to an environment variable named VIDEO based on the type of video adapter it determines in the workstation. Once this is determined, the program branches to the appropriate section and loads Lotus 1-2-3 with the correct video driver. This presumes that individual drivers named EGA.SET, CGA.SET and MONO.SET were created with the Lotus install utility and reside in the Lotus application directory. This batch file also includes software metering using the shareware METER program also supplied on this disk.

Listing:

```
@ECHO OFF
CLS
MAP L:=SYS:\APPS\LOTUS
NWHAT4 -DI -VNAME:VIDEO
IF "%VIDEO%"== "VGA" GOTO VGA
IF "%VIDEO%"== "EGA" GOTO EGA
IF "%VIDEO%"== "CGA" GOTO COLOR
CLS
ECHO OFF
ECHO DETECTED MONOCHROME MONITOR - LOADING LOTUS 1-2-3
L:
METER 123 MONO
GOTO END
:VGA
CLS
ECHO DETECTED VGA MONITOR - LOADING LOTUS 1-2-3
```

```
L:
METER 123 VGA
GOTO END
:EGA
CLS
ECHO DETECTED EGA MONITOR - LOADING LOTUS 1-2-3
L:
METER 123 EGA
GOTO END
:COLOR
CLS
@ECHO OFF
ECHO DETECTED CGA MONITOR - LOADING LOTUS 1-2-3
L:
METER 123 CGA
GOTO END
:END
F:
MAP DELETE L:
```

MAIL.ICO

Benefit:

This generic Mail Icon for use with Windows 3.0 brings E-mail programs fully into graphical Windows environment.

How to operate it:

Copy the file to your Windows directory. Specify `MAIL.ICO` when changing Windows icons under File Preferences for your E-mail program.

MNU

Benefit:

MNU is a shareware security and general-purpose enhancement tool for Novell NetWare. It operates much like the SYSCON utility and provides a number of utility services that NetWare does not.

Where to find it:

MNU and its documentation can be found on the Power Tools disk in a file called MNU.COM or in the CompuServe Forum.

Syntax: See "How to Operate It" below.

Price:

Shareware, $85 per server. Automatic updates are $20 per site per year, $5 if the survey with the program is filled out.

Restrictions?

None.

More information available from:

Mark Pfeifer
Bonsai Technologies
P.O. Box 6296
Rochester, MN 55903-6296

CompuServe ID: 73657,3203

How to operate it:

Installation instructions are contained in MANUAL.TXT. It is strongly recommended that you print and read the manual before installing the program. MANUAL.TXT is formatted for 1-inch margins on all sides and may be printed on nearly any printer by sending the file directly to the printer. For example, with a local printer, use `COPY MANUAL.TXT LPT1:`. To send to a network printer, use `NPRINT MANUAL.TXT /Q=LASER`.

The MNU requires a Novell network. Also, you need a modest level of expertise with DOS and Novell to configure the MNU.

The files contained in MNU.COM are:

README.TXT	This file.
MANUAL.TXT	The program documentation.
LICENSE.TXT	License agreement and warranty disclaimer.[**]
UPGRADE.TXT	Upgrade instructions.[**]
REGISTER.TXT	Registration Info & Form.[**]
INSTALL.TXT	Installation Instructions.[**]
APPNDX_J.TXT	Appendix J of the program documentation.
VERSION.TXT	Version history.
MNU.BAT	The batch file to execute menus.
MNU$MAIN.EXE	The menu execution program, called by MNU.BAT.
MNUINST.EXE	The installation/upgrade/registration program.
MNUCON.EXE	The MNU Configuration, used to set up info.
MNU$LOG.BAT	The batch file called to log out
MNU$HLP.HLP	The help file for use by MNUInst&MNUCon.

[**]The information in these files is also included in MANUAL.TXT.

Please direct any questions/concerns to:

Bonsai Technologies
PO Box 6296
Rochester, MN 55903-6296

The MNU Installation Instructions

Note: You must be running PC or MS DOS 3.3 to use the MNU.

The MNU was written for NetWare version 2.1x. It is known to operate correctly on 2.1x versions (2.10, 2.11, 2.12, 2.15). It should also operate correctly on version 2.0a—however, the authors have not verified this.

Installation and configuration of the MNU is not a trivial task if you are not familiar with both DOS and Novell. If you are not, we recommend that you enlist the services of someone who is.

1. Read the file LICENSE.DOC and agree to the terms presented for nonregistered users.

2. Login as SUPERVISOR or equivalent.

3. Copy MNUCON.EXE, MNU$HLP.HLP, MNU.BAT, MNU$EXEC.EXE, MNU$MAIN.EXE, and MNUINST.EXE to SYS:PUBLIC. Flag these files as Shareable Read-Only.

4. Copy MNU$LOG.BAT to SYS:LOGIN and flag as Shareable Read-Only. Also, make sure the group EVERYONE has ROS rights to SYS:LOGIN.

5. Run BINDFIX in SYS:SYSTEM to back up the bindery files. This step is necessary to allow you to restore your system to its original state in the unlikely event that you are using another application that uses the same nonstandard object types as the MNU.

6. Create a work directory for the MNU and give EVERYONE all rights except parental to it. We suggest that the work directory be SYS:MNU_WORK.

7. Modify the system login script. The MNU must have a drive mapped out to its work directory. Also, the environment variables must be set if the defaults are not used. Here is a sample script:

```
MAP F:=SYS:USERS\%LOGIN_NAME
MAP S1:=SYS:PUBLIC
MAP S2:=SYS:PUBLIC\%MACHINE\%OS\%OS_VERSION
MAP ins S1:=SYS:APPS
MAP W:=SYS:MNU_WORK
SET MNU_STATION=STATION
* These values are defaults, but we'll set them
* anyway.
SET MNU_WORK="W"
SET MNU_SEARCH="X"
SET MNU_USER="F"
```

See the Installation Reference section of the manual for more information. Please note the MNU_WORK environment variable must *always* be set. Also note that the syntax given is correct for Novell login scripts; if you are setting the env vars from a batch file, omit the "s (SET MNU_WORK=W)".

8. Run MNUINST and select Install The MNU.

9. Run MNUCON.

    a. Use Menu Information to create a base menu. We suggest that you name it BASE_MENU, put in your company name as the Description, and make EVERYONE an Authorized Object.

    b. Use Other Information to set options. Set Base Menu to the menu created in #7 (BASE_MENU). Set the Allow User Autho-

rization and Allow Escape to DOS as desired. See the Other
Information section of the manual for more information on
these options.

c. Create a Logout item: use Item Information to create an item
named LOGOUT per the following:

```
Description          Logout
Authorized Groups    EVERYONE
Menus Used In        BASE_MENU
Execution Method     Logout
```

10. The MNU is now usable. If you want users to load the menu
automatically when they login, put the command EXIT "MNU" in
each user's login script.

11. You may now create your full menu structure with MNUCon. Please
note that you must be SUPERVISOR or equivalent to run MNU.

What is the MNU?:

The MNU is a menu system designed specifically for use with Novell. It
was designed to be a logical extension of Novell's security system of Users,
Groups, and Trustees. In addition, program operation was designed to be
very similar to Novell's existing Menu Utilities; that is, MNUCon (the MNU
Configuration) operates very similarly to SYSCON (System Configuration). The MNU does not replace any of Novell's utilities, except for the
Novell Menu, but rather works hand in hand with them.

If you are familiar with the concepts of Novell's Groups and Users, you
will have no problem with the concepts of the MNU's Menus, Items, and
Programs. The MNU, for all it capabilities and flexibility, really is a very
simple program.

If you are familiar with Novell's SYSCON and other utilities, you will
have no problem navigating in MNUInst and MNUCon, as they were
designed to use the same user interface.

The best way to become familiar with the MNU is:

1. Skim Section 1, "MNU Basics," to get some background info.

2. Read Section 3, "The Wadget Example," to get an idea of what the
MNU can do (not necessarily how it does it).

3. Skim Section 2, "MNU Configuration," to get a general idea of what
you are going to do after the MNU is installed.

4. Install the MNU on your file server using Appendix G, "Installation."

5. Set up a simple version of your current menus using Section 2, "MNU Configuration," as a reference (or use the context-sensitive help).

Program Modules

The MNU consists of three modules:

MNUInst	MNU Installation (MNUINST.EXE,MNU$HLP.HLP)
MNUCon	MNU Configuration (MNUCON.EXE,MNU$HLP.HLP)
MNU	The MNU (MNU.BAT,MNU$MAIN.EXE)

MNUInst is used to initially install the MNU on a file server, enter registration information, and update existing MNU data. Please note that you must be SUPERVISOR equivalent to run this module.

MNUCon works with Menus, Items, and Programs in much the same way that SYSCON works with Users and Groups. Please note that you must be SUPERVISOR equivalent to run this module.

MNU is the user interface module. It is the module that each user will run to access the menu system.

MNU Objects

Items:

An item is simply a choice that appears on a user's menu. For example: Set Password, Word Processing, Logout.

You may specify which groups and/or users are authorized to use an item. In addition, you may specifically prohibit groups and/or users from using an item. Also, you must specify which menus the item is to appear on; for example, Word Processing would appear on the Applications menu, Set Password would appear on the NetWare Utilities menu, Logout would appear on the main menu.

Drive Mapping may be specified by an option; for example, for Word Processing, drive F: could be mapped to the WP subdirectory of the user's personal directory and drive G: could be mapped to a common data area. In conjunction with the Data drives, a Default Drive may be specified, so the item is executed with a specific drive letter as the default drive.

The program that the item uses may also be specified. This will allow a search path to the program files to be set up and also any data drives that the program needs. Also, license metering may optionally be utilized.

Items may also be used to standardize a set of instructions across other items through the use of Item Instructions. For example, you might set up an item called LASER_CAP to perform a printer capture to your laser printer. In the instructions for LASER_CAP, you enter the appropriate capture commands. Then in the instruction for your SPREADSHEET item, you insert an Item instruction before the Text instruction that loads your spreadsheet program. When the MNU encounters the Item instruction during execution of SPREADSHEET, it inserts all of the instructions from LASER_CAP. Please note that in this case Authorization and Prohibition are ignored for Item LASER_CAP (but not for Item SPREADSHEET).

Menus:

A menu is similar to an item in that you authorize and prohibit groups and users. Also, you specify which menus the menu is to appear in. However, a menu does not execute any programs or perform other actions and thus does not have Drive Mappings or Instructions. In a typical setup, you might have a Main menu, an Applications menu and a NetWare Utilities menu. The Applications menu and the NetWare Utilities menu would be used in the Main menu.

Programs:

A program is used to provide centralized license control, search path mapping, and data drive mapping. For example, if you have an accounting system that has three modules, GL, AR, and AP, you would set up a program called ACCTING that has a search path to where all the executables are and a Data Drive to where the centralized data files are kept. Then you would make separate items for GL, AR, and AP that all have ACCTING as the Program Used. If you later move the data and/or program files, you simply change the search path and drive mapping for the program and the items are affected automatically.

The license metering feature may be used to allow single-user programs to run on a network; the above accounting system is single-user and will not allow multiuser access to the data files. Simply specify the number of licenses as 1 on the program and only one person will be allowed into the accounting system at any time (you must also use the Exec execution method for this to work). Note that this setup, one program and multiple items, would not allow a user to access GL if another user is in AP, because both items use the same program.

The license metering feature also allows you to purchase fewer licenses for a program than the number of users on your network without violating your license agreement; on a ten-user network, you can buy five word processing licenses and use the license metering feature to allow only five users to use the program at the same time.

Help in MNUCon:

MNUCon has an on-line, context-sensitive help system. Whenever you need more information on something, simply press F1.

The Help Text is organized as an information tree that gets more and more specific as you move through it. The following is a guide to interpreting the Help screens:

The topic behind "::" is the title of the current page.

The topics behind ">>" are more specific help.

The topics behind "<<" are more general help.

Any highlighted text may be selected by moving the selection bar with the cursor keys and striking ENTER.

Highlighted text will generally appear after the ">>" and "<<" symbols. However, it will occasionally appear in the text also.

MNUCon Operation:

MNUCon consists of a series of menus and list selections.

When in a menu, use the up/down arrow keys to move among the options. Options that have a Quick-Select character will have that character highlighted. If you hit the Quick-Select character for an option, the cursor will move to that option. After the cursor is on your desired option, hit ENTER to execute the option.

When in a list selection, use the up/down arrows, home/end, pgup/pgdn to move the cursor through the options. Also, you may hit the first letter of an option. This will take you to the first option in the list with that first letter *except* if the current option has that first letter. Then it will take you to the next option with that first letter.

In addition to the cursor movement keys, one or more of the following may be active in a list selection: Enter, Delete, Insert, Mark (F5), Modify (F3). Hit the Help key while in the list to find out which keys are active.

Main Menu:

The Main Menu consists of the following options:

Group Information: This option allows you to add, delete, and edit Groups. The operations performed here are identical to those in SYSCON.

Item Information: This option allows you to add, delete, and edit Items.

Menu Information: This option allows you to add, delete, and edit Menus.

Other Information: This option allows you to edit the MNU's configuration information, such as the Base Menu, the Automatic Logout Timeout, whether or not to display the Station Number on the screen title, and so on.

Program Information: This option allows you to add, delete, and edit Programs.

Reports: This option allows you to print/display systemwide reports.

User Information: This option allows you to edit information pertaining to Users. The operations performed here are identical to those in SYSCON. Note that you cannot add or delete Users with this option; those functions must be performed in SYSCON.

Group Information

Selecting Group Information brings up a List Selection of Groups. The functions here duplicate those available in SYSCON. From this list you may Add, Edit, Modify, or Delete Groups.

Group Selection List

The Group Selection List has the following keys active:

Enter	Edit the Group under selection bar.
Delete	Delete the Group under selection bar or delete all marked Groups.
Mark (F5)	Mark/unmark Group under selection bar.
Modify (F3)	Change the name of the Group under the selection bar.
Insert	Create a new Group.

Edit Group

After you have selected a Group from the Group Selection List, the Edit Group menu is presented with the following options available:

Full Name   This option allows you to give the Group a descriptive name.

Group Members   This option allows you to add/delete users to/from this Group.

Summary   This option allows you to display/print a summary of this Group.

The *Full Name* option is used only to print reports. It has no impact on program operation. It does not need to be unique—two groups may have the same Full Name. The Full Name may consist of upper/lower case, spaces, and punctuation. This is the same Full Name that may be manipulated with SYSCON.

The *Group Members* information is used in many ways, both by the MNU and by NetWare. This is the same Group Members that may be manipulated with SYSCON.

Summary displays/prints a summary of the Group being edited. This Summary includes the Group's Full Name, Group Members, and Trustee Assignments.

Item Information

Selecting Item Information brings up a List Selection of Items. From this list you may Add, Edit, Modify, or Delete Items.

Item Selection List

The Item Selection List has the following keys active:

Enter	Edit the Item under selection bar.
Delete	Delete Item under selection bar or delete all marked Items.
Mark (F5)	Mark/unmark Item under selection bar.
Modify (F3)	Change the name of the Item under selection bar.
Insert	Create a new Item.

Edit Item

After you have selected an Item from the Item Selection List, the Edit Item menu is presented with the following options available:

Authorized Groups   This option allows you to specify which Groups are authorized to use this Item.

Authorized Users   This option allows you to specify which Users are authorized to use this Item.

Default Drive   This option allows you to specify a Default Drive letter for the Item to use as the default/current drive during execution.

Description   This option allows you to specify a Description for this Item. This Description is similar to Groups' and Users' Full Names.

Drive Mapping   This option allows you to specify the Drives that will be mapped when the Item executes.

Execution Method   This option allows you to specify an execution method for this item. There are several choices available, each with its own strong points relating to memory overhead, license metering support, and so on.

Instructions   This option allows you to specify the Instructions that this Item will use when it executes.

Menus Used In   This option allows you to specify which Menus this Item will appear in.

Prohibited Groups   This option allows you to specify which Groups will be Prohibited from using this Item.

Prohibited Users   This option allows you to specify which Users will be Prohibited from using this Item.

Program Used   This option allows you to specify which Program this Item uses, if any.

Summary   This option displays/prints a summary of this Item.

The *Authorized Groups and Users* is used to determine if an item will appear on a user's menu. There are three ways a user may be authorized to use an Item:

1. The user is in the Authorized Users list.
2. The user is security equivalent to a User in the Authorized Users list.
3. The user is a member of a Group that is in the Authorized Groups list.

Note that making a user security equivalent to another user does not transfer group membership (just like NetWare Trustee Assignments). Also see Prohibited Groups and Users.

The Default Drive option allows you to select the drive letter of the default drive during execution. If a default drive is not specified, the user drive will be the default drive.

Note that if the Item uses a Program that has a Default Drive specified, the Default Drive you specify for the Item will override the Program's Default Drive.

The *Description* option allows you to specify a Description that will be used when the item appears on a menu. The default Description is the Item Name (as it appears in the Item Information List). The Description is similar to Full Names for Groups and Users. It may be any combination of upper/lower case, numbers, spaces, and punctuation. It does not have to be unique (two items may have the same Description). In addition, this option allows you to specify a QuickSelect character. This character will appear highlighted on menus and may be used to move to the item with one keystroke. Note that this character must be specified in the same case (upper/lower) as it appears in the Description. Also, if the character appears more than once in the Description, the first occurrence will be used. Specify a space if you do not want a QuickSelect character for this item.

The *Drive Mapping* option allows you to specify drive mapping for data drives. Note that Item Drive Mapping overrides Program Drive Mapping for any Drive Letters that are used in both the Item and Program.

The *Execution Method* option allows you to specify the Execution Method for the Item. The following Execution Methods are available:

Shell   Very fast execution and return to menu, one-line instructions only, relatively high memory overhead (75–150K), license control is available.

Shell & Pause—Same as Shell, except program pauses before it clears the screen and returns to the menu.

Exec   Fast execution and return to menu, multiple-line instructions, low memory overhead (10K), license control is available.

Exit   Fast exit from the menu to DOS.

Batch   Execution and return to the menu is slower than other methods. License control is not available. This method exists only because there is no (0) memory overhead and so it is suitable for loading/unloading

TSRs and for running programs that won't tolerate even a 10K memory overhead.

Batch & Exit   Same as Batch except that the menu is not restarted after the item is done executing. The method is suitable for exiting to a local hard drive or starting another menu system.

Logout   Same as Batch except that after the item is done executing, MNU$LOG.BAT is called to log the user out of the network.

The following table summarizes these methods:

Method	Shell	Shell &Pause	Exec	Batch	Batch &Exit	Exit	Logout
Memory Overhead	75K	75K	10K	0K	0K	N/A	0K
Load TSR	No	No	No	Yes	Yes	N/A	Yes
License Control	Yes	Yes	Yes	No	No	N/A	No
Execution Speed	Fast	Fast	Slow	Slow	Slow	Fast	Slow
Return Speed	Fast	Fast	Fast	Slow	N/A	N/A	N/A
Multiple Instructions	No	No	Yes	Yes	Yes	N/A	Yes
Pause On Return?	No	Yes	No	No	N/A	N/A	N/A
Return to MNU?	Yes	Yes	Yes	Yes	No	No	No

Shell

This method is well suited for executing interactive programs that do not need a lot of memory to run. This method yields the best turn-around speed because the MNU does not need to be unloaded from memory; however, it executes only one instruction line. If more than one instruction line is needed, use the Exec method. This method does provide license control.

Shell & Pause

This method is the same as Shell except that it pauses for a keystroke before that screen is cleared and the menu restarted. It is well suited for use with noninteractive programs such as CHKVOL and DIR because it pauses and waits for the user to hit a key before overwriting the screen with the MNU.

Exec

This method is used for the great majority of Items. It has a low memory overhead, license control, and the return to the menu is almost instantaneous. It is slightly slower than the Shell methods because of the additional file I/O involved in multiple-line instructions and swapping the menu's memory space. It is much faster at returning to the menu than the Batch method because it does not have to reread all of the item and menu information from the file server.

Batch

This method is best for loading and unloading TSRs. The execution speed is similar to Exec but its return to menu speed is greatly impacted, because all item and menu information must be reread from the file server. License control is *not* available with this method. This method may also be used for programs that will not tolerate the 10K memory overhead of the Exec method.

Batch & Exit

This method is the same as the Batch method except that the MNU is not reloaded after execution. It may be used to transfer control to a local hard disk.

Exit

This method is used to provide an exit to DOS capability for nonsupervisor equivalent users when the Allow Escape to DOS is set to No. Note that supervisor-equivalent users may always escape from the base menu to DOS, regardless of the setting of Allow Escape to DOS. Any item instructions are ignored.

Logout

This method is used to provide a logout capability for items. It is somewhat more flexible than the Novell Menu !Logout because it uses the MNU$LOG.BAT file to log out. This file may be modified to provide a continuous login loop or display instructions about how to log back into the network. Also, MNU$LOG.BAT calls LOGOUT.EXE to actually log out, so the login statistics are displayed.

The *Instructions* option allows you to Add, Edit, and Delete the Instructions for this Item. Instructions may be straight text and may include instructions from other items. These instructions are normal DOS batch commands. User prompting for parameters may be done with the same syntax as the Novell Menu—put an '@' in the instruction, followed by the prompt in ""'s. For example, to do a copy: copy @"Source file spec" @"Destination file spec".

The Instruction List has the following keys active:

Enter	Edit the Instruction under selection bar.
Delete	Delete the Instruction under selection bar.
Insert	Create a new Instruction. The new Instruction will be placed immediately before the Instruction under the selection bar.

The *Menus Used In* option allows you to specify which Menus this Item will appear on. You may also specify that this Item will appear on a Menu by using the Menu Structure in Menu Information.

The *Prohibited Groups and Users* options are used in conjunction with Authorized Groups and Users to determine if an Item will appear on a user's menu. For an Item to appear on a user's menu, the user must first be authorized (see requirements in Authorized Groups and Users) and second, the user must *not* be prohibited. There are three ways a user may be prohibited to use an Item:

1. The user is in the Prohibited Users list.

2. The user is security equivalent to a User in the Prohibited Users list.

3. The user is a member of a Group that is in the Prohibited Groups list.

Note that making a user security equivalent to another user does not transfer group membership (just like NetWare Trustee Assignments).

The *Program Used* option allows you to specify which program will be used by this Item. Specifying a program to be used causes the program's search drives to be mapped when the Item is executed. It also enables license control when the program has it enabled and when a compatible execution method is used. In addition, the program's data drives and default drive are used. If the Item and program have the same drive letter mapped, the Item's mapping is used. Also, if the Item has a default drive specified (not a space), the Item's default drive is used.

The *Summary* option displays/prints a summary of the Item being edited.

Menu Information

Selecting Menu Information brings up a List Selection of Menus. From this list you may Add, Edit, Modify, or Delete Menus.

The Menu Selection List has the following keys active:

Enter	Edit the Menu under selection bar.
Delete	Delete Menu under selection bar or delete all marked Menus.
Mark (F5)	Mark/unmark Menu under selection bar.
Modify (F3)	Change the name of the Menu under selection bar.
Insert	Create a new Menu.

Edit Menu

After you have selected a Menu from the Menu Selection List, the Edit Menu menu is presented with the following options available:

Authorized Groups   This option allows you to specify which Groups are authorized to use this Menu.

Authorized Users   This option allows you to specify which Users are authorized to use this Menu.

Description   This option allows you to specify a Description for this Menu. This Description is similar to Groups' and Users' Full Names.

Menus Used In   This option allows you to specify which Menus this Menu will appear in.

Menu Structure   This option allows you to specify which Items/Menus will appear on this Menu.

Prohibited Groups   This option allows you to specify which Groups will be Prohibited from using this Menu.

Prohibited Users   This option allows you to specify which Users will be Prohibited from using this Menu.

Screen Position   This option allows you to specify where the Menu should appear on the screen.

Summary   This option displays/prints a summary of this Menu.

The *Authorized Groups and Users* option is used to determine if a Menu will appear on a user's menu. There are three ways a user may be authorized to use a Menu:

1. The user is in the Authorized Users list.

2. The user is security equivalent to a User that is in the Authorized Users list.

3. The user is a member of a Group that is in the Authorized Groups list.

Note that making a user security equivalent to another user does not transfer group membership (just like NetWare Trustee Assignments). Also see Prohibited Groups and Users.

The *Description* option allows you to specify a Description that will be used when the Menu appears. This Description is also used as the Menu's title when it is displayed on the screen. The default Description is the Menu Name (as it appears in the Menu Information List). The Description is similar to Full Names for Groups and Users. It may be any combination of upper/lower case, numbers, spaces, and punctuation. It does not have to be unique (two Menus may have the same Description). In addition, this option allows you to specify a QuickSelect character. This character appears highlighted on menus and may be used to move to the Menu with one keystroke. Note that this character must be specified in the same case (upper/lower) as it appears in the Description. Also, if the character appears more than once in the Description, the first occurrence will be used. Specify a space if you do not want a QuickSelect character for this Menu.

The *Menu Structure* option allows you to specify which Menus and Items will appear on this Menu.

The *Menus Used In* option allows you to specify which Menus this Item will appear on. You may also specify that this Item will appear on a Menu by using the Menu Structure in Menu Information.

The *Prohibited Groups and Users* option is used in conjunction with Authorized Groups and Users to determine if a Menu will appear on a user's menu. For a Menu to appear on a user's menu, the user must first be authorized (see requirements in Authorized Groups and Users) and, second, the user must *not* be prohibited. There are three ways a user may be prohibited to use a Menu:

1. The user is in the Prohibited Users list.

2. The user is security equivalent to a User in the Prohibited Users list.

3. The user is a member of a Group that is in the Prohibited Groups list.

Note that making a user security equivalent to another user does not transfer group membership (just like NetWare Trustee Assignments).

The *Screen Position* option allows you to specify where the Menu will appear on the screen. Both a Horizontal (Left,Center,Right) and a Vertical (Upper,Middle,Lower) position may be specified. The default is Middle,Center.

The Menu will be centered in the specified area of the screen. If the Menu is too big to be centered in the given area, the position will be adjusted automatically.

Summary displays/prints a summary of the Menu being edited.

Other Information

This option allows you to edit global operation parameters for the MNU. After selecting this option, the following options will be presented:

Allow Escape to DOS   This option selects whether or not pressing ESCAPE from the base menu will exit to DOS.

Automatic Logout Item   If you want to have an item execute when the Automatic Logout Timeout expires, specify it here. If none is selected, the user will still be logged out.

Automatic Logout Timeout   This option allows you to specify the number of minutes of inactivity before the user is automatically logged out.

Base Menu   This option allows you to specify a Menu to be used as a systemwide Base Menu.

Display Station Number   This option allows you to specify whether or not to display the station number with the user name in the screen title area.

Screen Saver Timeout   This option allows you to specify the number of minutes of inactivity allowed before the screen is automatically blanked.

Separate Menus from Items   This option allows you to specify whether or not Menus are separated from Items when they are displayed on the screen.

Summary   The option displays/prints this information.

The *Allow Escape to DOS* option allows you to select whether or not to allow an exit to DOS by pressing ESCAPE from the main menu. Note that Items with Execution Methods Exit or Batch and Exit will still exit to DOS after execution. Also, please note that SUPERVISOR equivalent users will always be able to escape to DOS from the Main Menu.

The *Auto Logout Item* option allows you to select the Item to be used for Automatic Logout. If you select <None>, the Automatic Logout will still function but no Item Instructions will be used. Please note that authorization checking is not performed for an Automatic Logout item. You must use Auto Logout Timeout to enable/disable the Automatic Logout.

The *Auto Logout Timeout* option allows you to select the Timeout for the Automatic Logout. Use a value of 0 to disable the Automatic Logout. The value is in minutes. The Automatic Logout is operational only when executing the Menu, not while in MNUCon or MNUInst. Also, it is not operational while in an application program.

The *Base Menu* option allows you to select the Base Menu, the Menu used by the program as the "main menu." Please note that everyone should be authorized to use this Menu.

The *Display Station Number* option allows you to select whether or not to display the Station Number after the User Name in the Title Block on the top of the screen. The Station Number is the current setting of the DOS envvar MNU_STATION, which should be the Connection Number.

The *Screen Saver Timeout* option allows you to select the Timeout for the Automatic Screen Saver. Use a value of 0 to disable the Automatic Screen Saver. The value is in minutes. The Automatic Screen Saver is operational only when executing the Menu, not while in MNUCon or MNUInst. Also, it is not operational while in an application program.

The *Separate Menus from Items* option allows you to select whether or not to separate Menu choices from Item choices when they are presented to the user. The separation consists of Sorting the Menus to the bottom of the list and inserting a separating line when the menu is presented to the user.

The *Summary* option displays/prints a summary of this information.

Program Information

Selecting Program Information brings up a List Selection of Programs. From this list you may Add, Edit, Modify, or Delete Programs.

Program Selection List

The Program Selection List has the following keys active:

Enter	Edit the Program under selection bar.
Delete	Delete Program under selection bar or delete all marked Programs.
Mark (F5)	Mark/unmark Program under selection bar.
Modify (F3)	Change the name of the Program under selection bar.
Insert	Create a new Program.

Edit Program

After you have selected a Program from the Program Selection List, the Edit Program menu is presented with the following options available:

Default Drive   This option allows you to specify a Default Drive letter for Items that use this Program to use as the default/current drive during execution.

Description   This option allows you to specify a Description for this Program. This Description is similar to Groups' and Users' Full Names.

Drive Mapping   This option allows you to specify the Drives that will be mapped when Items that use this program execute.

License Information   This option allows you to specify how many license copies you own for this program.

Search Path   This option allows you to specify the path where the executables for this program reside. The Search Path will be mapped when Items that use this Program execute.

Summary   This option displays/prints a summary of this Program.

The *Default Drive* option allows you to select the drive letter of the default drive during execution. If a default drive is not specified, the user drive will be the default drive.

Note that if an Item that uses this Program has a Default Drive specified, the Default Drive that is specified for the Item will override the Program's Default Drive.

The *Description* option allows you to specify a Description for the Program. The default Description is the Program Name.

Note that the Description for Programs is used only when printing reports and will never be seen on a user's menu (since only Items and Menus appear on user's menus).

The *Drive Mapping* option allows you to specify drive mapping for data drives. Note that Item Drive Mapping overrides Program Drive Mapping for any Drive Letters that are used in both the Item and Program.

The *License Information* option allows you to edit the License Information for the Program. The Number of Licenses sets the maximum number of users that may use the Program simultaneously. Note that if the Program is used from an Item with the Batch or Batch and Exit execution methods, the License Information will be ignored. Use 0 for an unlimited Number of Licenses.

The *Search Path* option specifies the location of the program files. This path will be mapped to a search drive (usually X:). Specify the full path including the volume name.

The *Summary* option displays/prints a summary of this Program.

User Information

Selecting User Information brings up a List Selection of Users. From this list you may Edit and Modify Users. These functions duplicate those available in SYSCON.

Note that you may not add or delete users; these functions must be performed in SYSCON.

Group Selection List

The Group Selection List has the following keys active:

Enter	Edit the Group under selection bar.
Delete	Delete Group under selection bar or delete all marked Groups.
Mark (F5)	Mark/unmark Group under selection bar.
Modify (F3)	Change the name of the Group under the selection bar.
Insert	Create a new Group.

Edit User

After you have selected a User from the User Selection List, the Edit User menu is presented with the following options available:

Full Name   This option allows you to give the User a descriptive name.

Groups Belonged To   This option allows you to add/delete groups that this User belongs to.

Security Equivalences   This option allows you to add/delete Security Equivalences for this User.

Summary   This option allows you to display/print a summary of this User.

The *Full Name* option is used only to print reports. It has no impact on program operation. It does not need to be unique—two users may have the same Full Name. The Full Name may consist of upper/lower case, spaces and punctuation. This is the same Full Name that may be manipulated with SYSCON.

The Group Belonged To information is used in many ways, both by the MNU and by NetWare. This is the same Groups Belonged To that may be manipulated with SYSCON.

The *Security Equivalences* information is used in many ways, both by the MNU and by NetWare. This is the same Security Equivalences information that may be manipulated with SYSCON, except that you cannot manipulate Group security equivalences with MNUCon while you can with SYSCON. However, MNUCon correctly maintains Group security equivalence while using this option and while using the Groups Belonged To option.

Summary displays/prints a summary of the User being edited. This Summary includes the User's Full Name, Groups Belonged To, Security Equivalences, Login Script, and Trustee Assignments.

Reports

This option allows you to edit display/print reports on the systemwide configuration. After selecting this option the following options are presented:

Complete System Config.   This option displays/prints a composite of the Menu Structure, MNU Configuration, and NetWare Configuration reports.

Menu Structure   This option displays/prints a report illustrating the systemwide menu structure.

NetWare Configuration   This option displays/prints a report of all the information relating to NetWare (Users, Groups, Trustee Assignments, system login script).

Complete System Configuration   This option displays/prints a composite of the Menu Structure, MNU Configuration, and NetWare Configuration reports. This report is complete enough to file as a paper backup of both your User/Group configuration and MNU configuration.

Menu Structure   This option displays/prints an illustration of the systemwide menu structure, without regard to Authorization/Prohibition.

MNU Configuration   This option displays/prints a complete report of the MNU's information on your system. This report prints the equivalent of a Summary report for all Items/Menus/Programs and a Summary of Other Information.

The *NetWare Configuration* option displays/prints a complete report of NetWare's User/Group information on your system and prints the system login script and all user login scripts. This report prints the equivalent of a Summary report for all Users and Groups.

MONITOR

Benefit:

MONITOR is a memory-resident utility (4K) that will keep track of all DOS file actions taken by any program. Loaded into the workstation, MONITOR logs the information to a file of your choice on the server. This information is useful if you encounter difficulty running application software on the network. MONITOR gives the network adminstrator a better idea of what the program is doing—what file may or may not be accessible to the application, and so on.

MONITOR is a LANSMITH utility that will track all file opens and searches. You can load MONITOR, run the application in question, and then unload MONITOR. You can then examine the log file to see how the application behaves.

Syntax:

```
MONITOR
```

or

`MONITOR /?` for a help screen of the available options.

In most cases, you simply enter the command `MONITOR` to load the program. When loaded this way, MONITOR will produce a log file named MONITOR.TXT. There are, however, a few command-line parameters for MONITOR. To view a list of the parameters supported, enter `MONITOR /H` (for help) or `MONITOR /?`

- The /P parameter changes the log file name to a user-defined file name.

- The /Q parameter causes MONITOR to not print the copyright screen.

- The /S parameter displays the status of MONITOR, showing the version number, the name of the log file being used, and some memory-usage statistics.

- You can unload MONITOR by using the /U or /R parameter. If you have loaded any memory-resident programs after MONITOR, you must unload them before unloading MONITOR.

MONITOR log file:

Below is a simplified version of a log file produced by running Word-Perfect version 5.0.

```
Monitor Utility Program - v0.0A
Copyright (c) LANSMITH 1990
```

Monitor shows the following files were OPENED or SEARCHED:

```
SEARCH of file   --> wp.???
OPEN of file     --> C:\WP50\WP.FIL
SEARCH of file   --> C:\WP50\WP{WP}.SET
OPEN of file     --> C:\WP50\WP{WP}.SET


...
SEARCH of file   --> C:\WP50\WP{WP}??.*
OPEN of file     --> C:\COMMAND.COM
```

Price:

Commercial, Monitor is part of a +6 NetWare package that sells for $395.

Restrictions?

None

More information available from:

LanSmith
406 Lincolnwood Place
Santa Barbara, CA 93110
(805) 687-1271
(800) 552-4567

MSGS.BAT

Benefit:

Saves keystrokes for a frequently used CC:Mail function. This utility provides a message listing by CC:Mail user. Other related files included are:

```
ADMIN.BAT
DIRECTOR.BAT
RECLAIM.BAT
DIAGS.BAT
USERS.BAT
```

Syntax: MSGS

How to operate it:

This batch file, along with the other CC:Mail administration files, are placed in the CC:Mail CCADMIN directory and are run from there. Alternatively, they could be put in a batch subdirectory on the search path and invoked with the alternate listing shown below. Substitute the name of your mailbox for MBX_NAME, and the location of the CC:Mail CCADMIN and CC:Mail CCDATA directories to match your directory structure. You will be prompted for the mail box administrator's password.

Examples of usage:

With the %1 variable in the batch file, you can redirect the Messages report to a printer by typing MSGS>LPT1: or to an ASCII text file by typing MSGS>MSGS.TXT.

Listing:

```
CHKSTAT MBX_NAME Y:\APPS\CCDATA MESSAGES %1
```

Alternate listing:

```
Y:\APPS\CCADMIN\CHKSTAT MBX_NAME Y:\APPS\CCDATA MESSAGES %1
```

NET.BAT

Benefit:

This is a universal batch file that loads the user's network shells and logs him or her into the correct server. Virtually every workstation should have one.

Syntax: NET

How to operate it:

NET.BAT must be on the DOS search path. Substitute the name of your file server for FS and change USERNAME as appropriate. This batch file also changes logical drives and tests for the existence of LOGIN.EXE. This is useful, particularly on NetWare 286, as user's home directories may be H:, and upon loading the network shells, the first network drive is F:. If the user logs out from the home (H) drive, the first network drive on the next login is H, not F. Users can execute this batch file for subsequent logins. Alternate drive letters can be changed as necessary.

   If used in conjunction with SHELL.CFG that contains the statement:

```
PREFERRED SERVER = FS
```

it is not necessary to name the file server in the login command line. The PREFERRED SERVER option of SHELL.CFG is available only with the DOS client shell version 3.0 or greater.

Listing:

```
@ECHO OFF
CLS
IPX
net3
F:
IF EXIST LOGIN.EXE GOTO LOGIN
G:
IF EXIST LOGIN.EXE GOTO LOGIN
H:
IF EXIST LOGIN.EXE GOTO LOGIN
:LOGIN
LOGIN FS/USERNAME
CLS
```

NET_MGR

Benefit:

NETmanager is a utility patterned after Carbon Copy(R) but instead works across a network. This tool is designed for support personnel and will generate trouble tickets to help you track network problems. With NETmanager, you can see the screen of a remote user across the building, across the county, or across the state - whatever the boundary of your LAN. Unlike some networking packages on the market now, NETmanager will let you see screens even in VGA graphics modes.
Other features of NETmanager include the ability to:

- Control any other PC on your LAN via your PC's keyboard
- Look at and solve user's application program problems without running around your building.
- Maintain configuration information about each PC and user on your LAN (i.e., option cards installed, application software, type of disks, etc.)

NETmanager operates as if you are sitting at the keyboard of the PC that you are controlling, even though you never leave your desk.

Syntax:

Price:

Commercial, $1,495

Restrictions?

NETmanager is fully compatible with the following LAN operating systems:

- Novell's Advanced NetWare 2.01 or 2.1
- IBM PC Network Program
- Ungermann-Bass Net/One
- 3Com 3Plus
- AT&T StarLAN

This fully functional demo version is limited to only 25 trouble tickets.

Available from:

Brightwork Development, Inc.
766 Shrewsbury Avenue
Jerral Center West
Tinton Falls, NJ 07724
(800) 552-9876
(201) 530-0440

How to operate it:

Installation

Install NETmanager by first creating a subdirectory for the program files
to reside. For example, the following command creates a subdirectory
called BRIGHT:

```
MKDIR C:\BRIGHT
```

Then, run the included installation program. The syntax for this command
is:

```
A:INSTALL d:\dir_path
```

where d: is the drive where you want the files to reside and dir_path is the
name of the subdirectory that you just created for the program files.

With Novell networks, you must have a login for NETmanager on each
server that you will be supporting.

NETmanager uses the login to gain access to the server for user
information. The login does not have to have any file access privileges.
NETmanager uses a default login of GUEST with no password. If you
already have a GUEST login on each server, with no password, you do not
have to perform any additional steps.

You can replace the GUEST login with one you prefer provided you
configure NETmanager with the new login you select. Also, if you assign
a password to this login, you must similarly enter this password into
NETmanager.

If you do not have a GUEST login on each server, use the Novell
SYSCON utility to create one. Refer to the Novell NetWare documentation for information on how to create a login on a server.

Next, go to a PC that does not have the NETmanager files loaded on it.
This PC will be any one that you wish to "listen" to. Insert the NETmanager
distribution diskette into the A: drive and type A:NRLISTEN. If the
program loads successfully, you'll see a message stating "NRLISTEN
loaded. Waiting for a call." Remove the disk from the drive and return to
your PC.

At your DOS prompt, type NETMAN. Since this is the first time that NETmanager has been run, it will take a moment for the database files to initialize.

To take control of the PC that you just loaded the NRLISTEN program onto, highlight "Control Another PC" from the main menu. If you have loaded NRLISTEN onto more than one PC, you will see a listing of all of the PCs that you can "listen" to. Move the cursor to the name of the PC that you want to control and press the Enter key. At this point, you should see exactly what is appearing on the other PC. For example, you can type DIR to get a DOS directory on the other PC.

Now, to terminate a call with NETmanager, press the F1 key. At this point, you can either chose to "Hang up" or "Hang up and log trouble." The difference is that with the latter you can log the call for future reference. Another option at this screen is the ability to view the other PC's equipment

Once you understand the basics of NETmanager, you can begin to install it so that NRLISTEN will automatically be loaded on each workstation that you might want to listen to. NRLISTEN has several optional parameters that you can modify that serve to tune the performance of the program.

Once you have logged several "help" calls, you can also print out reports that provide detailed listings of logged calls, user information, and equipment configuration. The reports are stored in dBASE III file format so you can use the output of NETmanager and prepare any additional type of report.

NWHAT4

Benefit:

"Network What" is a batch file enhancement tool that gets various pieces of information from a Novell network and returns this information to a batch process in the form of an error level or by writing the result to the DOS environment table as the NWHAT variable.

NWHAT also allows dynamic branching within a batch file or Novell menu based on the workstation and user information it can supply. It also allows users to edit login scripts with a text editor instead of going into SYSCON. Users also can change printer configurations with PRINTCON without having to log in as users. Use NWHAT to log in Network Assistant printer servers onto the network when a user logs out.

Where to find it:

NWHAT can be found on the Power Tools disk under the file name NWHAT4.COM.

Syntax: NWHAT—command [argument]. Note that running NWHAT without a proper command will produce a help screen.

Price:

$20 per server.

Restrictions?

None.

Available from:

Precision Data Consultants
NE 1670 Old Belfair Hwy
Belfair, WA 98528

How to operate it:

Result codes: (General)

NWHAT will return an error level of zero (0) if the command completed successfully.

Errors that keep the program from completing correctly return an error level of one (1). These errors include:

```
"Not attached to the Network"
"Out of Environment Space"
"Invalid Command"
"Invalid or Missing Argument"
```

Commands that require a simple yes or no result return error levels; all other commands output their results to the NWHAT variable in the DOS environment table. If the variable does not exist, it is created. If it does exist, it is overwritten with the results of this command. The information written to the NWHAT variable can then be read by a batch file using the %NWHAT% syntax or viewed by entering a SET command at the DOS prompt.

Commands:

A command must be entered preceded by a dash (-) or slash (/). Only the first two characters of the command are required. Improperly entered commands cause a help screen to be displayed.

Command	Purpose
NAME:	Returns the user's LOGIN NAME. Returns ERRORLEVEL 2 if you are not logged in to the network.
FULL	Returns the user's full name as entered during the MAKEUSER process. Spaces are translated to underscore (_) characters to be compatible with the operation of the SET command. "UNKNOWN" is returned to the environment if no full name was ever entered for the user. If no argument is entered, NWHAT returns the full name of the user logged in at this workstation. Otherwise NWHAT will return the full name of the user with that LOGIN NAME. Returns ERRORLEVEL 3 if no user by that LOGIN NAME exists on this server.

Command	Purpose
ID	Returns the user's mail box ID. This is the name of the subdirectory under \MAIL on the SYS volume where the user receives mail. This is also where the user's login script and PRINTCON configuration files are kept. If no argument is entered, NWHAT returns the mail ID of the user logged in at this workstation. Otherwise NWHAT will the return the mail ID of the user with that LOGIN NAME. Returns ERRORLEVEL 3 if no user by that LOGIN NAME exists on this server.
STATION	Returns the logical station number that this workstation is attached to on the file server.
PHYSICAL	Returns the physical station number (usually the network interface card number) of this workstation.
DISPLAY	Returns the video display type: VGA, EGA, CGA, MCGA, MGA (Hercules), or MDA. Defaults to CGA if card type is unknown.
LOGGED	Returns ERRORLEVEL 0 if the workstation is logged in to a file server. Returns ERRORLEVEL 2 if the network shell has been loaded but the workstation is not logged in.
ATTACH	Returns ERRORLEVEL 0 if the workstation is attached to the file server specified in the argument. Returns ERRORLEVEL 2 if the workstation is not attached to the named file server.
FSERVER	Returns the name of the file server mapped to the default disk drive or to the drive specified in the argument. If the drive is not mapped to a file server,the primary file server name is returned. If no argument is entered, the current default drive is assumed.
VOLUME	Returns the name of the disk volume on the file server mapped to the default disk drive or to the drive specified in the argument. Returns ERRORLEVEL 2 if the drive is not mapped to a file server volume. If no argument is entered, the current default drive is assumed.
MAP	Returns the network map specification (including the volume name) of the default disk drive or the drive specified in the argument. Returns LOCAL if the drive is mapped to a local DOS drive. Returns ERRORLEVEL 2 if the drive is not a local drive and is not mapped to a file server.
NETBIOS	Returns ERRORLEVEL 0 if NETBIOS is loaded. Returns ERRORLEVEL 2 if NETBIOS is *not* loaded.

Command	Purpose
USER	Used to tell if another user is logged in to this file server. Returns ERRORLEVEL 0 if the Login ID is valid and the user is now logged in to the server. Returns ERRORLEVEL 2 if the Login ID is valid for this file server but the user is not logged in. Returns ERRORLEVEL 3 if the Login ID is invalid for this file server.
MEMBER	Returns ERRORLEVEL 0 if the logged user is a member of the group specified in the argument. Returns ERRORLEVEL 2 if the user is not a member of the named group.

Additional information:

NWHAT writes the results to the "REAL" DOS environment table. NWHAT searches back through the running programs to find the root COMMAND.COM. The search technique used works fine on PC-DOS version 3.3 and Vectra DOS version 3.3 but has not been tested on other versions of MS DOS. It was adapted from an assembly routine written by MicroSoft, so it should be pretty reliable.

The results of NWHAT will *not* be written to the environment of a secondary COMMAND.COM! This won't be a problem if you are running the secondary COMMAND.COM in the single command mode (the /c switch). Most programs that allow you to run a DOS command from within them (such as the dBASE RUN command) use this mode. However, programs such as Lotus 1-2-3, which run a secondary COMMAND.COM, will give you erroneous results. The NWHAT results will not appear in the environment table of the secondary COMMAND.COM.

NWHAT overwrites the results of a previous command only if the current command completes successfully, so you should always test for an error level of zero to make sure the NWHAT variable has been updated. This is particularly important when you are using commands with optional parameters, because these are most likely to fail from "Invalid or Missing Parameter" errors.

Examples of usage:

Example 1:   This batch file demonstrates a controlled auto login process.

```
REM NET.BAT


echo off
cls
Rem See if the user is attached to the network.
NWHAT -logged
```

```
If ERRORLEVEL 2 Goto LOGIN
If ERRORLEVEL 1 Goto SHELL
NWHAT -fserver
echo This work station is attached to server %NWHAT%
NWHAT -station
echo as station %NWHAT%
NWHAT -name
echo Login ID is %NWHAT%
Goto END
:SHELL
IPX
NET3
:LOGIN
LOGIN %1 %2
:END
```

Example 2:   Sending and receiving files through mail directories. This batch file transfers a file into a user's mail directory.

```
Rem SENDMAIL.BAT
Rem Command line Usage
Rem SENDMAIL filename LoginID
echo off
cls
NWHAT -id %2
If ERRORLEVEL 2 GOTO NO_USER
If ERRORLEVEL 1 GOTO NO_NET
MAP M:=SYS:MAIL\%NWHAT%
COPY %1 M: /V
MAP DELETE M:
Echo Mail file %1 delivered to MAIL\%NWHAT%.
Goto END
:NO_USER
Echo %2 is not a valid User ID for this server.
Goto END
:NO_NET
Echo You must be logged into the network to send mail.
:END
Rem VIEWMAIL.BAT
Rem Get a directory list of the files in your Mail Box.
echo off
cls
```

```
NWHAT -id
If ERRORLEVEL 1 GOTO NO_NET
MAP M:=SYS:MAIL\%NWHAT%
DIR M: /P
Pause
MAP DELETE M:
GOTO END
:NO_NET
echo You must be logged into the network to view your
Mail Box files.
:END
Rem GETMAIL.BAT
Rem Copy a file from your mail box to the current
directory
Rem Usage: GETMAIL filename
echo off
cls
NWHAT -id
If ERRORLEVEL 1 GOTO NO_NET
MAP M:=SYS:MAIL\%NWHAT%
IF NOT EXIST M:%1 GOTO NO_FILE
COPY M:%1 /V
MAP DELETE M:
GOTO END
:NO_NET
echo You must be logged into the network to view your
Mail Box files.
Goto END
:NO_FILE
echo The file %1 is not in your Mail Box.
:END
```

Example 3:   Edit a login script file without going into SYSCON. This batch file uses the TED editor from PC Magnet but would work with anything else.

```
Rem EDLOGIN.BAT
Rem Allows SUPERVISOR (or User) to edit a LOGIN script
Rem Usage EDLOGIN LoginID
echo off
NWHAT -id %1
```

```
If ERRORLEVEL 2 GOTO NO_USER
If ERRORLEVEL 1 GOTO NO_NET
MAP M:=SYS:MAIL\%NWHAT%
If NOT EXIST M:LOGIN. GOTO NO_FILE
M:LOGIN.
MAP DELETE M:
Goto END
:NO_FILE
Echo There is no LOGIN script file to edit for this user.
Goto END
:NO_USER
Echo %2 is not a valid User ID for this server.
Goto END
:NO_NET
Echo You must be logged into the network to edit a LOGIN
script.
:END
```

Example 4:   Saving and restoring a drive map.

```
NWHAT -map L:
If ERRORLEVEL 2 GOTO SET NWHAT=NONE
If ERRORLEVEL 1 GOTO END
Rem Sample of Program map and execution
MAP L:=SYS:APPLICS\WS50
L:
WP
IF %NWHAT%==NONE GOTO DEL_MAP
MAP L:=%NWHAT%
Goto END
:DEL_MAP
MAP DELETE %1
:END
```

Example 5:   Keeping an ASSIST print server online when a user logs out. We use PS for our print servers. When the user logs out, this batch file logs the print server in so printing can continue normally.

```
LOGOFF.BAT
echo off
SET PS=NONE
NWHAT -physical
IF %NWHAT%==AA2700010100 SET PS=PS
IF %NWHAT%==346700010100 SET PS=PS
```

```
IF %NWHAT%==451000010100 SET PS=PS
IF %PS%==NONE LOGOUT
LOGIN PS
```

Example 6:   Edit a print configuration file without logging in as the user.

```
Rem PCON.BAT

Rem Allows SUPERVISOR or Group Manager to edit a user's
printer Rem configuration without logging in as the user.
Rem Usage PCON LoginID

echo off
NWHAT -id
If ERRORLEVEL 1 GOTO NO_NET
MAP H:=SYS:MAIL\%NWHAT%
H:
Copy PRINTCON.DAT PRINTCON.SAV
NWHAT -id %1
If ERRORLEVEL 2 GOTO NO_USER
If ERRORLEVEL 1 GOTO NO_NET
MAP M:=SYS:MAIL\%NWHAT%
If NOT EXIST M:PRINTCON.DAT GOTO NO_FILE
COPY M:PRINTCON.DAT
PRINTCON
COPY PRINTCON.DAT M:
Goto END
:NO_FILE
Echo There is no printer configuration file to edit for
this user.
Goto END
:NO_USER
Echo %2 is not a valid User ID for this server.
Goto END1
:NO_NET
Echo You must be logged into the network to edit a LOGIN
script.
Goto END2
:END
MAP DELETE M:
:END1
COPY PRINTCON.SAV PRINTCON.DAT
:END2
```

P0.BAT

Benefit:

This batch file is a sample of several files used to redirect users' printers. Each user on a network could have menu entries for each of the attached printers or printer queues. If one printer was tied up with a long job, users could redirect print jobs to another printer from a menu.

Syntax: P0

How to operate it:

Invoke directly from a network prompt, or call from a menu.

Examples of usage:

Names for the batch files can relate to physical printers (P0, P1, etc.), refer to the name of the user near the printer (SARAH.BAT), or have the name of the queue that they service. Timeout (TI), banners, tabs, form feeds and other capture switches can be modified as necessary.

Listing:

```
CLS
ECHO OFF
CLS
ECHO
capture p0 nb ti=1 nt nff
CLS
ECHO OFF
ECHO YOUR PRINTER OUTPUT HAS BEEN RE-ROUTED TO SARAH'S
LASER PRINTER
pause
```

RECLAIM.BAT

Benefit:

Saves keystrokes for a frequently used CC:Mail function. This utility will reclaim disk space freed up in the CC:Mail database when users delete messages. Other related files included are:

```
ADMIN.BAT
DIAGS.BAT
DIRECTOR.BAT
MSGS.BAT
USERS.BAT
```

Syntax: RECLAIM

How to operate it:

This batch file and the other CC:Mail administration files are placed in the CC:Mail CCADMIN directory and are run from there. Alternatively, they could be put in a batch subdirectory on the search path and invoked with the alternate listing shown below. Substitute the name of your mailbox for MBX_NAME and the location of the CC:Mail CCDATA directory to match your directory structure. The CC:Mail instruction manual cautions that the administrator must have exclusive use of the mail database while running the reclaim utility. You will be prompted for the mail box administrator's password.

Examples of usage:

Run this utility regularly to conserve disk space.

Listing:

```
RECLAIM MBX_NAME Y:\APPS\CCDATA
```

Alternate listing:

```
Y:\APPS\CCADMIN\RECLAIM MBX_NAME Y:\APPS\CCDATA
```

SHELL.CFG

Benefit:

The SHELL.CFG file gives you the ability to custom configure your network shell. This configuration allows you to set a preferred server, and will show directory dots [..] when running Windows 3.0 on a network.

Syntax: No syntax—this is a configuration file and is not executable.

How to operate it:

SHELL.CFG must reside in the same directory as NETx.COM and is read when NETx.COM is loaded. Some options, such as the ones shown in this example, are new and work only with the DOS client shells version 3.0 or later. Consult your NetWare manual for other options.

Listing:

```
SHOW DOTS = ON
PREFERRED SERVER=FINANCE
```

STACKEY/BATUTIL

Benefit:

STACKEY/BATUTIL provides a very powerful set of utilities to enhance batch files. These two programs provide "buffer-stuffer" services and enhanced batch file processing commands for simple menus and so on. BATUTIL also enhances the ability to manipulate the environment and to have a path that is longer than 127 characters.

What STACKEY does:

STACKEY is a keyboard stacker that lets you automate feeding of keystrokes to applications. It is a TSR taking about 1.3K of memory. As in previous versions, it has a simple intuitive syntax so that F1 is, er, well, F1 rather than the \059 that most other stackers require. As in earlier versions, this one allows stacking of EGA/VGA color changes and lock keys. Among its many new features, STACKEY can:

- Stack shift presses and so call up SIDEKICK and others.
- Pause a script waiting for a certain string on screen.
- Pause a script waiting for a hot key.
- Stack a Carousel partition swap or DV menu callup.
- Load high with 386max or QEMM.
- Toggle to send to standard output mode and replace SEND.
- Allow the buffer to be up to 60K for large filekey scripts.
- Insert beeps and pop-up messages in a script.
- Insert in-line code to a script if you are an ASM programmer.
- Disable print screen (great for laptops).

The program includes a 106-page manual on disk and an 18-screen on-line help summary. STACKEY still includes its utilities mode to do such things as swap ports, reboot, and so on.

What BATUTIL does:

BATUTIL is a nonresident program for adding power to your batch files. It has almost 100 commands for returning some kind of information either in the errorlevel, display, or the environment. It will access and directly manipulate the DOS environment. Among its high points:

1. `Batutil {menu choice1 choice2 ....}` will pop up an elegant menu with the user's choice returned in the error level.

2. It has a get key using the STACKEY intuitive syntax: for example, F1 for F1 with default choices after timeout if you want, and a count time of remaining time on screen if you wish.

3. Lots of display options including colors, large characters, and cursor location control.

4. Ten tunes and ten sounds.

5. Can ask for a string and place it in the environment.

6. Can ask for a filename and get it from a pop-up file list box, in the Windows style.

7. Supports environmental variables including path and prompt up to 255 characters.

8. Special support for manipulating path via batch commands or interactively.

9. Can return in the error level information on free disk space, memory, and so on—up to twenty-six aspects of your system in all.

10. Can return in the error level or environment the Carousel, DESQVIEW, or Omniview partition, DOS or 4DOS version, LIM version, Himem version, day of week, date, month, year, time, status of locks, number of files matching a file spec, whether a file is a device.

11. IF EXIST is extended to search path.

12. Includes a 115-page manual on disk and a 120K help program.

Where to find it:

On the Power Tools disk under the name STACKEY.COM or on CompuServe, IBM Systems Forum (GO IBMSYS), Library #3, SKEY30.ZIP. (Note: CTRLALT Associates, creators of this utility, will support its products including BATUTIL and STACKEY in section 12 of PCVENA go PCVENA.) Relevant PPNs are Barry Simon 76004,1664 and Rick Wilson 73007,3221. Or you can send us MCImail or write them at:

CTRLALT Associates
260 South Lake Ave., Suite 133
Pasadena, CA 91101

Syntax: See below.

Price:

Shareware, $39 (includes both the STACKEY and BATUTIL files).

More information available from:

Support Group, Inc.
P.O. Box 130
McHenry, MD 21541
1 (800) 872-4768
1(301)387-4500 (outside Continental U.S.)
FAX 1(301)387-7322

Purpose:

BATUTIL, along with its companion program STACKEY, is a program with two purposes: to give you power inside your batch files and to give you more control over the DOS environment. Included in the information that you can get returned in either the DOS errorlevel or an environmental variable are:

- current time, date, day of the week
- total amount and amount free of disk space, memory and EMS
- CPU type and type of coprocessor if present
- whether a file exists not only in the current directory but on the DOS path and if it exists on the DOS path, the actual directory can be returned in another environmental variable
- whether a file has today's date or not
- whether one of two files is older than another
- the ability to parse a filespec into individual components

While some of these options may seem simplistic at first, they give you the tools to create flexible and powerful BAT files for both LAN administrators and users.

STACKEY will automatically place keystrokes in your keyboard buffer. It is intended for use in connection with BATch files. Here is a typical example of a BATch file "lot.bat" for use with 1-2-3 using STACKEY:

```
stackey W18 CR"/FR%1.wk1" CR
123
```

Entering "lot mysht" at the DOS command line starts the BATch file with mysht as %1. STACKEY has the command line passed to it by the BATch processor with %1 already replaced by mysht. Thus STACKEY places in the keyboard buffer the text: "/FRmysht.wk1" followed by a carriage return. The initial W18 tells STACKEY to pause about 1 second to allow 123 to load. If it weren't there 123 would happily remove the keystrokes from the buffer before allowing any input. These characters wait in the buffer until a program requests keyboard input. The BATch file then loads 123 which requests input and gets it from STACKEY. /FR calls up a dialog to retrieve a worksheet and %1.wk1 followed by a CR loads that worksheet. The CR after the W18 will banish the opening logo screen in those versions with an opening logo.

How to use it:

Additional information about BATUTIL and STACKEY can be obtained from the extensive documentation that accompanies the program on disk. In addition, you can get interactive help for BATUTIL and STACKEY by typing

```
BATUTIL ?
```

or

```
BATUTIL !
```

at the DOS prompt. BATUTIL looks for the first two non-blank characters following the ? (or!) and if they are a valid BATUTIL command, you will be immediately sent to the help for that command; otherwise, the main help menu will be displayed. For example

```
BATUTIL ? SE
```

would display help for BATUTIL's SET command. BATUTIL ? displays the menu oriented help with various special effects.

Seventeen screens of help for STACKEY are available if you type in

```
STACKEY ?
```

To get help, the file STACKEY.HLP distributed with STACKEY must be available either in the default directory or in your path.

374 NOVELL NETWARE POWER TOOLS

Basic Concepts: BATUTIL

You give BATUTIL a series of commands on the command line. There are about 100 different commands—lest that overwhelm you, we note that many are just giving different pieces of hardware information which you'll rarely want and even the most complex idea (menus) are controlled by one basic command and fewer than ten commands which effect options like whether the menu explodes. Chapter VII is a detailed alphabetical command reference. When you invoke BATUTIL's help, one option is an alphabetical list of co mmands which will give you a panel with syntax and parameters for each.

The basic syntax is

```
BATUTIL {command1} {command2} ...
```

Each command is placed inside braces {}. The braces are critical—it doesn't matter whether you have spaces between } and the next { or not. truncation. That is all commands are distinguished already in the first two symbols and any substring of the command that has at least two letters will work. For example, the basic command to get a report on the environment is

```
BATUTIL {envrep}
```

The minimal truncation for that is EN so we'll often write ENvrep to emphasize this. Thus

```
BATUTIL {en}
```

or

```
BATUTIL {envr}
```

would work just as well as the full name. The basic commands are not case sensitive so {EN} or {En} or even {eNvRe} would do the same thing as {envrep}.

Roughly fifty of the commands return to the user (i.e. you as a batch file writer) a number from 0 to 199. If the command in question appears inside {} then that number is stored in the environmental variable RC (short for "return code"; environmental variable are discussed at the start of chapter 5). If the command appears in [], then BATUTIL will exit without running the rest of the command line and place this integer in the DOS errorlevel where you can test it with batch commands like

```
if errorlevel ....
```

Some commands will take optional parameters which also appear inside the braces for that command. Thus @Disk gives the free disk space. If no parameter is specified, then the current default drive will be used. Otherwise you can specify a drive as in

```
BATUTIL {@D C}
```

BATUTIL will object to incorrect syntax so if you tried

```
BATUTIL {@D 3}
```

then BATUTIL will exit (with an appropriate message if Verbose mode is on). You can separate the command from the first parameter by any of the following:

```
<space>,<comma>,= or  :
```

Rules of separation of multiple parameters for those few commands which accept multiple parameters depend on the commands.

Basic Concepts: STACKEY

The first time that STACKEY is invoked, it loads a small resident portion which becomes permanently resident taking almost exactly one kilobyte of RAM for code plus whatever buffer size you choose. By default the buffer size is 128 'keystrokes' or 256 bytes. This can be changed; see chapter 3—indeed many of the new features takes 3-10 keystrokes of buffer space and some considerable more so you may want a larger buffer. It displays the message:

```
Resident part of STACKEY now in place.
```

and proceeds to read its command line. At later times, STACKEY will find itself in memory and only read its command line. If you are using a hardware or software protocol that allows loading in high memory (386MAX, QEMM, etc), you'll want to use SKRES rather than STACKEY as you will if you want a buffer with over 10000 keystrokes, see Section III.11.

STACKEY will place keystrokes in its stack according to the rules of syntax described below. If there is a syntax error, it will exit with no keyboard stacking and give an erro message. For example, saying

```
stackey "hello "CRthere
```

will result in an error message. An arrow will point to the first place on the line that STACKEY was unable to interpret. The command line to send hello on one line and there on the next should have said:

```
stackey "hello "CR"there"
```

START.BAT

Benefit:

START.BAT is a sample file that can be nested from accompanying LOGIN.INC or invoked from user login script. Concepts presented here can be combined with concepts presented in INIT.BAT.

Syntax: This file is invoked by the LOGIN.INC file included on this disk, or can be invoked from a Network prompt, or by the command:

```
EXIT "START"
```

from a user login script.

How to operate it:

This file can be invoked using the EXIT command from the system login script. It allows individual users to create an AUTOUSER.BAT file, which is essentially the network equivalent of the AUTOEXEC.BAT file. It also provides a check for the existence of a MESSAGE.DAT file, a GREET-ING.DAT file, and even a JOKE.DAT file. If it finds any of these files, it will display them. By placing the AUTOUSER.BAT file in a user's home directory, the user gains some control over what happens on his or her machine at the completion of the login script.

Notes:

Cursor positioning used in this file assumes ANSI.SYS is present in memory. Mappings may have to be adjusted to match your network directory and mapping structure.

Listing:

```
rem START.BAT
ECHO OFF
   ECHO [0m[u
   IF NOT .%MN% == .          SET PROMPT=%MN% in $p$_$_
   IF      .%ID% == .SNA      GOTO START
   IF      EXIST Y:MESSAGE.DAT TYPE Y:MESSAGE.DAT
   IF NOT EXIST Y:GREETING.DAT GOTO NOGREET
   DISPLAY < Y:GREETING.DAT
:NOGREET
   IF EXIST Y:JOKE.DAT ECHO [1mType JOKE for the Joke of
```

```
    the Week ! [0m

      ECHO
      PAUSE
rem   ECHO LOGIN %ID% >> Z:\PUBLIC\STAT\STAT.DAT
rem   V:DT >> Z:\PUBLIC\STAT\STAT.DAT
      PATH Z:.;Y:.;X:.;W:.;V:.
      SET PTR=L
      GOTO START
:START
rem Set the Home drive to H:
        MAP H:=I:  > NUL:
        MAP DEL I:  > NUL:
      IF EXIST H:AUTOUSER.BAT AUTOUSER
      Y:MENU
```

TSRW31

Benefit:

This is a very useful program for network shells. Users first set a "mark" in memory and then load any TSR normally. At any point, they can release any program that occurs after a "mark" and reclaim that memory. This is a general-purpose utility that can work with any memory-resident software.

Where to find it:

On the Power Tools disk under the name TSRW31.COM or CompuServe IBM Systems Forum (GO IBMSYS), Library #3, TSRW31.ARC.

Syntax: Varies with utility.

More information available from:

Tom Gilbert's Heart and Mind
7127 Lafayette Avenue
Kansas City, KS 66109
Phone: (913)299-2701

How to operate it:

LoadTSRs

LoadTSRs is *not* a program. It is a *system*. The LoadTSRs system consists of three BAT files and an EXE assembly language program. The TSRmenu.BAT (first BAT file) invokes the MenuTSRs.EXE program that creates the Load2TSR.BAT (second BAT file). Load2TSR.BAT loads TSRs selected from a menu of TSRs displayed by the MenuTSRs.EXE program. The last line of Load2TSR.BAT chains to a KillLoad.BAT (third BAT file), which deletes the Load2TSR.BAT file.

The LoadTSRs system, as you receive it, contains only the TSRmenu.BAT and KillLoad.BAT files plus the MenuTSRs.EXE and its source code. While explaining this system, the LoadTSRs.DOC file may help you learn more about operating your computer.

Although the LoadTSRs system, such as ShowTSRs, UnMark, ReMark, and so on, are provided for programmers, novices can be "programmers" in our definition of the target audience. All that is necessary for you to benefit is a willingness to learn to program.

First, let's review some BAT file concepts.

With version 3.3 of MS-DOS, a BAT file can "call" another BAT file. What does that mean? BAT files commonly have a line that invokes a program. The line in TSRmenu.BAT that reads MenuTSRs is an example. When the operating system encounters this line, it loads and executes the program. When the program ends (terminates), the operating system resumes in the BAT file right after the "MenuTSRs" line with the program termination code in a BAT variable known as "ERRORLEVEL". The BAT file then continues with its next line.

It is as if the BAT file said, "Go To this program AND come back with the result." Here, for example, is the TSRmenu.BAT file:

```
Echo Off
MenuTSRs
IF ERRORLEVEL 1 GoTo Exit
%MrkDir%\Load2TSR
:Exit
```

Notice the blank line at the end. This says "done" and prevents a double prompt caused by the BAT file processor going back for a line that does not exist. The BAT file test for an ERRORLEVEL will be TRUE for a specified or any higher level. Only when MenuTSRs exits with 0 ERRORLEVEL will the jump over the %MrkDir%\Load2TSR NOT take place.

MS-DOS versions before 3.3 do *not* provide for calling another BAT file. If the Load2TSR.BAT file line is invoked, the label ":Exit" will never be reached. It is as if the TSRmenu.BAT file had said "Go To Load2TSR.BAT AND DON'T come back!" The operating system BAT file processor handles only one BAT file at a time. When the next BAT file is "chained," the processor starts all over again. This is *not* bad. In fact, it is GOOD! Starting over lets DOS update itself.

Application:

You are considering hiring a consultant to train your computer users. Ask the applicant to write your AutoExec.BAT file and give a long list of preparation actions required before the user receives control at the DOS prompt. If the applicant produces a multipage AutoExec.BAT file, write "unqualified" on the application. If the applicant's AutoExec.BAT file is short and begins a series of "chained" BAT files, with the secondary BAT files placed at logical points, hire him or her.

Our AutoExec.BAT contains only a virus protection system. If an infection is found, it chains one way. If the system is okay, it chains to a

SetPaths.BAT that, in turn, chains to a StartUp.BAT, which has a number of alternatives. Suppose that the next chain is LoadTSRs.BAT, which contains:

```
Set TSRdir=C:\TSRs
Set MrkDir=G:
FMark %MrkDir%\Watch
Watch
MenuTSRs
TSRmenu
```

The BAT file processor substitutes the Environment String that was set to "G:" for the variable %MrkDir%. The FMark line would be "FMark G:\Watch". Note that the backslash "\" is literal.

This might be a good time to use the MS-DOS "TYPE" command to see the MenuTSRs.EXE HELP screen. Do this:

```
C:>TYPE MenuTSRs.EXE
```

"You can't TYPE an .EXE file!" you say. Well, do it anyhow.

See how the sample LoadTSRs.BAT file sets the requirements for the LoadTSRs system. Use ShowTSRs, after the sample LoadTSRs BAT file. You will see that the operating system CONFIG.SYS, DOS SHELL, and DOS ENVIRONMENT are followed by FMark G:\Watch, Watch and a 128 byte LoadTSR line. MenuTSRs is a TSR itself! It "signals" that requirements have been met for loading TSRs from a menu. The "LoadTSR" line shows 6 instead of 5 under the files column because the Load2TSR.BAT file is counted.

Naturally, you will need to put your TSR.COM files in the TSRdir directory and have a MrkDir directory for the FMarks and the Load2TSR.BAT file. TSR.EXE files and TSRs *not* in the TSRdir or on the menu can still be loaded without using MenuTSRs.EXE; but it is important that each be preceded by an FMark. We prepare for changes to the TSR configuration by using FMarks. UnMark can be used to remove and TSRmenu can then re-load TSRs to meet your desires.

Using BAT files to UnMark or ReMark TSRs depends on the BAT file chaining process. When the BAT file processor switches BAT files, it gives DOS an opportunity to recover its breath between such operations. It really is better, however, to UnMark or ReMark from the command line. After all, you are the system driver, *not* a passenger!

Now for the bottom line on BAT files. The LoadTSRs system does *not* use BAT files just for the heck of it. If MenuTSRs.EXE loaded the TSRs while it was running, they would be installed above it (leaving a hole in memory when MenuTSRs terminated). If installation was done by the resident MenuTSRs, it would require a large resident for all the code. The use of BAT files allows DOS to do the installation. Each set of TSRs loads in the memory just vacated by MenuTSRs when the Load2TSR.BAT is chained on termination back to TSRmenu.

There are some interesting procedures in MenuTSRs.ASM that are worth consideration. The GetDirs Proc not only reads the master DOS environment but corrects it if either the TSRdir or MrkDir directories contain an ending "\". If you have *not* preset the variables, this procedure takes your input (ensuring at least 2 bytes and no trailing "\"), and puts it into the DOS ENVIRONMENT. There is a hazard in this! Your DOS Master Environment may not have sufficient space for the additions. To ensure that it is big enough, you will want to have a CONFIG.SYS SHELL = C:\COMMAND.COM C:\ /E:1024 /P or similar entry. My "E:1024" entry provides an environment size of 1k. You may need less or want more.

The IfPSPA PROCedure is used to test TSRfileNames from either the residents found in memory or your input against the list of files in your TSRdir directory. Notice the care used to make sure that the STACK is back UP to the RETurn address whichever way the procedure reaches its RETurn ending point.

The MakeBAT and EndBAT PROCedures demonstrate creating, writing to, and closing a file. MakeBAT is called before the decision as to whether to install or update the resident MenuTSRs so that an error will not occur as a result of no Load2TSR.BAT file being found on the initial call that installs MenuTSRs as a TSR.

The BP2PSPA PROCedure and the NBX2ASC PROCedure demonstrate displaying a value as HEX or as DECIMAL ASCII. These are commonly required assembly language routines. You may use or modify them for your own programs.

All programs of the TSRwrk series accumulate a table of MCBs with a WORD size value for each MemoryControlBlock address, the Address of the Block which it controls, the size of the block and flags. This table demonstrates how DOS keeps track of what is resident in its memory. The last MCB or currently running program has a Memory Control Block identified with a "Z"; all others begin with an "M". These paragraphs (16 byte blocks of memory) are what DOS uses when you Install TSRs or Release them.

WorkTSRs' programs are *not* intended for "passive users." They are provided with source code because they are for users who "take charge." Any comments or suggestions that help Tom Gilbert's Heart and Mind to learn and grow will be welcomed.

WorkTSRs is an all assembly language replacement for a series of programs written by TurboPower Software to manage TSR programs.

Because TurboPower Software is in the business of providing Turbo-Pascal utilities, its six major management programs were written in the Pascal. The assembly language replacements were written as exercises. They are placed in the public domain for educational purposes. Use the WorkTSRs if you prefer them; but, the credit for this TSR management system belongs to Kim Kokkonen and The TurboPower Software company. Some TSRCOM ASM programs were also rewritten.

FreeRAM differs from RAMFREE only in that it uses the CHKDSK algorithm and places a comma between the thousands and hundreds places. Rick Housh finds its report to be more accurate on his system. Take your choice.

Mark.COM Placing a MARK TSR before other TSRs that you load allows TSR removal without making a "hole" in memory or losing the INTerrupt chain. The WorkTSRs Mark releases its environment block to be used by subsequently loaded programs. When used with the WorkTSRs Watch, there will be *no* spurious INTerrupt Vectors associated with it. The Mark is simply a data area. Actually, Mark is obsolete. Even the so-called advantage of "Protected!" marks is eliminated by the use of File Marks. File Marks or the MarkNet counterpart for networks stored in a RAM disk directory dedicated to Marks is the best of all methods.

FMark.COM The FMark and its replacement program reduce the memory used by storing the Mark data in a File. FMark means FileMark and is more efficient.

MarkNet Has been left to TurboPower along with its RelNet RELEASE counterpart until we start using networks.

DeviceS Shows we are thinking about it. See DeviceS.Doc.

UnMark.COM The replacement for the RELEASE.EXE program. It is more efficient but has different options. Enter UnMark ? or /? or use >TYPE UnMark.COM to see them. The /Keep and /EMS left alone RELEASE options are not used because the first panders to user laziness and the second is a "kludge" for inadequate EMS systems. The /R option is for use with DOUBLEDOS and /D can be used when you want to see the blocks. The /S(tuff keyboard buffer) with a command is limited to the 15 Character PC design INCLUDING Carriage Return. Put BAT files in your path versus "d:\bat\filename" <- TOO LONG.

ReMark.COM The replacement for the DISABLE.EXE program. It returns a zero ERRORLEVEL when the status is as desired so that batch processing can continue and ERRORLEVELs of 1, 2, or 3 depending on what is wrong IF the batch file SHOULD terminate. If an invalid TSR

Name or PSP is entered, for example, the ERRORLEVEL is 2. No Watch installed returns 1 and No Room in Watch returns 3. The / options can be /D to DisAble or /A to Activate after the TSR has been DisAbled. A valid Name/PSP returns the current status with no "/" option. When you call ReMark with no Command Line, it gives HELP.

Watch.COM   Added to the TurboPower system to permit the DIS-ABLE program to make a TSR inactive while it remains in memory. It is essential that Watch be loaded before any TSR that you will disable. The replacement does *not* capture INT 16h but uses a different means to avoid reinstallations. Its data area is kept clear for ease should you wish to examine the ChangeBlocks. As TSRs are added, removed, or made inactive, Watch is kept up to date. ShowTSRs uses it to know *all* the interrupts a TSR has captured. Watch is the best part of the system and Watch.COM Version 3.1 releases its environment.

ShowTSRs.EXE: Replaces MapMem.EXE. The WorkTSRs series began with a desire to be able to scroll the MapMem data. The experience of translating Pascal to assembly language for that project induced a desire to replace RELEASE and DISABLE as well.

ShowTSRs was upgraded to version 3.1 to accommodate the LoadTSRs system described below. It displays a "LoadTSR" line when MenuTSRs has been installed.

The source code has been streamlined. There is less parameter passing by stack frame. Efforts to improve the English in comments and the HELP message were extensive. Testing the Shareware Command.Com replacement "4DOS" forced improved programming techniques. The environment is now searched "top-down" for the "owner" name and the MCBs are now fully sorted. 4DOS is recommended.

MenuTSRs.EXE   A program that displays all .COM files in a TSRdir directory. It allows you to select one from the menu including any parameters writing a Load2TSR.BAT file with each of your selections. When you have finished choosing TSRs to LOAD or UpDate, the program exits. MenuTSRs is invoked from a TSRmenu.BAT file. When it returns to the TSRmenu.BAT file without error, the TSRmenu.BAT file "chains" to the Load2TSR.BAT file that was created by MenuTSRs. Load2TSR.BAT calls on DOS to FMark and LOAD or UpDate the chosen TSRs. A final KillLoad.BAT file is "chained" at the end of Load2TSR.BAT to delete it from the directory where it was created. Be sure to read LoadTSRs .DOC before trying to use the system. Whether this system is useful to you or not is your own choice. Again, any "power user" will profit by studying the concept.

TSRmenu.BAT: Has six lines. See LoadTSRs.DOC.

KillLoad.BAT: Has four lines. See LoadTSRs.DOC.

Some notes for programmers:

The DeviceS program, besides having a more gaudy display, takes a different approach to finding and presenting the Device Chain. A typical approach is to find the NUL device as the first device in the chain and present the devices in the order of the chain until the device at the end of the chain. The resulting addresses make it appear that the NUL device is off in a segment of its own and that devices added by Config.Sys are loaded ahead of the standard DOS devices. We wanted the devices in the order that they occupy memory. The DOS Devices should start with CON, end with NUL, and be followed by any Config.Sys loaded devices in the order loaded rather than the order of the chain.

Certain remarks seemed appropriate even when just translating the Device Attribute word. The decision as to what remarks would be useful and meaningful consumed hours of planning time and may not be over yet. In case you choose to comment, the criteria were:

```
Tue  May 30, 1989 14:20 d:\work>devices
Address Strat Inter Attr Type Device   Name        Remarks
0070 014E 03CD 03D8  8013 Character    CON         Replaced Device
0070 0160 03CD 03DE  8000 Character    AUX
0070 0172 03CD 03F2  8000 Character    PRN
0070 0184 03CD 0410  8008 Character    CLOCK$      System Date/Time
0070 0196 03CD 0416  0840 Block Drives A - F       Mappable Drives
0070 01A8 03CD 03F2  8000 Character    LPT1
0070 01BA 03CD 03DE  8000 Character    COM1
0070 01CC 03CD 03FC  8000 Character    LPT2
0070 01DE 03CD 0406  8000 Character    LPT3
0070 01F0 03CD 03E8  8000 Character    COM2
0070 2D08 14C6 14CC  8004 Character    NUL
0A27 0000 0036 0041  8000 Character    EMMXXXX0 Expanded Mem Mgr
0C8D 0000 277B 2786  8013 Character    CON
0C8D 001C 277B 2786  8000 Character    FCON
14FA 0000 0012 0021  2800 Block Drive  G
1529 0000 0017 0022  4000 Block Drive  H
1579 0000 0017 0022  4000 Block Drive  I
15C9 0000 0030 003B  C000 Character    4DOSSTAK
```

To those who would argue that "System Date/Time" for CLOCK$ and "Expanded Mem Mgr" violate the first rule, we offer two thoughts that show that the decisions are not easy. The Clock Device is *not* guaranteed to have a name as obvious as "CLOCK$". A device that replaces it could have *any* name. "EMMXXXX0" certainly does identify the Expanded Memory Manager device to most of us, but we let rule 2 overcome the doubts caused by rule 1.

Much of what could be said about Disk Drives was accomplished by identifying the Drive Letter(s). The user already knows which of these drives take removable media and what capacities and whether any of them are RAM drives. If a system was part of a network, then "NetWork" would appear as the "Name". Additional remarks to the network line await your input. If your system uses HI-MEM by Microsoft as an Extended Memory Manager, it will be identified. Also, those character devices that report "busy" when accessed through IOCTL will show "Busy Rpt", giving you many remarks.

Examining the DeviceS.ASM code will answer most questions about what has been included and how it has been accomplished. If you are interested in programming, be sure to see the DevSort code.

The TurboPower Device.EXE program was patterned after Dev.EXE by Chris J. Dunford. Looking at the first ten DeviceS.ASM code lines you will see a pattern variation at the outset. We look for the CON device first in order to scan the appropriate segment for the NUL device. In the DevFind PROCedure, the header for NUL fills level 1 of the DevS data array. The data for all devices is then stored at subsequent levels until the end of the chain. With 32 levels (counting the 0 level, which will be used when sorting) and the large stack for overflow, there should be no catastrophes. Anyone with 32 or more devices please let us know, however!

While data from the device header is being stored, the attribute word is also interpreted for remarks. You'll see most of that from the DoName: label to the end of the DevLine PROCedure. The possible Block devices include NetWorks as well as disk drives. In the case of disk drives, the number of Units is stored for future interpretation as drive letters.

Upon return to the Main PROCedure, the program ends with an error message and ErrorLevel if *no* devices were entered into the array. Otherwise the Heading Line is displayed. The ShowMsg PROCedure is the one that interprets Units into drive letters and so we'll save it for review last.

Novice programmers were invited to examine and use the DevSort PROCedure earlier. The algorithm can be coded in any language. The "Sinking Bubble Sort" was developed for teaching because a "bubble sort" can be explained with only two hands whereas the more efficient algorithms require sophisticated demonstration aids. The "Sinking Bubble Sort" is only a little harder to explain and is much more efficient. The "bubble sort" must process the array as many times (minus 1) as there are members in the array. The "Sinking" technique raises "Bubble Sort" efficiency so that no perceptible time is taken with as few as 32 members.

Imagine that the array to be sorted is an apartment house that assigns each floor according to the value of the furniture. The furniture is initially moved to the next available level starting with the ground floor. No intermediate floors are left vacant. The furniture on each floor is tagged with a value. The basement floor is reserved for temporary storage, and the floors above the top floor that is used are sealed off with an infinite furniture value tag. The movers aren't very smart but they can compare two values and they sure can move furniture!

In the "Sinking Bubble Sort," the movers know two limits. They know that the first floor is level 1 and they know the number of the top level. In fact, their freight elevator won't go past the highest level occupied with furniture. They know that if they get all the furniture in value order from the Ground level to the Top floor, their work will be done.

There are 61 lines in the DevSort PROCedure. In the first five, the movers advance from their Basement. When they find that the next floor to examine is ABOVE the Top floor of furniture, they go to the fifty-ninth line of DevSort from which they end their day by returning to the Basement.

Checking the middle lines of code, you will see labels for "sink, down and done". They mark the test for, end of, and start of "sinking" points. See how the movers get to the DSsink: label. While working from the Ground to Top floor, the movers check the furniture value tags. If the value of the tag they read on the floor that they are working is less than the one they find on the floor above, they can advance without any moving to the floor above *unless* that floor is sealed off. If all of the furniture was initially stored in order of value from the ground to top floors, their day's work would consist only of checking tags and *no* moving.

DeviceS has two possibilities. If your system has no devices installed by Config.Sys, then NUL will chain to CON and, each in turn and in order, will chain to your last DOS device. (That device, by the way, will be the highest COM device that your DOS version supports. Our screen example shows COM2 for the DOS 3.2 version. Your DOS 3.3 version might show COM4.)

In this first possibility, all devices are in order except for the NUL device. As the movers examine the NUL furniture and CON furniture tags, they realize that the NUL furniture must move to the second floor in place of the CON furniture. To accomplish this, they first move the CON furniture to the Basement (as done by DevSort lines 13–19). After moving the NUL furniture to the old CON floor (20–24), they move the CON furniture from the basement to floor #1 (lines 25–29). Noting that they are on the

Ground floor, they see that there is *no* sinking to do and therefore advance to floor #2.

Floor #2 contains the NUL furniture that has a higher value than the AUX furniture on level 3. They take the AUX furniture to the basement, move the NUL furniture to floor #3, and then bring the AUX furniture to floor #2 just vacated by moving NUL to floor #3. Now on floor #2, they compare the AUX furniture to CON. Since CON is lower priced, they recover their place (still on floor #2, at DSdone:) and advance to floor #3.

Guess what? Guess what? Guess what? and so on. The NUL furniture, being higher priced, replaces all the other devices furniture until it is on the top floor. Sinking down each time finds that each device below NUL is already in proper order. This simple situation is unusual and probably doesn't apply to your DeviceS. If Config.Sys has loaded any devices, they will chain from NUL and the FIRST Config.Sys device loaded will chain to the DOS CON device. In other words, NUL will be out of order at the top as in the simple case, but it will be followed by the LAST device in memory and ALL others out of order until reaching CON.

When the movers go to work on this mess, they find NUL to be properly located below the LAST device in memory. After that, the floor #2 (last device) will begin to move upward in floors. As it moves up, the devices loaded after NUL will move down until the first floors contain the NUL furniture followed by all of the Config.Sys loaded devices' furniture in memory order. The next floor at that point will contain the CON device furniture. Not only will it be replaced by the LAST device furniture, but the sink routine will really begin to operate at full power. Once the CON device furniture is moved below the last device furniture, the DSdown: comparison will find that it is also lower than each of the other devices in turn until it has reached Ground level.

This sequence of sinking will repeat until the last COM device is sunk below the NUL device and above all other DOS devices.

When the "Sinking Bubble Sort" goes into the sink mode, it does exactly the same thing that it does in the conventional rising mode except that it does it top down instead of bottom up. The sink mode moves furniture from the current position down as far as the Ground floor, if necessary, to ensure that furniture values are in ascending order. In the conventional "bubble sort" the bottom-to-top exchange repeats until the ordering of furniture is completed. "Sinking" any out-of-order value when it is first encountered eliminates the need to go back and start from that Ground-floor position.

Sinking has two conditions that will stop the movers' exchange of furniture from a lower out-of-order position through the basement to the current "sink" position in exchange for the furniture at that position. The primary condition is that the furniture at the two levels is already in order. The absolute stopper is that the lower level is the basement. Whenever data is moved in computer memory, only a copy is moved. The original remains until overwritten by the exchange. When completed, the sort routine will have left a copy of the last moved furniture in the basement. If you run DeviceS.EXE in a debugger, a set of NUL device furniture will be found to remain in the basement as well as at the proper level when the sort is complete.

Two little auxiliary routines, "SI2BX" and the 3 "AX2ASCh" parts, provide means to copy either characters or ASCII representations of numbers into the DevS array. These routines are ubiquitous in assembly language programs. The AX2ASCh trio are nearly the same as used by Chris J. Dunford in his Dev.EXE program. Nobody has a copyright on such common routines, and you are free to use both or either in any program that will benefit from them.

ShowMsg Proc is quite specialized. The last part of it from the label SMnext: to ShowMsg EndP simply makes a double call to BIOS routines to display each character by "teletype" in the same way that TYPE at the DOS prompt does, except it initializes the space that will be used by each character to the attribute that is appropriate for where it is in a line of text. The NOT Found device header error message and heading line will be underlined for mono video or black and white on color, but the data lines are displayed in white on blue for the first forty-eight characters and white on red for the last seventeen.

The special part of ShowMsg occurs only for lines *not* starting with a space. These record lines *may* contain the data for block disk drive devices. If this is the case, then the Units number is converted to a drive letter. SMproc: decides if this is to be done. SMmore: begins by looking for the next drive letter in the "Kind" string. The first drive device will start with "A:" and the letters will increment depending on the number of Units. In our screen example, the first Disk Device is a Zenith driver that controls two floppies and four hard disk partitions. Even if you had only one floppy drive and one hard disk partition, it would still reserve letters "A:" and "B:" for floppies and "C: to F:" for your hard drive partitions. So Units = 6 becomes (count 'em) drives "A–F". Updating the second word of FlgS to six readies the string so that "G" is the next drive, and so on.

USERS.BAT

Benefit:

Saves keystrokes for a frequently used CC:Mail function. This utility provides a user listing along with numbers of messages stored. Other related files included are:

```
ADMIN.BAT
DIRECTOR.BAT
RECLAIM.BAT
MSGS.BAT
USERS.BAT
```

Syntax: USERS

How to operate it:

This batch file and the other CC:Mail administration files are placed in the CC:Mail CCADMIN directory and are run from there. Substitute the name of your mailbox for MBX_NAME and the location of the CC:Mail CCDATA directory to match your directory structure. You will be prompted for the mail box administrator's password.

Listing:

```
CHKSTAT MBX_NAME Y:\APPS\CCDATA USERS
```

VIRDET

Benefit:

VIRDET is a program that was created to detect whether a Novell network has been attacked by a Jerusalem B virus. The presence of the virus leaves a signature in RAM. If the program detects the signature, it returns with an error level of 1; if it finds no virus, it returns 0. You can use a program like BATUTIL (included on this disk) to check the error level and take appropriate action.

Only if no virus is found should you consider replacing all occurrences of LOGIN.EXE with LOGIN.BAT, which runs VIRDET and will continue to run the normal login file, renamed to ~LOGIN.EXE.

We have included the source so that you can be sure the program has not been doctored. You might use DEBUG to unassemble the .COM as a quick check that all is well.

This program is particularly useful during the period of disinfection to avoid the possibility of a supervisor logging on from a machine with an infected NET3 or IPX file.

Note this program will not detect the virus if it is loaded above 512K. So it will not work if you have users who use memory managers to get NET3 or IPX above 640K.

Syntax: Run from a batch file similar to the one shown below:

Listing:

```
VIRDET
IF ERRORLEVEL=0 GOTO LOGIN
ECHO JERUSALEM-B VIRUS DETECTED LOGIN ABORTED.......
ECHO CONTACT YOUR SYSTEM ADMINISTRATOR
GOTO END
:LOGIN
CLS
@ECHO OFF
ECHO NO JERUSALEM-B VIRUS DETECTED - PROCEEDING WITH LOGIN
CD\NET
IPX
NET3
F:
LOGIN
:END
```

WORD5.BAT

Benefit:

This file will load Microsoft Word for DOS (version 5.0) with the correct video driver for any video standard.

Syntax:

WORD5

or

WORD5 /L (for Word to load last document), etc.

How to operate it:

Microsoft Word for DOS (version 5.0) was supposed to be a network-"aware" application. However, Microsoft assumed that once MS Word was installed for a user, he or she would always use the same video standard whenever word processing. That, of course, isn't always the case. Using this batch file, users can log in from virtually any workstation and be assured that they will have the correct video driver support. The file that contains the video drivers for Word 5 is named SCREEN.VID. This batch file:

1. Creates a network search path for the Word directory.
2. Checks the type of video card in the workstation with the NWHAT4 utility included on this disk. This utility will return an environment variable VIDEO and set it with the type of video card found on the workstation executing the batch file.
3. Echoes a message to the user telling what type of video card was found.
4. Changes to a document subdirectory under the user's "home" directory.
5. Copies the correct version of the video driver (EGA.VID, CGA.VID, VGA.VID, or MONO.VID) to the current directory, starts Word with the /N (network) option, and makes provision for one variable to be passed to Word.
6. Moves the user back to the home directory upon exit from the application, and deletes the search path set in step 1.

Notes:

1. Mappings may have to be adjusted to match your network's directory structure and mappings.

2. NWHAT4 must be on the search path.

3. The network administrator must install MS Word for each video standard to be supported, then rename the generated screen.vid to the appropriate name. For example, install MS Word for CGA. Upon completion of installation, rename SCREEN.VID to CGA.VID. Repeat the process for Monochrome, EGA, and VGA. These files should reside in the Word application subdirectory.

Listing:

```
@ECHO OFF
CLS
MAP INSERT S1:=sys:\apps\word5
nwhat4 -di -vname:video
IF "%VIDEO%"== "VGA" GOTO VGA
IF "%VIDEO%"== "EGA" GOTO EGA
IF "%VIDEO%"== "CGA" GOTO COLOR
cls
echo off
echo LOADING MICROSOFT WORD 5.0 (MONOCHROME)
f:
cd doc
COPY Z:\APPS\WORD5\HERC.VID SCREEN.VID
WORD /n %1%
cd ..
GOTO END
:VGA
cls
echo LOADING MICROSOFT WORD 5.0 (VGA)
cd doc
COPY Z:\APPS\WORD5\VGA.VID SCREEN.VID
WORD /n %1%
cd ..
GOTO END
:EGA
cls
echo LOADING MICROSOFT WORD 5.0 (EGA)
cd doc
```

```
COPY Z:\APPS\WORD5\EGA.VID SCREEN.VID
WORD /n %1%
cd ..
GOTO END
:COLOR
cls
@ECHO OFF
ECHO CGA MONITOR
cls
echo LOADING MICROSOFT WORD 5.0
cd doc
COPY Z:\APPS\WORD5\CGA.VID SCREEN.VID
WORD /n %1%
cd ..
GOTO END
:END
map delete s1:
```

XMETER

Benefit:

XMETER is a software metering program for Novell networks. It's simple, uses *no* RAM, and does not require any VAPs or NLMs running on the server.

XMETER uses Novell's semaphores to monitor program usage. You first create a BATCH file to load your software. You open a semaphore on the way in and close it on the way out. The batch file must be programmed to restrict access to the program. XMETER returns DOS error level codes to control batch files.

Where to find it: On the Power Tools Disk as XMETER.COM or in CompuServe Novell A Forum (GO NOVA), Library #17, XMETER.ZIP.

Syntax:

Usage:

```
XMETER <Semaphore> <MaxUsers> /O/C/U/L
```

Semaphore is any name you want to give a semaphore. MaxUsers is the maximum number of users allowed to use the semaphore or the name of a meter list file.

/O	Open Semaphore.
/C	Close Semaphore.
/U	Return number of Semaphore users.
/L	Outputs status line for log file redirection.

Price:

Shareware, $95 per server.

More information available from:

Computer Tyme
216 South Glenstone
Springfield, MO 65802
(800) 548-5353 Sales
(417) 866-1222

How to operate it:

Using a meter list file: XMETER can use a special text file to limit semaphore access. To use this method, substitute the name of the list file for the MaxUsers parameter as follows:

```
XMETER Lotus METER.LST /O
METER.LST
Lotus 10
Wordstar 15
dBase 9
```

This allows you to maintain the number of copies of each program in a single list.

Usage Tracking:

XMETER provides usage tracking by outputing a comma-delimited ASCII line for each semaphore open and close. You must select the /L switch to activate this feature. The line must be redirected to a usage log file and you must write your own reporting program.

Example:

```
XMETER TEST METER.LST /O/L >> USAGE.LOG
```

This command appends the following line to the file USAGE.LOG:

```
"MARC","254:41","2","LOTUS","1","O","Y","08-26-90","17:43:22"
```

The line contains nine fields as follows:

1. User Name
2. Semaphore Name
3. Number of Semaphore users after execution
4. Command, O=Open C=Close
5. Success Status, Y=Success N=Failure
6. Date
7. Time
8. Internet Address of WorkStation
9. Logical Connection Number

Tricks:

When XMETER creates semaphores, it adds the letters XM- to the front of the semaphore name. So semaphore TEST is really XM-TEST. The idea here is so that all XMETER semaphores can be identified from other NetWare semaphores.

Whenever a workstation first uses XMETER, it creates a semaphore named XM-XMETER. This can be used to see how many users are using XMETER software. This semaphore can be cleared by using the command:

```
XMETER
```

XMETER/C

Benefit:

If a user turns off the computer while running an application, Novell will release his or her semaphores after fifteen minutes. All semaphores are also released when the user logs out. If a user reboots within fifteen minutes, the semaphores are cleared upon login.

Examples of usage:

```
XMETER TEST 10 /O
```

This opens semaphore TEST if less than 10 users have it open, otherwise it returns to DOS ErrorLevel 1.

```
XMETER TEST /C
```

This closes semaphore TEST allowing others to use it.

```
XMETER TEST METER.LST /O/L >> USAGE.LOG
```

This opens semaphore TEST if less than the number of users specified in METER.LST have it open, otherwise to returns DOS ErrorLevel 1. Log information is redirected to append log file USAGE.LOG.

Index

IBM Compatible 5.25" Diskettes

This Bantam software product is also available in an IBM compatible 5.25"/1.2M format. If you'd like to exchange this software for the new 5.25" format, please:

- Package your original 3.5" diskette in a mailer.
- Include a check or money order for US $7.95 ($9.95 Canadian) to cover media, postage and handling (California and Massachusetts residents add sales tax). Foreign orders: Please send international money orders; no foreign checks accepted.
- Include your completed warranty card.

Upon receipt Bantam will immediately send your replacement disk via first class mail.

Mail to: Bantam Electronic Publishing
            666 Fifth Avenue
            New York, NY 10103
            Attn: NPT/5.25 Disk